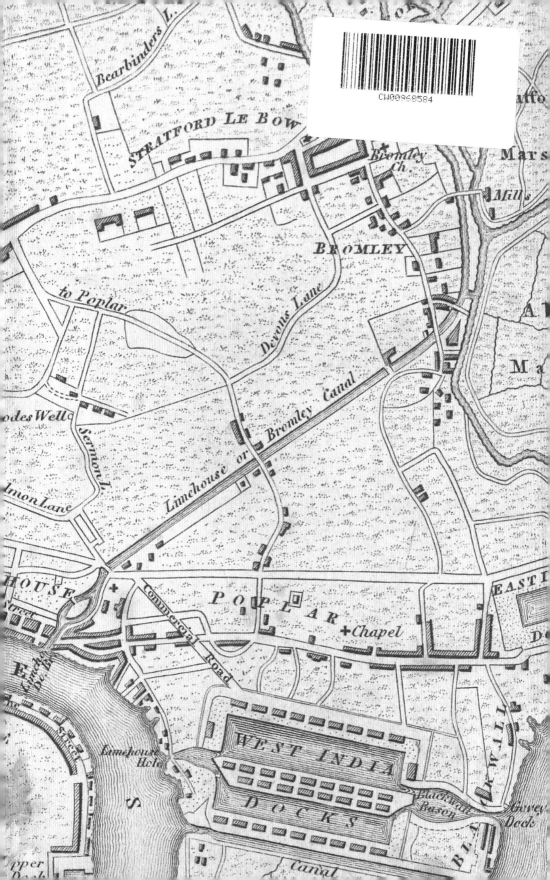

BEYOND THE TOWER

JOHN MARRIOTT

BEYOND THE TOWER

A HISTORY OF EAST LONDON

YALE UNIVERSITY PRESS
NEW HAVEN AND LONDON

U.S. Office: sales.press@yale.edu   yalebooks.com
Europe Office: sales@yaleup.co.uk   www.yalebooks.co.uk

Set in Minion Pro by IDSUK (DataConnection Ltd)
Printed in Great Britain by TJ International Ltd, Padstow, Cornwall

Map by Martin Brown Design

Library of Congress Cataloging-in-Publication Data

Marriott, John, 1944–
    Beyond the Tower : a history of East London / John Marriott.
        p. cm.
    Includes bibliographical references.
    ISBN 978-0-300-14880-0 (cloth : alk. paper)
    1. East End (London, England)—History. 2. London (England)—History.
3. Popular culture—England—London—History. 4. East End (London, England)—Social conditions. 5. London (England)—Social conditions. I. Title.
    DA685.E1M33 2011
    942.1'7—dc23
                                                                                        2011026749

A catalogue record for this book is available from the British Library.

10 9 8 7 6 5 4 3 2 1
2015 2014 2013 2012 2011

Contents

List of Illustrations

Picture section

Acknowledgements

This book has been over thirty years in the making. Since the late 1970s, when I embarked on doctoral research into the political history of West Ham, I have lived and worked in East London, and have had the immense good fortune to write about it. In the early days I would not have had the temerity to attempt a broader history of the area; even now it has been a challenging prospect, but it has been eased by many kindnesses. My debt to the Bishopsgate Library over the years is incalculable. Not only does the library contain one of the great national collections on London history, but here I encountered Stefan Dickers, Liz Pinnel and David Webb, whose extensive knowledge and unbridled generosity provided a wonderful working environment. Thanks are due also to Frank Sainsbury and Howard Bloch, both sadly with us no longer, Jenni Munro-Collins at the Newham Heritage and Archives Service, Chris Lloyd at Tower Hamlets Local Studies Library, and staff at the British Library, Cambridge University Library, and the Bodleian Library, Oxford.

The book owes much to discussions with Peter Claus, Chris Ellmers, Michelle Johansen, Philippa Levine, Susan Pennybacker, Katy Pettit and Sarah Wise, and to Gareth Stedman Jones, who since acting as my supervisor has continued as a source of inspiration. Comments from anonymous readers were supportive and insightful. I have leant heavily on colleagues and friends at the Raphael Samuel History Centre, University of East London, particularly those involved in cutting-edge research on London history. At Yale University Press, Phoebe Clapham enthusiastically supported the project from the outset, but thankfully was sufficiently astute to rein me in where necessary, and direct the arguments when I went astray; without her intervention the book would have been the poorer. And the whole project was made possible by my agent Maggie Hanbury.

Some time after starting on the book my twins Kabir and Karishma were born. Much to my alarm, they soon managed to find my papers, and set about rearranging them. Perhaps I can now make it up to them, as I can to Kanta, who has taken more than her fair share of parental responsibilities while I have been submerged.

John Marriott
East London and the East Riding, March 2011

To Kabir and Karishma, who were born and grew with this book,
and to the people of East London

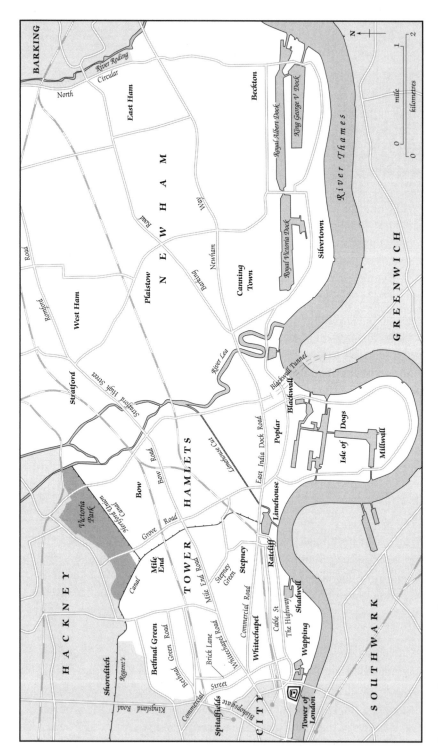

East London as it is today

Introduction: O Thomas Cook

IN THE summer of 1902 the twenty-six-year-old Jack London set off for East London. Best remembered for adventure stories such as *White Fang* and *Call of the Wild*, London was also an accomplished journalist who reported on a range of social and political issues. Now in the immediate aftermath of the death of Queen Victoria he was on a quest to explore the East End disguised as a vagrant American sailor. But first he had to find it. Friends were of little help; they claimed to know nothing of the place, gestured vaguely to the east and recommended he approach the police. Not wishing to involve the authorities, London resisted the suggestion but then made a decision – which was greeted with universal relief – to seek guidance from the Cheapside branch of the renowned travel agents Thomas Cook & Son. Here, however, he met the same ignorance; never having received a request to take travellers to the East End, Cook's stated that they knew nothing whatsoever about the place. London responded with characteristic disbelief:

> But O Cook, O Thomas Cook & Son, path-finders and trail-clearers, living sign-posts to all the world, and bestowers of first aid to bewildered travellers – unhesitatingly and instantly, with ease and celerity, could send me to Darkest Africa or Innermost Thibet, but to the East End of London, barely a stone's throw distant from Ludgate Circus, you know not the way![1]

The fable is a good one, and well told, but it does touch on an important truth, namely, that at the end of the Victorian era when the metropolis stood as a great world and imperial city, the whole of East London was in the minds of many middle-class inhabitants as remote and inaccessible as the far corners of the empire. It may be tempting to explain this remarkable ignorance by referring to the ways in which a distinct mythology had been created in the nineteenth century within which the East End was seen as a site of danger, depravity and destitution, and hence one to be avoided by genteel and respectable persons. There is something to this (and later we shall have reason to return to the origins and nature of this mythology), but this can be only part of the picture, because despite the modern impulses of the twentieth century which blew away the cobwebs of Victorianism, and developed new forms of social scientific research and mass communication, East London remained largely unknown.

This book is an attempt to answer the question that must have been uppermost in the mind of Jack London as he made his way to Thomas Cook: 'Where, what and when is East London?' In so doing we shall make many careful journeys through its streets, and meet thousands of its inhabitants. We shall learn how it was built and rebuilt, why people lived there, why people moved, and how they laboured; we will listen to those who recorded their thoughts on East London from within and without; and we will consider how it stood in relation to other areas of London, to Britain, and to the empire. The first journey, like so many others, begins with history, for history is, and will remain, our most trusted guide.

This book thus seeks to provide a history of East London since its emergence as a distinct area of the metropolis in the eighteenth century to its postwar decline and potential regeneration. It would be impossible in a single volume to write a truly comprehensive account, and so I have focused on those moments of change which have held a particular significance for the metropolis or indeed the nation as a whole. The stories are fascinating, full of larger-than-life characters who have entered into English folklore, and historical episodes which reveal the vivid experiences of people at the lower levels of metropolitan life. But apart from this, why study East London in the first place? Arguably, it is one of the best- and least-known parts of England. For most the East End conjures up a rather odd mix of contradictory images. To the outsider East London remains a working-class area, made up largely of unskilled and unemployed workers living in mean streets, and speaking in barely intelligible versions of the English language. The optimistic and sentimental look back to a golden age when East End life was an endless round of barrel organs, pearly kings and queens, jellied eels, donkey carts, benign grandmothers, rhyming slang, cockneys with hearts of gold, extended families, good neighbours and enthusiastic responses to all things royal. The long-running soap opera *EastEnders*, which has defined East London for a new generation, may have dispensed with the quainter trappings, but enough survives in its emphasis on community and family values to resonate with older memories. Pessimists, on the other hand, point to the persistence of fascist currents, prostitution, lawlessness, violence, suspicion of strangers, endemic poverty, chronic overcrowding, racial conflict, and dirt in the street and on the faces of children.

The popular sense of East London's history is equally replete with fragments of a half-remembered past, much of which is handed down from generation to generation as part of a common folklore. There is no overall narrative of historical development, only a profound sense of loss amongst an indigenous population which fondly recalls an age when we could walk the streets in perfect safety and leave doors unlocked. Tales of episodes and events come to stand for a history. Thus the East End was Chinese opium dens in Limehouse, Jewish tailors in Whitechapel, dockworker strikes, rowdy but good-natured music halls, slums eradicated by clearance schemes, postwar migrations eastwards to new estates in Essex, that archangel of retribution Jack the Ripper, fortitude during the blitz, sing-songs in pubs, day trips to Southend, the battle of Cable Street, momentary triumphs of West Ham Football Club, Oxbridge residents of Toynbee Hall, and colourful Petticoat Lane, the origins of which are lost in time.

Such a picture, however, captures little of what East London is, and nothing at all of its historical significance. It is true that when compared with London as a whole, the history of the East End is rather brief, and yet East London was created at precisely that moment when London embarked on a journey which would lead to its role as a great world metropolis. So closely tied were the timings of these historical transformations that it is tempting to impute a direct relationship between them. And with good reason, for it was during this period that East London emerged as the manufacturing and commercial heart of the metropolis. The workshops of Whitechapel and Spitalfields provided products such as clothing, furniture and footwear which satiated the ever-increasing demands of wealthy Londoners for such accessories, and the massive gas, chemical, engineering and munitions plants of Poplar and West Ham helped serve the needs of an advanced industrial and imperial nation; but also an extensive communications infrastructure of river, rail and dock became a gateway between England and the world through which passed an endless stream of raw materials, manufactured goods and human cargoes.

From the outset East London expanded because migrant labour from other parts of the country was attracted by the promise of employment – gainful and otherwise – and thus it came to be seen as a place of refuge for displaced persons; with the opening up of trading links with empire, this expansion was augmented by foreign migrants and refugees. So great was this movement of people that East London became, and remains, an epicentre of diasporic communities, a vital site of multiculturalism. I teach at the University of East London, where the student body comprises people of 120 nationalities. I live in Manor Park on the outer fringes of the East London of the nineteenth century. Opposite is a superstore owned and run by Gujurati Hindus which sells the cheapest rice and spices in the area, while a little further down the Romford Road is the Turkish Istanbul, good for fresh fruit and vegetables at any time of the day or night. My hair is cut by Iraqi Kurds, my car fixed by Sikhs; take-away meals are provided by a Pakistani shop, most of my domestic repairs are done by Polish builders, and internet facilities are offered by Somalis. Within 150 metres of my house are a Nigerian Episcopal church, a Bangladeshi mosque, a Tamil mandir, a Sikh gurdwara and a Baptist community centre. This is so typical an experience for anyone living in East London that it is easy to take it for granted; it is only when we venture out into the provinces that the thought of the world in East London comes to mind.

Politically, culturally and socially East London has also played a major part in the history of the metropolis and nation. Sport, in particular those working-class pursuits of soccer, speedway, darts and boxing, has always featured, and created a host of stars from James Parrott, who in 1770 reputedly ran the first four-minute mile, to David Beckham, the golden boy of English soccer. Because of what were considered the problems of chronic poverty, East London attracted many of the outstanding social reformers who were to lay the foundations of social reform and the welfare state. Samuel Barnett, William Booth, William Beveridge, Thomas Barnardo, Thomas Fowell Buxton, Frederick Charrington, Richard Tawney, George Peabody and Clement Attlee all devoted many years of their lives to helping the poor of the area. As a centre of political and religious dissent from the seventeenth century, East London fostered the thinking and careers of many outstanding figures including William Penn, who left for Delaware in 1682 and whose 1701 Charter of Privileges was marked in 1751 by the casting of the Liberty Bell at the world-renowned Whitechapel Bell Foundry, Jeremy Bentham, Mary Wollstonecraft, Annie Besant, Charles Bradlaugh, Sylvia Pankhurst, Will Thorne, Keir Hardie and George Lansbury, as well as the extraordinary political culture that gave rise to Jewish anarchists, headed by Rudolph Rocker, and provided temporary refuge for revolutionaries such as Lenin and Stalin.

Our understanding of East London is hampered also by a geographical uncertainty arising from endless disputes on where its boundaries are to be drawn. There is nothing new in such speculation. In *Life and Labour of the*

People of London, the classic work of social investigation undertaken in the closing stages of the nineteenth century, Charles Booth adhered to the administrative boundaries of the London County Council in taking East London to be the area stretching from the course of the ancient City wall in the west to the River Lea in the east. Within this broad area he distinguished the 'inner ring' of East London which included Shoreditch, Bethnal Green, Whitechapel, St George's-in-the-East, Wapping, Shadwell, Ratcliff, and the western portions of Mile End.[2] Thirteen years later, when further work had revealed a more complex picture of demographic change, the boundaries used by Booth were more fluid, for he now defined the 'outer East London' of Stepney, Bethnal Green and Poplar as the 'true East End of London'. Here was an area, he proceeded, that lay 'beyond those districts that usually go by that name', and he went further in referring to what was unmistakably the new borough of West Ham situated over the Lea in Essex as a

> quarter rapidly forming, equally populous and no less poor. The district differs for the better in many ways both from the old East End of the past and the new one that is coming into being. It contains a solid English industrial population endowed with a noticeable vigour and independence of character. It is almost altogether poor in the sense that among the residents none are rich, and that the middle class are leaving, but except in a few special parts it is in no way poverty stricken.[3]

It was at this time that Walter Besant, the most popular writer on London, published *East London*. Attracted to the idea that London was not a city but an extraordinary collection of overgrown villages, he spread the boundaries widely. According to his rough-and-ready calculations, East London was simply the area east of Bishopsgate Street and north of the Thames, and included the 'densely populated suburb, lying east of the River Lea' and the 'aggregation of crowded towns ... formed by the once rural villages of Hackney, Stoke Newington, Clapton, Old Ford, Stepney, Bow and Stratford'.[4] Later, in an imaginative move which for many overstretched the conventional mapping of London, he claimed that the 'suburbs of East London' included Chigwell, Chingford, Theydon Bois, and villages surrounding Epping Forest.[5]

Half a century later Robert Sinclair, a writer of novels, social commentary and film scripts, also thought expansively. For him East London comprised the boroughs of Stepney, Poplar, Bethnal Green, Hackney,

Shoreditch, West Ham, East Ham, Walthamstow, Leyton, Wanstead, Ilford, Barking and Dagenham. These boundaries, he reasoned, form neither a notional area to suit his convenience, nor municipal divisions, but rather define a distinct industrial geography with common social and cultural problems.[6] Such speculation and the ever-increasing boundaries to which it seemed to give rise created rather more problems than it solved. Sensitive to these problems, Millicent Rose's fine study of the East End advised us from the outset that 'no term in London phraseology is more inaccurately used'.[7] Those frequenting the fashionable and journalistic life of London have for many years secluded themselves in the far west of the city and have little knowledge of other parts of London; for them, as for Cook's, the East End is an unknown area somewhere to the east of where they reside. Thus, for example, when royalty visits Bermondsey, press and radio broadcasts report mistakenly that their highnesses have spent the day in the East End. To address this sorry state of affairs, Rose reinstated the importance of the ancient physical boundaries: East London is bounded to the south by the Thames, to the east by the Lea, to the west by Aldgate and the lines of the City wall, and to the north by Clapton Common within which the boroughs of Stepney, Poplar, Bethnal Green and Hackney were included.

There are of course no definitive answers to this conundrum, and no doubt it will continue to animate conversations, but for the purposes of this book, I choose to consider East London as the area covered today by the boroughs of Tower Hamlets and Newham. In doing so, I offer my apologies to those readers in Hackney, Barking and Dagenham, even Waltham Forest, who cherish an identity with East London. These areas are mentioned, but only in passing. Although Tower Hamlets and Newham may have different timelines, they are united – and simultaneously distinguished from their neighbours – by a shared history of industrial development and demographic change forged from the crucible of the Thames, the City and the empire.

After years of decline and neglect we have witnessed the mixed benefits of Docklands regeneration, and are now poised for two other massive programmes. East London will be part of the government's Thames Gateway regeneration scheme, which is the largest in Europe and over the next twenty years will transform the Thameside areas through provision of a new communications infrastructure and thousands of houses. Furthermore, the London Olympics of 2012 will take place around Stratford. It is perhaps too early to say precisely what impact these schemes will have, but their combined influence on the built environment, economy and cultural land-scape will be considerable. All we can hope for is that any such change is mindful of the rich history of East London, and treats it with respect.

CHAPTER 1

The Parish of Stepney to 1700

A S THE seventeenth century opened, roughly 200,000 people lived in London, making it by far the largest city in the realm.[1] The continuities with the past were powerful. John Stow, whose *Survey of London* was first published in 1598 and set the standard for all subsequent accounts, looked back on a city little different from that recorded by William Fitzstephen some four hundred years earlier. It was geographically and symbolically divided between the City of London, bounded by ancient walls and inhabited by merchants, traders, financiers and craftsmen, and the City of Westminster, the ancient seat of the Court, government and established religion. Between them ran The Strand, which closely followed the course of the Thames through a right-angled bend. Across the river the lowly settlement of Southwark was just beginning to take shape.

London was in many respects a large country town. Its houses were constructed of wood; many had gardens, and there were green fields and farms close by. None was far removed from the Thames. Livestock were driven through the streets, and smaller animals and fowl were kept in back yards to supplement family diets. The network of streets had been laid down haphazardly in mediaeval times; most were narrow, ill-paved and ill-lit, more suited to the wheelbarrow and the pedestrian than the large cart. Water and refuse presented seemingly intractable problems. Since few adequate defences had been constructed, land by the Thames was subject to flooding. Natural supplies were the only source of water for human consumption. There was no effective means of disposing of refuse, human and otherwise; instead offensive laystalls (rubbish heaps) and cesspits pock-marked the landscape. For the time being, London was still small enough to be grasped as a totality in the imagination of someone like Stow who was prepared to take the trouble to walk the length and breadth of its streets.[2]

To the east was the parish of Stepney (or Stybbanhythe, later Stebunheath), a populous area stretching from the Tower and the City wall to the River Lea

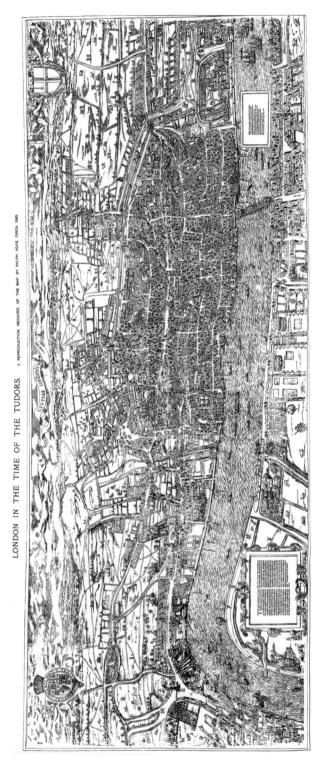

LONDON IN THE TIME OF THE TUDORS.   A REPRODUCTION, REDUCED, OF THE MAP BY RALPH AGAS, CIRCA 1560.

The Agas map of London, c. 1590. To the east, the ancient city wall headed north of the Tower, beyond which stood the Parish of Stepney, with early residential development along the Thames.

on the border with Essex. Over the next century Stepney was to become a commercial and manufacturing centre of such importance that contemporary observers referred to it less as the place eastwards of London than as East London itself. The events which led to the incorporation of the parish into the space of the metropolis are where the story begins.

He spake evil English

Stepney had ancient origins. Founded as a manorial estate by the Normans, it attracted institutions which were clearly unwanted by City authorities in their back yard, and which have survived only in the names of districts. Spitalfields (literally, hospital fields) derived from a priory founded by Walter Brune and his wife Rosia in 1197, which provided for the needs of sick and poor travellers until its dissolution in 1534, at which time it was found to have 180 beds. The site was subsequently occupied by 'many fair Houses builded, for Receipt and Lodging of worshipful and honourable persons'.[3] Nearby, in 1247 a wealthy City merchant, Simon Fitzmary, donated a parcel of land outside the City wall to the monks of St Mary of Bethlehem on which they built a priory. For the next 750 years, on different sites around London, what became the Royal Hospital of Bethlem (more popularly, Bedlam) incarcerated, treated callously and later provided care for those suffering from mental disorders.[4]

The Manor of Stepney was held by London bishops until 1550, when it was confiscated by Henry VIII during his campaign to dissolve the monasteries, and given to Lord Wentworth. The last incumbent was 'bloody' Bishop Bonner, who had supported Henry's break with Rome, but under Mary was reconciled to Catholicism, and gained a reputation as a ruthless persecutor of Protestant dissent. The Wentworth family retained possession until 1720; then, after a brief period, use was granted to Sir George Colebrooke, and was held by his descendants until the abolition of the manorial system in 1926.[5] With its fine mansions and pleasant countryside offering recreation to a wealthy elite, the manor was in many respects typical of those found in pre-modern England. It was a favoured retreat of many notable Londoners. In addition to the long line of London bishops who occupied the manor house, Thomas Cromwell, Thomas More, Sir Henry Colet and his son John, Sir Martin Frobisher, William Penn, Sir William Ryder, Sir William Burrough and Sir John Cass lived in Stepney. John Stow, writing somewhat nostalgically at the end of the sixteenth century about an age in the history of the city that was rapidly disappearing, suggested that the parish had an even wider appeal among the general populace:

I find also that in the moneth of May, the Citizens of London of all estates ... had their seuerall mayings, and did fetch in Maypoles, with diuerse warlike shewes, with good Archers, Morice dauncers, and other deuices, for pastime all the day long; and toward the Euening they had stage playes, and Bonefiers in the streetes: of these Mayings, we read in the raigne of *Henry* the sixt, that the Aldermen and Shiriffes of London being on May-day at the Bishop of Londons wood in the parish of *Stebunheath*, and hauing there a worshipfull dinner for themselues and other commers ...[6]

Hunting had long taken place in that part of the bishop's wood later occupied by Victoria Park and its surrounds. When in 1292 the bishop attempted to enclose it for his own private parties, he provoked a mass protest among Londoners. A petition successfully submitted to the king claimed that from time immemorial citizens had hunted in the woods for 'hares, foxies, conies, and other beasts'. As late as the nineteenth century, these popular hunting rights continued to be asserted symbolically on Easter Monday by chasing a stag on foot through the countryside.[7]

The ancient church of St Dunstan, rebuilt in the tenth century by the Bishop of London, and the only parish church in Stepney until the construction of St Mary Whitechapel in the early fourteenth century .

During the Tudor period, many local popular recreations took on distinctly militaristic aspects. Tournaments were staged in the neighbourhood of Bishop's Hall and Mile End Green, while practice sessions at archery butts in Shoreditch and Stepney Green created such skilled archers that Henry VIII established the order of Knights of Prince Arthur's Round Table with responsibility for organizing annual pageants at which the 'Knights' staged mock battles. And at Mile End Green in 1539, London's citizen army mustered before marching to Westminster for review before Henry. It must have been an impressive occasion, as Richard Grafton recalled:

euery Alderman in order of battaile with his ward came into the common field at Mile Ende, and then all the Gonnes seuered themselves into one place, the Pykes into another, and the Bowmen in another, and likewise the Bilmen, and there rynged and snayled, which was a goodly sight to behold: for all the fields from white Chappell toe Myle ende, and from Bednall Greene to Ratclyffe, and to Stepney were all couered with harnesse, men and weapons, and in especiall the battaile of Pykes seemed like a great Forest.[8]

The reference made by Stow to the enactment of stage plays was no aside, for at the time of his survey, Stepney and neighbouring Shoreditch were at the vital heart of English theatre during its formative period. Since mediaeval times a large variety of dramatic productions, including miracle and mystery plays, mummings, pageants, dances and jigs, had been performed by strolling players in towns and the countryside wherever a suitable site could be found. Most of the productions were ephemeral, had little status and were therefore rarely published. During the late Elizabethan age, however, the work of a handful of entrepreneurs, proprietors, actors and playwrights led to the brilliant flowering of a new cultural form – even though there were few at the time who recognized the significance of the moment.[9] Theatre became increasingly professional, secular and cosmopolitan. Classical drama was revived, tragedies made their appearance, and there was a considerable appetite for straight history, all of which was staged with comic interludes.

Beyond the reach of City censorship and taxation, and yet close enough to attract audiences, Stepney and Shoreditch were well situated to host such entertainment. The staging of plays in the courtyards of inns had long been established but in 1567 John Brayne, a grocer, opened what was arguably the first purpose-built theatre with a stage and galleries at the Red Lion in Whitechapel. It was designed to provide a venue for touring companies, and had some commercial success, but within a year had closed down. Undeterred, Brayne teamed up with his brother-in-law, the tragic actor Richard Burbage, to finance the building of a new theatre. Constructed on the site of the Holywell Priory, Shoreditch, in 1576, and named simply The Theatre, it accommodated a permanent company of players, and enjoyed such an immediate success that in the following year Burbage built another theatre – The Curtain – nearby.

Drama had always provided space for dissent, and productions at the new public theatres were no exception. The Theatre soon attracted the notice of City authorities. A letter from the Lord Mayor dated 12 April

1580 informed the Lord Chancellor that 'great disorder' had been committed at The Theatre on Sunday last, and that it was his

> duty to inform him that the players of plays, used at the Theatre and other such places, and tumblers and such like, were a very superfluous sort of men, and of such faculty as the laws had disallowed; that the exercise of the plays was not only of great hindrance to the service of God, but also a great corruption of youth, with unchaste and wicked manners, the occasion of much incontinence, practices of many frays, quarrels and other disorders, within the City. He therefore begged that order might be taken to prevent such plays, not only within the City, but also in the liberties.[10]

The Lord Mayor did not have to wait long. Early in 1581 Brayne and Burbage were charged in the Middlesex Quarter Sessions that on 'divers occasions' they

> brought together and maintained unlawful assemblies of the people to hear and see certain colloquies or interludes called playes … at a certain place called The Theatre … By reason of which unlawful assembling of the people great affrays assaults tumults and quasi-insurrections and divers other misdeeds and enormities have been then and there done and perpetrated by very many ill-disposed persons to the great disturbance of the peace of the Lady the Queen.[11]

The charges were exaggerated – but only slightly. One remarkable eye-witness account provides us with a rare glimpse of the audience at these early theatres. The Venetian Ambassador, Foscarini, often attended productions, perhaps to gauge the popular mood of the English. On a visit to The Curtain, he was accompanied by a Florentine, Antima Galli, who reported:

> He often goes to the plays in these parts. Among others, he went the other day to a playhouse called the Curtain, which is beyond his house. It is an infamous place in which no good citizen or gentleman would show his face. And what is worse, in order not to pay a royal, or a scudo, to go in one of the little rooms, not even to sit in the degrees that are there, he insisted on standing in the middle down below among the gang of porters and carters, giving as his excuse that he was hard of hearing – as if he could have understood the language anyway.[12]

That evening the Ambassador faced a near riot. He was invited by the players to announce the next performance – a choice that proved so unpopular that the audience, thinking he was a Spaniard, turned on him and drove him out.

In the ensuing years, outbreaks of the plague were used conveniently to justify restrictions on stage productions in and around the City, but the Lord Mayor and his lieutenants were well aware that Henry VIII and Elizabeth I, together with large sections of the population, took delight in the theatre, and so an uneasy compromise was reached allowing productions at certain times of the week 'without danger of infection'. One notable playwright and actor joined the company when he arrived in London in 1592, and thus it was that many of the plays of William Shakespeare, including *Henry VI, The Comedy of Errors*, and *Romeo and Juliet*, had their premieres on the stages of The Theatre and The Curtain. At this seeming high point in the history of British theatre the attacks from City authorities intensified, no doubt prompted by the unprecedented popularity of the various venues. A petition against a theatre that had been converted from a private house in Blackfriars was submitted by constables to the Lord Mayor in 1596 and provides a wonderful insight into the nature of their concerns. The petitioners declared that

> there was daily such a resort of people and such a multitude of coaches (many of them Hackney coaches bringing people of all sorts), that at times the streets could not contain them, they clogged up Ludgate Hill also, so that they endangered one another, broke down stalls, threw down goods, and the inhabitants were unable to get to their houses or bring in their provisions, the tradesmen to utter their wares, or passengers to get to the common water stairs without danger of life and limb; quarrels and effusion of blood had followed, and other dangers might be occasioned by the broils, plots and practices of such an unruly multitude.[13]

In 1595 the Lord Mayor requested the magistrates of Surrey and Middlesex to suppress plays on the Bankside in Southwark because of recent increases in crime. Two years later The Theatre and The Curtain were singled out in another letter.[14] When combined with the refusal of the landlord to extend the lease on The Theatre, the suppression led to its forcible closure. Legend has it that when it was demolished the timbers of The Theatre were carried across the Thames and used to build the Globe Theatre in Southwark. In June 1600 the Privy Council ordered that the only theatres allowed to continue were the recently built Globe at Bankside and the Fortune at Golden Lane on the eastern edge of the City; despite this The Curtain survived until 1610.

The appearance of Protestant dissent in the early sixteenth century represented another vital strand of Stepney's resistance to the established order. England was a Catholic country, with levels of church attendance as high as anywhere in Europe. There were, however, significant and mounting undercurrents of disaffection with the conduct of priests. At a time when most in the country lived meagre lives, lavish expenditure on ritual and ornamentation, the corrupt practice of selling indulgences to pardon past sins, and the unwarranted interference of ecclesiastical law into people's lives created deep resentment. This dissent gained momentum when the German monk Martin Luther launched his revolt against the Papacy. Lutheran religious tracts and ideas soon reached across the Channel – at first a trickle and then a flood – carried by the considerable trade between England and Germany and the Low Countries. Unsurprisingly, therefore, southern and eastern ports were among the first to be exposed to dissent, and throughout the century the powerhouse of Protestantism was located in the south-east.[15]

From the outset, Stepney was responsive to the stirrings of reform. Leading Christian humanists including Richard Fox and John Colet found enthusiastic audiences amongst parish congregations before moving on to bigger things. Others paid a high price for their beliefs. In 1540 William Jerome, who had been appointed vicar of St Dunstan's, Stepney, three years earlier, was burned at Smithfield as a Lutheran. And Edward Underhill, known as the 'hot gospeller' for the fervour of his Protestant ballads during his time at Limehouse, was imprisoned by Mary, and later fled Stepney to avoid further persecution.[16]

At this early stage the desire for separation from the Catholic Church was hardly a movement, let alone a revolution. Lutherans, Anabaptists, Puritans, Seekers, Independents, Brownists and Barrowists were among many sects that eventually unified, albeit uneasily, into the concerted resistance which brought about the Reformation.[17] Such internal schisms, however, did not seem to allay the fears of civil and religious authorities, who did what they could to persecute dissent in its various manifestations. As part of the oath taken by every freeman of the City was the requirement that 'ye shall know no gatherings, conventicles nor conspiracies made against the Kings Peace'.[18] Beyond the City, the riverside areas of Stepney attracted attention for they offered a degree of refuge and, more importantly, were the first ports of call for continental emigrants seeking to spread the message of religious dissent.

The ideas of Luther and Calvin in particular found fertile soil in the Stepney hamlets, where congregations grew rapidly during the reign of Mary.

Fearing persecution, they took steps to avoid detection. An instance of martyrdom compiled by John Foxe and included in his remarkable *Acts and Monuments* provides insight into the clandestine activities such congregations were forced to adopt in Stepney. In 1558 Cuthbert Sympson, deacon of the 'Christian congregation in London', who had been charged with attending 'assemblies and conventicles where there was a multitude of people gathered together to hear the English service', was tortured by Bishop Bonner before being burnt at the stake. The case against Sympson relied in part upon evidence submitted by a spy and other lowly informants. James Mearing testified that 'The meeting sometimes is at Wapping, at one Church's house, hard by the waterside; sometimes at a widow's house at Ratcliff, at the Kings-head there; sometimes at St. Katherine's at a shoemaker's house, a Dutchman called Frog'.[19] The widow was Alice Warner, who herself provided evidence of what appeared to be clandestine meetings of foreigners at her house:

> That upon a Sunday, six weekes agone, a certain company of Frenchmen, Dutchmen, and other strangers, and amongst them Englishmen, appearing to be young merchants, to the number of a score, resorted to her house of the Kings-head at Ratcliffe; requesting to have a pig roasted, and half a dozen faggots to be brent. In the meantime the said company went into a back house ...; the said multitude called one another 'brother' and did every one, to his hability, cast down upon the table money, which was two pence per piece, said money was disposed ... to the use and relief of the poor. And this examinate thinketh it was a Frenchman, or some other outlandishman, because he spake evil English.[20]

Following the death of Mary Queen of Scots in 1587 a degree of religious freedom for dissent prevailed in which various sects were able to gain congregations in Stepney. Among the most important was that led by Thomas Helwys, who on return from a period of refuge in the Netherlands founded the first Baptist congregation in England at Spitalfields. While there he published *A Short Declaration on the Mystery of Iniquity* (1612) which stoutly defended the principles of religious liberty. A copy sent to James I contained a handwritten declaration that the king was mortal and had no power to make laws over his subjects. All this clearly transgressed the boundaries of tolerance; Helwys was imprisoned in Newgate, to die there four years later.

The great confluence of people

The culture of dissent was sustained by social changes within the early modern parish. Despite legal restrictions, Whitechapel and Spitalfields continued to attract large numbers of migrant labourers, street sellers and illicit traders who were barred from the City but found that they could survive on its rich pickings. After dissolution of the priory in 1534, the focal point of Spitalfields had shifted to Spital Square, which became a site of wealthy residence and, along with St Paul's, the most important pulpit in England: 'In place of this hospital, and near adjoining, are now many fair houses built for receipt and lodging of worshipful persons,' observed Stow.[21] To the west stood the Artillery ground on a site used previously to grow teasels and erect tenter frames for the manufacture of cloth, to the east a large field (Spitalfield) which was occasionally taken over by a large fair, and to the south Whitechapel, which continued to host a sizable itinerant population.[22]

Whitechapel and Spitalfields were adjacent to highways dating back to Roman times, the most important of which passed from London to Colchester and came to be known as the Whitechapel Road after the name commonly attached to St Mary Matfelon Church erected just outside the City wall in 1329. This eastern route had for centuries been the meeting place of town and country, and was frequently congested with carts transporting produce, and with animals being driven to abattoirs. Coaching inns and taverns had been built to cater for this traffic, and by the close of the sixteenth century houses began to spread along this and other eastbound thoroughfares. Stow may have celebrated the plebeian culture of the time, but it was a celebration increasingly tempered by deep anxieties held by all shades of polite opinion, most particularly by the City merchants, that the rapid growth of the area would bring the poor and attendant social problems.

The fears were real enough. In Elizabethan times large numbers of the 'poorer sort of Trades and Occupations' had migrated to London from other parts of the country. Barred from entering the City by the authority of the various livery companies, they exercised their 'illicit' trades in the immediate vicinity of the City walls. According to John Strype, they made 'counterfeit indigo, musk, saffron, cochineal, nutmegs, wax, steel and other Commodities; but they were but Bunglers at their Business'.[23] They flouted the rules governing indenture by taking an 'abundance of Apprentices' who rarely served their full term, as a result of which 'few became sufficient Workmen'. Overall, the increase in this population was seen as a threat to the well-being and commerce of Londoners: for 'besides that the Sickness was often increased, the Suburbs were abused by false and often insufficient Wares; and deceits were practised by them, having none appointed to oversee them and their Works'.

Whether it was the 'encouragement these petty Traders and Artificers met with', reflected Strype, 'or the multiplying of the meaner sort of People … a great number of Edifices were erected in the Suburbs, where before were Fields, and void Places; especially in the Eastern part of the City'.[24] This was a situation that the City authorities could not allow to continue, and so, following a series of forceful complaints, Elizabeth I issued a proclamation in 1580 that sought to restrict further growth. The proclamation opened sternly by describing how her 'principal care under Almighty God … to have her people not only well governed by Ordinary Justice, to serve God, and obey Her Majesty', had been rendered virtually impossible 'without device of more new Jurisdictions and Officers for that purpose; but to be also provided of Sustentation of Victuals, Food and other Necessaries for Mans life, upon reasonable Prices; without which no City can continue'. Besides the problems posed by public order and inflation in the prices of essential goods, there was an enhanced danger threatened by the plague:

> Yet where there are such great Multitudes of People brought to inhabit in small Rooms; whereof a great part are seen very Poor; yea, such as must live by Begging, or by worse Means; and they heaped up together, and in a Sort smothered with many Families of Children and Servants in one House or small Tenement; it must needs follow, if Plague or Popular Sickness should … enter among those Multitudes, that the same would not only spread itself and invade the whole City and Confines, as great Mortality should ensue the same …; besides the great Confluence of People from all Places of the Realm, to the manifest Danger of the whole Body thereof.[25]

The proclamation closed by imposing a ban on the building of all new houses and tenements within three miles of the gates of the City 'where no former House hath been known to have been in the Memory of such as are now living'. This was the first legislative restriction on the growth of buildings. Coming as it did in the late sixteenth century, it represented a determined attempt to strangle the growth of those parts of Stepney adjacent to the City, but Whitechapel and Spitalfields continued to grow seemingly untroubled by the attention of City authorities. Indeed, as the redoubtable Dorothy George has argued, such restrictions, especially when faced with the multitudes of the poor who flocked to live in the area, actually encouraged the construction of inferior accommodation. Few builders were willing to invest heavily in houses that could be razed to the ground if they were found to have infringed the proclamation; instead, they constructed or patched up cheap and wretched hovels, hidden from view in small courts and alleys, in full knowledge that in the absence of alternative accommodation people in desperate circumstances would be forced to live there.[26]

John Stow wrote shortly after the proclamation and was well aware of its failure to prevent further urbanization. In surveying changes that he had witnessed in Stepney he may have lamented for a lost age in the history of the city, but there is little reason to suggest that the record was unreliable. His account of the Whitechapel Road leading out of Aldgate, for example, captured a sense of how slum housing was intruding on pleasant common land, leading to a loss as dramatic as any act of enclosure:

> both sides of the streete bee pestered with Cottages and Allies, euen vp to White chappel church: and almost halfe a mile beyond it, into the common field: all which ought to lye open & free for all men. But this common field, I say, being sometime the beauty of this City on that part, is so incroched vpon by building of filthy Cottages, and with other purprestures, inclosures, and Laystalles (notwithstanding all proclaimations and Acts of Parliament made to the contrary) that in some places it scarce remaineth a sufficient high way for the meeting of Carriages and droues of Cattell, much less is there any faire, pleasant or wholesome way for people to walke on foot.[27]

The next hundred years was punctuated by a series of largely unsuccessful attempts to restrict the growth of inferior houses in the eastern suburbs of London. Enacted in Tudor and Stuart royal proclamations and statutes, they provide us with valuable insights into the range of contemporary concerns promoted by the settlement of the poor in areas beyond the control of City authorities.[28] In 1583 an example was made 'in some very public manner' by the public punishment of individuals who had transgressed the proclamation, although the law was 'too short to pull down the houses that were already built'.[29] Ten years later a statute was introduced against new buildings and the subdivision of houses to create new extra tenements; exempted was accommodation for the 'better sort' and, more significantly, for the mariners, sailors and shipwrights in the riverside districts.[30] As her reign came to an end, however, Elizabeth retrospectively surveyed over twenty years of endeavour to control suburban growth, and concluded that 'manifold mischiefs ... were like daily to increase for want of due execution of the said [1580] proclamation'. Perceiving 'great delay, negligence and partiality' in applying the proclamation, she commanded the Lord Mayor and other authorities 'faithfully and diligently' to execute nine articles designed to eliminate the construction of dwellings on new sites within three miles of the City walls, and lay down punishments for any transgressors.[31]

Rarely in the history of English law could the desired effect of a royal proclamation have proved so misplaced in so short a time, for early in the following year London was stricken with a devastating outbreak of the bubonic plague. Widely thought at the time to have migrated from the suburbs, it killed 30,000 before it finally receded. Thomas Dekker, one of an outstanding corpus of Tudor pamphleteers, left us with the most vivid and poignant of contemporary accounts. In *The VVonderfull Yeare*, published as the last victims were being buried, he captures the peculiar suffering of the eastern suburbs:

> Imagine then that all this while, Death (like a Spanish Leagar, or rather like a stalking *Tamberlaine*) hath pitcht his tents, (being nothing but a heape of winding sheetes tackt together) in the sinfully-polluted Suburbs: the Plague is Muster-maister and Marshall of the field.[32]

Such horrors were no doubt intensified by the panicked exodus from London of thousands fleeing the plague, the vast majority of whom passed through the suburbs:

> for away they trudge thicke & threefolde, some riding, some on foote, some without bootes, some in their slippers, by water, by land, In shoales swom they west-ward, many to *Graues-end* none went vnless they were driven, for whosoeuer landed there neuer came back again: Hacknies, watermen & wagons were not so terribly imployed many a yeare; so yt within a short time, there was not a good horse in Smithfield, nor a Coach to be set eye on … In this pitiful (or rather pittilesse) perplexity stood *London*, forsaken like a Louer, forlorne like a widow, and disarmd of all comfort.[33]

Finally, continuing a practice that had existed for centuries, the east beyond the City walls was used as a dumping ground for the dead and afflicted:

> let vs see what doings the Sexton of *Stepny* hath: whose ware-hovses being all full of dead commodities, sauing one: that one he left open a whole night (yet it was half full too) knowing yt theeues this year

were too honest to break into such cellars. Besides those that were left
there, had such plaguy-pates, that none durst meddle with them for
their lives.[34]

For James I, who had just acceded to the throne, this outbreak must have
seemed untimely, and with great alacrity he took up the cause of Elizabeth to
rid the suburbs of undesirable elements. He determined that because the
'great confluence … of excessive numbers of idle, indigent, dissolute, and
dangerous persons' in small habitations in and about the City had been 'one
of the chiefest occasions of the great plague and mortality', the articles of the
1602 proclamation be carefully and speedily executed, and no tenement
infected by the plague be reoccupied.[35] The panic over, and ever mindful of
the need for profitable housekeeping, James turned his attention to the
general state of London's buildings. A proclamation of 1605 ordered that any
new house within a mile of the suburbs be built wholly of brick and stone:
any suggestion that this was solely a means of improving the built environment, however, has to be tempered by recognition that James was largely
inspired here by the necessity of preserving timber for the maintenance of
the 'Shipping and Navie of this Realm'.[36]

Whatever the motive, this proclamation, like its predecessors, proved
futile. Further proclamations followed which grew ever more complex in
the demands made of new building. Occasionally campaigns were launched
to prosecute offenders, as in 1616 when proceedings were taken out against
several defaulters. Among them was the hapless William Hearne of
Whitechapel, who, following a petition submitted by parishioners, was
charged with building 'diverse tenements of an auntyent stable in a common
Inn called the Redd Lyon in Whitechapel street, directly contrary to his
Majestie's proclamation, and to the great annoyance and charge of the rest
of the parishioners by bringing poore people there to inhabit, who in dying
leave their children to be maytayned by the parish'. Hearne was ordered to
dismantle the chimneys he had built and return the building to the original
stable.[37] What is interesting about this particular case is that it was prompted
not by fears amongst parishioners of disease and disorder, but by the threat
of increased rates, and it tended to suggest that the targets were not necessarily the large developers, many of whom paid handsomely for permission
to build, but early manifestations of the jerry-builder. Indeed, ultimately it
was the imperatives of speculative house builders of the kind that came to
be associated with the excesses of the nineteenth century that frustrated all
attempts to restrict the growth of inferior accommodation in the eastern
suburbs of the seventeenth century. As a contemporary tract reveals:

The desire of Profitte greatly increaseth Buyldinges and so much the more for that this greate Concurse of all sortes of people drawing nere unto the Cittie, everie man seeketh out places, highe-wayes, lanes and coverte corners to buylde upon, yf it be but sheddes, cottages and small tenements for people to lodge inn, wch have not any meanes either to lyve or to imploye themselves about any other manner of thinge, than either to begge or steale, by wch meanes of Idleness, it cometh to passe that in some one parrishe ther are above two thousand people wch doe lyve without any man's knowledge howe, not useinge any manner of Art or Trade. This sorte of covetous Buylders exacte greater renttes, and daiely doe increase them, in so muche that a poore handie-craftsman is not able by his paynefull laboure to paye the rentte of a smaller tenement and feede his familie.[38]

It is easy to assail these practices, and such builders have rightly been taken to task for what they did, but it has to be remembered that they operated in structures and systems that were not of their choosing. It was the custom of the Manor of Stepney to grant leases of only thirty-one years, effectively discouraging the construction of better accommodation or even the regular maintenance of existing accommodation.

The Civil War temporarily brought an end to house building, but then parliament, while wishing to revive development, took steps to prevent its worst excesses. Noting that 'New Buildings, Outhouses and Cottages' were a 'great Annoyance and Nusance to the Commonwealth', and that, despite previous legislation to the contrary, the 'growing Evil was multiplied and encreased', an Act of 1656 forbade new buildings within ten miles of London with less than four acres of land attached. Predictably, this failed to prevent another major outbreak of the plague in 1665, but by this time authorities were close to acknowledging that restrictive legislation was ineffective, and towards the end of the century the campaign was more or less abandoned.[39] A Bill of 1709 to prevent the construction of houses on new foundations provoked animated petitions from influential local land-holders with ambitious development plans and as a consequence was never implemented.[40]

Ancient divisions

By the end of the century the population of London had nearly trebled to 575,000 – twice that of all the other major urban centres in England combined. This figure, however, disguises variations which reveal more precisely the uneven nature of the dramatic growth that had taken place. Most notable was the massive shift in the balance of the population to the outlying suburbs. In 1560, three quarters of London's residents were to be found in the City limits; by 1680, and despite a slight increase, the population of the City made up only a quarter of the total.

What is clear, therefore, is that the increase in London's population was due largely to expansion of the suburbs beyond the older boundaries. Of these suburbs, the eastern grew strongest, as a result of which its population of 140,000 in 1680 was fourteen times that of 120 years earlier, and was now more than double that of any other suburban area to the west, south or north.[41] London acted as a powerful magnet at a time of rural depopulation when tens of thousands of people displaced by enclosures and developments in capitalist agriculture sought regular work. Many of those who migrated to London discovered, contrary to popular belief, that its streets were not paved with gold, but then the wages offered to artisans in London were up to fifty per cent higher than in the provinces, and the spell cast by London on the nation's imagination remained.[42] For the less skilled the mere prospect of employment in labouring, service and transport was enough to persuade many to journey there. London also drew migrants from continental Europe. Since the fourteenth century the Court had made repeated attempts to attract skilled workers from overseas in the hope that their expertise would be passed on to English artisans, thereby improving the quality of finished goods. Among those attracted were silk weavers from France and the Low Countries who since the mid-sixteenth century had migrated in a steady stream to be granted naturalization and even to be admitted as full members to the London Weavers' Company.[43]

The extraordinary transformation in the population and size of London suggests a change in kind, not merely of degree, for we can detect here signs of the birth of a modern metropolis. Expansion westwards bridged old geographical separations, most notably that between the City and Westminster, which merged into a single continuous town. The built fabric shifted as brick and stone replaced wood. Much of this was driven by a virtue made out of the necessity to rebuild London after the catastrophic Great Fire of 1666, but the Stuarts were well aware of the desirability of more secure structures and had already issued several royal proclamations to that effect. The victory of parliament over Stuart rule in the Civil War of the 1640s would have been impossible without the solid support of the citizens of London. That, however, was not the only victory, for London emerged as a Protestant city in which past religious tensions were overlain by a degree of unanimity that laid the foundations for progress into a modern age.

Integral to this vision was recognition of the urgent need to address the inconvenient and filthy state of London's streets. In 1662 Charles II introduced an Act 'for repairing the High wayes and Sewers and for paving and keeping clean of the Streets in and about the Cities of London & Westminster'.[44] The problem that it addressed must have been a familiar one to many Londoners. The roads, declared the preamble, are so 'miry and foul' as to be a danger to the inhabitants and travellers passing through. To solve these problems the Act proceeded to order the appointment of commissioners with powers to repair or construct sewers and pavements, and to remove encroachments which had hindered free movement, the costs of which would be met by the owners of the houses adjoining the streets, who, it was assumed, stood to gain most from the improvements. Faced with the 'great quantities of Sea-coal-ashes dust dirt and other filth which of late times have beene and daily are throwne into the Streets Lanes and Allies', inhabitants also were charged with the responsibility to sweep and cleanse the streets in front of their houses twice per week, removing all the 'soyle dirt and other filth' ready to be taken away by the scavenger, and to repair or pave the streets from time to time at their own expense.

Soon after, the destruction of large swathes of congested and ill-constructed housing by the Great Fire did more to improve London's built environment than any such legislation, but by 1690 it seemed that many of the old problems remained, particularly in those areas unaffected by the conflagration. An Act 'for Paveing and Cleansing the Streets in the Cityes of London and Westminster and Suburbs and Liberties thereto'[45] sought to restore the provisions of the 1662 Act, which had by then expired. Without compulsion, inhabitants had refused to pay the rates levied for scavengers, as a result of which the 'poorer sort of People' were found to 'dayly throw into the said Streets all the Dirt Filth and Coale-Ashes ... by reason whereof the said streets are become extremely dirty and filthy soe that their Majestyes Subjects cannot conveniently pass through the same about their lawfull Occasions'.

Perhaps most importantly, London was on course to global supremacy as a great commercial and imperial city. It had provided the platform for Britain's age of exploration, during which powerful merchant trading companies such as the East India, Levant and Muscovy exploited their monopoly rights to good effect. England's overseas trade soared during the seventeenth century, the vast bulk of it handled by the Port of London and subsidiary wharves downstream. A century earlier London had been a satellite to the great port of Antwerp; now at the dawn of the eighteenth century it threatened to become the centre of European trade, challenged only by Amsterdam: within another hundred years it would be the commercial and financial capital of the world.[46]

The nursery of navigation

For the more perspicacious observers of the seventeenth century, the making of East London merely confirmed that its economic and political fortunes were inextricably tied to those of the metropolis as a whole. So what precisely was East London at the moment of its assimilation? The rapid growth of the seventeenth century was shaped by physical boundaries. The Thames was a natural barrier, but at the same time the interface between the river and abundant supplies of cheap land close to London encouraged a variety of trades centred on the river and the sea that were critical to the nation's commercial prosperity. The other barrier, manmade and of more recent origin, was the line of the City wall which formed the western limit to the growth of East London, and served to define the line between the order and wealth of the City and an outlying region seemingly beyond the reach of the authority of the City and its livery companies. Here the dead, the dying and the insane of past centuries had been disposed of, and here fledgling trades seeking freedom from restrictive legislation were to seek refuge as the wave of modern metropolitan expansion took off.

Reaches by the Thames had been particularly favourable to the development of a maritime economy; indeed, the first reference to Stybbanhythe – hinting at the probable origin of its name – appeared in c. 1000 when mention was made of a hithe, or landing place, on the gravel by Ratcliff, which was one of the few suitable sites below London Bridge before the outlying marshes were embanked.[47] This section of the river became also an important centre of shipbuilding. We have no evidence of precisely when this was established, but related activity was recorded in the mid-fourteenth century, when timber was purchased at Ratcliff for the king's ships, and carpenters were coerced to work on ships and barges being built there.[48] Although private shipbuilding in Stepney can be traced to mediaeval times, the tradition of Thames shipbuilding effectively began in the sixteenth century with the siting of the royal dockyards on riverside locations at Woolwich, Deptford and Erith to build the large ships commissioned by the navy and trading companies. The first major contract for the Woolwich yard, for example, was the flagship *Henri Grace à Dieu*, completed in 1513 and then fitted out at Erith, where the draught of the Thames was adequate. The smaller private yards also expanded to supply and fit modest ships for the various overseas and domestic coastal trades, as did the army of local smiths, coopers, sail-makers, rope-makers and carpenters whose livelihood came to depend upon the fledgling industry.

One area is worth particular attention since its development trans-formed the industrial and social landscape of the region as a whole, and in important respects defined its relationship with both nascent imperial endeavour and the financial powerhouses of the City. Early in the seventeenth century Blackwall was an unprepossessing site. Situated in a cul-de-sac formed by the rivers Thames and Lea, and therefore somewhat isolated from the eastward development along the riverside, it seemed to offer few advantages. However, it did provide sheltered moorings for offshore ships and was therefore a convenient place of embarkation and disembarkation for travellers wishing to avoid the awkward journey around the Isle of Dogs, and an important anchorage for outward-bound vessels taking on victuals. During the sixteenth century many of the great voyages of discovery had departed from Blackwall, and in 1606 three ships set sail from there filled with passengers who would colonize Virginia. Despite the absence of a purpose-built dock, Blackwall was a favoured location for the repair of the Tudor fleet.[49] In 1614 it was chosen by the East India Company as the site for a new dockyard, and so began the making of Poplar.

The Company had been granted a charter by Elizabeth in 1600 confer-ring monopoly trading rights with India, China, Japan, Sumatra and Java. These rights were exploited to the full. The five ships used on the Company's first voyage had been purchased from private individuals, but the ambitions of the Company, coupled with the demand for larger ships capable of sustaining the rigours of an arduous return journey to the East, encouraged the directors to consider building their own fleet. William Burrell, a Ratcliff shipbuilder, was appointed as Company shipbuilder, and acquired the lease of the Deptford Yard in 1607 on behalf of the Company. Such was the demand, however, that by 1614 Burrell was instructed to build a new dock adjacent to the existing one. Instead, he recommended a new site at Blackwall, where the land was cheap, the river of sufficient depth to accommodate larger ships, and the circuitous journey around the Isle of Dogs was rendered unnecessary. The dry dock was completed two years later along with an iron foundry, spinning house, storehouses, and slaughter- and salting houses to provide for the long voyages. A twelve-foot-high wall was built to provide a degree of security to the yard, but clearly warehouses were considered at risk in such an isolated location, for the Company continued to use various repositories in the City.[50] So rapid was the progress of the yards that in 1621 Thomas Mun, an eminent

London merchant and director of the Company, felt compelled to refute claims that they were draining resources from the king's navy:

> In trade of Merchandize our Ships must goe and come, they are not made to stay at home; yet neuerthelesse, the *East-India* company are well prepared at all times, to serue his Maiestie, and his Kingdomes, with many warlike prouisions, which they always keepe in store; such as Timber, Planks, Iron-workes, Masts, Cordage, Anchors, Caske, Ordinance, Powder, Shot, Victualls ready packed, Wine, Sider, and a world of other things, fitting the present building, repairing and dispatch of Shippes to Sea: as may be plentifully seene in their yardes and storehouses at *Deptforde*, and more especially in those at *Blackewall*; which are growne so famous, that they are daily visited & viewed by strangers, as well as by Embassadors, as others; to their great admiration of his Maiesties strength, & glory, in one onely Company of his Merchants, able at short warning to set forth a fleet of Ships of great force & power.[51]

At this stage, however, Blackwall was not developed as a residential area. Most of the labourers lived closer to London and had to make their way to the yard along Poplar High Street. When salters petitioned the Company for an increase in wages because of the daily journey from London they were granted 1d per night to help towards lodgings close by.[52] The remoteness of residential accommodation was clearly an inconvenience for the Company and its labour force. Soon after the yard opened Burrell purchased the adjacent causeway with a view to its residential development. After a protracted dispute with the Company over ownership a compromise was reached. House construction began in the early 1620s and continued throughout the century.[53]

The impact of the yard on local communities was considerable. Mun suggested that its trade with the East would maintain 2,500 mariners, and shipbuilding and repairing 500 carpenters, caulkers, joiners and other labourers.[54] He was not far wrong: in 1618 the workforce was reckoned to be 232, a number that increased, as more Company ships were commissioned, to nearly 400, making the yard the largest single employer of labour in the London area.[55] In addition, the Company saw itself as a generous local benefactor. '[A]re not many poore Widdowes, Wiues, and Children of *Black-wall, Lime-house, Ratcliffe, Shadwell* and *Wapping*,' inquired Mun,

> often relieved by the *East India* Company, with whole Hogsheads of good Beefe and Porke, Bisket, and doales of money? Are not diuers of

their children set on work to pick Okam, with other labours fitting
their age and capacitie? What might I not say of repayring of Churches,
maintenance of some young Schollers, relieuing of many poore
Preachers of the Gospell yearely with good summes of money; and
diuers other acts of charitie, which are by them religiously performed,
euen in the times of now of their worst misfortunes?[56]

This was a rather optimistic picture. Local inhabitants were allowed to
enter the yard to receive old food distributed as charity, and gather wood
chips for firewood, but when the Company discovered that some took the
opportunity to steal bolts, spikes and other portable items, the practice was
discontinued. Security was clearly its priority. Despite the high wall, Burrell
was instructed to appoint watchmen and turn mastiffs loose in the yard
each evening.[57] In 1627, however, the Company did convert a brick house
with three acres of land at Blackwall into an almshouse for twenty-four
seamen who had served in its ships, two rooms of which were used as a
school until 1730.[58] And in 1642, spurred by a petition from local parishioners, it provided part of the almshouse land for the construction of a
chapel. Over time this was extended and finally consecrated as St Matthias
in 1866.

   As trade continued to increase so the dock was gradually enlarged to
take more and larger vessels, but following a financial crisis provoked by
Dutch rivalry, and mounting criticism that the yard had become a financial
liability, the Company sold the yard to the shipwright Henry Johnson in
1656. It proved a good investment, for in the aftermath of the Civil War
British naval and merchant fleets grew rapidly, including that of the
Company. Many Company ships were built at the yard in the second half
of the century, as a result of which Johnson and his son became rich and
powerful figures in Company affairs. The yard was systematically extended
such that by 1669 it housed the largest wet dock in England.[59]

   Whether it was because the Company, as one of the largest ratepayers
in Stepney, decided it was in its interests to have its voice heard in local
affairs, or because its servants were Godfearing men, it is striking just how
powerful its presence was on the vestry. Among vestrymen appointed in
1634, for example, were Christopher Browne at Ratcliff, who was previously a leading captain of the Company, Robert Fotherby at Poplar, a
manager of the Blackwall yard, and John Ducy at Poplar, a measurer of
timber at the yard.[60] Among the churchwardens of seventeenth-century
Stepney were Robert Salmon, a Company director, and Humphrey
Robinson, Robert Bell and Walter Whiting, all Company merchants.[61]

Although the East India Company was by far the most active of the merchant adventurer companies, many ships of the Muscovy and Levant had also set sail from Stepney yards, captained by the likes of Hugh Willoughby, Richard Chancellor, Humphrey Gilbert, William Burrough, and Martin Frobisher, and manned by local seamen. Trinity House had been founded by Thomas Spert at Stepney in 1514 with responsibility to promote the safety of British shipping, and in addition to East India Company men recorded as active in the affairs of the parish were a host of renowned shipbuilders including members of the Pett and Burrell families, and Henry Johnson.[62] This community – part of a long tradition of seafaring, and standing at the very heart of Britain's commercial and imperial ambitions – was singled out for lavish praise by contemporary observers. John Strype, again writing in a celebratory mood of a London recovering from the traumas of Civil War, remarked of south Stepney

> that it is one of the greatest Nurseries of Navigation, and Breeders of Seamen in *England*, the most serviceable Men in the Nation; without which *England* could not be *England*. For they are its Strength and Wealth. And by how much the more Honour and Use our mariners are to us, so much the greater fame Deservedly accrues unto this Parish, that breeds and brings them up in such great Numbers.[63]

To meet the needs of this rapidly increasing water-borne population and the host of labourers who built and maintained their vessels, houses were strung along the riverside south of the Ratcliff Highway. Starting at the Tower, they gradually extended through St Katharine's, Wapping, Shadwell and Limehouse to Blackwall, so laying the foundations of distinct communities that were to play their part in the history of the area. The settlement was also promoted by a degree of self-interest, skilfully exploited by the Commissioner of Sewers. In 1571 the Commissioner decided that the construction of houses in Wapping would help secure the southern part of the manor from the age-old problem of flooding, for tenants could not but attend to their properties by erecting effective defences. 'The plan succeeded,' claimed Thomas Pennant in 1790, 'and in our days we see a vast and populous town added to the antient precincts (which had stagnated for ages).'[64] Much of the housing, however, occupied as it was by those on the lowest rungs of the maritime hierarchy and those employed in the various associated trades, was little better than slum properties found in other parts of the capital. Stow, situated at the cusp of this transformation, recognized well the forces that signalled early stages in the making of East

London while expressing the prevailing sense of unease about the spread of such properties:

> From this precinct of S. *Katheren* to Wapping in the Woze, the vsuall place of execution for hanging of Pirats & sea Rouers, at the low-water marke … was neuer a house standing within these 40 years; but since the gallowes being after remooued farther off, a continuall streete, or filthy straight passage, with Alleyes of small tenements or cottages builded, inhabited by saylors victualers, along by the riuer of Thames, almost to *Radcliffe*, a good mile from the Tower … Radcliffe it selfe hath beene also encreased in building eastward (in place where I haue knowne a large highway, with fayre Elme trees on both sides) that the same hath now taken hold of Lime Hurst, Lime Host, corruptly called Lime House, some-time distant a mile from Radcliffe … The first building at Radcliffe in my youth (not to be forgotten) was a fayre free schoole, and Almes houses … But of late years shipwrights and (for the most part) other marine men, haue builded many large and strong houses for themselues, and smaller for Saylers, from thence almost to Poplar, and so to Blake wal.[65]

We know little of the plebeian culture of Stepney. It was overwhelmingly oral, that is, it was passed on by word of mouth rather than by written testimony, and so no written evidence provides us with direct access; instead we have to rely on folk tales and the information contained within official accounts such as police and court reports, poor law records, the writings of contemporary middle-class observers, and newspaper accounts. Some insight is provided, however, by the popular ballads of the time. From as early as the sixteenth century aspects of the maritime tradition which dominated Stepney's river-side hamlets featured strongly. In *The Merry Wives of Wapping, or, The Seaman's Wives Clubb*, published as a broadsheet during the 1670s, we learn of a group of wives who, lamenting the absence of their husbands at sea, meet each week to drown their sorrows in hard liquor:

> A knot of women in Wapping do meet,
> One day in a week each other to greet;
> To tell you the truth they do call it a clubb,
> Where they at the Bottle do merrily bub.

> Each one her husband's absence doth bemoan,
> Complaining that they are forc'd to lye alone;
> And that they want what other women have,

Although they are married to seamen brave;
At length being flusht with brisk reviving brandy,
Their sorrows melt away like sugar candy.[66]

Each in turn related how difficult it was to remain faithful to their husbands, especially when presented with distractions:

Now then, quoth the fourth give ear to my tale,
Within a month after my husband set sail,
I could have had proffers, though tempte I be,
Of gallant young gamesters, some 1, 2, & 3.

But enter my apron I would not permit,
The best of them all for to meddle a bit;
Though since in my mind I perhaps might repent,
That faithfulness hindered my real intent.

No such anxieties shrouded the sexual exploits of lone seamen with money in their pockets seeking female company while on shore leave. *The Taylor's Wanton Wife of Wapping*, published about 1683, recounts the story of a seaman who, while ordering a coat, espied the tailor's fair wife:

My dearest creature, said he, I had rather
Have thee, than any fair lady I know;
Therefore this night we will both lodge together,
Home to the taylor my dear shall not go:
We will enjoy the raptures of pleasure,
A sweeter creature sure never was known;
I will endow thee with part of my treasure,
And let the tailor this night be alone.

As was so often the case, however, the sailor was being tricked into losing his hard-earned cash. In other ballads celebrating the exploits of seamen ashore, frequent use is made of playful but thinly disguised sexual innuendo. *The Rigs and Sprees of Ratcliffe Highway and Wapping*, published around 1830 but almost certainly much older, is a good example.

I am a jolly sailor bold,
And always in motion

Have passed the flying Dutchman
Oft, when sailing on the ocean.
Have sailed the globe all round,
And in foreign lands been stopping:
Have crossed the line, but never found
Such a charming place as Wapping.

I met a frigate in full sail,
No calm could her be stopping,
She ran a-head, and anchored in
A dirty bay at Wapping.
She lowered her gib, her mainsail furled,
And tacked about larboard;
She fired a gun, then bang she ran
In a little port to starboard

She ran her bowsprit into me,
So cleverly and handy,
Then I ran on her quarter-deck,
And fired at her gangway.
I broke her poop and holloed – whoop,
And let her cables loose, sir;
They ran away and sailed into
The port of Paddy's Goose sir.[67]

This picaresque maritime culture was also captured in popular tales, including Richard Head's *The English Rogue Described in the Life of Meriton Latroon*.[68] First published in 1667, this was an early example of rogue literature, much imitated in the eighteenth century. Although troubled by the censor for descriptions of sexual exploits, the book was essentially a moral tale designed to expose the traps open to unwary travellers. It tells of the adventures of a young man who falls in with an itinerant band of gypsies to fornicate and cheat his way around the country. Among the places in London visited by the hero was Wapping. Attracted there by the offer of employment as a warehouseman for a merchant with a plantation in Virginia, and befriended in a local alehouse by a seaman and his companions, he eventually realizes that he is being sold, like many of his contemporaries, into maritime slavery, and escapes by capsizing the boat transferring him to a ship anchored in the Thames.

Women, & persons of meane ranke

By this time the early stirrings of religious dissent in Stepney had grown into a major force. For a time during the Civil War, the parish was dominated by Puritanism, although this did not prevent the appearance of colourful religious figures. William Greenhill of Magdalen College, Oxford, founded a body of Independent dissenters at Stepney in 1644, and with Jeremiah Burroughs – the so-called morning and evening stars of Stepney – gave daily lectures. An associate of Greenhill was Matthew Mead, who lived at Mile End and was appointed by Cromwell to a new chapel of Shadwell in 1658 before embarking on his series of Mayday sermons at Stepney Fair (p. 72).[69] Clerics expressing opposition to parliamentary rule, on the other hand, received unwelcome attention. When William Stampe was appointed vicar of Stepney in 1642 and made plain his opposition to the Long Parliament, which was beginning to challenge monarchical authority, he provoked outrage. Services were interrupted by unruly crowds gathered in the churchyard. One parishioner declared she would rather hear a barking dog or a creaking wheel than listen to him preach. Impeachment proceedings were taken against Stampe, who fled the parish to seek refuge in Oxford.[70]

The blossoming of religious sects was followed by a period of retrenchment in which nonconformity was actively discouraged by church and state. Puritanism lost much of its appeal for the middle and upper classes, while the remainder joined the ranks of nonconformist congregations, in particular Presbyterian and Independent. The Restoration therefore saw a flurry of legislation designed to enforce common forms of religious practice and bolster the authority of Charles II. The 1662 Act of Uniformity[71] required adherence to the Book of Common Prayer in all church services, the 1664 Conventicle Act[72] forbade all unauthorized forms of assembly for religious worship, most of which took place in small chapels, houses or even fields, and the 1665 Five Mile (or Oxford) Act[73] banned all persons approaching within five miles of any parish in which they had preached to an unlawful assembly. In 1669 the Archbishop of Canterbury, Sheldon, with the full support of Charles II, sought to chart and hence control what they viewed as the worrying rise of dissent, and to this end ordered Episcopal Returns to be taken of each parish detailing the nature and extent of religious observance among parishioners. In a letter to his archdeacon, Sheldon expressed his underlying fears:

> You cannot choose (as well as I) but be alarmed on all hands with the
> continual reports of the frequency of conventicles and unlawful

meetings of those who, under the pretence of religion and the worship of God, separate from the unity and uniformity of God's service, to the great offence of all, and fear of many of His Majesty's faithful subjects, who love and truly endeavour the peace and prosperity of Church and State.[74]

The returns provide us with insight into the popularity of conventicles in Stepney, for many of these illegal gatherings attracted significant numbers. Presbyterians met at a 'warehouse of Mr. Raymonds neere Ratcliffe Cross fitted for ye purpose', attracting a congregation of 200, while no fewer than 800 met in 'Spittlefields at a new house built for that purpose with pulpit and seates'. Quakers had congregations of 500 in Ratcliff and Spitalfields; Independents had 500 near Stepney Church, 300 at Wapping and an unrecorded congregation at Spitalfields, while Anabaptists were present in Limehouse, Poplar and Wapping.[75]

These numbers were not only much higher than those for other Middlesex parishes but were recorded with greater precision. Comments from religious observers, however, tended to play down their significance. 'Several meetings of ye same perswasion, consist for the most part of ye same persons,' declared one, while the meetings are 'much encreased by straglers that walk on Sundays for recreation, and goe in, out of curiosity. The generality of these meetings consist of women, & persons of meane ranke.' What was needed to deal with the problem of dissenting congregations, they concluded, was firm resolve at local and national levels:

> While the magistrates were active, they were rarely heard of, except Quakers, and those not a quarter ye number they are now. Many of these meeting people, especially Presbyterians and independents did, till of late, frequent ye Church: and will easily be reconciled again if they see the governmt resolute. Since the death of Sir William Ryder & Major Manly (who kept this parish in good order), there is no justice of peace in ye parish.[76]

There followed a period of renewed persecution. Between 1661 and 1689 more people were arrested for religious dissent in Stepney than in any other Middlesex parish.[77] And their meetings and places of worship were broken up; a few of what must have been many occasions were recorded. Over 1664–5, twenty successive Quaker meetings were disrupted by the constabulary, and members arrested, with much wanton destruction carried out by trained bands. Soldiers removed furniture from the Ratcliff meeting house in 1670, and later returned to confiscate wagonloads of materials before demolishing the house, and in 1682 troops smashed the fittings in the Stepney meeting house of the Independents. Preachers at conventicles were obvious targets. Matthew Mead and Samuel Annesley were convicted several times, and there were numerous arrests of others in Wapping, Limehouse and Spitalfields.[78]

By the 1680s, however, the tide was turning against continued persecution. In 1684 the churchwarden, several constables, supervisors of the poor, headboroughs and beadles of Spitalfields and Bethnal Green were fined for refusing to suppress conventicles in their parishes.[79] And then, in an effort both to promote commerce and to mitigate the powers of the Anglican Church, James II and William IV respectively introduced the Declaration of Indulgence (1687) and 1689 Toleration Act[80] granting to 'our subjects ... free exercise of their religion for the time to come, and add that to the perfect enjoyment of their property'.

The Quaker community had been sufficiently robust to survive persecution, and was further liberated when the 1689 Quaker Affirmation Act[81] declared that members refusing to swear an oath could no longer be imprisoned and their estates sequestered if they were prepared as an alternative to make a solemn affirmation. Approximately 10,000 Quakers lived in London at the end of the seventeenth century, and were distributed fairly evenly over the City and outlying parishes, although they tended to be concentrated geographically around their meeting houses. By that time, Quaker congregations had established meeting houses in Gracechurch Street on the eastern edge of the City, which became the focal point of the Quaker business and banking communities, and at Devonshire House in nearby Bishopsgate, which housed the executive body, and included a library and a variety of archives of the movement. Meanwhile, the smaller Quaker meeting houses in Wapping, Ratcliff and Spitalfields continued to grow steadily.

Many of the smaller and more zealous sects, however, collapsed during this period of political stabilization and the relaxation of restrictions on worship, undone in part by the incessant squabbling to which they were prone. Nationally, this may have encouraged the growth of Anglicanism as the state religion, but in Stepney a new challenge to the established church was mounted. An incident in the 1690s nicely illustrates this. In response to the increase in population, two Anglican tabernacles were established in Spitalfields, the second on the estate of the local dignitary Sir George Wheler, who anticipated exercising the type of privileges enjoyed by lords of country manors. He was immediately confronted with petitions to the

House of Commons from sections of the population claiming that these temporary places of worship outside the consecrated church were a deliberate and provocative effort to stall their plans for an alternative church and burial ground, and enforce the 'Rules and Rubricks of the Church of England'. One printed paper contended that Wheler's chapel was too small to seat the congregation and receive the corpses from the hamlet, and that Wheler had no right to dismiss a priest who had failed to conduct services according to his wishes, but then, one suspects, came to the nub of the matter:

> We own we have many *French* and *Walloons*, and many of them joyn in *Divine Worship* with us, and more would if they had *Room*, but there's not a *Dissenters Meeting* in the Hamlet, except one of *Quakers*, very few of which live in our Neighbourhood.[82]

Comments such as these reflect the increasing presence in East London of a distinctive religious and social group: the Huguenots.

Tawdery callico madams

For almost a century Protestants in France, known as Huguenots, had been granted substantial civil rights by the 1598 Edict of Nantes. However, Louis XIV, no enthusiast for religious toleration, encouraged the repression and forcible conversion of Huguenots and in 1685 formally repealed the edict, making Protestantism illegal in France. The subsequent persecution drove large numbers of Huguenots to leave the country, and a substantial community, many of them highly skilled silk weavers, settled in Spitalfields and the adjoining areas. As a direct result of this migration, not only did silk weaving become an industry of considerable magnitude, but its organization and the weavers' struggles against deteriorating circumstances presaged much of the industrial development of East London.

Large quantities of silk goods had first made their appearance in England in the thirteenth century. Laws protecting 'silk-women' from unscrupulous employers and the importation of foreign goods were introduced in the fifteenth century, although reference to 'laces, ribbons and fringes of silk' suggest that manufacturing was devoted to small wares and required little skill.[83] Encouraged by James I, the manufacture of broad silks began early in the seventeenth century and increased so rapidly that in 1629 the Throwsters' Company of London was incorporated to control employment and apprenticeship, the majority of which was within the

City. Indications of the size of the industry are unreliable, but it appears to have been considerable. In 1661 the Company claimed that it employed 40,000 men, women and children. This was probably an exaggeration, although it is supported by Daniel Defoe's estimate of 50,000 in 1679, and by J. Trevers' assertion of 1675 that 100,000 persons were dependent upon the London trade.[84]

This expansion created its own difficulties, particularly when James I's attempt to boost the domestic industry by introducing silk looms and foreign weavers was met with determined resistance from weavers who saw them as a threat to their livelihoods. A petition of 1616 voiced common resentment against the arrival of foreigners in London. Foreign weavers, it complained, had

> made bold use of late to devise engines for the working of tape, lace, ribbons, and such, wherein one man doth more than seven English men can, so as their cheap sale of these commodities beggareth all our English artificers of that trade that enricheth them.[85]

The King responded by affirming that despite 'steps taken in former times and in the present reign against aliens … they multiply so fast as to enhance the price of provision, lodging, &c, and by their ingenious machines &c usurp the trade from the English', and suggested that the 'benefit of laws be taken against them'.[86] But James recognized well that the future of the domestic silk industry depended upon the importation of foreign skills, and so no action was taken. Other unsuccessful petitions followed until the outbreak of the Civil War temporarily put an end to such representations. As a body, weavers enthusiastically supported the parliamentary cause, indeed it was the combined loyalty of such artisans which prevented London from falling into the hands of Royalist forces.[87] They joined the trained regiments, declared adherence to the ideas of popular sovereignty espoused by the radical John Lilburne, and were largely responsible for the rapid construction of fortifications around the capital when a contemporary observer, William Lithgow, noted some 4,000 weavers and other craftsmen marching with shovels and mattocks along the section running from Wapping to Whitechapel.[88]

Victory, however, brought no improvement in the conditions experienced by the main body of weavers. In 1650 a short pamphlet entitled *The humble Representation of the Commonalty of the Weavers Company* contended that the 'many thousands of the poorer sort of us … are like to perish' because 'thousands of intruders are suffered into our trade … aliens eate the bread out of our mouths [and] our inheritance is possest by strangers'. The blame for this resides not with parliament, but at the doors of the master weavers who make up the governors of the Weavers' Company:

[A]t the beginning of the war many of us and our servants engaged for the Parliament and in our absence, they, being generally malignant, staying at home, and keeping servants all of their own country, never employing any English ... by degree got all the trading, so that now the war is ended, and returned to follow our callings, we can get no employment. By which means many hundreds have been forced to leave the trade, as to be porters, labourers, water-bearers, etc., and many forced to take relief from the several parishes wherein they dwell.[89]

The plague and Great Fire of 1665–6 intensified the plight of weavers. It has been estimated that over 1,000 weavers and their families from the Spitalfields area perished.[90] One victim had carved on his gravestone in Stepney Churchyard:

Here lieth the body of Daniel Saul,
Spittlefields weaver; and that's all.

It was as eloquent an epitaph to the life and death of an East London artisan as we are likely to find. A petition in 1670 led to the introduction of a bill to prohibit the importation of foreign wrought silks and looms, but a counter-petition claiming the ban went against the interests of domestic industry by stifling invention and ingenuity prevented its passage and the importation of foreign labour continued.

By 1687 over 13,000 Huguenots had made their way to London, approximately 3,000 of whom were merchants and professionals, the remainder artisan weavers. They brought skills to manufacture a much wider range of fabrics, with appropriately exotic names, than had previously been possible. Lustrings, alamodes, brocades, satins, mantuas, velvets, watered tabbies and ducapes of the highest quality were now produced to meet the seemingly insatiable appetites of fashionable Londoners. A petition presented to parliament by the Weavers' Company in 1713 claimed that the level of silk manufacture was twenty times that of 1664, and the industry was worth £300,000 per year.[91] Further impetus was given in 1718 when Thomas and John Lombe were granted a patent for water-driven machinery capable of spinning organzine from raw silk with speed and efficiency.[92]

The majority of these weavers took up residence in Spitalfields, although as their numbers grew many later moved to the previously isolated areas of Bethnal Green and Mile End Town. John Strype observed the transformation of Spitalfields brought about by this settlement:

> Within this Parish, formerly, in the Memory of some, pleasant Fields for the Citizens to walk in and for good Housewives to whiten their Cloths: Now all but built into Streets, with a very convenient Market-place, and a Tabernacle for Divine Worship.[93]

The refugees seem to have been welcomed, at least by the authorities; Charles II gave them naturalization and equality before the law, the local community benefited from increased employment, and respectable opinion favoured the example they set. Strype argued (perhaps not dispassionately since he was himself born of a leading family of silk weavers which had fled persecution) that the nation as a whole was in their debt:

> Here they have found Quiet and Security, and settled themselves in their several Trades and Occupations: Weavers especially. Whereby God's Blessing surely is not only brought upon this Parish, by receiving poor Strangers ... but also a great Advantage hath accrued to the whole Nation, by the rich Manufactures of weaving Silks, Stuffs and Camblets: which Art they brought along with them; and this benefit also to the Neighbourhood, that these Strangers may serve for Patterns of Thrift, Honesty, Industry and Sobriety.[94]

There is little to suggest that Huguenots were considered a threat to the established church; on the contrary, they were granted a licence to build their own churches and follow their distinctive forms of religious practice. French churches had first been established in London during the sixteenth century, but with the wave of settlement during the late seventeenth century their number increased dramatically; in all, forty-eight had been established in London and its suburbs by 1702.[95] In the decade after 1687 new churches appeared at Swan Street, Shoreditch, and in Spitalfields at Crispin Street, Artillery Street, St John Street and Pearl Street.

For indigenous weavers, however, the newcomers posed a threat. In reaction against the government's decision in 1675 to allow large-scale Huguenot immigration, a weavers' riot broke out in Spitalfields and Shoreditch and rapidly spread to other parts of London and its surrounds.[96] The rioters formed into groups of between 30 and 200, and targeted machine looms, which they removed from the houses of master weavers and set alight. The London militia was called out to deal with the disturbance but many of the officers were sympathetic to the weavers and the initiative failed. Charles therefore ordered 3,000 guardsmen to the streets, a measure that eventually quelled the riot. In the aftermath civil authorities, including magistrates, were charged with negligence. Rioters were fined; many were released without charge. Governors of the Weavers' Company proclaimed their ignorance of the events and denounced the rioters.

These protests were rearguard actions against an inexorable tide of foreign competition. By now another, more menacing cloud had appeared which had slowly gathered in the course of the century, and was inextricably linked to the nation's imperial exploits. Since its formation in 1600 the East India Company had established its position as a significant overseas trader by importing wrought silks and dyed and painted calicoes from India into European markets.[97] These wares were relatively cheap and of high quality, and, equally importantly, came to be highly sought after by fashionable society. Printed calicoes, bright and colourful, swept away monochromatic dresses and linings. Although they were dismissed as vulgar and tawdry in some quarters, women with an eye to fashion were not to be deterred, and much of the imported cotton was within reach of the lower social orders. Special occasions attended by women of rank resembled embassies of Indian queens, although it was said that the gentry had difficulty distinguishing their wives from their servants.[98]

Weavers responded through a series of petitions. Attempts in 1680 to force a ban on the wearing of Indian cloth were unsuccessful, but in 1685 parliament agreed to an additional duty of 10 per cent on imported calicoes, which was doubled in 1690. These measures had no noticeable effect, and demands for a total ban were again raised. In desperation at worsening conditions, over 4,000 weavers and their wives marched to parliament during a debate on a bill in 1697, and threatened to invade the house. That same day a contingent stormed East India House in Threadneedle Street, breaking down the door and smashing windows. Three demonstrators were arrested and committed to Newgate. Further attacks followed. The house in Spitalfields belonging to the Deputy Governor of the Company, Thomas Bohun, was besieged by thousands of weavers, two of whom were shot dead by a trained band sent to quell the disturbance, and a large assembly in a Hackney field resolved to destroy Wanstead House – the grand mansion occupied by the all-powerful Governor of the Company, Sir Josiah Child – before the military were able to intervene to prevent them. Even more drastic was the series of assaults carried out on women quietly going their way about the streets of London. Any woman wearing calico – 'tawdery Callico Madam', according to a popular weavers' song – came under threat from weavers and their families of having her dress ripped to pieces, torn from her back, or even doused with nitric acid.

Although these actions were greeted with widespread opprobrium, weavers found a champion in Daniel Defoe. Launching the short-lived journal *The Manufacturer* in 1719, he offered to tell the weavers' story 'in a manner less offensive than they have been able to tell it in the street'.[99] 'Warmth may have been their mistake', but their warning was timely, for 'the whole manufacture of Great Britain will be destroyed by this Callico Plague as People are swept away by the General Infection'. And then in an appeal drawing upon imperial rhetoric he asks all mothers wearing calico to 'consider how many Families of Mothers and Children they help to starve by gratifying their Callico-Fancy … and employing Pagans and Indians, Mahometans and Chineses, instead of Christians and Britains'.

Opinion now swung in favour of the weavers' struggles. A bill prohibiting the use of all calicoes and linen manufactured outside Britain was passed by the commons only to be defeated by the Lords. A period of some tension passed in which thousands of weavers and their families from Spitalfields took to the streets; in 1721 the bill finally became an act. Any celebration was short-lived, for it soon became apparent that despite the threat of fines of up to £20 and continued assaults on the streets, women refused to be dictated to in the manner of their dress. The decades that followed therefore witnessed the deepening distress of silk weavers, to which they responded with petitions and sporadic acts of open violence against women wearing calico, engine looms, the houses of master weavers and parliament. Armed crowds of up to 4,000 were reported on the streets of West London; on several occasions only military intervention prevented loss of life.

One of the considerablest towns

The need to provide accommodation for a growing population in the eastern suburbs, and the emergence of speculative house builders and developers anxious to meet or anticipate that need, overcame all attempts to impose restrictions on further building. Indeed, the seventeenth century witnessed even stronger and more urgent growth which effectively transformed modest and isolated settlements into an urban district that could lay claim to its own identity. Contemporary maps by William Faithorne

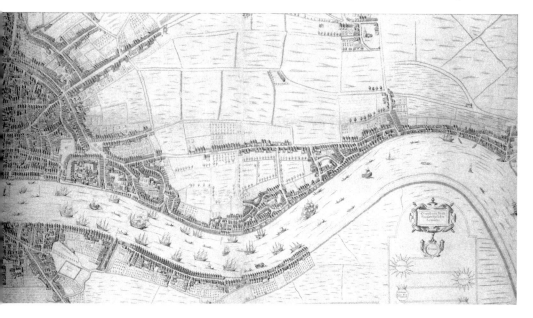

Extract from the Newcourt and Faithorne map of London, 1658. Stepney was now rapidly expanding, particularly along the riverside and around Whitechapel.

(1658) and Ogilby and Morgan (1681) revealed that the population settled in the two areas that had already been seeded. Along the riverside the thin ribbon of housing broadened and extended further to Limehouse, while around Whitechapel new developments spread north along Hog Lane (later and better known as Petticoat Lane) towards Spitalfields, south along the Minories to encroach on Goodman's Fields, and east as far as Mile End.

The social topography of East London predated its incorporation into the metropolis. A study of baptisms, marriages and burials recorded in the parish registers over 1606–10 revealed that the population was heavily concentrated in riverside sites. Over half the baptisms had taken place in the hamlets of Ratcliff (576) and Limehouse (423), followed by Shadwell (171) and Poplar (166). By comparison, the inland hamlets of Mile End (86), Bethnal Green (74) and Spitalfields (58) were small.[100] Burials exceeded births in all the hamlets, suggesting strongly that any increase in the population was the result of immigration, approximately three quarters of which was from London and the Home Counties. From the occupations recorded for the fathers of baptized children we gain some idea of the social composition of the areas. It might be expected that riverside hamlets would reveal a preponderance of those engaged in maritime trades, but the extent of the domination was remarkable. In Shadwell over 90 per cent were so employed, followed by Ratcliff (70 per cent) and Limehouse (67 per cent). None was recorded in Bethnal Green or Spitalfields; here the males employed were weavers, smiths, tailors, shoemakers and builders, or provisioners such as bakers, butchers and brewers.[101] It was notable also that middle-class individuals such as teachers, merchants and gentlemen were very much in evidence. In Bethnal Green a quarter of the total were middle-class; even in poorer hamlets such as Ratcliff and Limehouse they made up 5 per cent. Only in Wapping and Shadwell was none enumerated.

Inhabited by the poor, most of the accommodation was small and inferior. Made either of wood and Flemish lath and plaster, or timber and boards, a typical house had a life of about sixty years, after which it became unstable. More stable brick-built houses were the exception. A parliamentary survey carried out in 1650–51 for tax purposes indicated that they comprised only 8.8 per cent of all houses in Tower Hamlets. Wood had the advantage of cheapness and local availability, so that despite the move towards brick, particularly after the Fire of London in 1666, most of the poorer houses continued to be made as they had in the past. Approximately 90 per cent of the houses were small, typically two-storeyed with four rooms. Few had gardens. Their modesty is indicated graphically by the fact that in 1662, when the hearth tax was introduced, 70 per cent of the houses in Whitechapel, 47 per cent in riverside districts and 45 per cent in Spitalfields were non-chargeable, that is, they were rated in value at less than £1 per annum. Although houses across the district were uniform in size, there were strong contrasts in building patterns. In the sixteenth century, areas such as St Katharine's and Whitechapel had begun to develop unimpeded by planning norms. Here stood closely packed housing built in a seemingly haphazard fashion. Here tenements were frequently erected on vacant sites without the knowledge of the landowner. Riverside districts and Spitalfields, on the other hand, displayed more orderly development, for local landowners such as John Pennington and Sir William Leman laid out streets (often named after them) and let building plots according to an overarching plan.[102]

Stepney was not immune to the influence of Nicolas Barbon, the most rapacious of seventeenth-century developers. In a move revealing a somewhat ambivalent attitude to speculative building in the area, the Crown sold him large plots of land during the 1680s in the Old Artillery Ground, Spitalfields, Wellclose Square, Wapping and Tower Hill, all of which were close to residential building.[103] In ways that would become only too familiar in years to follow, Barbon believed in the operation of the free market and was prepared openly to flout the law in order to build further houses which, far from threatening the City, were to be of lasting benefit, not least, it has to be said, to the benefit of Barbon himself. Writing in 1685 he claimed that the rents in some of the outer districts had been 'considerably advanced by the addition of New Buildings'. Those, for example, in Bishopsgate had increased from fifteen and sixteen shillings per annum to thirty by the 'increase of buildings in Spittle-fields, Shadwell and Ratcliff-Highway'.[104] No reference is made to the adverse effects of such increases on the inhabitants, particularly in driving the necessity of subletting with all its attendant problems.

The ways in which these various tendencies came together is shown by the experience of seventeenth-century Shadwell. Dominated by flat pasture land crossed with ditches, the district was uninhabited until the beginning of the century, when it underwent such rapid growth that by 1700 it was almost totally developed, with a population well in excess of 10,000. The majority of houses were two-storeyed, although sheds had appeared alongside the Ratcliff Highway at the northern boundary, and a few larger houses inhabited by a small elite fronted the Thames. The economy centred on the sea and river. According to the 1650 survey, Shadwell had rope-makers, tan yards, breweries, smitheries and timber yards, and no fewer than four docks and thirty-two wharves along the four hundred yards of river frontage. Of the working population, 53 per cent were mariners, 10 per cent in ship-building, and 7 per cent lightermen.[105]

If there was a moment when East London was created, then this was it. The startling growth of London in the seventeenth century had forced a radical reappraisal of how its boundaries were to be defined. By 1700 it was no longer possible to think of London essentially as a mediaeval walled municipality with small outlying settlements; it was now a sprawling metropolis with an indeterminate centre of gravity, an expansive urban complex made up of districts with distinct characteristics. The transformation is captured in the two great surveys of London which conveniently straddled the period of rapid expansion. That of John Stow appeared in 1598 as the Tudor age was drawing to a close. In a section entitled 'The City of London divided into Parts' he claims that 'the ancient division of the city was into wards and aldermanries' and proceeds systematically to describe each of the twenty-six wards. Later, briefly and almost as a postscript, he gives an account of the 'suburbs without the walls' and the 'City of Westminster'. In 1720 John Strype published his updated and expanded version of Stow; here the ordering of a confident Protestant London is very different:

The dark side of the maritime economy: the body of the pirate William Kidd at Execution Dock, Wapping, 1701. In the remote background is the famous mast house of Perry's Dock at Blackwall, although it was not erected until the 1780s.

The city of London ... may not improperly be divided into four parts. The First is the City of *London* within the Walls and Freedom, which is inhabited by wealthy Merchants and Tradesmen, with a Mixture of Artificers, as depending on Trade and Manufacture. Secondly, the City or Liberties of *Westminster* ... which are taken up by Court and Gentry, yet not without a Mixture of eminent Tradesmen and Artificers. Thirdly, That Part beyond the *Tower*, which compriseth *St. Catharine's, East Smithfield, Wapping, Shadwell, Ratcliff, Limehouse,* and so eastward to *Blackwall*: Which are chiefly inhabited by seafaring Men, and those that, by their Trade, or otherwise, have their Dependence thereon. And, fourthly, *Southwark,* which ... is generally inhabited and fitted with Tradesmen, Artificers, Mariners, Watermen, and such as have their Subsistence by and on the Water: Besides Abundance of Porters and Labourers, useful, in their Kind, to do the most servile Work in each of the four Parts.[106]

What Strype described was a London comprising expansive areas ranked hierarchically according to the professions and trades of their inhabitants. Their boundaries may have been poorly defined, but they signalled the moment of East London's conception: no longer was Stepney merely eastwards of the city; it was an identifiable part of London itself and a suburban district in its own right:

Stepney may be esteemed rather a Province than a Parish, especially if we add, that it contains in it both City and Country: For, towards the south Parts ... it is furnished with every Thing that may intitle it to the Honour, if not of a City, yet, of a great Town; Populousness, Traffic,

Commerce, Havens, Shipping, Manufacture, Plenty and Wealth, the Crown of all. And, were it not eclipsed by the Lustre of the neighbouring City, it would appear to be one of the considerablest Towns of the Kingdom.[107]

Little wonder, therefore, that Strype now wished to lay claim to the area in his picture of a new London striding into the modern age.

CHAPTER 2

Industrialization and the Spirit of Improvement, 1680–1800

T HE SPECTACULAR growth of London in the seventeenth century could not be sustained indefinitely. Even by mid-century it was evident that the rate of population increase was slowing, and this trend was to continue into the next. Thus, while the population of London increased impressively from 490,000 in 1700 to 950,000 in 1800, when compared with the rapid growth of the previous century this represented a certain stabilization brought about by a weakening of the capital's hold over national life. Indeed, as London came under challenge from the manufacturing heartlands of the north and the Midlands, fast emerging as major urban centres through the early impact of the industrial revolution, its share of the country's population actually fell during the second half of the eighteenth century.[1] None of this suggests that London declined as a centre of production; on the contrary, it remained the single largest manufacturer throughout this period; increasingly at the heart of the capital's production lay East London, which entered into a phase of rapid industrialization, quite distinct in its trajectory and form.

The storm that broke elsewhere

East London witnessed the same deceleration of population growth as did London as a whole in the eighteenth century. In 1710–11 the total population of the Tower Division was 143,436, increasing to 188,609 by 1800.[2] Most of this increase was due to net immigration as migrant labour continued to flow into East London at the same time as many of its gentry sought refuge in more salubrious parts of the City. Individual parishes revealed movements away from older settlements to areas that had previously been only sparsely populated (see table opposite). Thus Limehouse, Spitalfields, Shadwell, Wapping and Ratcliff, all of which had seeded the original growth of East London, had reached the

Population of parishes and hamlets within the Tower Division of Middlesex, 1710–11 and 1800[3]

Parish	1710–11	1800
St Anne, Limehouse	7, 020	4, 678
St Botolph, Aldgate	–	6, 153
Christchurch, Spitalfields	21, 420	15, 091
St George's-in-the-East	19, 020	21, 170
St John, Hackney	–	12, 730
St John, Wapping	7, 500	5, 889
St Leonard's, Shoreditch	13, 200	34, 766
St Mary, Whitechapel	18, 000	23, 666
St Mary, Stratford Bow	–	2, 101
St Matthew, Bethnal Green	8, 496	23, 310
Mile End, New Town (hamlet)	6, 462	5, 253
Mile End, Old Town (hamlet)	2, 820	9, 848
Norton Folgate (Liberty)	–	1, 752
St Paul, Shadwell	13, 002	8, 828
Poplar and Blackwall (hamlets)	5,136	4, 493
Ratcliff (hamlet)	21, 360	5, 666
St Katharine's, Tower (Liberty)	–	2, 652
Liberty of the Tower Without	–	563
Total	143,436	188,609

limits of their expansion, while the areas of significant growth included Shoreditch, Whitechapel and Bethnal Green, where there was space for development.

A comparison of contemporary maps tends to confirm these trends. Gascoyne (1703) and Strype (1720) show dense settlements in sites of locational advantage adjacent to the City boundary and the river. By the end of the century riverside settlement had falteringly reached Blackwall via Poplar High Street, while to the north of the parish Bethnal Green and its neighbour to the west, Shoreditch, both of which had in the recent past been open fields, were rapidly being transformed into residential suburbs. Contemporary descriptions of East London tended to affirm that most of the older settlements remained little changed. An early guide described a tour of the riverside communities, now consolidated by their continued reliance on maritime trades into an unbroken band of residential development:

Beyond the Tower, going down river, is St. Catherines: when passing Hermitage-Bridge, you come into Wapping; these two are very large

and populous suburbs. Here, for the generality, the captains or masters
of trading ships and vessels, and their sailors dwell: these places are
near two miles in length. Next adjoining is Shadwell, which lies also
along the river; lower down is Ratcliffe, and Limehouse, which is reckoned about four miles from London Bridge: these five places are
contiguous, and all the little streets, lanes and alleys and courts swarm
with people, and are so considerable, that they contain as many houses
as several capital cities in Europe, though there are no remarkable
buildings in them ...[4]

Mid-century Whitechapel to the north remained a place seemingly
dominated by the main thoroughfare linking the City to the eastern counties and the employment opportunities that the large itinerant trade
offered:

> Whitechapel is a spacious street for entrance to the City eastward, and
> somewhat long, reckoning from the lay-stall east unto the corner of
> Houndsditch West. It is a great thoroughfare, being the Essex Road,
> and well reported to, which occasions it to be well inhabited, and
> accommodated with good inns for the reception of travellers, horses,
> coaches, wagons, &c. Here on the south side is a hay market three
> times a week. The south side within the bars ... is taken up by a great
> many butchers, who carry on a great trade, both wholesale and retail.
> On the north side are divers considerable inns, much resorted to ...
> About the bars ply a great number of stage-coaches, for the conven-
> iency of carrying passengers to Stratford, Bow, Low Layton,
> Laytonstone, West Ham, East Ham, Walthamstow, Woodford,
> Wanstead, Barking, &c.[5]

We must be careful, however, not to overstate the degree of continuity
in such settlements, for there were significant changes brought about
by industrialization. The eighteenth century is conventionally viewed as
the harbinger of the industrial revolution which begat the great manufacturing centres of the Midlands and the north. In contrast to this experience, few large factories sprang up in London; the capital was simply too
remote from the coalfields and sources of iron ore, and its land too
expensive to enable it to compete successfully with the industrial concerns
of centres such as Birmingham, Manchester and Sheffield. 'The industrial
revolution', memorably remarked the social historian J.L. Hammond,
'passed like a storm over London but broke elsewhere.'[6] At first sight

Stepney from the Rocque map, 1749. The industrial and residential growth of East London was well under way, but open fields and market gardens were still much in evidence.

this orthodoxy seems to have weight. Despite the fact that London remained by far the largest manufacturing centre in Britain, its production was dominated by small-scale firms employing less than twenty-five persons. And so many of the commodities produced were specialist and luxury items to feed the insatiable demands of a metropolitan bourgeoisie by now enthusiastically embarking on a consumer revolution. But this is only part of a complicated story, for London also had its heavier and dirtier industries, most of which were concentrated in riverside sites to the east. Here were to be found chemical, engineering and transport industries, and shipbuilding and its associated concerns, some of which were of considerable size. Both Johnson's shipyard at Blackwall and the Royal Arsenal at Woolwich had workforces numbered in their hundreds during the eighteenth century.

To foreground industrial production in this way provides a too narrow view of London's modernization. Important though it was as a manufacturing centre, London grew rich and powerful because it was above all a commercial and financial giant. In the course of the eighteenth century London became the centre of the most extensive commercial and imperial network the world had ever seen, and occupied a position of seemingly unchallengeable authority. Furthermore, an emphasis on production tends to understate the importance of London's service sector, which probably contributed more to economic growth than manufacturing itself. So how did London's rather complicated story of growth manifest itself in the trades and industries of the eighteenth century? Dorothy George, as is so often the case, provides us with a useful starting point. London trades, she argued, were so promiscuous it would have been difficult to find one which was not represented. However, in general terms, they can be classified as follows:

1 Trades dependent upon access to the port in particular and the riverside in general. Shipbuilding and the many associated trades, including rope-making, carpentry, cooperage and ironmongery, first spring to mind, but important also were those businesses, such as sugar refining, armaments and engineering, which required the river to import raw materials or export finished goods, and those associated with the docks, including warehousing and lighterage.
2 Manufacturers of quality goods for an ascendant metropolitan bourgeoisie. Clocks and watches, scientific instruments, jewellery, furniture and clothing were all made in London, often to a higher degree of perfection than elsewhere in the country.

THE LONDON HOSPITAL
FROM AN ENGRAVING OF 1753 BY CHATELAIN AND W.H.TOMS AFTER A PICTURE BY WILLIAM BELLERS

London Hospital, Whitechapel Road, 1753. The isolated and rural nature of the environment was exaggerated. To the right stood a mound – the remains of the fortification built around London during the Civil War.

3 Overlapping with the above was an expansive sector that strove also to provide the needs of conspicuous consumers. Coffee houses, hairdressing, printing, millinery, shoemaking, tailoring, various branches of the building trade, retailing and of course domestic service, the largest single outlet for female labour, were concentrated among London's streets.[7]

To these we may well add a fourth which firmly established itself in the eighteenth century. Doctors, lawyers, civil servants, priests, accountants, architects, teachers and other members of what became known collectively as the professions found rich pickings in a city which was at the centre of the cultural, legal and administrative life of the nation. Together they made up over a quarter of London's middle class.

   Although many of these trades were to be found in every part of London, their precise distribution was shaped by the complex interplay of space, tradition and the law. It made good economic sense for most suppliers of goods and services to be close to their potential consumers.

Manufacturers of clocks and jewellery, for example, were concentrated in Clerkenwell in the east of the City, and cabinet-makers and brokers in the rich parish of St James.[8] The great engine powering the ascent of the metropolis to its pre-eminence as a global city, however, was East London. Here remained a site with privileged access to the Thames, an abundance of relatively cheap land and labour, and a refuge from restrictive legislation, which was conveniently close to the financial corridors of the City, and yet remote from the entrances of fashionable residences in the West End. To the south stood the Port of London. Comprising 'legal quays' which were mediaeval in origin, and had changed little in the previous two hundred years, supplemented by 'sufferance wharves' which were constructed downstream past the Tower, the eighteenth-century Port was required to accommodate such a dramatic increase in commodities that towards the close of the century it was brought to the edge of a crisis that threatened not only its own future but that of the great commercial metropolis (see Chapter 4).

High on the list of vital commodities was coal. Few of the Londoners burning coal in their domestic hearths late in the sixteenth century could have anticipated the role it would play in London's industrial revolution, but in the eighteenth the signs were unmistakable.[9] Since London was remote from significant coalmines, coal had to be brought from elsewhere, most notably the coalfields of the North East. Between 1650 and 1750 the tonnage of coal shipped from Durham and Newcastle doubled to approximately 650,000 tons per annum, and the infamous London smog appeared.[10] While domestic consumption continued to account for the bulk of the imports, fledgling industries that relied increasingly on coal as a source of motive power were in evidence. Early experiments in converting coal to coke took place in the mid-seventeenth century, when John Winter and Thomas Peyton established works at Greenwich and Deptford.[11] Crowley's iron manufacturers migrated to Greenwich in 1704 to supply a range of ironware including anchors, nails, locks and cannon to the local naval shipyard and the yards at Blackwall and Deptford responsible for the fleets of the East India Company .[12] And nearby was the great Royal Arsenal with its own considerable foundries for the manufacture of a diverse range of artillery and ammunition.

The maritime economy of East London prospered in the course of the eighteenth century. The shipyard at Blackwall, originally built by the East India Company and taken over by Henry Johnson until his death in 1683, expanded under the proprietorship of Henry Johnson junior and his younger brother William. With Henry's death in 1719 the yard entered a period of uncertainty when few ships were commissioned: 'Blackwall ... is gone very much to decay', declared an observer in 1723.[13] By then the East India Company had transferred its shipbuilding back to Deptford, and in a rare period of peace the demand for naval vessels fell. Although formally severing its connections with the yard, the Company continued its relationship with Blackwall indirectly through other means. When management was eventually assumed by the Perry family, they exploited connections with the Company, and the yard returned to prosperity. Between 1756 and 1767, for example, Perry & Company built 31 large ships at Blackwall, no fewer than 27 of which were Eastindiamen of approximately 650 tons each. When the yard came up for sale in 1779 the Perry dynasty had accumulated enough money to buy it, and with the confidence gained from a full order book soon set about extending the dock, most notably by building a fourth dry dock, and a large wet dock to the east of the yard on marshland owned by them. This wet dock, the most ambitious private dock initiative of the eighteenth century, was named the Brunswick Dock; together with the shipyard it was 'the greatest private dock in all Europe'.[14] Its opening in 1790 heralded a dramatic new phase in the history of London docks, as we will shortly discover.[15]

More generally, the riverside parishes of Wapping, Limehouse, Shadwell and Ratcliff became the most vital centres of the mercantile economy of the metropolis as a whole. Not only shipyards and docks, but a great variety of offices and workshops sprang up in order to service the needs of the Royal Navy and the merchant fleets which made their way up the Thames. Thus amidst the influential community which developed were to be found ship repairers, timber merchants, victuallers, scientific instrument makers, contractors, cartographers, accountants and insurers, many of whom had large personal estates.[16] Extensive commercial networks were forged which revealed the complex interconnectedness of their members' interests. Take, for example, the important Wapping-based firm of John and William Camden, Anthony Calvert and Thomas King. Primarily ship owners engaged in the Caribbean slave trade, they were able to establish social and business partnerships, often at the highest levels of commercial and financial power in the City, and so extend their operations on a truly global scale.[17] They became involved in the development of the Pacific whale fishing industry, the transportation of convicts to Australia, sugar refining, provisioning of merchant and naval fleets, the East India trade, and insurance (Calvert and King were among the founder members of Lloyds).

In large part dependent upon such trading activities, sizable local manufacturing firms were established. The Hermitage Pothouse, founded late in the seventeenth century, was one of the largest producers of tin-glazed pottery ware in London, and the Red Lion brewery, owned by Sir John Parsons, Lord Mayor in 1703, was the most valuable of the brewing houses before being overtaken by the Truman brewery in Brick Lane late in the eighteenth century. Few industries, however, could match the numerous sugar refineries associated with the growing Caribbean slave trade. They varied greatly in size, from the refinery of Hayer and Riners insured for £500, to Camden, Lear and Thelluson valued at £6,000, and Thomas Slack and associates valued at £9,900 in 1767.[18]

To the north of East London around Spitalfields, silk weaving continued to enjoy good fortunes as production and the number of silk weavers steadily increased during the early decades of the eighteenth century. The masters remained in the City or upmarket areas of Spitalfields, while the poorer and more numerous labouring weavers and spinners of both sexes were forced to seek accommodation and employment in nearby Bethnal Green, Shoreditch and Mile End New Town, which were fast emerging as residential and manufacturing suburbs. In 1750 it was estimated that there were 500 master weavers around the parish and its environs, approximately 15,000 looms, and at least 50,000 locals dependent upon the trade.[19] The problem was, however, that the manufacture of silk cloth was extremely sensitive to the whims of fashion, seasonality, interruptions in supplies of raw materials and threats from foreign imports. Even at times of general expansion there were short-term downturns which could create widespread distress in the locality, thereby promoting industrial unrest. Proposals to establish a charitable fund as early as 1706 drew attention to the fact that:

> Many manufacturers, and especially London weavers and other workmen who keep several men at work, are sometimes much straight-ened for money, either to pay their men's wages or to find goods to employ them, especially at the dead time of the year … and thereupon, being forced to pawn some of their goods for what pawnbrokers are pleased to lend on them, they do not only impoverish themselves, and turn away their men, who, for want of work, do with their families become a burthen to the public, but it also discourages the said manufacturers.[20]

Protective tariffs levied on the import of foreign silks were only in part successful, for, as well as Italian organzine, French silks continued to find their way to London. Fearful of this continued threat to their livelihoods, weavers campaigned unsuccessfully to raise import duties; instead, the importation of French-manufactured silks including ribbons, stockings

and gloves was prohibited in 1766, and in 1773 magistrates were empowered to regulate – and thereby maintain – the wages of journeymen
weavers, and in 1811 those of female weavers.[21] These so-called Spitalfields
Acts benefited from the support of employers and notable authorities such
as the Lord Mayor and Sir John Fielding. No doubt designed to provide
some degree of protection to the industry and security to the poorest-paid,
in practice, the acts imposed restrictions which hindered improvements in
technology, fatally weakening local industry and forcing many masters to
relocate elsewhere. The laws were repealed in the 1820s, by which time the
industry was in terminal decline, and Spitalfield weavers suffered distress
as severe as that experienced by any workforce in the modern capital.

Prominent among other industries in East London were sugar refining,
distilling and brewing. Many breweries and distillers were to be found in
eighteenth-century London, for this was a thirsty capital, a thirst in part
created by the ready availability of cheap and intoxicating ales and liquors.
The 'manufacturers' ranged from backstreet distillers to magnificent breweries in the vanguard of capitalist development. Many distillers were able
to operate freely on payment of a low excise duty, but even here owners of
outlets such as brandy and gin shops in the poorer areas of London could
set up stills seemingly beyond the reach of the few authorities which chose
to take their responsibilities seriously.[22] A report published by the Middlesex
Sessions in 1726 recorded 7,044 retailers, 2,105 of which were unlicensed.[23]
Most of these were to the east, where above eighty trades such as chandlers,
carpenters, barbers and shoe-makers were found to sell spirits. In Bethnal
Green alone there were over ninety weavers and 'other persons of inferior
trades … concerned in our manufactures'. East London also contained
many small breweries such as the Red Lion and the Three Kings which
produced a variety of ales, but they were completely overshadowed by the
great brewhouses. The Black Eagle brewery was founded by the Quaker
Joseph Truman in 1680 on a small site by Brick Lane, and expanded rapidly
in the course of the eighteenth century to become the largest brewery in
London, employing at its peak in excess of 1,000 people. Early in the nineteenth century it was taken over by Sampson Hanbury and Thomas Folwell
Buxton and was renamed Truman, Hanbury, Buxton and Co. Whitbread &
Company was established by Samuel Whitbread in 1742, also along Brick
Lane, but moved to larger premises in Chiswell Street on the eastern edge
of the City in 1750. It was the first mass-production brewery, which by
1786 had the capacity to produce over 150,000 barrels of strong, unadulterated beer annually, and provides another example of a modern industrial
dynasty with roots in East London.

Many of these industries had first settled in the eastern suburbs because here they found a certain refuge from controls exercised by the guilds, and their owners a degree of freedom from religious persecution. By the eighteenth century these considerations were less apparent. Faced with market forces quite beyond their control, the guilds relinquished their authority to become little more than hospitable members' clubs, and Quaker manufacturers and financiers in particular were gradually becoming assimilated into the metropolitan economy. It is unlikely that this transformation unduly influenced the fortunes of East London, the indigenous industries of which were expanding rapidly, because it continued to provide relatively cheap rents. The suburbs also provided suitable locations for a variety of less desirable callings. So-called offensive trades were discouraged by a series of by-laws from operating within the City walls and so settled in East London where few such laws existed, or were applied with less rigour, but here again early capitalism played a part. Whitechapel, for example, situated as it was at the boundary between the City and the rural culture of the eastern counties, had long contained numerous slaughterhouses which in turn gave rise to ancillary trades including bone-boilers, glue-makers, leather workers and tallow-makers. Small manufacturers of chemicals and related trades such as dyes, ink, paint and tar were ubiquitous. And there were thousands of men and women on the edge of criminality who eked out an existence of sorts.[24]

Symptomatic of the sense of unease created by the rising population of Stepney were the attempts early in the eighteenth century to assert Anglican authority. Starting with Shadwell in 1669, and followed by St George's-in-the-East, Spitalfields, Limehouse, Stratford-at-Bow and Bethnal Green, hamlets separated to form their own parishes. The 1710 Fifty Churches Act[25] also helped consolidate Anglican authority by funding the construction of Nicholas Hawksmoor's magnificent edifices of Christ Church, Spitalfields, St George-in-the-East and St Anne's, Limehouse. Despite this, Protestant dissent – particularly, as we have seen, by Quaker and Huguenot communities – continued to exert an influence throughout the eighteenth century, although in the longer term, with the decline of silk weaving and the integration of Quaker businesses into the economy, both traditions of Protestant dissent were assimilated into the dominant order.

To continue in ruins

Data from baptism records reveal the extent to which the social compositions of the different parishes of East London were determined by their industries. The differences may not have been so pronounced as those of the early seventeenth century but they were still striking. Of the occupations of adult males in Spitalfields, 64 per cent were in clothing, while in the riverside areas 46 per cent were in maritime trades.[26] This population was dominated by members of the working class. A survey of parish registers for 1813 revealed that 13 per cent of the male labouring population were skilled, 40–50 per cent semi-skilled, and 14–20 per cent unskilled. Approximately 40 per cent of adult males and their families lived in extreme poverty, while the proportion of upper and middle class in East London was low compared with the City (approximately 50 per cent) and Westminster (approximately 43 per cent). In the ensuing decades the industrial landscape of East London would be transformed; its class structure, however, would prove to be rather more resilient.

Much of the housing for the labouring population in these older areas was by now dilapidated. Built originally in haphazard fashion with little regard for regulations or the quality of materials, houses soon became ruinous and ramshackled, leaving them prone to collapse, often on the unfortunate heads of the poor who had sought temporary shelter therein. Just as Tudor and Stuart building regulations had proven singularly ineffective in preventing the spread of such accommodation, so eighteenth-century legislation failed to halt the destructive consequences of speculative house building and poor estate management. This was peculiarly so in East London, for Stepney and Hackney were still regulated by ancient manorial customs over property rights which came into conflict with local and public statutes, thereby creating confusion over management and responsibility. At times of economic uncertainty this could have a drastic impact on the availability and quality of accommodation, in turn contributing to a decline in population.

Take, for example, the various attempts that were made in the eighteenth century to develop a large estate in Ratcliff. John Entick, one of the most meticulous of London's surveyors of the time, recalled that the origins of the estate were unclear but early in the century its fortunes took a turn for the worse. Trade in the area had declined, a misfortune compounded when control of the ground and building leases passed into the hands of the Committee of City Lands. The committee mismanaged the estate by letting the premises to some 'necessitous and artful people' on condition that they repaired and maintained them. In the event, the tenants absconded with the rents and sold what they could of the material fabric of the houses. The committee resolved to let the houses again to the highest bidder. Mr Beezly, a sugar baker, took the leases for the considerable sum of £640 per annum in the hope that a ferry over the Thames recently established by Act of Parliament, with a road leading to the estate, would revive its fortunes. But the ferry was little used, forcing Beezly to foreclose the lease. At the time of writing (1772), several houses along Rose Lane had fallen down, and others were ready to follow. Those facing Broad Street had been burnt down, and were likely 'to continue in ruins'. Entick closes with an appeal for a national scheme to encourage 'men of fortune and integrity' to embark with a lease that 'shall encourage them to lay out their money to advantage'.[27]

Quite apart from the ruinous state of many houses, their ill construction, proximity to local industries and congested layout meant that they were at constant risk from fire. In the immediate aftermath of the Great Fire of 1666 regulations were introduced to reduce fire risks in new buildings. Old buildings, however, were exempt and, in part as a result of this, East London – which had largely escaped the ravages of 1666 – witnessed frequent conflagrations during the eighteenth century, many of which destroyed considerable numbers of houses. A few examples must suffice from a six-year period mid-century. In 1757 fire broke out at Mr Godfrey's distillery in Limehouse Hole, but since his premises were detached from the street the fire was quickly extinguished without damage to neighbouring houses.[28] Other incidents had less fortunate outcomes. In September 1758 there was a great fire at Gun Dock in Wapping which consumed twenty houses; three days later a fire at Wapping broke out but was brought under control 'with the loss of four houses only'.[29] In May 1761, thirty-four houses and eight laden barges and lighters were destroyed to the value of £50,000 when fire broke out at a biscuit baker's in lower Shadwell.[30] An even more serious fire occurred there in July 1763, when eighty-seven houses were entirely lost. Its course demonstrated vividly the alarming speed at which such conflagrations spread in congested districts. The fire began in a stable or outhouse in a rope-maker's at New Crane dockyard in Shadwell. Spreading to an adjoining loft full of dry reeds, it took hold of a ship in the dock and then the 'very old and dry' houses next to the water along Wapping Wall. Before water and engines could be mobilized the fire crossed the street, and in a few hours all the houses on both sides of the Wall were entirely consumed. On the north side the fire eventually stopped at Star Street but not without damaging several houses in New Gravel Lane, among which was a 'remarkable well-built new brick house and cooperage'.[31]

It seems that few lessons were, or could be, learnt from these incidents. In July 1794 a fire broke out in Ratcliff whose destructive power exceeded any witnessed since 1666. It was caused by the boiling over of a pitch kettle in a barge-builder's yard, and rapidly spread to shipping on the river and then to several ranges of warehouses filled with combustibles, including one belonging to the East India Company which contained 200 tons of saltpetre. Before the fire was spent the warehouses together with over half of the 1,200 houses in Ratcliff had been completely destroyed at a cost of over £1 million. Hundreds of families were made homeless and thrown on to public benevolence. Tents were provided for many, a subscription was opened at Lloyd's Coffee House, and contributions from the thousands who travelled to view the devastation raised more than £16,000, but none of this prevented the dramatic fall in the population of Ratcliff.[32]

The most significant growth in this period was witnessed in the northern districts of East London. The transformation of Spitalfields brought about by the settlement of silk weavers and other poor labourers in the latter half of the seventeenth century continued apace. By the 1680s the hamlet was largely built up and thought sufficiently populous to be granted a market by Charles II. A market house and marketplace were established between Bishopsgate and Whitechapel, but in the early years the inaccessibility of the site meant that the market had little of the vibrancy of other London markets; only later, with better communications, did Spitalfields market become London's premier market for fruit and vegetables.[33] The migration of Huguenot weavers after 1685 and the additional employment they provided led to further increases.

Accommodation struggled to keep pace with demand. Master weavers built impressive houses to the north of the parish, many of which survive to this day in Elder and Fournier Streets, but the majority of inhabitants were of lesser means with no access to decent housing. Towards the close of the seventeenth century, Barbon and the family of the local estate owner Sir William Wheler had developed streets around Brick Lane with lines of small and cheap houses, and yet in the period of expansion that followed, local builders with limited resources were more active; by mid-century the parish was completely built over.[34] Under these circumstances any pressure from increases in population was relieved by subletting, which by 1749 had become a problem for the rating authorities of the parish.[35]

The other solution was for migrants to seek accommodation nearby, most notably in the neighbouring parish of Bethnal Green. Like other hamlets within Stepney, Bethnal Green had provided a pleasant country retreat for members of the metropolitan bourgeoisie; indeed, early in the seventeenth century it included a proportionately larger number than any other apart from Mile End.[36] Within a matter of decades it was subject to the unwelcome presence of increasing numbers of the labouring poor who migrated from Spitalfields or who came to Bethnal Green in search of work nearby. Of the 520 people assessed there in 1694, 100 were Huguenot.[37] Throughout the following century population levels increased steadily, in the process of which many of the previously settled middle-class residents were displaced. Houses to accommodate these migrant labourers were built by local tradesmen on small plots of freehold land bought from London merchants. As always, the poor turned to subletting as a means of paying the rent. When 1,800 houses were assessed in 1743 they were found to contain an average of 8.3 inhabitants.[38]

Shoreditch was a small suburban parish which because of its proximity to London began to develop in the sixteenth century. In the ensuing decades development was modest and piecemeal. Market gardens appeared, as did large houses built by London merchants seeking a rural retreat. By the mid-eighteenth century the hamlets of Hoxton, Moorfields and Holywell to the south of the parish contained approximately 1,900 houses.[39] But from then on new roads were laid to a coherent plan, and the area grew rapidly as a manufacturing and residential suburb containing a mix of artisans and tradesmen, some of whom were an overspill from the crowded silk-weaving centre of neighbouring Spitalfields.[40] With a degree of inevitability, it also attracted large numbers of the poor, endowing parts of Shoreditch with a reputation for crime and squalor typical of the other dangerous enclaves of the late-eighteenth-century metropolis.[41]

Stinks of the whole easterly pyle

Such congestion promoted demographic shifts away from the older riverside sites, but of greater consequence in the longer term for the social topography of London was the exodus from East London of the metropolitan bourgeoisie. Whereas previously employers and landlords had tended to reside close to their businesses and properties, the steady growth of industry and poorer accommodation blighted what they had found to be congenial environments, prompting them to migrate to more suitable locations even if more remote from their sources of livelihood. In the City, the signs had been evident even earlier. Sir William Petty, renowned economic philosopher of the seventeenth century, saw the gradual shift westward as part of the modern urban experience:

> Now if great Cities are naturally apt to remove their seats, I ask which
> way? I say, in the case of *London*, it must be Westward, because the
> Windes blowing near ¾ of the year from the West, the dwellings of the
> West end are so much more free from the fumes, steams, and stinks of

the whole Easterly Pyle; which where Seacoal is burnt is a great matter. Now if it follows from hence, that the Pallaces of the greatest men will remove Westward, it will also naturally follow, that the dwellings of others who depend upon them will creep after them.[42]

His contemporary John Graunt, also noting that 'the City of *London* gradually removes *westward*', provided an alternative – and yet still partial – explanation. The King, he argued, had moved court to Westminster, and with him large sections of the gentry and its retinue of vendors. The old City was bedevilled with narrow and congested lanes which impeded the passage of carriages, while open spaces and gardens had been crammed with houses which shut out light and air.[43] Prompted by the belief that it was no longer necessary to live close to work, eighteenth-century metropolitan elites thus escaped the narrow and dingy lanes of the City by migrating to the streets and squares that were being constructed in open fields to the west. Some found residence in the imposing squares of the West End; others, less well placed, migrated to the building estates that were springing up alongside the New Road from Paddington to Islington.[44] By mid-century it was widely believed that this migration was sapping the economic vitality of the easterly part of the City and its suburbs, and thus demands were voiced 'to prevent the disagreeable effects already felt from the shifting of the inhabitants and trade to Westminster and its Liberties' by considering the most effective means of building a new bridge at Blackfriars. For a time the scheme was delayed by 'a little jealousy arising between the Eastern and Western parts of the City, lest one should by such improvements get the advantage over the other in point of situation for trade', but opposition was overcome and the enabling act passed in 1756.[45]

Demographic trends in the City were soon replicated in East London. By 1720 John Strype had identified geographical divisions which were based largely upon local trades and occupations, notably maritime, silk and other manufacturing trades, and which were inhabited for the most part by the working and itinerant poor. As a pre-modern parish, Stepney included also significant numbers of bourgeois families, who found in its ancient estates and mansions a retreat from the dirt and bustle of the City, and those who worked in locally based commerce, manufacture and professions. Historically, like much of London, the parish had comprised villages with strong senses of local identity. Centred on the church and local government, they provided agreeable neighbourhoods for the middle classes.[46] Many survived into the modern period. Thus in Mile End Old Town, Stepney, Spitalfields and Limehouse, and further out in Stratford,

Plaistow and West Ham, could be found men and women of real social and economic worth. Among those who had settled in these early days were Francis Bancroft, Master of the Drapers' Company and social benefactor, Sir Richard Gresham, mercer and Lord Mayor, and Lord Morley, politician and philanthropist, all of whom had made their mark at the Court or in the City. Notable also was the presence of maritime power. Sir Henry Palmer, who commanded a ship against the Armada, Sir Thomas Bladden, the Surveyor of Victuals for the Navy, Sir Michael Greene, Master of Trinity House and Surveyor of the Navy, Laurence Sulivan and Sir George Colebrook, both chairmen of the East India Company, and Sir John Gayer, former Governor of Bombay, can all be found in local records. Later, as East London's population grew, some of these gentry retreated further afield (literally) to create magnificent estates in neighbouring districts. Samuel Gurney, Quaker philanthropist and founder of a financial empire, lived for most of his married life at Ham House in West Ham, and Sir Josiah Child, one of the most rapacious and powerful figures in the history of the East India Company, built Wanstead House, which in its splendour and opulence was rivalled only by Blenheim.

If residential segregation existed, it was highly localized. In the course of the eighteenth century, however, the middle classes of East London as a body moved out, effectively reshaping its social landscape. To explore the point further let us consider the experience of Mile End Old Town. As a semi-rural retreat, some distance from the manufacturing and trading centres of East London, but close to the main thoroughfare from the eastern counties, Mile End had attracted wealthy merchants, professionals, landowners and mariners since the early seventeenth century. Stepney Green was particularly popular, and around it appeared fine houses with stables and carriageways.[47] Many of the families which occupied these houses in the eighteenth century had direct and convenient links to the trading and shipbuilding activities of the East India Company in nearby Blackwall, and tended to remain in the region for two or three generations before migrating to town houses in the West End or to country estates in Essex and Hertfordshire.[48] Captain William Fitzhugh lived in Mile End with his wife Mary from the 1720s. He made several voyages to India, and accumulated an impressive holding of Company stock. Their son Thomas served the Company for thirty years, ending up as superintendent of the cargo with a fortune of £60,000. He retired to Portland Place in West London some time after 1780 and died there in 1800. Laurence Sulivan, who with an unrivalled knowledge of Company affairs was appointed director and emerged as one of its most powerful figures in the eighteenth century, moved in 1738 to Mile End, where he had a villa on Stepney Green.

After a spell of duty in India from which he emerged an even wealthier man, he returned to the villa until 1761, when he bought Ponsborne Manor in Hertfordshire, and a couple of houses in the West End, living there until his death in 1786.[49] The examples of Fitzhugh and Sulivan were typical and indicate that numerous Company servants, slave traders and brokers lived in Mile End for various periods of time in the eighteenth century before moving to more fashionable areas. The trend was unmistakable.

Contemporary observers began to draw attention to the broad effects of the residential segregation attendant on the westward migration of the metropolitan bourgeoisie, and in so doing defined a fundamental geographical and cultural separation between what were now referred to as the East End and West End of London. Joseph Archenholtz, a visitor to London from Germany in the 1770s, noted this migration, and was clearly struck by contrasts in the two Londons that were being created. Within the past twenty years, he declared,

> an actual emigration has taken place from the eastern parts of London towards the western; thousands have left the former, where they do not erect new buildings, for the latter, where the most fertile fields and most agreeable gardens are daily metamorphosed into houses and streets. The City, especially along the shores of the Thames, consists of old houses, the streets there are narrow, dark and ill-paved; inhabited by sailors and other workmen who are employed in the construction of ships and by a great part of the Jews who reside in London. The contrast betwixt this and the western parts of the metropolis is astonishing: the houses there are almost new, and of excellent construction: the squares are magnificent; the streets are built in straight lines, and perfectly well lighted: no city in Europe is better paved.[50]

Archenholtz was an astute observer, for the trends he identified were real enough; the populations of Marylebone, St Pancras, Hammersmith, Kensington and Chelsea had increased dramatically since the beginning of the century.[51] And he was no doubt largely reliable in describing contrasts in the built environment. A problem arises, however, when spaces such as the West End and the East End come to be defined – often in relationship to one another – as mythical sites, and enter thus into the public imagination. As we shall see, it was from this moment that East London was represented and accepted by respectable opinion as a site of poverty and danger, in contrast to the gentility, wealth and glamour of the West End. In part, these myths sprang from a profound ignorance of East London, heightened by the eighteenth-century exodus of local elites. Writing of the time, J. Richardson retrospectively observed:

> Fifty years ago this metropolis … did not contain above one million of inhabitants. The extent … was commensurately small; and yet the inhabitants of the different districts were less acquainted with each other and more distinct in their manners, habits and characteristics, than they are these days. The inhabitants of the extreme east of London knew nothing of the western localities but from hearsay and report and vice versa … There was little communication and sympathy between the respective classes by which the two ends of London were occupied … Each district was comparatively isolated, the state of isolation produced peculiarities, and the peculiarities corroborated the isolation, and thus the householders of Westminster … were as distinct from the house-holders of every sort of Bishopsgate Without, Shoreditch and all those localities … as in these days they are from the inhabitants of Holland and Belgium.[52]

Few of us today would subscribe to the view that location is all-important in determining life-style and behaviour, and the extent of isolation is probably exaggerated. Nevertheless, Richardson was correct to highlight the existence of distinct communities in London, based on particular trades and industries, and largely ignorant of others to be found just a few miles away. This had far-reaching consequences, for out of this ignorance a number of sites came to be identified as of intense concern to eighteenth-century metropolitan authorities.

Noisome dangerous and inconvenient

As a magistrate in eighteenth-century London, Henry Fielding had closer contact than most with its criminal elements, and in 1751 described well the impending sense of unease about these various sites:

> Whoever indeed considers the Cities of *London* and *Westminster*, with the late vast Addition of their Suburbs; the great irregularity of their Buildings, the immense Number of Lanes, Alleys, Courts and Byeplaces; must think, that, had they been intended for the very Purpose of Concealment, they could scarce have been better contrived. Upon such a View, the whole appears as a vast Wood or Forest, in which a Thief may harbour with as great Security, as wild Beasts do in

the Desarts of *Africa* or *Arabia*. For by *wandering* from one Part to another, and often shifting his quarters, he may almost avoid the Possibility of being discovered.[53]

In singling out the suburbs Fielding was part of a long tradition which looked with disfavour upon their uncontrolled growth and propensity to attract the poorest elements of the population, but what was perhaps new was his concern to identify their inherent criminality. As early as 1724 an Act was introduced to 'prevent violences and outrages being committed by any persons under pretence of sheltering themselves from debt … within the Hamlet of Wapping-Stepney'.[54] The preamble declared that

> it is notorious that many evil-disposed and wicked Persons have, in Defiance of the known Laws of this Realm, and to the great Dishonour thereof, unlawfully assembled and associated themselves in the Hamlet of *Wapping-Stepney*, and places adjacent in the County of Middlesex, under the pretence of sheltering themselves from Debt, and have committed great violence and outrages upon many of his Majestys good subjects, and by force protected themselves and their wicked Accomplices against Law and Justice.

To prevent such conspiracies the Act made illegal, under penalty of transportation for seven years, any assembly of three persons or more gathered to obstruct persons attempting to serve a writ or court order.

The reputation of many of these sites was further sullied by associations with London's sex trade. The riverside locations of Stepney had long been centres of prostitution where a mobile seafaring population could find solace in the numerous bawd houses and taverns, but during the eighteenth century other parts of East London came to be recognized as equally disreputable, not merely because of the concentration of brothels therein but also because they supplied large numbers of prostitutes for the City. *Satan's Harvest Home*, a hugely popular book, putatively written in French by a Catholic priest, and first published in 1734 with the aim of exposing the 'Present State of Fornication, Whorecraft and Aduleration' in Protestant Britain, reflected on the source of the many prostitutes to be found each night on the streets of London:

> When a person unacquainted with the Town passes at night thro' any of our Principal Streets, he is apt to wonder whence the vast body of *Courtezans*, which stands ready, on small Purchase, to obey the Laws

of Nature, and gratify the Lust of every drunken Rake-hell, can take its
Rise. *Where the Devil do all these B-ches come from?* being a common
Fleet Street phrase ... when each revolving Evening sends them up
from White-Chapel to Charing Cross.[55]

And when Henry Fielding's blind brother John, who was also a magistrate,
gave evidence to a parliamentary committee worried about the policing of
the metropolis, he singled out Whitechapel and the area in the immediate
vicinity of the Goodman's Fields Theatre as infamous centres of disorder
providing pimps, prostitutes and thieves with convenient shelter.[56]

At a time when the policing of London was rudimentary and its streets
dark and ill-lit, these criminal enclaves thus represented spaces where
thieves, prostitutes and beggars found refuge from the authorities and the
public gaze. The Clink and the Mint in Southwark, Whitefriars and Alsatia
at the City's south-eastern boundary, Spitalfields and Whitechapel,
Shoreditch and the Ratcliff Highway were among sites which acquired fearsome reputations for criminal activity, exacerbated by the strategies of
mutual protection adopted by their inhabitants which discouraged
unwanted intruders. In modern parlance, they were no-go areas.[57]

It was at this moment that the gospel of improvement took shape and
began to resound through the ranks of London's authorities. Disputing
conventional wisdom that the late eighteenth century witnessed the onset
of a dark age brought about by industrialization and urbanization during
which the standards of life were systematically degraded, Dorothy
George's classic *London Life in the Eighteenth Century* contended that this
period in London's history was marked by a decline in violence and
brutality, mortality rates, pauperization and drunkenness. George was
perhaps too optimistic about the extent of metropolitan reform, for
despite the real progress achieved grievous problems remained that
blighted the lives of the poor. But the spirit of humanity which promoted
such improvements, allied to a greater knowledge of social conditions,
can certainly be traced back to the mid-eighteenth century when legislation proliferated and the powers of local authorities – including those to
raise the necessary finance – were greatly extended. Had the opportunity
been seized after the Great Fire to rebuild London along planned and
rational lines then little of this would have been necessary, but it was
squandered and the chaotic topography of London's streets laid down in
mediaeval times remained as an inconvenient and incongruous feature of
a metropolis fast emerging as a world centre of trade, empire and
commerce. Thus legal and parochial authorities again strove to transform

the streetscape by providing vital space for Londoners and visitors to meet, converse and pass in a secure and congenial environment, and the impulse of improvement gathered momentum.[58] In 1754, frustrated by the piecemeal reform of previous decades, which had done little to resolve its narrow, irregular and dirty streets, John Spranger outlined plans which sought to transform Westminster. 'In all well-governed Countries', he argued,

> the first Care of the Governors hath been to make the Intercourse of the Inhabitants, as well as of Foreigners, sojourning in the Country, safe, easy and commodious, by open, free and regular *Highways*. This is more especially incumbent on *Trading* Nations, as, without a free and safe Intercourse between Place and Place by Land as well as water, *trade* cannot subsist, much less flourish.[59]

Spranger proposed that responsibility for the state of London's streets should be taken out of the hands of individual householders and ineffective local authorities, and invested in commissioners with powers to make by-laws, raise funds through the rates and punish offenders. By making such provisions, the resultant Act[60] guaranteed an unprecedented uniformity in the cleansing, paving and lighting of London streets. By the end of the century the transformation was well under way; streets were straighter, better paved and lit, and cleaner – in short, more civilized and modern.[61] One impressed observer in 1787, for example, commented that the paving of Westminster streets had introduced 'a degree of elegance and symmetry … that is the admiration of all Europe and far exceeds anything of the kind in the modern world'.[62]

Although much of this spirit of improvement was directed to the ancient – and bourgeois – areas of the City and Westminster, the eastern suburbs did not escape attention. Nineteenth-century accounts testify to the persistence of extensive slums, suggesting that some places were beyond the redemptive powers of legislation, but a good many thoroughfares were opened up to traffic, thereby creating swathes of light and air through dense rookeries. A few examples from Whitechapel must suffice. In 1768 'An Act for better Paving the part of the High Street in the Parish of St. Mary Matfellon'[63] described this vital thoroughfare as 'extremely ill paved' and 'greatly obstructed by posts and projections' which had rendered it 'incommodious and dangerous to persons passing through'. Commissioners were appointed to undertake the work of clearing and paving it.

The other important artery was Brick Lane, which travelled south–north, conveying goods carriages from the waterside areas through Whitechapel to Spitalfields, Bethnal Green, Bishopsgate and Shoreditch. Mediaeval in origin, and, like many such streets, ill-paved and obstructed because the necessary finances and legislative powers were not in place, the lane and its tributaries were subject to a series of improvement acts which systematically tackled their various sections. In 1772 An Act for Paving, Cleansing, &c. the Squares, Streets, &c. within the Parish of Christ Church[64] declared that since Brick Lane was 'much out of repair it would be of great benefit to have the whole paved'. The sum of £14,000 was to be borrowed to finance the necessary work. Similarly, in 1778 An Act for Widening and Improving a certain avenue called Dirty Lane and part of Brick Lane[65] proposed to pave part of the lane and several of the smaller streets and passages leading to it. Four years later An Act for making a Passage for Carriages from Spitalfields to Bishopsgate Street[66] argued that the passage would be of great public utility, and listed the houses that would need to be demolished in the process. The scheme was to be financed by taking £9,000 from the Orphans Fund. By 1788, however, it was apparent that the original scheme to widen Brick Lane had encountered problems. An Act to Explain and Amend an Act in 12 Geo. III[67] stated that the £14,000 initially borrowed had proven insufficient; debts had mounted which could not be repaid, and therefore further loans were required. The authors were also sensitive to the peculiar problems faced in such an area – located as it was between the commercial might of the City and an ancient rural culture – and serve to remind us that improvement was also about the preservation of public order. Penalties were to be exacted for slaughtering livestock in the streets, and for keeping swine. Wandering cattle were to be impounded.

As in the City and Westminster, the changes brought by such improvement were greeted with a sense of disbelief. John Entick, who was not normally given to hyperbole, wrote in 1772 that

> As you enter the eastern part of London, the passenger … will meet with objects of wonder and amazement; considering the shortness of the time in which these improvements and the new pavements have been completed. The same kind of pavement has been continued … in Whitechapel, from the north end of the Minories, as far as the bars or bounds of the City Liberties; and again down Houndsditch, in which street an opening has been made into Bevis Marks for the carriages to pass into St. Mary Axe and Leadenhall Street … As soon as we enter

where Aldgate once stood, there appears on the left hand a spacious broad and open street, and well built, running southward as far as Crutched Friars which was lately impassable, and a terror to the native inhabitants.[68]

Apparent here is a distinct sense of relief, for Entick was writing in troubled times and may have seen in these improvements signs of a more stable future. If so, his optimism was misplaced, for East London was being rent by tumultuous riots, the last of which had yet to be witnessed. We now turn, therefore, to the nature of this unrest and the criminal propensities of the population of East London that it putatively revealed. For here were laid the foundations of a certain mythology that continues to haunt East London to the present.

CHAPTER 3

The Culture and Politics of Dissent,
1700–1800

EIGHTEENTH-CENTURY East London was transformed by the experience of industrialization and urbanization which laid the foundations for the continued expansion yet to be witnessed in the nineteenth. As vestiges of the local middle classes fled to more congenial parts of London or the countryside, social structures were increasingly shaped by the presence of a nascent labouring poor. We must now turn to the question of how these changes impacted upon the cultural landscape of East London, in particular, how a tradition of dissent inherited from pre-modern times found new modes of expression.

A very superfluous sort of men

The origins of popular culture can be traced back to the mediaeval carnival, which was enacted throughout Europe, and survived well into the twentieth century despite the profound social and economic changes that had taken place in the intervening period.[1] It was a boisterous, bawdy, blasphemous, grotesque and excessive celebration of life which sought to challenge the established order by inverting it. Consumption of alcohol, meat and pancakes seemed to know no bounds; excited people played music on improvised instruments, and danced in the streets, often in the costumes of wild animals, clerics, devils and fools with grotesque masks. There was no clear distinction between players and spectators. Flour and fruit were thrown about randomly, and people were struck with pigs' bladders and sticks. Plays – profoundly irreverent, even unruly – were staged, using the whole of the town as a backdrop. Matches, jousts and tournaments – often extremely violent – were organized. Carnival was a holiday celebration to mark liberation from the austerities of Lent, but equally it was a powerful symbol of challenge to debilitating social structures and norms underpinning the everyday world of pre-modern societies. As such the spirit of carnival was embedded in many leisure activities. Thus the Lord of Misrule and the World Turned Upside Down were among popular phrases which somehow captured the carnivalesque to be found in popular humour, literature, music, recreations and sport, particularly when set against the grain of middle-class respectability. 'What is high humour at Wapping', noted John Brown in 1751, 'is rejected as nauseous in the City'.[2] As we entered the modern era, the disgust felt by religious and civil authorities, together with the unwelcome disruption to industrious labour, prompted an intense campaign to outlaw what were considered excessive forms of popular pleasure which had been inherited from the carnival. Plebeian 'sports' such as cock-fighting and bull-baiting were banned, stage plays were censored, riots were brutally suppressed, and the most obvious sites of carnival – the fairs – were eventually closed down.

The eighteenth-century gospel of improvement provides a good example of the clash between respectable opinion and the vestiges of a plebeian culture in East London. Take, for example, the 1788 Act for 'paving, cleansing, &c. squares, streets, &c. within the Parish of Christ Church and for removing nuisances and obstructions therefrom'.[3] At first glance this was part of an attempt to improve road communication in the interests of commerce, but the offences identified reveal that it was simultaneously an attack on forms of an older popular culture that had no place in a modern metropolis. 'If any cattle, beast or swine be found wandering about any of the streets or public places within the said Parish it shall be lawful … to impound such', declared one clause against the dogged survival of rural customs. Attention was also devoted to the more carnivalesque activities of local inhabitants. Any person would be deemed to have committed an offence who

> shall throw, cast, or lay … any dung, ashes, dirt, dust, filth, soil or rubbish … or shall throw at oranges, or any cock, pigeon, or fowl, or set up oranges or any duck, pigeon, or fowl to be thrown at, or shall make or assist in the making of any fire or fires commonly called bonfires, or shall set fire to, or let off, or throw any squib, serpent, rocket, or fireworks whatsoever in any of the said footways or carriageways.

The relative freedom of fairs had also encouraged the carnivalesque. Stepney Fair was born in 1664 when the Lord of the Manor, the Earl of Cleveland, secured a patent from Charles II for a weekly market at Ratcliff Cross and an annual fair at Mile End Green. Stepney Fair was a latecomer on to the metropolitan scene, for it had long been preceded by the more famous fairs of Bartholomew, Smithfield, Greenwich and Southwark, but with the growth of the parish it prospered. The entertainment on offer at numerous stalls included dancers, peep shows, menageries, jugglers, performing animals, freak shows and theatrical booths. Among the curiosities displayed were

> A little black man, 3 feet high, aged 32, his wife, the little woman, not 3 feet high, aged 30, known respectively as the Black Prince and Fairy Queen; she gave general satisfaction to all that saw her, by diverting them with dancing, being big with child … Then there was a Turkey Horse 2 feet odd inches high and above 12 years old, and a Monstrous Creature from the Deserts of Ethiopia.[4]

Some of these entertainments clearly transgressed the boundaries of respectable taste, and so from its early days the fair attracted the attention of religious and civic leaders. The Stepney Meeting House preacher Matthew Mead gave an annual Mayday sermon at the fair. On one occasion he recalled that he had originally been invited to deliver the sermon by a gentleman who had often suffered 'grief of his soul to behold the vicious and debauched practices of youth on that day of liberty'. In the hope that many might be induced to 'spend their time in listening to a sermon, than in drinking and gaming, &c', Mead agreed and his sermons had met with 'great success'.[5] In 1708, the City's Court of Common Council noted that St Bartholomew's Fair had of late seen

Bartholomew Fair in the eighteenth century. The entertainment on offer at makeshift stalls travelled around London fairs.

the Erecting and Setting up of Booths in Smithfield of extraordinary Largeness, not occupied by Dealers in Goods, Merchandises, &c., proper for a Fair; but used chiefly for Stage-plays, Musick and Tipling (being so many receptacles of vicious and disorderly Persons), Lewdness and Debauchery have apparently increased, Tumults and Disorders frequently arisen, and the Traffick of the said Fair, by the Traders and Fair-keepers resorting thereto, greatly interrupted and diminished.[6]

The Council resolved that in future the fair be restricted to three days. But fairs were resilient to such censure, for they were deeply embedded in – even expressive of – the social and economic life of the community. Many fairs had emerged from, and still retained, the role of markets, and so existed to the mutual benefit of local traders, entrepreneurs and their customers. Taverns, for example, had much to gain from nearby fairs. Thomas Dale, drawer of beer at the Crown Tavern, Aldgate, and proprietor of the Turk's Head Musick Booth, offered his customers at Smithfield Fair 'a glass of good wine, etc.' and the promise of entertainment with 'musick, singing and dancing'. 'You will see,' he added, 'a Scaramouch Dance, the Italian Punch Dance, the Quarter Staff, the Antick, the Country man and Country woman's dance, and the Merry Cockolds of Hogsden.' Another enterprising landlord announced 'a dance of three bullies and three Quakers, and a cripple dance by six persons with wooden legs and crutches'.[7]

There was also an intimate relationship between fairs and theatres. All fairs featured theatrical booths providing opportunities for professional players to reach a wide audience, and it was this which tended to sustain a broader theatrical culture. Stepney and Shoreditch had been at the heart of a nascent English theatre at the end of the sixteenth century, before the forced closure of The Theatre and The Curtain and later the Puritan ban on stage productions. Smaller, transient theatres, however, did rise again after the ban had been lifted. One was located in Goodman's Fields, Whitechapel, as early as 1703. Goodman's Fields was an unprepossessing area at the time, for the most part surrounded by lowly housing and near to the notorious Rag Fair. *The Observator* of that year clearly saw the benefits the theatre offered to members of the local middle classes:

It is a very good place in the Rosemary Lane precincts, and I know of no reason why the quality at both ends of the town should not have the same diversions. This will be a great ease to the ladies of Rag Fair, who are now forc'd to trudge as far as Lincoln's Inn Fields to mix themselves with the quality.[8]

From that point the theatre disappears from the historical record, but in 1729 another was opened by a small entrepreneur, Thomas Odell, who converted an old bookshop in Whitechapel. The Goodman's Fields Theatre soon built up a sizable audience for the type of respectable plays shown in the West End.[9] With the audience came a 'halo of brothels which drove away the industrious inhabitants' and raised the concerns of local religious leaders, including the vicar of St Botolph, who in a sermon condemned the theatre, and local merchants who feared that it would corrupt their apprentices.[10] Having failed to persuade the Lord Mayor and aldermen to take action against a theatre beyond their jurisdiction, local dignitaries approached the Lord Chamberlain. But Odell was not easily deterred and challenged the legality of the action, forcing its withdrawal. Now free from threats of closure, the theatre had a successful first season offering a mix of popular contemporary plays, such as Farquhar's *The Recruiting Officer*, and Shakespeare. This very success, however, provoked hostility from rather more dangerous quarters; the large theatre managers, who had seen their own audiences fall, united to oppose the Goodman's Fields Theatre, in the face of which Odell decided to sell up in 1731. The astute actor/manager Henry Giffard took over, and it was under his proprietorship that a new theatre with the same name was erected the following year on a plot of land leased from Sir William Leman.

For three seasons Giffard survived on a staple fare of plays and musical entertainments. The timing, however, was not propitious, for the political tide was turning once again against popular theatres. Giffard departed three years later for Lincoln's Inn Fields, leaving the theatre to be used for acrobatic and juggling performances until its forced closure by the 1737 Licensing Act, which, ironically, he had helped to bring about. The architect of the act was the influential Sir Robert Walpole, who had good reason to feel aggrieved; the government was vulnerable to criticism and he himself had been singled out in recent stage productions as a corrupt and egotistical minister. The decisive moment came when Walpole was passed the manuscript for *The Vision of the Golden Rump*, which launched a vicious and scurrilous attack on him and George II using a huge pair of the latter's buttocks as a set from which the players made their entrance. It was rumoured that the messenger was Giffard, to whom the manuscript had been submitted for consideration, and who was duly awarded a thousand pounds for his loyalty. Whatever the source, Walpole used the evidence of *The Vision of the Golden Rump* to rush through the 1737 Act, which transformed the English theatre by requiring future stage productions to be approved by the Lord Chamberlain. This measure effectively curtailed the smaller and more radical theatres, whilst promoting the patent theatres of Covent Garden and Drury Lane as the only legitimate playhouses.[11]

There were always loopholes, however, one of which was exploited by Giffard. Following an appeal to the Lord Chamberlain, and perhaps in recognition of services rendered, he was restored as manager of Goodman's Fields in 1740. The following season opened with a 'Concert of Vocal & Instrumental Music', in the middle of which he offered *Richard III* without charge, effectively circumventing the Act. In the title role was 'A GENTLEMAN who never appeared on any stage'. By the end of the season this 'gentleman' was the best-known actor in London, attracting such an enthusiastic audience that the carriages of the nobility and gentry reputedly stretched from Temple Bar to Whitechapel.[12] 'Did I tell you about Mr. Garrick,' inquired the poet Thomas Gray in a letter to a friend, 'the town are gone mad after? There are a dozen dukes of a night at Goodman's Fields sometimes.' The unprecedented success of David Garrick sealed the fate of Goodman's Fields, for patent theatres, once again fearful of the competition, made representations to the Lord Chamberlain, forcing its closure in 1742. The last production at Goodman's Fields was *The Beggar's Opera*. The theatre was demolished in 1746, and another built on the site, but it had little success and was soon converted into a warehouse before being destroyed by fire in 1809.

The closure of Goodman's Fields marked the end of any theatrical tradition in East London which had claim to respectability. The small venues operated by tavern keepers remained, offering a varied diet of farce, dance and music, and fairs continued to provide outlets for the more enterprising. Thomas Doggett, manager of Drury Lane Theatre, and his fellow actor/manager Thomas Penkethman performed regularly at fairs, earning more, it was said, in twelve years than a waterman earned in the course of a lifetime. Plays such as Doggett's *A New Droll called the Distressed Virgin, or the Unnatural Parents* fed the taste of popular audiences for bawdy reverie. Fairs, however, although licensed, always had the potential to push at the boundaries not only of respectability but of the political order, especially when other avenues had been closed off. Because of this they too were subject to a general assault in the course of the eighteenth century. Southwark Fair was forced to close in 1762, and while others survived well into the nineteenth century, they too eventually succumbed to a determined campaign organized by all shades of middle-class reforming zeal against the challenges posed to the moral and political order.

Rather more enduring were the public houses, for they remained at the very core of popular recreation. Pubs provided not only copious amounts of alcoholic beverages to suit all tastes, but also warm, convivial atmospheres. Here friends could meet to talk and play games, conduct societies, hold meetings or be entertained by musical and theatrical acts. Pubs also served a vital socio-economic role within the community by providing accommodation and a convenient place to strike agreements over employment and deals of various descriptions. Having links with local businesses, fairs, markets and theatres, pubs were thus deeply embedded within the mechanisms and structures of local life, and it is this which helps to explain their popularity and extraordinary longevity.

There is nothing peculiarly urban about the pub, but whereas in rural environments they were scattered, in areas such as East London which witnessed rapid increases in thirsty populations their number and density tended to increase dramatically. In the course of the nineteenth century, under the censorious gaze of Victorian social reformers, it was oft cited as a source of concern that East London had more pubs per square mile than any other place in England. The origins of this rise are difficult to trace, since the presence of so many of the early pubs in the records has not survived, but it is possible to gain some idea of the extent of the increase in the early modern period from estimates recently made for the parish of Bethnal Green.[13] In 1552 there were 4 alehouses, rising to 74 in 1716, and 84 in 1785.

Many pubs were considered disreputable, as prosecutions for unlicensed activity suggest, and yet they were vital to the consolidation of a more respectable working culture. This is nicely illustrated by the alacrity with which the pub was embraced by Huguenots after their settlement in the late seventeenth century. The seventy-four-year-old Joseph Roquez recalled in 1840 that in his youth there were about half a dozen public houses kept by Frenchmen, and chiefly frequented by French patrons.[14] Included were members of the numerous benefit clubs and friendly societies established by Huguenots soon after their settlement, which formed the model for the great friendly societies of the nineteenth century.[15] The Society of Parisians, for example, was founded in 1687 as a mutual benefit society run by and for exiles from Paris living within three miles of Christ Church, Spitalfields. The society met monthly in a local pub. This example was followed by the Bachelors Benefit Society (1697), the Norman Society (1703), the Society of Lintot (1708) and the Friendly Society (1720), all of which met regularly in East London pubs. By 1813 approximately 3,000 people in Bethnal Green alone belonged to benefit societies, thereby helping to sustain the pub-based culture.

Alehouses were also integral to the tradition of radical politics. Many debating clubs met there, encouraging an ethos of inquiry and bonds of solidarity among their members. The more radical venues such as the Seven Stars and the Three Sugar Loaves in Spitalfields attracted the uninvited attention of the local rector, who complained of the suspicious characters who gathered there. At times of religious turmoil pubs could provide a refuge for persecuted congregations. Equally, during industrial struggles, most notably the weavers' riots of the 1760s, pubs fast became the headquarters of the various committees which met to coordinate protest and action.

The experience of early friendly societies served to remind us that Huguenots brought a distinct culture to East London, one remote from the carnivalesque pursuits of the largely unskilled and uneducated labouring population: serious, intellectually vigorous and virtuous, it remained an important presence until the decline of silk weaving in the first half of the nineteenth century. In the longer term, Huguenot culture helped define the cultural pursuits of the respectable indigenous working class. This tradition of self-improvement through education, a tradition shared with Quakers, was capable of brilliant achievement. Take, for example, the Spitalfields Mathematical Society, founded in 1717 by a retired mariner, Joseph Middleton, who wished to teach the mathematics of navigation to sailors. Over time, the society's membership and interests diversified as it became a major centre for scientific experimentation. Weavers comprised approximately half of the membership (which varied from fifty to eighty); the remainder was made up of skilled workmen from other local trades, typically brewers, braziers and bakers. Several society members emerged as significant figures in eighteenth-century science. John Dollond, a weaver of Huguenot descent, brought to the society a passion for optics, invented a telescope and founded the firm Dollond and Aitchison. Thomas Simpson, a self-taught mathematician who started his working life as a weaver, pioneered the use of calculus, in recognition of which he was elected to a Fellowship of the Royal Society in 1745.[16] Another FRS was John Canton, son of a weaver, who worked on electricity and magnetism. Members met weekly to discuss mathematics and solve mathematical puzzles, and ambitious lecture programmes were organized. The society amassed a library of 3,000 volumes and a collection of scientific instruments which were freely borrowed by members. Early in the nineteenth century, with the decline of the silk-weaving community, the fortunes of the society changed for the worse, and it was eventually taken over in 1845 by the Royal Astronomical Society, at which point its membership stood at nineteen.[17]

Huguenot weavers and their families partook in a wide variety of recreations that in later years would be described as rational. In evidence to the 1840 Hand-loom Weavers' Commission, Edward Church, a long-time solicitor in Spital Square, recalled the existence of flourishing Historical, Floricultural, Musical, Recitation, Entomological and Columbarian Societies. The weavers, he claimed, were virtually the only botanists in London, and were the first entomologists in Britain. They were great bird fanciers, particularly of pigeons, and breeders of canaries, which were kept by their looms to cheer them, and were considered the best bird catchers in London, in great measure supplying the market with linnets, woodlarks, goldfinches and chaffinches. They were also passionate gardeners, cultivating not only their own gardens but pioneering the use of allotments. One six-acre plot of land in Bethnal Green was enclosed and divided up into about 170 small gardens, most with summer houses where families would dine on Sundays and holidays. Flower competitions were regularly held, dahlias and tulips being particularly prized.[18]

This was a culture, however, of what may be described as an aristocracy of labour, and so was not representative of weavers or indeed the labouring poor more generally. As Church reminds us with a rhetoric characteristic of the time, the weavers as a body were deeply divided between this self-conscious cultural elite and the large majority:

> We are not, however, to suppose that the whole of them spent their time and money in this way. Intellectual enjoyment is not suited to the taste of the bulk of mankind in any station. With a large proportion of the weavers the animal enjoyments adapted to their condition were the chief objects of their desire.

This artisan culture was therefore somewhat exclusive; not only did it cater for the tastes of relatively few Huguenot exiles, but it was remote from an indigenous popular culture having very different lineages and contrasting attitudes towards 'rational' recreation. In the course of the eighteenth century popular religious dissent in East London faded, in part because sects were assimilated into the dominant order, in part because the struggles against the excesses to be found in popular recreations around fairs, theatres and public houses had largely been won. In its stead, East London witnessed the eruption of nascent struggles within the industrial and political spheres which reshaped the internal divisions of the working population.

*Stepney, 1769. By now Whitechapel and Spitalfields were congested, and residential develop-
ment was beginning in neighbouring Bethnal Green.*

Warmth may have been their mistake

The most intractable problem faced by the authorities in eighteenth-century East London was that created by militant – at times, riotous – forms of industrial struggle. Here, as before, silk weavers facing desperate circumstances were in the vanguard. Despite a sustained growth of the industry in the seventeenth century, conditions of weavers had shown little sign of improvement, and it had needed only a change of fashion or a new challenge from foreign competition to plunge weavers into destitution, thereby provoking various forms of militancy, from petitions and attacks on women wearing calico to large-scale riots (pp. 39–40). The eighteenth century witnessed little improvement, for the industry in East London remained vulnerable to foreign and increasingly provincial competition, ever threatening the livelihoods of local weavers. It was against this backdrop that new forms of combined action emerged within the industrial sphere.

At moments of particular tension the labour force turned in on itself to reveal fissures along lines of race. Previously, resentment had been directed against Huguenot settlers, but with the migration of large numbers of Irish labourers willing to take work as journeymen weavers and coal heavers at low wage rates, anti-Irish sentiment among other sections of the labour force rapidly mounted. It only needed a spark to ignite such simmering hostility into open riots such as those that erupted in East London during the summer of 1736. Amidst general concern about a Jacobite conspiracy to overthrow the Hanoverian regime and restore the Stuart dynasty, crowds of between 2,000 and 4,000 rampaged through Shoreditch, Spitalfields and Whitechapel shouting 'Down with the Irish' and attacking at will the houses and businesses thought to be Irish-owned. Attempts to disperse the crowds by reading the Riot Act proved ineffective, but when the Tower Hamlets militia was summoned the rioters vanished into the night. For a time promises made by local employers to discharge Irish workers brought an uneasy calm, only to be broken a few days later by renewed rioting when crowds converged on Goodman's Fields, Rosemary Lane and along the Ratcliff Highway.[19]

Typical of the disturbances was that of the night of 30 July, when a crowd of 'several hundreds', armed with clubs, sticks and stones, and chanting 'Down with the Irish. Down with them', attacked a number of houses and shops in Whitechapel, smashing the shutters and breaking windows. One victim was James Farrell of Rose and Crown Alley. Awakened by the noise of knocking next door, he looked out of his window only to be spotted by some rioters who cried out 'd—n ye that is not the House'. Urged on by the wife of one of the leaders with the words 'd—n them, have their heart's blood', the crowd started to break down his door, at which point he escaped by jumping out of a window. Three of the rioters were captured by the militia, tried, convicted and sentenced to imprisonment.[20] The riots evaporated as rapidly as they had started, and for a time more restrained modes of protest were adopted. Even in 1745, when a climate of fear and suspicion provoked by the threat of a Jacobite invasion spread through London, evidence of Catholic persecution was slight. There were suggestions of a Jacobite underground among the Irish weaving community, but any such movement was marginalized by the extraordinary level of surveillance to which areas with Catholic populations were subject in this period.[21] In East London – both then, and in subsequent episodes such as Jewish immigration – religious antagonisms were invoked at times of more fundamental work-based tensions, serving to complicate the picture.

Matters came to a head late in 1769. The 1760s was a crucial decade marked by the playing out of new economic and technological regimes in silk weaving that irreversibly affected the relationships among weavers, employers and the state.[22] In 1762 the weavers published a book of prices laying out standard rates of pay for a range of jobs. Compliance was strictly enforced; any weavers accepting work below the standard were subjected to ritual humiliation, while any employers seeking to drive down rates risked having their looms smashed and cloth cut. Increased numbers of armed and disciplined weavers, augmented by striking artisans in other trades, took to the streets. By the end of the decade, the shadow of insurrection hung over East London; the authorities, genuinely fearful of a breakdown in the political order, decided something had to be done. On 18 October 1769 John Doyle and John Valline (or Valloine) were tried at the Old Bailey for the crime of feloniously breaking into the Spitalfields house of Thomas and Mary Poor 'with intent to cut and destroy a certain quantity of silk manufactory in a loom, and also … to cut and destroy a loom'.[23] It was alleged that they had nominally led a raiding party of seven weavers which had deliberately and selectively destroyed the work of only one master weaver who had not given a fair price. The total loss was estimated at just over £100, almost all of which was from the cutting of bombazine cloth.

What emerged from the trial of particular interest were details of the complex social networks that sustained silk weaving.[24] The Poors were impoverished master weavers who, having worked and eaten with the cutters over the past four years, knew them all well, claiming to be able to recognize their faces and voices even in the darkness and even if disguised. For a time, they refused to report the incident. Mary attempted to negotiate with the cutters a price for her silence, but the offer of 30 guineas was rejected. Fearing ritual humiliation within the community, she fled to Limehouse, where she learned that a reward of £500 had been offered by one of the richest master weavers, Lewis Chauvet, for information leading to the prosecution of those responsible for a raid on his house when seventy-six of his looms were cut. The cutters returned to the Poors' house on 31 August to destroy utensils, goods and shuttles. The Poors were out seeking nightly refuge, but their son William was at home, and gave evidence at the trial, reporting that his pleas for mercy stopped one of them cutting him up. The Poors reported the raids to the constabulary, and Mary wrote to Chauvet 'having heard he was a sufferer'.

The trials of Doyle and Valline, and later of William Horsford, were replete with contradictory and circumstantial evidence. Mary Poor in particular was an unreliable witness who was determined to settle old scores, and if possible gain a reward. A number of former employers testified to the industrious character of Valline, but three influential master weavers – Traqaun, Dumoissur and Chauvet – condemned him as being of riotous disposition. Doyle and Valline were found guilty and sentenced to death; Horsford was given the same sentence on 6 December 1769. These were the first capital sentences meted out for this type of crime, and so they were clearly intended to set an example. The dramaturgy, however, did not end there.

In a move similar to the unprecedented hanging of coal heavers off the Ratcliff Highway in July 1768 (p. 85), it was decided that the executions should take place not at Tyburn but at Bethnal Green. Adjacent to Spitalfields and home to many poor weavers, Bethnal Green was well chosen as a site 'to strike Terror into the Rioters'. The radical MPs John Sawbridge and James Townsend, who were riding high on the popularity of the campaign to confirm the legitimacy of John Wilkes' victory in the recent parliamentary election at Brentford (p. 89), disputed the decision. They appealed to the Secretary of State for information, and wrote to the King requesting a reprieve. Respites were granted, but following an adjudication by Lord Mansfield the sentence was carried out on 6 December at the watchhouse opposite the Salmon and Ball pub (which still stands on the corner of Bethnal Green Road). The scene was described by John Entick:

> They were therefore this morning taken in a cart from Newgate through the City to Whitechapel, and thence up the road to Bethnal Green, attended by the Sheriffs &c, with the gallows, made for the

purpose, in another cart; it was fixed in the cross road, near the Salmon and Ball. There was an inconceivable number of people assembled, and many bricks, tiles, stones &c thrown while the gallows was fixing, and a great apprehension of a general tumult, notwithstanding the persuasion and endeavours of several gentlemen to appease the same. The unhappy sufferers were therefore obliged to be turned off before the usual time allowed on such occasions, which was about eleven o'clock; when, after hanging about fifty minutes they were cut down and delivered to their friends.[25]

Doyle's last words were a plea for vengeance: 'Let my blood lay to that wretched man who has purchased it with gold and them wretches who swore it falsely away.'[26] His call was heard by the assembled crowd, for between 4,000 and 5,000 of them marched in a 'riotous and tumultuous manner' to the house of Lewis Chauvet in Crispin Street, Spitalfields, where they broke the windows and burnt his furniture. The King offered a reward of £50 and a pardon for the apprehension of the offenders; it was not claimed.[27] Not wishing to risk further trouble, the authorities hanged Horsford at Tyburn later that month.

This was the last riotous act of Spitalfields weavers. It would be tempting, albeit dispiriting, to see this closure as the successful implementation of state 'terror' on the population of East London. The reality was more complicated, for early in the 1770s rising levels of general unemployment provoked petitions and threats of disorder from weavers and sections of riverside labour. Following a joint approach to parliament by master and journeymen weavers, supported actively by the Lord Mayor and the City magistrate Sir John Fielding, the first Spitalfields Act[28] was passed. It required the Lord Mayor and magistrates to 'settle, regulate, order and declare the wages and prices of work of the journeymen weavers' in the City and parishes of Middlesex, effectively taking the matter out of the hands of master weavers, and so laying the foundations for fifty years of industrial calm, despite the steadily worsening plight of those weavers who had been most involved in the previous period of turmoil.[29]

A happy effect

The other work-based communities in East London displaying a propensity to riot in the period leading to the end of the eighteenth century were the maritime and riverside trades. Congregated in Wapping, Shadwell and Ratcliff, they comprised a mobile population with direct links to international networks of trade and commerce, had a strong Irish presence, and inhabited enclaves virtually beyond the reach of the authorities. 'When one goes into Rotherhithe and Wapping,' wrote the blind magistrate John Fielding,

> which places are chiefly inhabited by sailors, but that somewhat of the same language is spoken, a man would be apt to suspect himself in another country. Their manner of living, speaking, acting, dressing, and behaving are so peculiar to themselves.[30]

Perhaps because of this, their exploits are poorly documented; nonetheless, their role in the making of East London was important and needs to be examined.[31] Strype may well have noted the maritime tradition of Stepney as one of the 'greatest Nurseries of navigation' (p. 28), but this celebration of the wealth and glory brought by ascendant sea power paid little heed to the lot of those who provided the manpower. The life of an able seaman was tough and uncompromising. Often pressed or kidnapped into service, separated from families and friends, subjected to harsh disciplinary regimes on long voyages, fed on meagre diets, frequently exposed to danger, and paid a pittance, sailors had good cause to harbour resentments, which sporadically erupted into open revolt. In 1626 seamen discharged from the navy without pay rioted in the riverside hamlets where they were temporarily billeted, and in 1635 the Wapping Shipwrights' Company reported a revolt of seamen who refused to promise not to serve in foreign navies. Further disturbances were witnessed when seamen from Ratcliff, Limehouse and Blackwall participated in riots at Southwark in 1640, in a mutiny downriver in 1648, and in a riot at Wapping and Tower Hill in 1653.[32]

Those discarded from service found themselves on the streets. Forced to fend for themselves many took to crime, for which some unfortunates paid the ultimate price. Henry Johnson, for example, found it difficult to gain sufficient work in the merchant fleet and so stole lead from the roof of the Rev. Hugh Colley in Mile End Green, for which he was hanged in 1739. Robert Legrose of Whitechapel had served in the navy and merchant fleets but on one shore leave stole clothes from a haberdasher and sold them to Margaret Frame in Rag Fair. He was hanged in 1741. And Richard Eades from St George-in-the-East found himself in poverty after discharge from the navy. He resorted to street robbing around Cable Street, and was hanged in 1741.[33]

Coal heaving attracted none of the celebratory epithets written about maritime labour and yet its role in sustaining the economic success of

London was no less vital. Coal was the life-blood of the capital as industri-alization took off in the eighteenth century, and its continued flow depended in part upon the manual strength and dexterity of the coal heavers who unloaded the cargoes of the collier boats that had sailed from the coalfields of the North East. It was dirty and punishing work, but open to any who had sufficient strength and will to endure the conditions. The Irish did, as a result of which they were heavily represented amongst the coal-heaving community.

Combined action amongst heavers in pursuit of better pay and security was made difficult by the seasonality of the work, the high turnover of labour and punitive sanctions levelled against strikes and go-slows. And the anti-Irish riots of the 1730s severely damaged any prospects of uniting different sections of the labouring population of East London. By the 1750s, however, heavers began to agitate against a systematic undermining of their work conditions. A petition was sent to parliament in 1757 against coal contractors who, it was claimed, had colluded with collier owners to hire labour through ale-house keepers and other informal means, so undercutting the collective strength of the heavers. In response, the 1758 Coal Act[34] required Alderman William Beckford to manage the heavers by allocating work and administering wages, so, it was hoped, providing a degree of stability. Seeing a corrupt system that served none but contrac-tors, a Middlesex magistrate, Ralph Hodgson, set up a rival scheme which successfully drove up the wages of the heavers. Not to be out-manoeuvred, the contractors appointed by Beckford recruited large numbers of Irish heavers at reduced rates, so precipitating a series of murderous struggles. One contractor, John Green, was laid siege to by heavers at a public house in Shadwell before the military intervened to disperse the angry crowd.[35] Green's house was attacked on the following day, when he shot two of the assailants before making his escape. In subsequent trials Green was acquitted of murder; in contrast, John Grainger, Daniel Clark, Richard Cornwall, Patrick Lynch, Thomas Murray, Peter Flaharty and Nicholas M'Cabe were found guilty of riot and hanged at Sun Tavern Fields off the Ratcliff Highway on 26 July 1768.

Further provocation followed when contractors engaged sailors to unload coal. Open war broke out when the sailors were attacked by heavers at Shadwell Dock, and, in a series of skirmishes, scores were killed. 'In short,' wrote a contemporary observer, 'to so great a height was this insur-rection got, that the inhabitants of Wapping were perpetually under the most direful apprehensions.'[36] A detachment of troops was posted to the area, taverns were raided and fugitive Irishmen sought. Nine heavers were

apprehended and charged for the murder of an apprentice sailor, John
Beattie, who had been stabbed to death in one of the frays. After a hearing
before Sir John Fielding, they were committed to Newgate. Four were
brought to trial; James Murphy and James Duggan were found guilty, and
hanged at Tyburn on 11 July. In total, therefore, nine heavers were executed
that month, an example, suggested John Entick, that 'produced a happy
effect; the tumults immediately ceased, and peace and industry supplied
the place of resentment and mischief'.[37]

Entick spoke prematurely, for, as we have seen, the weavers' struggles
had not yet ceased. And even if the execution of weavers in the following
year did herald a period of relative industrial calm, this was to be rudely
broken in June 1780, when the most serious metropolitan insurrection of
the eighteenth century erupted. The Gordon Riots need concern us only in
passing, for they were a London-wide phenomenon rather than specifically
or exclusively of the east. The immediate cause was a petition organized by
Lord George Gordon against what were perceived to be concessions to
Catholics in recent legislation, in support of which large demonstrations
marched to parliament. Gordon had insisted that only the more respectable middling sort and tradesmen should take part, but invocation of anti-
Catholic sentiment stirred slumbering popular hostility that had previously
awoken, and more riotous crowds appeared. Over six days Newgate was
attacked, liberating hundreds of prisoners, Catholic churches and houses
were destroyed or damaged, including those of Sir John Fielding and Lord
Mansfield, and businesses were plundered.

The work of George Rudé and Peter Linebaugh has done much to
remind us that we must exercise a degree of caution in seeing these riots as
the expression of a bigoted mob. The term mob tends to suggest a
dangerous rabble acting with neither restraint nor reason. The Gordon
Riots, like the anti-Irish riots of 1735, displayed violence, not in a random
fashion but chiefly against the property of the rich in the City and
Westminster; in contrast, the congested Catholic districts of St Giles and of
riverside hamlets were unscathed. Nearly 300 people were killed in the
riots of 1780, and 160 were brought to trial. Those charged were not dominated by the criminal or vagrant poor, but represented a cross-section of
the labouring population as a whole – journeymen, apprentices, domestic
servants and craftsmen were among their numbers.[38]

There were riots during that fateful month, however, that are difficult
to see as other than racially motivated. Take, for example, the trial of Mary
Roberts, Charlotte Gardiner and William Macdonald at the Old Bailey on
28 June 1780. They were charged that on 8 June, with fifty or sixty others,

they demolished the house of John Lebarty, an Italian who owned a public house and slop shop in St Catherine's Lane, Whitechapel. Lebarty claimed that he knew the two women, who lived close by. Roberts, he declared, came with the mob to his house and called to him, 'You outlandish bouger, I will have your house down: you outlandish Papist, I will have your house down.'[39] Other witnesses apparently had no doubt that Gardiner, a black woman, was also a leader. Lebarty's neighbour, Letitia Harris, testified that thirty or forty times Gardiner had removed items of furniture to place them on the fire outside: 'she worked as if she had been an horse; she pulled off her shoes and stockings … crying more wood for the fire, more wood for the fire'. Macdonald also was easily recognizable since his left arm was in a sling following discharge three months earlier from the Guards Regiment. The rioters then proceeded to remove the wainscoting and pull down the house, brick by brick. All three were found guilty and hanged at Tower Hill. In total twenty-one people were executed for their participation in the Gordon Riots.

Wilkes and coal heavers forever

The forms of popular culture found in East London prior to 1800 tend to suggest a culture of protest, whether by dissident Protestants against the established church, by weavers and coal heavers against threats to their livelihoods, or by theatres against the censorious gaze of City authorities. Much of this protest drew upon the carnivalesque to push at the boundaries of the law, often overstepping them. Although the arena of parliamentary politics was formally legal and accessible to a rather small section of the population (the franchise, after all, was generally restricted to men of the middle and upper classes), occasionally, issues were thrown up which galvanized popular sentiment and led to important shifts in the political landscape. The campaign for parliamentary democracy led by John Wilkes placed the question of popular rights firmly on the agenda, and seemed with a measure of inevitability to attract the attention of the people of East London.

The campaign, summed up well by the radical slogan 'Wilkes and Liberty', was relatively short-lived. Provoked in 1763 by an article in issue number 45 of the satirical periodical *The North Briton* for which Wilkes was charged with seditious libel against the King, the campaign quickly became a national issue of political democracy, reaching a sort of closure in 1774, when Wilkes was finally accepted as a rightful member of parliament.[40] The campaign thus coincided with an extraordinary period of industrial struggle waged by the London labouring population, and although we must be careful not to draw too precisely the links between the political and industrial spheres, there can be little doubt that in London at least the dramatic support for Wilkes was an expression of more general grievances. During the trial Wilkes invented himself as a champion of English liberty for 'all peers and gentlemen, and, what touches me more sensibly, that of all the middling and inferior set of people, who stand most in need of protection'.[41] Such a champion had not existed since the revolutionary turmoil of the mid-seventeenth century; this, combined with Wilkes' considerable skills as a journalist and orator, clearly touched on a deep current of sentiment among those who felt excluded from the oft-trumpeted rights of freeborn Englishmen, with the result that he enjoyed extraordinary levels of popular support, particularly among the industrial and commercial out parishes to the north and east of the City.

Unsurprisingly, popular support was most evident in the late 1760s, as the phase of industrial struggle reached its dramatic climax. Spitalfields weavers were much in evidence in the Middlesex election campaign of 1768. They gathered in Piccadilly, handing out the blue cockades of Wilkes and distributing handbills proclaiming 'No. 45, Wilkes and Liberty'. A scuffle broke out with supporters of the rival candidate, Proctor, during which his coach was pelted. Later in the year the temporary release of Wilkes from prison following indictment for libel coincided with the turbulent struggles of coal heavers against the introduction of a new contract system. Witnesses in the trial of John Green (p. 85) testified that the mob was chanting 'Wilkes and coal heavers forever'. Thomas Axford, publican of the Swan and Lamb nearby, reported that some of the mob ran to houses calling out 'd–n you, light up your candles for Wilkes; upon which I went ... and light up one candle below stairs in the front, and illuminated my house above; I went to the door and saw every house round me was illuminated'.[42] An open declaration of political allegiance, however, had its dangers. Thomas Overstall visited a barber, and then decided to have a drink with a friend. They discovered that the public house was shut, and while deliberating about their next move they were approached by about six men who began discussing politics: 'Who are you for?' they asked one another. 'One said I am for Wilkes; d–n you, said others, I am for Bute; after that they began to swagger with sticks to one another over their heads.'

The difficulty of inferring political intent is nicely illustrated by an incident which took place at Limehouse in May that year. About five hundred rioters, mostly sawyers, marched to the recently erected sawmill of Charles Dingley, to be met by the works superintendent, Christopher Richardson, who inquired of their demands. The sawyers replied that the mill was working when 'thousands of them were starving for want of bread', and proceeded to destroy the machinery at a cost of £5,000.[43] Seen thus, the incident appears as another act of machine-breaking performed in broad daylight in defence of the right to work: indeed, an anti-Luddite Act[44] against the vandalism of mills, engines, bridges and fences was passed in the following year. And yet Dingley was a well-known and prosperous Russia merchant in the City who had established a considerable timber import business, and who had declared his opposition to Wilkes and was later to contest his candidature.[45] He also organized a lobby of 'loyal' City merchants, traders and stockbrokers, including the Spitalfields master weaver Lewis Chauvet, who was soon to play an instrumental role in the prosecution of John Doyle and John Valline (p. 82).[46]

By now the social and geographical base of Wilkes' support was broadening. His candidature at the Brentford election of 1769 attracted cavalcades which marched peacefully through London. One set out from Poplar and Mile End with three hundred horsemen and met up with a contingent at Bishopsgate Street before riding to Brentford. On the way they 'hailed' Dingley at the Royal Exchange.[47] When Wilkes won but was denied his place in parliament a series of meetings took place around London, none better attended than at Mile End Assembly Room. On 17 April an audience variously estimated between 1,750 and 2,500, with a crowd of 5,000 outside, decided to establish a committee to prepare a Bill of Grievances and Apprehensions. The main speakers were John Sawbridge, MP for Hythe, and James Townsend, MP for West Looe, both sheriffs of London. Among Wilkes' staunchest supporters, they also actively supported the plight of weavers, receiving deputations, objecting to the stationing of troops in Spitalfields, and intervening to delay the execution of Doyle and Valline.

With the decline in industrial militancy after 1769, and the eventual election of Wilkes in 1774, the popular political voice of East London fell silent. Wilkes was an ineffectual member and became, with age, increasingly resistant to reform. During the Gordon Riots he defended the Bank of England by shooting rioters, and he later greeted the French Revolution with horror. Created in part by an ability to give voice to popular radicalism, Wilkes then suffered from its demise. By the time radicalism experienced a new dawn in the 1790s he was an ailing figure, eventually dying in 1797.

Cartoon of Charles Dingley at his sawmill in Limehouse, 1769. Dingley had been involved in a bitter dispute over the introduction of machinery, and put himself forward as a rival candidate to John Wilkes at Middlesex.

The Spitalfields genius

This chapter would be incomplete without mention of the cultural landscape of the social elite of East London. We know little of the quotidian lives of these people, but they were neither exceptional nor significantly different from those of other City merchants. Outside work, their limited time – and therefore that of their wives – was taken up with networking and socializing, and beautifying their houses and gardens, with the occasional visit to the theatre and other respectable forms of recreation. Church attendance was obligatory, while the more socially aware devoted time to managing local affairs and various acts of public philanthropy. This elite culture, important though it was to the early development of East London, had little significance in the longer term. By the end of the eighteenth century the outward migration of the local bourgeoisie was gathering momentum (p. 60); by the end of the nineteenth a few grand houses and street names were all that remained of past opulence.

Into the spaces vacated by this exodus sprang a body of local elites whose collective presence by the end of the century was a powerful reminder of the vitality of religious dissent. Quaker congregations had been among the largest of nonconformist sects in the early history of Protestant dissent in Stepney (pp. 14–15). By forcing Quaker congregations to live beyond established cities, the Five Mile Act of 1665 operated to their advantage since they could pursue commercial interests without interference from City authorities and guilds. They survived the religious persecution under Charles II to emerge in the eighteenth century as an influential business community, particularly when the Affirmation Act (1696) opened up opportunities for involvement in London affairs.

Quakers drew members from across the social hierarchy. Most were from the humbler industrial crafts and trades of London, but a minority were from the financial and commercial sectors, and comprised a closed cadre of gifted individuals. William Allen, scientist and social reformer, Samuel Gurney, banker and philanthropist, Elizabeth Fry, prison reformer, Ben Truman, brewer, Thomas Fowell Buxton, brewer and political campaigner, and their associates bestrode the financial, social and philanthropic life of East London like no others. As Quakers they moved within complex social and business networks largely set apart from the structures of what was considered acceptable society, and were inspired by a deep religious conviction to do good works. Barred from careers in government, law, universities and the church, Quakers sought creative outlets for their energies in commerce. Here they saw no incongruity between philanthropy and the pursuit of profit; indeed, they were interlinked. At a time of corruption, fraud and sharp practice in the spheres of finance and commerce, Quakers established a reputation for integrity and honesty; on the back of such trust they founded banking empires, including Lloyds and Barclays, and large businesses such as Cadbury, Rowntree and Bryant and May.

One of the first notable local Quakers was Silvanus Bevan, who in 1715 established a pharmacy at Plough Court adjacent to the Gracechurch Quaker Meeting House at the eastern edge of the City.[48] The successful firm passed into the hands of Joseph Gurney Bevan, who in 1792 recruited as a clerk the remarkable William Allen. Allen had been born in Spitalfields to a prosperous silk manufacturer, and through diligent pursuit of his passion for chemistry became a partner in Bevan's firm three years after joining. It was at this time that Allen also took up studies at Guy's Hospital and set up the Askesian Society where young scientists met to advance chemical knowledge through discussion and experimentation. Its members included Luke Howard, who became a partner with Allen at the pharmacy before establishing a laboratory for the manufacture of nitric and sulphuric acids and liquid ammonia at a more remote and hence safe site in Plaistow, West Ham. Allen was to emerge as a scientist of some repute. He co-founded the Pharmaceutical Society, became a lecturer at the Royal Institution, and for his work on carbon was elected as a Fellow of the Linnaean Society in 1801 and the Royal Society in 1807. It was not always easy at that time for such people to maintain an equitable balance between science and religious conviction, but Allen did so by constantly reminding himself of their ulti-mate importance. '[T]he pursuits of science,' he wrote, 'properly conducted, tend to enlarge our views, to banish narrow prejudices, to increase our love of truth and order, and give tone and vigour to the mind.' And yet scientists must beware 'lest chemistry and natural philosophy usurp the highest seat of the heart'.[49] Thus despite his eminent scientific career Allen somehow found the time and vigour to pursue interests in philanthropy, education and the abolition of the slave trade.

Close to home, he viewed with dismay the desperate plight of silk weavers, and with the London magistrate Patrick Colquhoun established a Soup Society in Spitalfields early in 1798, the first of its kind in the country (p. 112). Allen, however, reached beyond the intimacy of Quaker circles to collaborate with prominent radical reformers. His commitment to progres-sive education, largely inspired by the ideas of Joseph Lancaster on the monitorial system as a means of providing education for the poor, culmi-nated in his appointment in 1810 as treasurer of the Royal Lancastrian Society, renamed the British and Foreign School Society in 1814.[50] He was a close friend of the abolitionists Thomas Clarkson and William Wilberforce, served on the committee of the Society for the Abolition of the Slave Trade,[51] collaborated with Robert Owen in establishing the model commu-nity of New Lanark, and with James Mill published a quarterly journal, *The Philanthropist*, which included articles by Mill himself and another Spitalfields-born reformer, Jeremy Bentham.[52]

Allen's friend Samuel Gurney moved in the same social and political circles. Heir to a family bank in Norwich, Gurney was brother to the redoubtable Elizabeth Fry and Hannah Buxton, and after his marriage lived at Ham House, West Ham. With wealth acquired by inheritance and through marriage, Gurney progressed rapidly in the London bank of Richardson & Overend. By 1809 the bank, now Overend Gurney, was on course to becoming the largest discounting house in the world, making its fortune by borrowing money from other banks to relend to firms and households. Once established, Gurney devoted much of his energy to philanthropy and reform, working with Allen in the British and Foreign School Society and the Anti-Slavery Society, and pioneering famine relief in Ireland, prison reform and African freedom. It was largely under his influence that the Poplar Hospital for Accidents, the first hospital to treat injured dockworkers, was opened in 1855.

As with earlier elites, however, the influence of these Quaker dynasties in East London was eventually to decline. Allen moved to Stoke Newington shortly after marrying for the second time in 1806. Gurney remained at Ham House until his death in 1856, but the financial empire he built was mismanaged by his successors; it crashed in 1866, bringing widespread devastation to the staple industries of the area (p. 212). By this time Quaker financial and business interests were fully integrated into the national economy.

The collapse of the staple industries of East London may have been provoked by the 1866 crash, but this was merely the final act in a protracted story of decline brought about by the rationalization of production as the forces of the industrial revolution took hold. The direct impact of this rationalization on the course of industrial change in East London during the nineteenth century was dramatic, and next demands our attention.

CHAPTER 4

Modernization and its Discontents,
1800–1860

DESPITE THE continued growth of East London, an observer of the
late eighteenth century would have been forgiven for thinking
that the area and the majority of its people clung on to the past
rather than looked to the future. Continuities with a previous age tended
to prevail. Employment to the north of the parish in Spitalfields and
Whitechapel was still dominated by silk weaving, which after the passage
of the Spitalfields Act in 1773 was enjoying a period of relative tranquillity.
There were also multitudes of labourers and semi-skilled workers in trades
such as tailoring, shoemaking, cabinet-making and upholstery who worked
long hours in small, poorly lit rooms.

Employment in the riverside area to the south was dominated by
maritime trades. It has been estimated recently that in the early eighteenth
century a quarter of London's population relied directly or indirectly on
the Port, while in 1800 the magistrate Patrick Colquhoun could claim
that 120,000 men were directly employed there. Even if this figure is
exaggerated, it suggests that a significant percentage of East Londoners
found employment in the Port at some time in the course of a year.[1] It
was not merely the Port – important though it was – which provided work,
but also a host of ancillary trades such as shipbuilding, rope-making,
coopering and inn keeping. Although rather smaller than the Port in terms
of the numbers employed, shipbuilding in late-eighteenth-century East
London was heir to a long and honourable tradition of skilled labour.
Roughly ninety per cent of all Thames shipbuilding was located on the
stretch between London Bridge and the Woolwich ferry.[2] The first and
some of the largest private yards were to be found there, including those
owned by the Pett family at Limehouse, and the East India Company yard
at Blackwall.

The changes witnessed by this industrial landscape in the first half of
the nineteenth century confront conventional wisdom on the nature of the

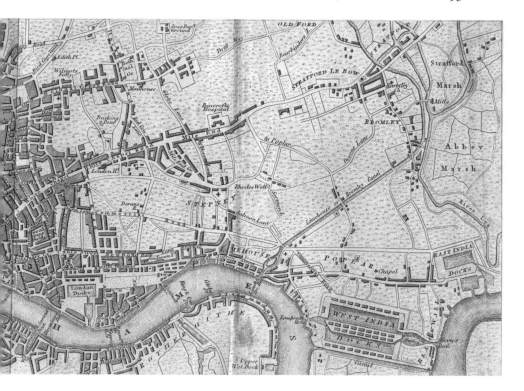

Allen map of East London, 1829. The first phase of the development of the docks was complete, and growth was extending eastwards into areas such as Mile End which were previously rural retreats for the wealthy.

industrial revolution, for here the revolution was not the familiar story of cotton, iron and steam and the emergence of factory production; rather it was of the intensification of small-scale production, the unremitting pressure to reduce wages by use of less skilled labour, struggles of staple industries to survive in the face of domestic and overseas competition, and the imperative of retaining imperial authority. This last matter impelled a remarkable transformation of the riverside area, which is where the story begins.

A region of half land, half water

Maritime and associated trades in the riverside areas of Wapping, Shadwell and Limehouse had changed little since the seventeenth century. The Port of London had hardly emerged from its mediaeval foundations. The landing and shipping of merchandise were carried out at the legal quays which had punctuated the stretch of riverside between the Tower and London Bridge since Elizabethan times. These were supplemented with sufferance (licensed) wharves to the east of the Tower, which were meant to accommodate increases in shipping but in fact were never able to keep pace with demands for more wharfage. The problem was not merely one of space, however, for the whole system needed radical overhaul if London was to retain its position as a great trading centre. Every member of the merchant community recognized this to be the case; indeed, it was a small group of merchants with interests in Caribbean slave plantations which in the 1790s determined to provide a solution by building the largest, most secure and technologically advanced docks complex in the world, and in so doing effectively transformed the physical and industrial landscape of the area.

In the course of the eighteenth century, Britain emerged as the greatest trading nation in the world. At its heart stood London, which, enriched by commercial and imperial endeavour, had emerged as a truly global city by the end of the century. This rise was reflected well in the statistics of London's maritime trade, which had trebled during the century. In 1700 the value of imports was £4,875,538, that of exports £5,387,787. By 1794, imports had soared to £14,863,238, and exports to £16,578,802. This trend was broadly reflected in the amount of cargo transported. Over the same period the aggregate tonnage of British ships entering the Port increased from 80,040 in 839 ships to 429,715 in 2,219. When the coastal trade (mostly colliers from the north feeding London's insatiable appetite for coal), which since 1750 had increased from 511,680 tons in 6,396 ships to 1,176,400 tons in 11,964, is added, we gain a sense of the scale of merchandise now passing through the Port.[3]

Because of better policing, administration of customs duties, and proximity to the capital, legal quays tended to handle the more valuable cargoes such as tea, sugar, indigo, spirits, coffee, firs, tobacco, silk and fruits on which high duties had to be paid. Restricted to the 1,464 feet of river frontage, there was simply no room for expansion to meet rapidly increasing demand. Sufferance wharves were used to land high-bulk, relatively low-value cargoes such as timber, corn, rice, fish, bricks and coal. More extensive than legal quays, they nonetheless found it difficult to provide adequate facilities. The inevitable result was overcrowding. In 1796 a pilot of Trinity House, Edward Nicholls, surveyed a sorry state of affairs. He estimated that the port had the capacity to moor 545 ships, and yet on an average day 775 ships were to be found there.[4] Little regard was paid to safety or mutual convenience when docking. Many ships were anchored so close to one another that in blustery conditions they collided, causing damage. Some were crowded into such shallow water that after an ebb tide they rested on their anchors and were severely damaged or lost. At times the river was so congested with shipping that there was no room to pass; on one occasion it took Nicholls seven days to sail from Deptford to the Port.[5] Outward journeys were little better. While historically there was good reason to locate the Port as close to the city as practicable, the circuitous route around the Isle of Dogs made navigation difficult. Dangerous eddies and shoals had caused many ships to run aground, tiers of ships queuing to be unloaded obstructed the progress of other vessels behind, and journeys were delayed as pilots were forced to await changes in the wind in order to negotiate the dramatic bends in the river.

The protracted delays to which ships were subject provided opportunities for plunder and fraud. The custom of taking samples from cargoes of rum and sugar, of masters disembarking before discharge of their cargoes, of permitting persons on board with all manner of loose attire

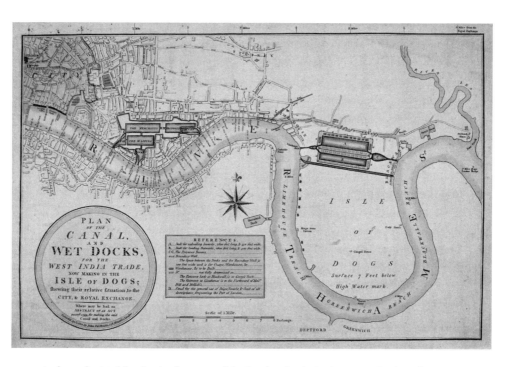

A plan submitted for the development of the London Docks in the 1790s. By then the system of legal quays and sufferance wharves along the riverside had become hopelessly inadequate in coping with the traffic.

suited to secreting goods, fostered a culture of open theft and smuggling, often with the connivance of the Revenue Officers, who seemed determined to have their share of the 'perquisites'. In effect, pilfering took place at every point of the cargoes' delivery. Matthias Lucas, a master ligh-terman (and if anyone should know, he would), claimed that most thefts occurred from lighters conveying goods between ship and quay, and since 700 people were employed in lighterage at any one time the scale of plunder was potentially considerable.[6] Even if the goods were landed without mishap, they were frequently forced to remain on the quays and thereby exposed to pilferage before they could be removed to secure ware-houses some distance away.

At stake, however, were not simply the profits of individual merchant traders, but the commercial viability and competitiveness of the Port itself, and hence the future of London as a centre of world trade. John Inglis, a London merchant, claimed that the legal quays presently accommodated a third of the demand, and were a 'species of monopoly, degrading and inju-rious to the merchants' because they had artificially raised and maintained wharfage costs. The proposed docks will 'establish a competition essential to the security of the trade, and to the dispatch and economy which is necessary to provide for the trade of the Port of London in its present extended circumstances'.[7] Comparison with Liverpool revealed that charges for unloading sugar, cotton, coffee and ashes at the Port were approxi-mately three times higher. Threats from continental ports were yet more worrying.

Plans were drawn up by the West India Merchants Committee for a new wet dock at Wapping. Fearing loss of control, the City Corporation proposed a rival dock across the Isle of Dogs, an intervention which prompted the government to set up a parliamentary committee to 'enquire into the best mode of providing sufficient accommodation for the increased trade and shipping of the Port of London'.[8] A total of eight plans were submitted by persons who had a direct and personal stake in their success.[9] The protracted debates which followed centred on the relative merits of the Wapping and Isle of Dogs schemes, which were submitted in the form of rival bills later in 1797, only to be deferred.[10] Largely because of its prox-imity to the City, Wapping seemed to hold sway, but then Robert Milligan, a leading West India merchant who had previously refused to lend support to any of the plans, persuaded key committee members that the West India trade should be accommodated by extensive docks on the Isle of Dogs, and that adjacent warehouses were the only means of guaranteeing the security of the merchandise. In this respect, the remoteness of the site was a distinct advantage; not only did most plunder take place in the upper reaches of the Port, but it would render obsolete the need for the circuitous journey round the Isle. Milligan also won over the City Corporation, but the rest of the merchant community proved more recalcitrant. Eventually, a select committee was set up in 1799 to decide between the schemes. It expressed regret that 'though this subject has now been under consideration for several years no measure should have been taken for remedying the evils so universally felt'. Noting that the Wapping docks would benefit small ships, and the Isle of Dogs docks large ships of the East and West India trades, the committee recommended that both schemes be adopted, and the latter should immediately be put into effect.[11] With astonishing alacrity, the Act for Rendering more Commodious and for Better Regulating the Port of London[12] was drafted and received royal assent the following month.

The West India Dock Company was established by the Act to build and administer the new dock on the Isle of Dogs. An initial capital of £500,000 was raised without difficulty. Subscribers included banks, the City Corporation, and a wide range of maritime interests; they acted in full knowledge that their investment was protected by a Consolidated Fund which, in an unprecedented move, had been set up by the government using public monies, and for at least twenty years the dock exercised a monopoly over trade with the West Indies.[13] Construction began early in 1800, and despite the massive scale of the undertaking was virtually completed in the summer of 1802. The opening on 27 August was an appropriately extravagant affair. Among an estimated audience of 30,000 were many national figures. Such a gathering at a location which at the time appeared remote, even in the wilds, must have cut an odd spectacle, but the press greeted the occasion enthusiastically. The *Morning Chronicle* saw in the opening a rightful celebration of Britain's imperial commerce:

> Yesterday the magnificent Docks at Blackwall, which in size and accommodation to shipping exceeds everything that now exists, were opened for the reception of the shipping in the West India Trade. By eleven o'clock the various avenues and roads leading to the Isle of Dogs were crowded by multitudes, some on horseback, others in gigs and curricles, but the great number were pedestrians. The bustle and confusion in repairing to Blackwall were astonishing; such was the

anxiety of some individuals, that they pushed boldly on without slacking rein until they were stopped by the soldiers planted at the various points leading into the Docks ... The whole of the scene indeed must have been highly gratifying to every well-wisher to the greatness of this Country. In the space of two years, by the energy, the spirit, the wealth, and the perseverance of individuals, this imperial work, the proof of past and the pledge of future prosperity, has been begun and almost finished ... While property is thus rendered active by liberty and maintained secure by law, (and what other source has commerce had in this country but liberty and law?) it is impossible to set bounds to its operations and to its success.[14]

Though the site on the Isle of Dogs had eventually been favoured by West Indies merchants, it was evident that the original plans for a dock at Wapping were not going to be abandoned; indeed, even before the docks were completed, work had started on the Wapping or London Docks as part of the wider scheme of the redevelopment of the Port of London. Much of the ancient hamlet of Wapping was excavated to make room for the docks, warehouses and high wall, a process involving the London Dock Company in a relatively high initial outlay which remained a financial burden for years to come. When completed in 1805, the docks comprised separate Eastern (or Shadwell) and Western (or St George's) docks linked by a small tobacco dock, and enclosed a total of thirty-five acres of water, providing room for 300 vessels.[15]

The third major development which took place along the East London riverside in this period was construction of the East India Docks. The East India Company had a long history of involvement with the Blackwall site, which during the eighteenth century had passed into the hands of the Perry dynasty, under whose direction the Brunswick Dock was constructed in 1790 (p. 53). These facilities met the needs of the Company; the large Eastindiamen had for decades conveniently moored in the deep stretches of river by Blackwall, unloading their valuable cargoes into secure lighters which carried the merchandise to the quays and wharves, later to be transferred to the Company warehouses, which were built like fortresses. The success of the West India Docks coupled with growing suspicion that thieves were now turning their attention to the cargoes of Eastindiamen prompted plans for similar docks at Blackwall.[16] A scheme was drawn up by a group of leading East India merchants and ship owners with the tacit support of the Company. Since there were no rival schemes, and no public monies were involved, the protracted debates leading up to the decision on the West India Docks were not repeated. With seeming ease, the Act 'for further improvement of the Port of London, by making Docks and other works at Blackwall for the Accommodation of the East India shipping in the said Port'[17] was passed in July 1803.

Most of the finance came from the directors of the East India Dock Company and their associates, including £6,000 from John Perry himself, and £1,000 from the Chaplain of the Company almshouse.[18] Plans were drawn up by John Rennie and Ralph Walker, both of whom had been actively involved in the construction of the West India Docks and so brought valuable experience to the new scheme. The East India Docks were centred on the Brunswick Dock, which was converted into the new export dock. When completed in 1806 the area of the water contained was 30 acres, making the entire dock about half the size of the West India Docks. But then fewer ships were required for the India trade than the Caribbean trade because cargoes for the former tended to be of smaller bulk and higher value than for the latter.

The East India Docks were opened in August 1806 with a grand ceremony. At least 15,000 people attended, including 'such an assemblage of British dames in all the pride of beauty, grace, dignity and dress, as was scarcely collected together', the *Gentleman's Magazine* reported. The Lord Mayor turned up unexpectedly, and hurried moves were made to turn out the front row of spectators, not without protest.[19] The Docks were plain in design, remotely located, and notably had no warehouses. The Dock Company was granted a monopoly for twenty-one years, according to which all vessels trading to India and China were required to use the docks, and all cargoes unloaded must be housed in the East India Company's warehouses.

By the end of the opening decade of the nineteenth century the first, and arguably most important, phase of London's modern dock complex was complete. Each of the three separate docks was granted a compulsory clause enabling them to exercise a twenty-year monopoly over the landing and warehousing of dutiable cargoes. The dock companies made full use of such advantageous conditions to strengthen their positions, although this was mitigated by other problems of their own making. The East and West India dock companies paid off the construction costs and were able to build up reserves which enabled them to pay high dividends to their shareholders for longer than was warranted by performance alone, while the London Dock Company was saddled with long-term indebtedness brought on by high initial costs and delays in completion.[20] Seemingly committed to an ethos of free trade in the docks as in silk weaving, parliament refused

St Katharine's Dock, 1846. Opened in 1828, the docks could not accommodate the larger vessels and were forced to amalgamate with the London Docks in 1864.

to renew monopoly rights in the 1820s, and so transformed the situation. The most immediate effect of this refusal was to open up competition not only among the companies but also with other wharves and warehouses in the Port. It also prompted the construction in 1828 of the St Katharine's Dock, seeking to take advantage of the new conditions. In this new competitive environment, company dividends fell, and amalgamations ensued; in 1828 the East and West India Dock Company was formed. The London and St Katharine followed in 1867.

The companies shored up their share of trade by offers, including free towage to shipping companies, or by lowering their rates in the hope of gaining competitive advantage. Nothing could be done, however, about the impact of steam-powered ships from the 1830s, and the rapid growth in the size of vessels thereafter. These larger vessels could not readily be accommodated by upriver docks without massive investment in new facilities, but even then there was a risk that modest extensions of existing docks would be overtaken by the spectacular growth in the size of ships. When in 1870 the East and West India Company opened the south-west dock on the Isle of Dogs, for example, it was hailed as highly advanced; by 1882 it was generally recognized to be inadequate.[21] The only solution was to construct an entirely new dock downstream which could not only take the larger ships but also meet their owners' increasingly strident demands for speedier discharge and loading of the cargoes. Thus the Victoria Dock was completed in 1855. Situated in West Ham, beyond historic East London, it was the largest dock in the world, capable of taking the latest steam vessels. It was acquired by the London and St Katharine Company, which then proceeded to build the adjacent Albert Dock in 1888. These developments gave the company a decisive advantage over the East and West India, and from 1865 it soared ahead of its rival in the quantities of cargo landed.

Apart from the financial, commercial and employment gains attendant on the expansion of the docks in this period, the great advantages of riverside sites ensured that East London also remained prominent as a site of Thames shipbuilding. This supremacy was if anything consolidated from the 1830s, when iron and steam superseded wood and sail, for London not only retained its influential merchant community, attracted by the reputation of Thames shipbuilders, but also had at its disposal unrivalled expertise provided by important engineering firms such as Penn, Rennie and Maudslay.[22] New yards opened, even in areas which had previously been thought unsuitable for shipbuilding such as the Isle of Dogs. Following excavation of the docks, more than a dozen shipyards were established here, including the famous names of Scott Russell, Millwall Ironworks, which in 1858 launched Brunel's *Great Eastern*, J.D. Samuda and Yarrows.

The largest of the shipbuilders, the Thames Ironworks and Shipbuilding Company, had its origins in the firm Ditchburn and Mare, which in 1836 established a shipbuilding yard adjacent to Blackwall on the Poplar side of Bow Creek. Initially, the company relied on supplies of coal and iron from the north of England, but as they became more costly Mare decided to take advantage of the new coal wharves constructed by the Northumberland and Durham Coal Company on the West Ham side of the creek. With contracts from the Admiralty for naval vessels, and several for private yachts and steamers, the firm prospered, but following heavy losses on contracts for supplying ironwork for the new Westminster Bridge and vessels for the Crimean War, Mare became insolvent. Renamed the Thames Ironworks and Shipbuilding Company, the firm was taken over by P. Rolt, under whose direction the firm again expanded with regular orders from the P & O shipping line and the Royal Mail Steam Navigation Company. Then in 1860 the Thames Ironworks guaranteed entry into the annals of shipbuilding history by constructing HMS *Warrior*, the first British iron-hulled warship, thought at the time to be the most powerful warship in the world.[23]

This period of growth saw the emergence of sizable firms employing considerable numbers of workers and making important contributions to the metropolitan economy. This portrait of East London industry contrasted starkly with the small-scale workshops conventionally held to characterize East London of the mid-nineteenth century. By 1865 Wigram and Green, who had taken over the old yard at Blackwall, employed 1,500, Scott Russell, later the Millwall Ironworks, 5,000, Samuda 2,000, and the Thames Ironworks 6,000. In total, the numbers employed in Thames shipbuilding soared from 2,500 in 1831 to 27,000 in 1865, the majority of them located on north riverside sites.[24] This was the zenith of the industry, however, for by then the rival shipyards in north England and Scotland were beginning to attract an increasing share of the orders.

Picturesque in their dirt

Virtually all the trades of the area were vulnerable to trade cycles, seasonality of production, the fickleness of fashion, and provincial and foreign competition. Employment was rarely guaranteed; members of the workforce were thrown back on to the informal and predatory market as soon as demand for their labour fell. Operating outside the market were large numbers who lived by their wits as street sellers and entertainers, prostitutes, and those operating within the criminal underworld. It is difficult to know with any certainty whether the conditions endured by the poor of East London deteriorated in the first half of the nineteenth century. High levels of underemployment persisted, occasioned by the fragmented structure of the labour market and the continued importance of relatively small employers, but we would need to scrutinize closely the changing fortunes of individual trades to build a more reliable and complete picture over this period. What is clear, however, is that the numbers of the poor gradually increased, and that through various surveys they became better known to contemporary observers.

Amidst periodic recessions plunging sections of the population into destitution stood the various London docks which seemed to possess extraordinary symbolic power. They, more than any other feature of the industrial landscape, came to represent metropolitan modernization; it was as if at last the dark shadows of a pre-modern past were being dispersed by an unfaltering march into the bright dawn of a new commercial future. Some sense of this can be gleaned from the public enthusiasm which greeted the opening of each dock, but it was evident also in the numerous guides listing places of interest to visit. Fifty years later, in one such guide published to mark another great event in the history of the imperial metropolis – the Great Exhibition of 1851 – the docks were singled out to the unwary visitor as a site of strange awe:

> The visitor who desires to appreciate the power, the wealth, and the world-wide commerce of London, in all its varied phases, will naturally be desirous to see the docks, the shipping, and the river below bridge, in which are to be found concentrated the evidence of a commerce, and of a concourse of nations, the like of which has never yet been seen, and is calculated to astonish the most heedless observer. A more striking contrast than that between the appearance of the east and west ends of London, can scarcely be conceived: instead of the numerous fashionable equipages, and the gaily-dressed throngs of pedestrians, which crowd the spacious and handsome streets of the west end, the stranger will find himself in a region, half land, half water, in which the population are chiefly sailors and jews, and the business all that pertains to ships and shipping; and, a bowsprit, thrusting itself between the houses into the street, while the atmosphere is an olio of smell more powerful than savoury, and justifies a doubt as to our basis being on terra firma.[25]

A rather more intimate picture is painted by George Sala, one of the most prolific and well-paid journalists of the time. After one of his many peregrinations in the early 1850s he described what he encountered in the neighbourhood of the London Dock:

> Not in one visit – not in two – could you, O reader! Penetrate into the tithes of the mysteries of maritime London; not in half a dozen papers could I give you a complete description of Jack alive in London. We might wander through the dirty mazes of Wapping, glancing at the queer, disused old stairs, and admiring the admirable mixture of rotting boats, tarry cable, shell-fish, mud, and bad characters, which is there conglomerated. We could study Jack alive in the hostelries, where, by night, in rooms the walls of which are decorated with verdant landscapes, he dances to the notes of the enlivening fiddle; we

might follow him in his uneven wanderings, sympathise with him
when he has lost his register ticket, denounce the Jews and crimps
who rob him … Ratcliffe and Shadwell, Cable Street and Back
Lane, may be very curious in their internal economy, and very
picturesque in their dirt; but it cannot be a matter of necessity that
those who toil so hard, and contribute in so great a degree to
our grandeur and prosperity, should be so unprotected and so little
cared for.[26]

The effect of the docks on local communities was merely hinted at in such
celebratory accounts of the modernization of East London, but it was a
vital issue. When the docks were first opened the companies decided
to recruit a permanent and respectable body of dock labour controlled by
an authoritarian disciplinary regime. With tales of large-scale pillage still
fresh in their memories, and mindful of the fact that wages and salaries
were the largest single running cost, it seemed advisable to create a
workforce which was reliable and trustworthy by offering steady employment rather than inflated rates. The West India Dock Co., for example,
initially appointed two hundred permanent labourers at a rate of 3s 6d per
day, which was about average for a labourer.[27] While they prospered under
privileges of the compensation clause introduced in the originating acts as
a means of guaranteeing returns on investments, companies did maintain
an improved labour force; with the withdrawal of monopoly rights,
however, economies had to be made, the easiest of which was to take
advantage of the glut of labour created by Irish immigration and the
decline of silk weaving. The dock labour force was thus casualized, measures that had been introduced to mitigate the damaging effects of casualization were abandoned, and the numbers of permanent men reduced to a
minimum.

Any calculation of the numbers actually employed in the docks was
fraught with difficulties. One investigator estimated that at least 20,000
were employed but had to admit that since most dock companies were
reluctant to give him the required information this was nothing more than
a rough guess. Part of the problem was that the dock force was divided
between the permanent and casual ranks, and that the latter in particular
were subject to enormous fluctuations in demand related to the numbers
of ships arriving in the port. In 1798, for example, ship arrivals from the
Caribbean varied from 111 in August to 0 in December.[28] Construction of
the modern docks, the eradication of monopoly privileges and increased
trade dampened the fluctuations, but only to a limited degree. In 1849,

ships entering the East and West India Docks (now amalgamated) during any one week varied from 209 to 28, the handling of which required labour forces numbering 4,000 and 1,300 respectively.[29] At St Katharine's Dock, daily workforces varied between 1,700 and 500, and at London Dock 3,000 to 500. If account is taken also of ancillary labourers, including lightermen, shipwrights, caulkers, carpenters and porters, who depended upon the docks for employment, then approximately 30,000 labourers faced lengthy periods of unemployment during slack periods.

The vast body of casual labourers struck at the very heart of the social, moral and political concern exercising the minds of nineteenth-century middle-class observers in London, who thus singled out the figure of the casual dockworker as the most degraded form of human existence. It was during the time of mounting concern in the 1840s that the greatest social investigator of the nineteenth century, Henry Mayhew, set himself the task of charting the work and lives of the labouring poor of the metropolis. He soon came to appreciate the futility of this massive task, and abandoned it, but not before he had undertaken an extraordinary series of studies of particular sections of the metropolitan labour force.[30] It is not merely that Mayhew provided detailed information on wage rates, hours of work, rents and so forth, but importantly he gave the poor a voice. Mayhew relied for much of his evidence on interviews conducted with the poor, who for the most part he treated with sympathy and understanding, and in turn gained their trust. But it appears that even he found it difficult to empathize with casual dock labourers, referring to them as 'this most wretched class'.[31] He described the London docks as a home colony to Spitalfields, for many unemployed weavers migrated there in search of work, and yet he acknowledged that the docks provided opportunities for employment to an entire range of working people who had fallen on hard times:

> we find every kind of calling labouring at the docks. There are decayed and bankrupt master-butchers, master-bakers, publicans, grocers, old soldiers, old sailors, Polish refugees, broken-down gentlemen, discharged lawyers' clerks, suspended government clerks, almsmen, pensioners, servants, thieves – indeed, everyone who wants a loaf, and is willing to work for it.[32]

Because of fluctuating demands for labour, each casual faced the daily struggle to find work at the dock gates. Crowds of dock labourers gathered early each morning in the hope of being 'called', that is, picked out and offered work for the day. This uncertainty created a scene of greedy despair: 'I could not have believed,' wrote Mayhew of a call at the London Dock, 'that there was so mad an eagerness to work, and so biting a want of it, among so vast a body of men.' Compared with the patient misery of the silk weaver, more heroic than desperate, the plight of the dock labourer was tragic and sublime.[33] And it was of course Mayhew who attempted to record the conditions casual labourers endured. He begins with the testimony of a Dorset man, literate, who had found work as a navvy and porter before a series of setbacks forced him to seek work in the docks. Here he was able to earn 14s in a week, but most of the time, because his face was not known, he earned less than 3s, surviving on penny loaves and what he could get through begging.[34]

Casual labourers are the 'most intemperate and improvident of all'. They inhabit low lodging houses to be found in the small courts and alleys close to the docks, and frequent public houses, most of which are named the 'Jolly Tar' or something similar. The contrast between the superabundance of the docks and the destitution of the surrounding area bewilders the mind, claimed Mayhew, although few who come to see the riches of the far-famed Port know of its underside.[35] And yet he understands well that the habits of casual labourers are due not to any moral weakness but to the precarious nature of their work:

> It is a moral impossibility that the class of labourers who are only occasionally employed should be either generally industrious or temperate – both industry and temperance being habits produced by constancy of employment and uniformity of income.[36]

The lot of the casual dock labourer deteriorated in the course of the nineteenth century. Faced with declining fortunes, dock companies introduced labour-saving machinery and exploited more intensively this reserve army of labour. But this was not a problem of the docks alone; the use of casual labourers was endemic in the industries of East London, and as the logic of capitalist rationalization took hold, so their conditions worsened and their chances of regular employment fell.

Crape, gauze, bandanna and bombazin

In some contrast to the impulses of commercial and industrial modernization witnessed in the riverside areas, the silk-weaving centre of Spitalfields remained tied to small-scale production using mechanical looms. Towards the end of the eighteenth century the silk weaver was confronted with ever-increasing difficulties. Changing fashions, increased competition from the provinces and abroad, and a determination among master weavers to drive down wages created conditions which had driven weavers to destroy looms and woven cloth in riotous acts born of desperation. In response, the 1773 Spitalfields Act[37] was introduced as a means of providing stability to the earnings of weavers by enabling magistrates to determine piece rates for a range of tasks, so placing on a firm footing a practice which had operated in a rather haphazard manner for many years (pp. 54–5).

While the Act had praiseworthy aims, like so many others it had consequences which were largely unintended. Since the Act applied only to London and Middlesex, there was nothing to prevent employers moving their production to Essex, or further afield to Coventry and Macclesfield, where they could get away with paying no more than two thirds of Spitalfields rates.[38] And while the smaller masters were Spitalfields men who favoured the Acts because they prevented the district from a precipitous decline into pauperism, the industry was increasingly dominated by large City operators. These employers considered regulation as undue interference in the market, an encouragement to combinations among weavers, and a disincentive to innovation since the same rates were paid whether or not labour-saving devices were used. The increasing stranglehold of the City was to lead to the demise of silk weaving in Spitalfields late in the nineteenth century, but for now weavers continued to struggle against mounting odds.

In evidence to an 1818 parliamentary committee set up to inquire into complaints of hardship detailed in several petitions of ribbon weavers, William Hale, a local silk manufacturer employing hundreds of Spitalfields weavers, asserted that while the Act had prevented riotous behaviour, during trade depressions it had encouraged manufacturers of fancy goods to move where labour was cheaper, much to the cost of local journeymen weavers.[39] Weighing up an argument that captured well something of the complexity of the debate on legislation, Hale stated that some employers believed that general conditions would improve if the Act were repealed since work at a reduced rate is preferable to none, but he predicted that it would tempt many to screw down wages so much that weavers would be driven to seek poor relief, and become alienated from 'that country and government under which they could not live by honest means'. Stephen Wilson of Lea, Wilson & Company – one of the largest manufacturers – declared that the Act 'unsettles the workmen, repels the artist, blunts

industry, disgusts the consumer, discredits the seller, and ruins the enter-
prize', evidence for which was the fact that the manufacture of fine silk
trades such as crape, gauze, bandanna and bombazin (sic) had recently
been forced out of Spitalfields.[40]

Weavers themselves remained resolute in support of the Act. Using the
experience of earlier combinations of journeymen, they formed societies
representing particular trades in silk weaving to expose and prosecute
through the courts employers who evaded payment of the fixed rates, and
to provide insurance for members sacked for demanding the appropriate
rate. The Good Intent, for example, could claim eighty-three members in
1813 with over £5 'in the box'.[41] At a general meeting of another society
held in September 1817, when an appeal was heard for higher contributions to enable it to continue, the committee reported that in the past nine
months they had been successful in restoring the lawful price of work to at
least fifty weavers whose employers had refused to pay it.[42] Manufacturers
counterclaimed that the societies had exerted illegal pressure on their
members to enforce the Act, and forced divisions between weavers who
could rely on comfortable earnings and those who starved for lack of work.
Ambrose Moore, of Wilson & Moore, a silk manufacturer employing
several hundred, produced a paper showing that during the depressed year
of 1816 a family of five weavers earned £262 while others were forced on to
poor relief, simply because the Act dictated 'You shall rather starve than
take less than your full wages'.

The Parliamentary Committee disagreed, and decided not only to
allow the Act to remain in force but also to extend it to Coventry for a trial
period of a few years. This extension was never implemented, however, for
the forces of free trade were rapidly gathering momentum, and one of their
favoured targets was Spitalfields. A House of Lords committee on foreign
trade in silk and wine criticized the Acts as restricting the free employment
of labour and capital. Within two years a bill appeared before the Lords'
Committee to repeal the Spitalfields Acts; after amendment and a fierce
rearguard action among weavers who organized petitions and demonstrations to the Commons it received royal assent in 1824.[43] Driven by the
mantra of free trade, the government soon resolved to reduce drastically
the duties on imported silks, and for a while the domestic silk industry
witnessed rapid growth. Most of the growth, however, was in Lancashire
and Derbyshire, where wage rates and other running costs were lower than
in London, and there were more power-driven looms. Early scepticism,
particularly among weavers themselves, that such looms would not be able
to resolve the considerable technical problems had receded in the face of

Family of Spitalfields silk weavers, 1833. The industry was in terminal decline, and most weavers were plunged into destitution.

evidence that the latest machines could not only weave all cloths with the possible exception of velvet, but they could do it more efficiently. It was reckoned that a woman on a power loom could produce twice as much as a man on a hand-loom.[44]

Spitalfields manufacturers were slow to adapt to change; most faced a choice between bankruptcy or relocation to a silk-weaving town where wages were lower and machines more advanced. A report submitted by W.E. Hickson to the Commission on the Condition of Hand-loom Weavers (1838) declared that silk manufacture was no longer centred on Spitalfields but instead on Manchester, Macclesfield and Coventry. Although wages were lower in the manufacturing districts, the conditions of the weavers were on the whole better, simply because rents, provisions and fuel were much cheaper. During the harsh winter of 1838, for example, coal in Spitalfields was approximately three times the price of that in Manchester. Furthermore, open competition with foreign manufacturers had fostered such improvements that Coventry weavers could now produce ribbons of a quality and beauty never previously known in England, and little inferior to those of France.[45] Spitalfields could no more compete with France than with Manchester, so that when a commercial treaty was signed in 1860 abolishing duties on imported silks the end was in sight. In 1824, 60,000 London weavers had consumed 1.5m pounds of silk yarn in production; sixty years later the numbers were respectively 4,000 weavers and 80,000 pounds of silk yarn.[46]

Before 1860, therefore, and despite its continued troubles, silk weaving remained the single most important industry in the northern parishes of East London. Its common description as a Spitalfields trade is misleading, for by the end of the eighteenth century its looms and weavers could be found not only in Spitalfields but in Shoreditch, Bethnal Green, Whitechapel, Bishopsgate, and Mile End New Town.[47] Although, as we have seen, the industry expanded steadily in the closing decades of the century, its growth was built on unstable foundations and was never able to guarantee the relatively favourable rates of local weavers, artificially maintained as they were by the Spitalfields Acts and duties on foreign imports. During downturns large numbers of weavers experienced distress so severe that the Spitalfields weaver came to symbolize an artisan in the direst poverty. In 1795 the radical John Thelwall recounted their fate:

> Even in my short remembrance, bare-foot ragged children ... in that part of the town were very rare ... I remember the time ... when a man who was a tolerable workman in the fields, had generally, beside the apartment in which he carried on his vocation, a small summer house and a narrow slip of garden, at the outskirts of the town, where he spent his *Monday*, either in flying his pidgeons, or raising his tulips. But those gardens are now fallen into decay. The little summer house and the Monday's recreation are no more; and you will find the poor weavers and their families crowded together in vile, filthy and unwholesome chambers, destitute of the most common comforts, and even of the most common necessaries of life.[48]

It was in response to the deep recession of the final years of the century, that a group of Quaker philanthropists led by William Allen and Patrick Colquhoun established a soup kitchen in Spitalfields. Funded largely through voluntary subscriptions, including £500 from Lloyd's Coffee House, the society opened a shop in Brick Lane from which it sold nutritious soup to around 3,000 families facing starvation.[49] By 1811 the operation was on a thoroughly professional footing. The committee was dominated by Allen and members of prominent Quaker families, and could report subscriptions of over £4,000, most of which had been taken out by Quaker firms, and from which nearly half a million quarts of soup had been distributed not only from the shop but also directly to the houses of the poor. This was not indiscriminate relief, however, for in ways that were to prefigure patterns of poor relief later in the century, the society visited approximately 1,500 claimants' families to satisfy itself that none of the relief was given to 'unworthy subjects'.[50] Details submitted on individual cases, however, tend to suggest that few weavers were unworthy, for only the most distressed ever had recourse to poor relief in any form:

> EB has a wife and five children: only one loom's work: badly employed. They said that they had been almost starved through want of work; and that, were it not for the soup, they must go to the workhouse, which was so repugnant to their feelings that dire necessity alone would make them submit to it. MB has four of five looms unemployed, and when the silk trade is tolerably brisk can not only support his family respectably but can contribute to the relief of his poorer neighbours. He bears a respectable character. Through want of employment he has been brought to the last degree of distress: his wife and children exist almost entirely on soup, having disposed of almost everything that is moveable.[51]

In 1812 a group of leading evangelicals established the Spitalfield's Association. Growing out of the experience of the soup kitchen, it sought to ameliorate local distress by providing relief on a more systematic basis than private charity. The district was surveyed, divided up, and the poor visited in their own homes on a regular basis to assess their eligibility. One of the founder members, Thomas Fowell Buxton, gave an address to a fund-raising event in November 1816, when the distress was most acute. He brought the audience's attention to 'scenes of deeper misery, of darker horror' than those of ruin and hunger. Families were on the verge of starvation, wretched creatures sought nightly refuge in the baskets and sheds of the market, and an old man was discovered days after collapsing, too weak to move, and infested with 'vermin of all kinds'.[52]

Silk weavers had always been affected by periodic downturns, but by the mid-1830s the impact of the repeal of the Spitalfields Acts threatened the industry's survival. A series of petitions from hand-loom weavers prompted a select committee. William Hale was again called to give evidence and claimed that poor weavers had become 'much more distressed and indigent; they almost go in rags, and have very little to keep them'.[53] In addition to being a silk manufacturer, Hale was the treasurer of the

Whitechapel Poor Law Union, and brought an informed, if exaggerated, sense of how the wider community had been affected:

> The consequence to Spitalfields of the loss of the minimum rate of wages, and the attempt to compete with foreigners, has been ruinous to the manufacturer, and reduced the wages of the workmen one-half. The effect of this competition which is attempted, without any protection whatever to the workmen, in the shape of a minimum rate of wages, is to destroy a great deal of the manufacturing capital, to degrade the condition of the working people, to increase the poor-rate, to make bankrupts of persons who supply them with provisions, &., and to produce a great deal of misery and disease, a great deal of discontent among the population, and to destroy the morals of the poor.

By now the plight of Spitalfields was of national concern, and Dr James Kay, Assistant Poor Law Commissioner, was directed by the Commissioners to report on the conditions therein. The focus of his inquiry was silk weaving, but he recognized from the outset that the problems encountered were far wider. The availability of cheap accommodation, either in lodging houses or sublet rooms, he argued, attracted a large population of casual labourers from the docks, builders' labourers, porters, shoemakers, hawkers and similar workers who were mixed with the mass of the weavers. Weavers themselves were satisfied with meagre diets and scanty clothing, but in order to survive many were forced to work in the docks or become porters at Billingsgate fish market. A considerable number, however, were too feeble for such bodily exertion and resorted to hawking fish and fruit around the streets.[54]

Spitalfields weavers also attracted the attention of Henry Mayhew. Over the past ten years, he reported in one of his letters to the *Morning Chronicle*, the price of weavers' labour had fallen twenty per cent, and the average day's work was fourteen hours. According to some weavers the deterioration of conditions was the result of competition among masters, and if affairs were allowed to continue 'the fate of the working man must be pauperism, crime or death'.[55] But perhaps the most vivid contemporary narrative of the terminal decline of a once proud tradition of Huguenot silk weaving comes from an interview with William Bresson, a velvet weaver and loom broker. Bresson was fifty-two years old at the time of the interview. The great-grandson of a Huguenot who took refuge in Spitalfields, where his family and subsequent generations settled, Bresson had seen the distinctive culture of the French weaver gradually disappear, largely through intermarriage. His annual receipts over the years 1822–37, which had fluctuated from £101 9s 9d in 1825 to £26 6s 1d in 1837, suggested that trade had been precarious and uncertain. Every five or six years it had suffered from a downturn lasting for two years before a recovery set in. Since 1818 there had been a steady decline in wages, chiefly because of the impact of the Jacquard loom which, by using punched cards to control its operation, enabled less skilled weavers to manufacture fancy fabrics with considerable facility. This decline, however, had not provoked the militancy seen in the eighteenth century when so much damage was done by cutters to woven cloth; indeed, every form of combination among weavers had disappeared. Since the repeal of the Spitalfields Acts attempts had been made to prevent wages falling, but this had proved impossible because there were so many weavers entering Spitalfields who had previously been cotton and linen weavers before being superseded by the introduction of power looms, and many Irish weavers prepared to take lower wages. The rational amusement of weavers had been badly affected by the loss of open spaces to new buildings. Not only had this led to a decline in traditional pursuits such as gardening, but to physical deterioration – few weavers were above five feet two inches in height. Despite this steady decline in circumstances the moral state of hand-loom weavers had remained favourable.[56]

Slop employment

In terms of employment the docks, shipbuilding and silk weaving were the most important East London industries in the first half of the nineteenth century, but there were other sources of employment which need to be considered to arrive at a more complete picture of the changes taking place. Although there were large numbers of women in silk weaving, female employment was dominated by domestic service, especially for the young: in the London of 1851 servants comprised approximately half of employed females between fifteen and nineteen, a proportion which fell rapidly with age, and especially with marriage. Needlework took approximately a quarter of those in their twenties, while laundry work employed up to a fifth, the numbers increasing with age; by the time women reached fifty, laundry work was the most important source of employment.[57] These women were among the most heavily exploited. The work was long and tedious, and the pay low, even by contemporary standards. It was not unusual for a laundry worker to rise at four in the morning and work through to midnight for less than a male labourer on a fourteen-hour day.

Street selling also attracted large numbers of women, their ages depending upon their marital status. This work offered a degree of freedom and opportunity to single and widowed women, and provided wives of male street sellers and labourer with a means of supplementing the family income.[58] Seafood, fruit, vegetables, flowers and a range of small personal items and household goods were sold by women, largely because of their ease of transport. Female sellers resided in the immediate neighbourhoods of street markets. Mayhew finds them in the streets of Spitalfields and Bethnal Green mixing with 'slop-employed' cabinet-makers, tailors and shoemakers. One of his informants in Whitechapel had counted a hundred married women in 'different branches of open-air commerce', only two of whom had husbands in regular indoor employment. A tailor's wife sold watercress, and expected to be joined by her husband in the near future because of his failing eyesight.[59] The circumstances of female street sellers were of unremitting toil. In a famous interview with a watercress girl aged eight, Mayhew talks of someone who had lost all childish ways. All she knew was watercresses and what they fetched. She had been taken out of school by her mother when she discovered that the master had beaten her across the face with a cane. Now she stood early on a cold morning in a thin cotton gown and with a threadbare shawl around her shoulders, with no expectation of pity or kindness.[60]

The reference in Mayhew to slop trades reminds us that small-scale production in East London was also underpinned by the use of cheap labour, often in overcrowded and unsanitary conditions. On 6 November 1849 he began his Letter VI to the *Morning Chronicle* by suggesting that his investigations into the London poor had almost blunted him to sights of ordinary misery. 'Still I was unprepared,' he proceeded, 'for the amount of suffering that I have lately witnessed. I could not have believed that there were human beings toiling so long and gaining so little, and starving so silently and heroically, round about our very homes.'[61] Nowhere was this more apparent than in tailoring. Mayhew estimated that 21,000 tailors resided in London: of these, 3,000 belonged to the 'honourable' part of the trade, heir to a long tradition of skilled work; the remainder were 'sweaters', who acquired the necessary skills quickly and were prepared to work long hours for pay below standard rates. After reassuring sceptical readers that the account was based on first-hand knowledge and information, Mayhew described a visit to a group of nine slop tailors sitting cross-legged in a small room off a narrow court, eight feet square, stitching various dress and frock coats. In the past week they had worked from seven in the morning to eleven at night. For that they were paid 13s, from which rent and the cost of trimmings were deducted, leaving 7s 3d. Women tailors earned between 3s and 6s net per week, which Mayhew claimed was hardly enough to keep them. One shirtmaker who worked from five in the morning to nine at night, taking a nap of five or ten minutes in the day ('The agitation of mind never lets one lie longer'), never made more than 2s 6d. Little wonder then that the slop trade was the ruin for many, since without adequate income women workers were forced into prostitution. Never, claimed Mayhew, had he heard anything as solemn and terrible as the tales recounted by such women.[62]

By the mid-nineteenth century such wretched conditions were evident in the growing presence of sweated trades which soon came to dominate the economy of East London. There is a tendency to see sweating as a response to a glut of labour and the introduction of mechanization in the second half of the century, but its origins were rather earlier. With the decline in the power of the guilds to control labour, and the concomitant collapse of the apprenticeship system, entry into previously protected trades was opened up to less skilled labour prepared to work at lower rates of pay. As was the case with silk weaving, new masters moved in to impose a capitalist logic to production, making full use of the labour which was now freely available. Mayhew was informed that until 1834 the labour of tailors was regulated at twelve hours a day, on the employers' premises, providing each tailor with the opportunity of earning a decent living. But then masters began to break with tradition and take on increasing numbers of sweaters. A strike saw the defeat of the tailors, leading to an acceleration in the employment of underpaid workers and the immiseration of the skilled to the point of desperation.[63] Shoemaking and the furniture makers, which were also at the heart of the sweated trades of East London, underwent similar experiences.[64] 'There are not many stronger contrasts,' remarked Mayhew in his report on cabinet-makers, 'than that between the abode of the workman in a good West-end establishment, and the garret or cellar of the toiler for a "slaughter-house" [sweat shop] at the East-end.'[65]

These trades were important to London because their products commanded the largest and closest market in the country. And unlike factory production, which required significant amounts of space and capital, much of the work was carried out in small workshops or domestic rooms. As land increased in value during the nineteenth century, this was to prove decisive to the survival, indeed growth, of sweated trades. The industrial revolution which transformed production through the introduction of mechanization did not therefore create a factory system in East London; instead the use of relatively simple hand-driven machines intensified the division of labour, and thereby the growth in the employment of cheap, semi-skilled workers, many of whom were women and later immigrants.[66] If East London was not in a position to take advantage of factory production, the new capitalist masters were able to reduce production costs to a minimum in this way. Sweated labour was the result of the operation of this particular logic. A new mass market created by the demands of a more comfortable working class for less expensive 'luxury' items may have fuelled this drive,[67] but equally it could have been that the success in reducing production costs fostered the market. The second half of the century witnessed the collapse of staple industries such as shipbuilding and silk weaving in East London, leading with a degree of inevitability to an intensification of sweating. In the meantime, a more familiar form of industrialization took off in the hinterlands (Chapter 6).

Superior persons

Thus far we have focused on changes in the more important industries and occupations of East London. The story has been one of an unremitting struggle against deteriorating conditions brought about by capitalist rationalization and the precarious nature of employment. We must, however, exercise a degree of caution in viewing nineteenth-century East London as a place of unmitigated poverty and desolation. *Life and Labour of the People of London,* an extraordinary survey undertaken by Charles Booth and his co-workers over the years 1886–1903, revealed something of the social composition of its working population. In stark contrast to the images of degradation spread by the myth of outcast London (Chapter 6), and despite the worsening of conditions for most of the working population, Booth found that approximately half of the adult males were in regularly paid occupations described as skilled, professional or merchant, while less than ten per cent were in irregular, casual employment, the remainder being semi-skilled.[68] East London in the late nineteenth century was therefore dominated for the most part by skilled and semi-skilled workers and their families, who tended to determine the course of industrial struggle; they also inhabited and largely controlled the area's cultural landscape. There were members of the labour force who possessed genuine levels of skill, and could command regular employment providing them with relatively comfortable means. For reasons that will become apparent in the next chapter, historical accounts of East London have neglected this stratum of skilled labour, and yet it is one which needs to be considered in order to provide a more complete – and complicated – picture of the social composition of the area.

Before Booth there were no reliable estimates of their numbers, not least because, with the labour market in a constant state of flux, a person claiming to be, say, a carpenter might be occupied as such for three months in the year, spending the remainder as a general labourer. An occupational census based on baptism registers in East London in 1813 reveals that approximately one third of the adult male population worked as casual labourers, and therefore endured extreme poverty. Another third could be considered semi-skilled, leaving the final third in the category of skilled.[69] The experience of women suggests that few were in skilled occupations. In 1851 London, three quarters of those between the ages of fifteen and nineteen and two thirds between twenty and twenty-four were domestic servants, laundrywomen or seamstresses; if we add others in sweated industries and retail then the unskilled become an overwhelming majority of the total.[70]

Skilled workers normally possessed particular skills acquired through an apprenticeship. Given the specialist nature of many of London's manufacturing trades, skilled labourers were in demand, and for the most part their ready substitution by others less skilled was virtually impossible. Their wages were relatively high, and, equally importantly, regular. Coopers, mechanics, weavers, lightermen, carpenters, shipwrights, glass-blowers and printers were amongst their numbers. Mayhew provided his customary insight into their conditions of work. One tailor he interviewed had worked in a first-rate house in the West End for fifteen years. His wages averaged approximately £1 6s per week, although during slack periods from August to October weekly income had fallen to 4s 6d. Recent increases in the demand for cheaper cloth, however, were forcing even first-rate houses into slop shops; if this continued then the journeyman tailor would ultimately be reduced to the status of a needlewoman.[71]

A shoemaker, also working for the West End trade, was a 'fine specimen of his class'. He was tolerant, dispassionate and philosophical in thought, and had a 'strong literary taste and love of reflection'. From the cleanliness of his home and three children, Mayhew claimed, he and his wife were 'very superior persons'. In the past thirty years the wages of shoemakers had fallen from 35s to 13s 6d per week, chiefly because of competition from footwear manufactured in France and in particular in Northampton, where factory production had been introduced. On average Mayhew's informant earned 27s per week, but for this he worked fourteen hours every day, and he was making steadily less each year. His wife considered that their means had fallen, and that if the situation failed to improve they faced the workhouse or forced emigration to America.[72]

Sawyers, many of whom served a seven-year apprenticeship, had been in constant demand, and could command wages averaging 35s per week. Since 1826, however, the introduction of horse- and steam-driven sawmills, which were capable of faster and more precise work, had superseded human labour; in East London numbers had fallen to less than 500, mostly employed in shipyards around Limehouse. This cursed machinery, according to sawyers who had been in the trade for over thirty-five years, benefited only the timber merchants, for sawyers were now idle and few apprentices were taken on; average wages had fallen to 18s per week.[73]

Carpenters also had encountered pressures from large masters to cut costs, with the same consequences. Twenty years ago, Mayhew was informed, it was normal for carpenters and joiners, having served an apprenticeship in the country, to make their way to London in the hope of higher wages and eventually of 'taking up their freedom' by being accepted into the Carpenters Guild. That migration had not diminished, but many found that the only work available was that provided by speculative builders who offered much lower wages. A 'new race' of employers had therefore emerged who forced carpenters in an overstocked labour market to work a third more in order to earn customary rates of pay. There were approximately 18,000 carpenters and joiners in London, a tenth of whom were 'in society', that is, part of a trade society for an artisan elite. Some of these could earn 35s per week with overtime, but with the introduction of machinery demand had fallen together with wage rates. Carpenters in the 'dishonourable' part making up 90 per cent of the trade were forced to work a twelve-hour day under a harsh disciplinary regime for approximately half this amount.[74]

I wish to end this chapter with a discussion of two trades that had a particular significance to East London. Mid-century there were approximately 9,000 cabinet-makers in London, deeply divided between a small artisan elite and the mass who laboured in East End 'slaughter houses'; between them, according to Mayhew, was a contrast stronger than in any other trade. The artisans of the best class were 'possessed of a very high degree of intelligence', and lived in the most comfortable houses, containing polished mahogany furniture and clean carpets. The East End toiler, on the other hand, lived in a single room with one item of furniture and bare floors. One from Bethnal Green stated he could not afford a chest of drawers, but then asked what he would do with drawers, since he had nothing to put in them. Guaranteed prices by a book drawn up in 1811, and protected by his trade society, an artisan could earn 35s per week, and this level had remained steady. The large majority of cabinet-makers were unprotected, however, and had witnessed a dramatic fall in income in the past twenty years brought about by the increase in the number of small masters who supplied both capital and labour, and who constantly attempted to reduce costs by cutting wage rates and rent. Thus, as in tailoring, much of the work was carried out in rooms in Spitalfields and Bethnal Green, and over long hours for piece rates that had fallen to a quarter of what they were earlier.[75]

Shipwrights numbered approximately 3,000 at this time, most of whom resided in Poplar and its neighbourhood. A ship joiner interviewed by Mayhew in a comfortable room surrounded by his family recounted what was a typical experience. Born in London, he was always expected to follow his father in the business, and having completed his apprenticeship had worked under contractors for thirteen years, earning between 33s and 38s per week. At this stage the early introduction of iron ships had not been harmful, since they needed a wood lining to back the iron plates.[76] Boat-builders, on the other hand, had declined in numbers, largely because of loss of contracts. The list of prices agreed in 1824 was now largely ignored, and their society was little more than a social and benefit club. One member who had completed his apprenticeship over thirty years ago claimed that at that time his earnings of 50s per week provided him with a comfortable home, but now, because of the irregularity of work, he averaged 22s. Despite the intelligence, soberness and frugality of boat-builders as a body, increasing numbers were being driven to drink by poverty and oppression.

This chapter has considered the profound changes to the industrial landscape of East London in the first half of the nineteenth century. East London came under immense pressure to meet increasing demands for cheaper housing, silk, clothes, shoes and furniture, and to modernize riverside communication, the obsolescence of which threatened the commercial prosperity of London. With abundant supplies of labour to hand, expensive rents, and worrying competition from the provinces and abroad, employers and contractors chose to intensify small-scale production. The result, therefore, was not a factory proletariat but desperate groups of small producers and itinerant craftsmen who possessed a degree of skill but were forced to work long hours in poor conditions for meagre rates of pay. Overall, therefore, it seems likely that the lives of the labouring population of East London worsened under the impact of the industrial revolution. One important indicator of this was the health of its inhabitants, a subject which therefore bears detailed examination in the next chapter.

CHAPTER 5

The Spectre of Cholera, 1830–1875

SINCE THE late eighteenth century doctors had occasionally speculated on the relationship between disease and both filth and poor ventilation, but it was not until the cholera and typhus epidemics of the 1830s that the government started to take this matter seriously.[1] It was not merely that reforming medical opinion came increasingly to believe that many of the deaths from epidemics were preventable, nor that state officials appointed to administer the new poor law recognized in their hard-nosed pragmatism that such diseases invariably gave rise to dramatic increases in numbers seeking relief, but also that the new Office of the Registrar General saw in the data compiled on death rates an opportunity to reveal the relationship between epidemics and the physical environment, and hence provide preventive measures. In concert, these comprised an extraordinarily powerful body of opinion which thrust metropolitan improvement back on the political agenda.

In no area of the country did the scourge of cholera have such a pronounced effect on the public imagination as it did in East London. The industrial revolution had a deleterious impact on the work conditions endured by all sections of the labour force, but it also promoted the rapid growth of an urban population forced to live in squalid and crowded accommodation located in districts where the sanitation was pitifully inadequate, and supplies of water not merely limited but all too often contaminated. Epidemics of 'fever' and cholera which preyed upon the population of East London, and the response of authorities to the carnage, were therefore as much a product of the industrial revolution as the systematic deskilling of work and decline of staple industries. But this is not merely a story of how epidemics stalked the courts and alleys of East London as they did many of the poorest districts of Glasgow, Liverpool and Manchester. East London was the battleground on which the struggle for sanitary reform was waged at a national level, and through that struggle the poor came to be viewed in troubling new ways.

As if a snow-storm had taken place

Cholera reached London early in 1832 when Daniel Barber, mate of the *Felicity* from Limerick, which had been laid up on the river by the London Docks for three weeks, died at 4 a.m. on 8 February. R. Bowie, a surgeon who at the time was practising at St George's-in-the-East, attended Barber on board shortly before his death, and found him in a state of collapse, blue, cold, pulseless and suffering severely from spasms. Over the ensuing fortnight, the majority of cases recorded were seamen engaged in domestic trade between the North East and London.[2] From there cholera spread to the wider community. Bowie subsequently attended merchants, wharfingers, seamen, dock officers and the poor of what clearly was a maritime community, from where the epidemic then spread to Limehouse and across the river to Southwark, which was hardest hit of the metropolitan districts. The conditions he encountered – which no doubt were seen to have contributed materially to the epidemic – were 'very bad'. Cellars of houses were flooded by water from the river, cesspools and sewers, accommodation was acutely overcrowded, and ventilation poor. Water, supplied by the East London Water Company to stand-pipes in courts on intermittent days, often 'smelt very offensively'. The streets were ill-paved; the cavities which appeared soon filled with stagnant water and decaying animal and vegetable matter.

This was an area frequently visited by epidemics. Bowie himself had attended seventy-two cases of typhus in 1828–9 and numerous cases of a malignant scarlet fever. And yet he strongly refuted the popular notion that the poor loved dirt. During the epidemic many had whitewashed the houses around Rosemary Lane; to those accustomed to the black courts and alleys, it 'seemed almost as if a snow-storm had taken place'.[3]

East London parishes, however, were ill prepared for 1832. The tragedy was that the vital matter of public health rested in the hands of local authorities. As in other areas of public service, a jealously guarded but misguided sense of local autonomy stalled initiatives from central government which might have proved more effective in tackling epidemics. When cholera approached ever closer to the shores of Britain, the government took the unprecedented step in 1831 of establishing a Central Board of Health to advise on the prevention of the epidemic. Consistent with contemporary opinion that the disease was contagious, the government ordered the Board to secure the cooperation of local authorities in all ports to enforce quarantine restrictions. Should cholera reach these shores, then 'all intercourse with any infected town and the neighbouring country must be prevented by the best means within the power of the magistrates'. Where families refused to be separated, then their houses should be marked 'Sick' for all to see.[4] Within a month, however, the Board decided, on the basis of similar experience on the continent, that such coercive measures were 'productive of evil'; instead local boards of health were recommended with responsibility to monitor the course of the epidemic, supervise extreme cleanliness and free ventilation, encourage habits of temperance, prevent panic, and above all establish cholera isolation hospitals.[5]

However well-intentioned, these measures were destined to fail. It was not only that they were based on ignorance of the nature of cholera, but also that the local boards had neither the power nor the funds to enforce them. It was not long before the Central Board began to receive desperate letters from local people who had taken its recommendations seriously.[6] W.G. Williams from the Brompton Board of Health declared that private benevolence had enabled them to move filth from the streets and houses, but it was an endless task, one that ought to be chargeable to property owners who heretofore had ridiculed such demands. East London parishes were also initially resistant to the recommendations, but in November they received news that cholera had arrived in the North East, and promptly established local boards. Most did their best to inspect their localities and clear rubbish from the streets. Poplar supplied brushes, buckets and white-wash to the poor, but with limited powers there was little else that could be done.[7] More ambitious initiatives involving the expenditure of ratepayers' money could prove disastrous. Thomas Barneby, Rector of Stepney and Chair of the Mile End Old Town Board of Health, recorded that at a meeting of local ratepayers convened by the Board to consider measures to be taken in the event of an epidemic, including construction of a temporary isolation hospital, a large majority decided that no funds should be raised since the measures contemplated were unnecessary. The Board was dissolved.[8]

Thus public health was left to the paving commissioners with responsibility for cleaning and repairing the streets, and the commissioners of sewers. In London alone there were approximately three hundred such bodies, all appointed from the ranks of local ratepayers, many petty oligarchies, which were parsimonious, corrupt and incompetent.[9] There was no accountability to the wider community, and few guidelines on where their responsibilities lay. Most damagingly, the supply of water was entirely in the hands of the water companies, which answered only to their shareholders, and over time, even when the links between cholera and drinking water seemed certain, displayed criminal irresponsibility in continuing to provide contaminated water. The provision of medical relief to the ill was similarly neglected. Some felt that when the boards of guardians were established by the Poor Law Act of 1832 they should assume responsibility for medical treatment of disease and insanity, but nothing came of it; indeed, so harsh was the regime that boards initially refused to provide any form of relief to the able-bodied afflicted. They did have the power, however, to appoint local medical officers of health to attend patients, and report and make recommendations on the general health of the union.[10] Most were poorly paid – and severely censured when through the diligent pursuit of their duties they proved troublesome.

Even when local bodies acted responsibly and with commendable speed, they were constrained by circumstances. Following the death of three poor women from suspected cholera who were 'buried at great depth in the corner of the church yard', the new local board of health at Limehouse determined to follow the advice of the Central Board.[11] Without adequate funds, however, there were strict limits on what could be achieved. Despite the parsimony displayed by ratepayers of Old Mile End, most of the other parishes in East London attempted to provide cholera hospitals on the cheap by converting rooms in workhouses or renting private accommodation. Their principal concern may have been to save lives, and yet there was a constant fear among local authorities that panic could spread as rapidly as cholera among local residents if nothing was done.

It is only with difficulty that we can assess the response of local residents to cholera. Rumours sprang out of, and were fed by, the prevailing ignorance surrounding the epidemic. Some local people argued that cholera was endemic to the riverside areas, and to prove the point they cited the cases of Wapping and Ratcliff, where cholera had struck 'to an alarming extent' in 1827 and 1830, and spread with such 'frightful rapidity that many persons died daily'.[12] And yet recorded incidents of panic or deep social unease were rare. In May 1832 an elderly woman died of cholera at a house in Mile End New Town. When her daughter, Mrs Downs, fell ill the parish doctor prescribed medicine, but her condition deteriorated. Friends, suspecting the medicine was responsible, fed some to a cat, which promptly died. Two pupils of the doctor then attended the patient, only to be attacked by an angry crowd which accused them of being poisoners. Mrs Downs died two days later, soon after which her husband and daughter also fell ill. Neighbours insisted they be removed to hospital, but Mr Downs refused, at which point a riot took place.[13]

In another incident at the time, an 'infuriated mob' assembled outside the cholera hospital in St George's-in-the-East, threatening to tear it down and kill the surgeon. Their grievance, however, was not about the presence of the hospital or the treatment of cholera, but the unfounded suspicion that doctors were selling the bodies of victims for dissection. When the leader was conducted around the hospital and witnessed for himself the level of care, he declared he was ashamed, and the mob dispersed.[14] Such confused pictures were probably sensationalized by the press and local opinion, for overall what tended to prevail was a calm resolve. It was inevitable that the symptoms of diarrhoea or fever were often diagnosed as the onset of cholera, but such unease never escalated into a wider unrest. A letter from B. Aldis of Limehouse captured the mood:

> In consequence of the Papers stating that the inhabitants of Limehouse were panic struck from the arrival of cholera in that neighbourhood, I went this morning, in company with a medical friend, in order to observe the formidable disease … I went to obtain some information respecting the individuals who had died there; the persons whom I saw did not appear at all alarmed; they stated that two deaths had occurred, but, as far as they knew, not occasioned by cholera. So much for the fear existing at Limehouse.[15]

Many purveyors – respectable and rather less so – exploited the situation by advertising remedies in the form of medicines 'used by the medical officers', and varieties of alcoholic concoctions. Mary Wilson, a 'dashing Cyprian', found an ingenious way of robbing her clients. When Captain William Fenwick, master of the collier *June*, landed at Shadwell, she gave him sundry doses of 'anti-cholera' which rendered him 'half seas over'. The good captain followed Mary to a house of ill-fame, where she robbed him of the considerable sum of £25 which he had on his person.[16]

The epidemic in London was short-lived and relatively mild, for by the time of its cessation in December 5,275 deaths had been recorded. Of these, poor areas south of the river were generally considered to have taken the brunt, but the picture was rather more uneven. Southwark had by far the highest mortality (891), followed by Whitechapel (470), the City of London (359), Lambeth (337) and Westminster (325), while notorious areas such as Bethnal Green (170) and St George's-in-the-East (123) escaped relatively lightly. Mortality rates broadly reflected this ordering.[17]

The Man in the Moon

In the immediate aftermath of 1832, a select committee was directed to inquire into the administration of sewers in the metropolis, largely at the behest of a petition submitted by the inhabitants of Limehouse.[18] The system had long been recognized as inefficient. Many of the sewers had been constructed in ancient times when parish populations were relatively small. Responsibility for their maintenance resided with a total of seven metropolitan Commissions of Sewers which had the power to levy sewer rates, but their members had little relevant knowledge or expertise, were unelected and virtually unaccountable.[19]

The consequences of this inefficiency for areas of East London had earlier been exposed by the rapid growth of population and the disruption caused by construction of the docks. In 1812 Limehouse residents made representation to the Commissioners to take responsibility for cleansing the common sewers which were in a bad state because inhabitants nearby had heretofore been expected to pay. Twenty-two years later, no meaningful reply had been sent.[20] In 1816 a case was presented to the Solicitor General that the Tower Hamlets Commission was in dereliction of its duty. An ancient public sewer in Wapping called the Man in the Moon had effectively been destroyed by the construction of the London Docks, as a result of which houses, shops and cellars in the neighbourhood were frequently inundated with water, and public streets became impassable. Applications for a new sewer were rejected by the Commissioners on the grounds that they had neither the power nor the inclination, since the area had been 'little better than a swamp since time immemorial, and the inhabitants were no more inconvenienced than they were forty years ago.'[21]

The 1832 cholera epidemic introduced an urgency to the matter. Evidence to the 1834 Select Committee conveyed a sense of the local conditions which prevailed. Residents of Limehouse, for example, submitted a petition to parliament in which they stated that

> the sewers, both public and private … are for the most part shallow, narrow, inconvenient, filthy, and out of repair, and being chiefly above ground, are exposed to every species of inconvenience and annoyance, and are, from constant exposure, liable to be choked up, and the waters thereof rendered stagnant from dead animals, offal, broken vessels and other refuse and materials of an offensive kind being deposited therein.[22]

W.T. Higgins, a surveyor to the trustees of the parish, testified that despite the construction of large numbers of new houses there were few sewers to serve them, largely because the Commissioners had built none over the past hundred years. Residents by the so-called Black Ditch near the Limehouse Dock had been given an assurance four years earlier that the

Commissioners would attend to their grievances, but nothing had been done. Even when cholera was much in evidence, the only improvement made by the Commissioners was to cover the open sewers in Ropemaker's Fields.[23]

Nothing came from the deliberations of the Select Committee. As time passed the interest in cholera faded; instead health reformers turned their attention to common fevers. From their ranks emerged Drs Thomas Southwood Smith, Neil Arnott and James Kay who, under the tutelage of Edwin Chadwick, came to define the official doctrine of sanitary reform. East London was again the focus of attention, for the formative experience of these physicians derived from their first-hand observation of fever cases around the London Hospital in Whitechapel, and it was from this platform that they successfully shifted the emphasis of reform towards the imperatives of cleanliness, ventilation and an efficient sewerage system. The typhus epidemic of 1837 provided the initial impulse. In the eyes of many authorities, the most alarming effect of the epidemic was not the loss of life, but rather the dramatic increase in numbers applying for poor relief. Faced with such increases, and in the absence of any appropriate public health authority, the poor law guardians of East London decided to devote funds to the alleviation of the fever by removing refuse from the streets and prosecuting negligent landlords. The auditors considered this an unlawful use of public funds, at which point the matter was referred to the Poor Law Commission. Its secretary, Chadwick, judging that the reduction of pauperism by prevention of epidemic diseases was within the remit of the Commission, authorized a series of studies of fever conditions in London.[24] He directed Arnott, Southwood Smith and Kay to undertake the work in full knowledge that they had a proven record of involvement in public health and so were unlikely to challenge his commitment to reform.[25] Their investigations of Wapping, Whitechapel, Bethnal Green and Ratcliff established the link between pauperism, filth and disease. In so doing they consolidated the official doctrine of epidemic disease, and provided the platform for Chadwick's determined campaign of health reform, culminating in his monumental *Report on the Sanitary Condition of the Labouring Population of Great Britain* (1842), and the 1848 Public Health Act.[26]

The studies on fever conditions appeared in the *Fourth Annual Report of the Poor Law Commissioners* (1837–8). The commissioners themselves introduced the reports by emphasizing the influence that the severe epidemics of the previous two years had had on destitution and claims for relief. Under such circumstances, they concluded, it has proved sound economy for local administrators to fund from poor rates the removal of

physical evils, or indict offending parties; such expenditure should hence-
forth be sanctioned by law, for now the 'most prominent and pressing' of
demands was to reduce charges on the poor rates 'caused by nuisances by
which contagion is generated and persons are reduced to destitution'.[27]

Arnott and Kay submitted a supplementary report on the physical
causes of fever in the metropolis. They singled out malaria as the chief
subject of concern, believing, in accord with the miasmic theory held by
most medical opinion of the time, that this was a generic disease including
a range of 'fevers' caused by rotting animal and vegetable matter close to
human habitation. Under different circumstances, malaria had given rise
to a range of fevers, including yellow fever, jail and ship fevers, and most
notably typhus, which since the Fire of 1666 had wiped out significant
sections of the metropolitan population in a series of epidemics. Included
also were brief reports from medical officers which indicated the extent to
which typhus haunted East London. Many parts of St George's-in-the-East,
for example, were rarely without fever, owing largely to the 'careless and
dirty habits of the lower order of people', while in Goodman's Fields fever
'has been most severe in those courts and alleys where there is no free
circulation of air'. In Spitalfields, the medical officer scarcely knew what
'portions to describe as the worst', for all lodging houses 'have been the
general and almost constant abode of fever for years past'; he considered
that the greatest benefit would derive from the opening up of more
spacious thoroughfares.[28] This situation had been exacerbated by the
inability of local authorities to finance the removal of nuisances, and when
these expenses were charges on the poor rates they were declared illegal,
with the result that even those irregular and inadequate attempts that had
been made would likely cease.

The report concluded by expressing confidence in boards of guardians
as the only authority capable of implementing the necessary measures. The
recent cholera epidemic and special boards of health had commanded
public attention, the report declared, and 'well-directed efforts were made
at that time, with considerable success, for the temporary abatement of
whatever noxious physical influences were found to impair the well-being
of the poorer classes'. The boards had been dissolved, but the investigations
undertaken produced an impression on the public mind which still
remained, and which would lead the more intelligent members of the
middle classes to welcome any effort the government might make to
procure a legal sanction to their efforts for the removal of these evils.
Under such circumstances, the guardians should be given the necessary
powers to tackle sanitary problems and prevent their recurrence. This

egregious picture of local conditions was supported by the report of Southwood Smith. Records of the London Fever Hospital, he proposed, proved that certain metropolitan areas were 'constant seats of fever, from which this disease is never absent', the very worst forms of which prevailed in Bethnal Green and Whitechapel.[29] In some streets almost every house was stricken; in some instances every room in every house. Whole families had been swept away, particularly among the wretched hand-loom weavers, but also among the middle class and even the wealthy.

In the following year Southwood Smith extended his inquiries to other poor metropolitan districts. Detailed figures on deaths from intermittent fever (ague), synochus (continued fever), typhus and scarlatina (scarlet fever) in twenty unions revealed that Whitechapel had the highest mortality rate (3.34 per 1,000), followed by Stepney (2.22), Bethnal Green (2.10) and Lambeth (1.73).[30] Relating fever incidence to those seeking parochial relief, he speculated that the returns provided evidence of the pauperizing influence of epidemics; nearly a half of those on relief in Whitechapel, and a third in Bethnal Green, currently were suffering from fever. Efforts might have been made, he concluded, to improve the physical environment of the metropolis by widening streets and providing sewerage, but no attention had been paid to districts inhabited by the poor. It was a false economy, for by preventing disease such improvements would ultimately cost less than maintaining families affected by its consequences.

Sanitary ramblings

The momentum of sanitary reform gathered pace in the 1840s. Driven by Chadwick, the pioneering epidemiologist William Farr at the new Office of the Registrar General, and like-minded reformers, important commissions heard evidence on the sanitary conditions of large urban centres, and reported on the advisability of improvements in the removal of nuisances, better ventilation and more efficient sewerage systems. East London continued to figure prominently in their deliberations. The Select Committee on the Health of Towns (1840) inquired into the dwellings of the poor in several large industrial cities, including parts of London.[31] Southwood Smith and Arnott gave evidence, or rather simply revisited the evidence they had recently supplied to the Poor Law Commission. Samuel Byles, Spitalfields resident and former medical officer of the Whitechapel Union, spoke of the failure of local authorities to improve woefully defective drainage, largely because of lack of power of enforcement, and the inadvisability of boards of guardians taking responsibility for sanitation.[32]

When Robert Heelis, medical officer for the Limehouse District, was asked for an instance of how want of such authority had failed to prevent disease, he told of the inadequate response of Sewer Commissioners to the cholera outbreak of 1832.[33] The committee concluded by recommending legislation in the form of a Building and Sewerage Act to enforce sanitary regulation, and the setting up of a Central Board of Health and local boards in every sizable town with an immediate remit to address not only the causes of disease, but also the problems of burial grounds, water supply, public spaces, lodging houses, open thoroughfares and spaces for public bathing.

Amidst the routine evidence, however, were glimpses of new concerns which were to become an increasingly menacing feature of perspectives on the metropolitan poor. There was a telling exchange between the Committee and Dr Arnott which is worth reproducing in full:

Do you perceive that where the drainage is better the habits of the people are more cleanly? – It will tend to that; where filth is unavoidable, it makes people careless of making a little addition to it; it does not shock their feelings as if all was clean.

With respect to the moral habits of the children, if they go to school and come back to a place filthy, does it affect them? – No doubt it has an effect upon them.

In these close and confined districts, where generation has been living after generation, has it had an effect upon the health of the children? – Yes; no doubt, in the fenny, marshy districts of England, the people acquire an appearance which distinguishes them from the inhabitants of the elevated districts … and no doubt the atmosphere of the town will operate on them in the same way. An individual, the offspring of persons successively living in bad air, will have a constitution decidedly different from a man who is born of a race that has inhabited the country any long time.

The race will continue degenerating? – Yes, to a certain extent.[34]

What we see here are the beginnings of an attempt to link physical environment to a range of moral and social pathologies. The squalid conditions inhabited by the poor were seen not only to affect their health but to lead to a moral and physical deterioration. The poor, in other words, were distinguishable by appearance and habits – a race apart which would continue to be prone to the process of degeneration. In this way emergent medical orthodoxy helped lay the foundations for the application of pernicious racial theory to the East London poor.

The Commission into the State of Large Towns and Populous Districts (1844) paid particular attention to putative improvements since the cholera epidemic. Southwood Smith claimed that little progress had been made since his evidence of 1838. A common sewer had been constructed through Whitechapel which had materially improved parts of the locality close to the main thoroughfares, but the most crowded and filthiest courts and alleys hidden from public view remained unaltered.[35] In such fever-ridden districts the poison to which inhabitants were exposed produced a mental apathy and physical listlessness which drove them to the use of 'the most pernicious amount of stimulants' such as 'ardent spirits' and opium. To Southwood Smith these places were not only the seats of disease but the great seats of crime:

> There is a point of wretchedness which is incompatible with the exist-
> ence of any respect for the peace and property of others; and to look in
> such a case for obedience to the laws when there is the slightest pros-
> pect of violating them with impunity, is to expect to reap where you
> have not sown … [I]n the most wretched hovels in these neglected
> districts … live our great criminals, violent and reckless men, who
> every now and then perpetrate in cold blood, with savage callousness,
> deeds which fill the whole country with disgust and horror.[36]

These authoritative expressions of the early sanitary movement gave rise to the first practical legislative action. In direct response to the oft-stated criticism that authorities were hampered in their attempts at improvement by the lack of genuine power, a series of acts were quickly passed. The 1846 Nuisances Removal Act,[37] to prosecute those responsible for filth, foul drains and squalid houses, the Public Baths and Washhouses Act of the same year,[38] to provide facilities for public bathing, and the 1847 Towns Improvement Clauses Act,[39] to define the right to lay water supplies and drainage schemes, rationalized and consolidated the move to reform.[40]

Since the desire to defend ancient liberties against the incursions of a centralizing state remained powerful, local authorities could and did resist this flurry of sanitary legislation. This inertia was cruelly exposed by Dr Hector Gavin, a committee member of the Health of Towns Association, who in a pioneering investigation of 1848 inquired into the conditions endured by the poor of Bethnal Green.[41] Convinced that Bethnal Green – which only thirty years previously had been largely open fields and gardens – typified the conditions found in many large towns, Gavin hoped that by revealing its true state he would raise the public profile of 'sanitary improvement and social amelioration', and hence mitigate the toll of the

lives of the poor.[42] Despite proof of the link between poverty and epidemic
fever established by inquiries over the past decade, it was clear to Gavin
that little had been achieved in real terms to improve the lives of the urban
poor. *The rich know nothing of the poor,* he declared; 'the mass of misery
that festers beneath the affluence of London and of the great towns is not
known to their wealthy occupants.' His aim, therefore, was better understanding of the causes of mortality, pauperism, immorality and crime so
that they could be tackled with greater purpose. When the local authorities
were acquainted with the evils created by neglect of sanitation in Bethnal
Green, for example, they would be impelled as a minimum 'to cleanse the
foul streets and filthy dwellings of their miserable fellow-parishioners ...
and effect an amount of good of which they have no conception.'[43]

Bethnal Green, according to Gavin, was one of the eastern districts
which were generally known as the unhealthiest of the metropolis.
The parish had a notorious reputation for its lack of sanitation, and yet was
bounded to the south by the still more neglected districts of Spitalfields,
Mile End New Town, Whitechapel and Mile End Old Town. The
Commissioners of Sewers could not plead ignorance of this, for petitions
from local residents had repeatedly been submitted. Street by street – and
in a way that was redolent of Southwood Smith's 1838 survey – Gavin
then detailed the conditions witnessed at first hand. A few examples must
suffice. The houses on Paradise Row presented what appeared to be decency
and comfort, but appearances were deceptive. Mr Knight, a gentleman,
had recently purchased one, only to die shortly after from an aggravated
form of typhus. On inspection Gavin found Paradise Dairy immediately
behind the house with sixteen cows and twenty pigs, whose refuse was
allowed to pile up and decompose, creating an offensiveness obvious to
every passer-by.[44] The damaging consequences of the persistence of a rural
economy were evident also in Globe Road, which was piled high with every
variety of manure at different stages of decomposition, forming a 'wholesale
manufactory of a poison, at once most disgusting and most deadly'. Even
this was surpassed by Pleasant Place (the irony of street names seems to
have passed Gavin by), which was a canal of a black, slimy compost of clay
and animal remains, whose filth and abomination had to be seen to be
believed.[45]

In the older part of the parish to the west by Spitalfields there were no
gardens. Here mechanics, weavers and labourers resided; the majority
earned little and were forced into overcrowded houses, sleeping as many as
fourteen to a room. Disease and death existed 'to an alarming extent'.
The streets were in a disgraceful state; rarely cleaned, they collected refuse.

Cutaway picture of a Bethnal Green house, 1848. This was included in Hector Gavin's Sanitary Ramblings, *as a means of conveying the desperate state of poor tenements.*

The drainage was inefficient, sewerage non-existent, and there were only two water closets in the whole district. Some of the worst slum property was cleared by the construction of the Eastern Counties Railway line from Liverpool Street, but the displaced poor had simply moved to the dilapidated and desolate houses nearby, rendering them even less fit for human habitation.[46] By far the most respectable district was that along the main Bethnal Green Road. The drainage here was good, although capable of improvement, and the best houses had privies and cesspools, and some new houses were fitted with water closets, a feature so rare that there were more attached to these few houses than in the thousand others in the parish. It was the only district seemingly exempt from fever and other epidemic diseases.[47]

Man's physical wants are few, Gavin concluded, but none was being satisfied among the poor of Bethnal Green. Light was excluded by densely congested housing, clean water provided by a monopoly exercised by the East London Water Company was scarce and expensive, food was meagre and of poor quality, houses were ill constructed and fuel little known. The result was unnecessary loss of life on a vast scale. The life expectancy of mechanics, servants, labourers and their families was 16, that of the parish as a whole 22. The blame for this appalling state of affairs was laid squarely at the door of authorities who not only seemed 'utterly incapable of designing, superintending or executing great public works, but ... cannot be led to conceive their necessity'.[48] Under such circumstances, improvements in housing and sanitation must be undertaken by central powers with the will and authority to drive them through.

The flurry of legislation was brought together and consolidated in 1848–9 with the passage of a revised Nuisances Removal Act,[49] the Diseases Prevention Act,[50] and the Public Health Act.[51] The last provided for the establishment of the General Board of Health under Chadwick which effectively marked the beginnings of centralized control of public health, even though the Board was not given the full weight of authority that Chadwick and his colleagues thought necessary. In practice, the Board could not impose its will upon local authorities, and only in exceptional circumstances could a Local Board of Health be made compulsory.

The Augustan age?

These early campaigns of health reformers and the shift in public consciousness they effected provided the context for the first determined attempts to address the pathological problems of the poorest urban environments. Metropolitan improvement of the eighteenth century had been a piecemeal affair, but improvers began to mobilize their forces during the 1830s for a renewed assault on the problems which beset London, in particular the citadels of contagion. How, then, did the gospel of improvement consciously affect the lives of East Londoners? Prompted by concern over incidences of fever and consumption, the cholera outbreak of 1832, and the administration of the poor law, public initiatives were taken to address the agenda mapped out by William Farr and his contemporaries in the medical world. Priority was given to the opening up of public space, resulting in the creation of a large park for the residents of East London, and the construction of new thoroughfares and railway lines through some of the worst slum areas.

The question of a public park had first been raised in the report of the Select Committee on Public Walks and Places of Exercise (1833). The report noted that with the dramatic increase in the population of London many open spaces had been enclosed, and the multitudes had little access to open and healthy places in which to walk. St James', Hyde, Green and Regent's Parks all provided 'inestimable advantages' as public walks to inhabitants of the West End, and it was thus a matter of some regret that no comparable space existed to the east, for there was 'no part of London where such Improvements are more imperatively called for'.[52] Some means must therefore be devised of providing space for the 'exercise and recreation of the humbler classes'; without it they would continue to cause great mischief by pursuing 'low and debasing pleasures' including drinking-houses, dog fights and boxing matches. This mission to wean the working class from traditional pursuits by offering as an alternative more rational forms of recreation was tempered by concerns over health. It was of vital importance to their health that opportunities should be available to enjoy the fresh air, and escape from the dust and dirt of the narrow courts and alleys by walking in comfort with their families.

Witnesses who gave evidence were unanimous in recognizing the benefits of more public space, particularly when so much of the land was being taken over by corporations which had no wish to provide access. Robert Sibley, for example, an architect and surveyor, explained that the Brewers', Mercers' and Ironmongers' Companies, Clare Hall, Cambridge and Eton College held large amounts of land. In some instances ancient rights of way had been threatened. A local magistrate, John Stock, recounted that a popular walk of three miles along the river bank between Limehouse Reach and Blackwall had been retained but only after many contests. The public had less success with another path crossing the Isle of Dogs, however, for the land had been acquired by the West India Dock Company, which then denied them access.[53]

Fearing that the whole process would stall, a group of the 'respectable inhabitants of Tower Hamlets' headed by George Young MP formed a provisional committee in 1840 to press the matter. They organized a series of meetings; at one such meeting in Bishopsgate attended by several members of parliament it was resolved to draw up a petition to present to the Queen.[54] Headed 'Tower Hamlets Park', the petition drew upon 'official documents' to declare that a large portion of the 400,000 people who resided in the area were exposed to privations and calamities which produced appalling ravages of death. No less revolting was the moral pestilence. 'Unable to breathe the pure air of Heaven with their families,' the petition declared, 'multitudes are driven into habits of intemperance, bringing in their train demoralization, disease and death.' Happily, these evils were not beyond remedy, for a Royal Park was likely to reduce annual deaths by many thousands. Some 30,000 inhabitants signed the petition, which was presented to Victoria by the notable health reformer the Marquis of Normanby.

Victoria not only approved enthusiastically but also offered practical support by authorizing the sale of York House to help finance the project. In 1842, the Victoria Park Bill was passed in parliament without opposition. James Pennethorne of the Office of Woods and Forests was appointed as the architect by a Board established at the Office, and after surveying the area recommended alternative sites. The southern site would stretch from the Mile End Road to the Thames at Limehouse, while the northern would be just east of Bethnal Green. In keeping with medical opinion that public spaces should be located in areas of densest occupation, Pennethorne preferred the southern site, but since it was likely to cost nearly twice as much as the northern he was overruled by the Board; and so 237 acres of land were purchased, most of which was open field of a rather inferior nature.[55] Following endless wrangles over the design, access roads, and sale of acquired land for redevelopment, Victoria Park was finally opened to the people of East London in 1845.[56]

VICTORIA PARK.—THE LODGE.

Victoria Park Lodge, 1846. The ideals of the park conveyed by the grandeur of its architecture and the recreations displayed were never quite realized, but tens of thousands of East Londoners gathered there on a regular basis.

The construction of railways and new thoroughfares was driven by commercial considerations. If they happened to pass through some of the poorest working-class areas it was because land was cheap, and tenants and landlords could more readily be persuaded to move with small bribes, but planners seized on the opportunity to argue that since large numbers of slum properties would be cleared there were also considerable potential benefits for public health.[57] The construction of an improved railway and road infrastructure in districts adjoining the City, including Whitechapel, Shoreditch and Bethnal Green, effectively cleared some of the most congested and impoverished sites in London. The first of the great railway schemes was the Eastern Counties line. Completed in 1839, it ran from Bishopsgate via Stratford to Norwich and Ipswich, effectively linking East London to the counties of East Anglia, which at the time, it was argued, supplied the needs of half the population of London. The London and Blackwall Railway started operation in 1841 by taking passengers between Fenchurch Street in the Minories on the eastern boundary of the City to the docks at Blackwall. These early lines were connected in 1849 by construction of a branch between Stepney and Old Ford at Bow, which was later extended by the London, Tilbury and Southend Railway in the 1850s.

Initially, the public were persuaded that such schemes had real social benefits in ridding areas of poverty and crime, but it soon became evident that the displaced poor needed to remain close to their sources of work. In any case, few could afford daily travel. And since no alternative accommodation was provided for them, the real effect was simply to intensify overcrowding and relocate slum areas.[58] In 1864, for example, the Medical Officer of Health for Bethnal Green complained of the consequences of the construction of Liverpool Street Station in Bishopsgate:

> Owing to the demolition of houses in the neighbouring parishes to make room for railways, a large influx of persons has taken place into our own, and has aggravated the greatest evil with which we have to contend, and that is overcrowding. The parish – always full – is now filled to excess, although a large number of dwellings have been recently erected. Houses even in a bad condition are sure to find occupants, and there is a great difficulty in procuring house-room, the tenants endeavour to conceal their sanitary wants, fearing that they will be compelled to remove while the needful improvements are being made.[59]

Housing stock was also reduced by the construction of warehouses and the conversion of residential accommodation into workshops and offices.

Whitechapel was particularly badly hit. Its proximity to the City, and possession of thoroughfares such as Commercial Street, Whitechapel High Street and Commercial Road, which were vital to the conveyance of commercial goods, encouraged dock, clothing and merchant companies to site their warehouses in the district.

The road infrastructure of Whitechapel was transformed by the construc-tion of the Commercial Road linking the docks to Christchurch, Spitalfields. There had been previous attempts to improve communication, as for example between Wapping Street and Ratcliff Highway in 1776,[60] but most expenditure was devoted to the paving, lighting and cleansing of local streets, and the repair of sewers.[61] Occasionally, when major repairs were required, considerable sums of money had to be borrowed by beleaguered local authorities.[62] In ambi-tion and cost, the plan to construct a major thoroughfare through a densely crowded district of Whitechapel was an entirely new venture. The scheme was first proposed by the Tower Hamlets Commissioners of Sewers, and submitted to the Select Committee which had been appointed to consider opening 'improved lines of communication between different parts of the Metropolis, for the purpose of affording increased facilities for the conveyance of merchan-dise, and for the passage of carriages and persons'.[63] It was clear, however, that the committee was acutely sensitive to other desiderata which made it more receptive to grand schemes of this nature. There were some districts in London, it suggested, of dense populations of the 'lowest class of labourers' which were entirely secluded from the gaze and influence of the better-educated, and therefore 'exhibit a state of moral and physical degradation deeply to be deplored'. More immediate communication would necessarily cure this evil, and at the same time a freer circulation of air would eradicate 'those prevalent diseases which are now not only so destructive among them-selves, but so dangerous to the neighbourhood around them'.[64] Although the plans would undoubtedly be expensive, few citizens would object to the outlay, since the benefits were likely to be great; a small duty on coal brought into London might be the most equitable means of raising the necessary funds.

The detailed plans were drawn up also by James Pennethorne, who, assuming the mantle of his old mentor John Nash, had established himself as the torch-bearer of metropolitan improvement.[65] Commercial Street, running from Whitechapel High Street to Christchurch, Spitalfields, parallel to Brick Lane a little to the east, was built over 1843–5.[66] That might have been it. There had been prevarication and undue delay caused by nervousness over the sums involved, but the Select Committee and Office of Woods and Forests could look back with some satisfaction at a challenging job well done. Except even before the first squalid house had been demolished to clear the way for the new street, dissenting voices had begun to express disquiet at the abandonment of the ambition of some of the early schemes. A devastating article in the *Westminster Review* ridiculed the plan for Commercial Street, pointing out that according to some absurd logic it ended at Christchurch as if the only object of the scheme were 'to enable sailors of our merchantmen to attend divine service on Sundays'.[67] Pennethorne's original plan, which took the street further north to Shoreditch, where it could link up with the newly constructed Eastern Counties Railway terminus and the road ringing the City, should not have been discarded on the grounds of cost alone. Unsurprisingly, Pennethorne agreed, and with the support of local residents put renewed pressure on the Commissioners to reconsider. In 1845 they acceded, and were subsequently empowered to build the northerly extension, although continued squabbles over budgets, and the difficulties in disposing of new sites fronting the street delayed completion until 1858.

In the ensuing decades, public anxiety mounted about the failure of such schemes to eradicate slums. Pressure was exerted with only limited success on the railway companies to provide alternative accommodation for those displaced by their schemes. More important was the compulsory introduction from the 1860s of workmen's trains offering cheap daily fares, which led directly to the growth of a ring of working-class suburbs, including West Ham, Walthamstow and Leyton. While this relieved some of the congestion of inner-city areas, the problem of accommodation for the casual poor, few of whom could afford even these cheap fares, remained. It was at this moment that charitable and philanthropic organizations decided to erect the vast working-class tenement blocks which became such a feature of the built environment of East London (p. 245).

Extraordinary duties

Heretofore, inquiries into the sanitary condition of urban centres had considered London alongside the great manufacturing towns, but in 1847 the rather peculiar problems faced by the metropolis were recognized when a Sanitary Commission under Lord Grosvenor was appointed with a remit to consider 'whether any and what special means may be requisite for the improvement of the Health of the Metropolis'.[68] Chadwick and Southwood Smith were included among the four commissioners. Had the Commission fulfilled its brief we might have an exhaustive survey of how drainage, street cleansing and paving, and refuse removal could be improved. In the event, however, the Commissioners' immediate attention was drawn to reports that cholera was again progressing towards Europe, and a decision was taken that the preparedness of the metropolis to deal with the impending danger should instead be explored. Much of the report was therefore devoted to identifying the lessons that could be learnt from 1832. Evidence was gathered on the previous outbreak, and any improvements that had followed. The Commission concluded ruefully that in general sanitary conditions were no better. When this revelation was combined with a medical orthodoxy which still held that 'the habitual respiration of impure air is an incomparably more powerful predisponent to epidemic disease' than poverty, it came as no surprise that the one safeguard identified was immediate and complete removal of filth from the principal thoroughfares and hidden courts and alleys.[69] If this measure were supported by improved drainage and a better water supply to maintain cleanliness, then it was likely that were cholera to break out again, its toll on human life in the metropolis would be greatly reduced.

These expectations proved wildly optimistic, for the cholera epidemic of 1848–9 was more terrible by far than that of 1832. Ironically, one of the first tasks of the new General Board of Health was to report on the epidemic. The notable social reformer Lord Ashley was named as one of the three authors, but the style of the report was unmistakably that of Chadwick and Southwood Smith. A comprehensive report on London compiled by R.D. Grainger mapped the course of the epidemic, and pointed to the failings of the authorities.[70] No fewer than 14,601 London cholera deaths were recorded between September 1848 and December 1849 (nearly three times the 1832 total). Districts in the south again were hardest hit, with Southwark (1,928) and Lambeth (1,824) recording the highest totals. Bethnal Green (976) and Shoreditch (899) had the highest mortality of East London districts, followed by Stepney (601) and Whitechapel (564). This order was broadly reflected in the corresponding mortality rates from all causes.[71]

In asserting the agenda of sanitary reformists, the report added little of originality. Cholera was seen to be subject to the same general laws as typhus; replicating the previous epidemic of 1832, it decimated the fever districts of the metropolis which were without sewers and drains, had no proper supply of water, and were never visited by the scavenger. Local authorities had to take a measure of responsibility for the epidemic because of their failure to carry into effect beneficent legislation, although they had often been forced to operate under trying circumstances. The redoubtable and indefatigable Dr Gavin, who on the outbreak was appointed as Medical Inspector for Bethnal Green and Shoreditch, submitted a detailed report to the General Board in which he recounted an interview with the chairman of the Bethnal Green Board of Guardians, who stated that 'they were quite sick of having charge of the medical arrangements for the relief of the poor, and that they would be heartedly glad to get rid of it. The clerks of the local guardians universally complained of

> the hardship inflicted on the guardians by the Act which imposed on them the responsibility of carrying into effect the arrangements for the prevention of disease. They contended very earnestly, that the administration of the law for the relief of the poor had nothing whatever to do with the arrangements for the prevention of disease; and that the Boards of Guardians were not the parties fitted to undertake such onerous and responsible duties ... [T]heir ordinary duties under the Poor Law were such as to prevent their fulfilling the extraordinary duties imposed upon them by the Nuisances Removal and Diseases Prevention Act; and that though such duties might be imposed, it would be impracticable to carry them out with any efficiency.[72]

WEST-HAM UNION.
Notes to the Poor on CHOLERA.

EXPERIENCE having proved that "CHOLERA" is not contagious, let no one fear to render assistance to his Neighbour, or any Fellow-Creature who may be attacked with it.

Keep the mind at rest, trusting in God, and "fear not the Pestilence though it walk in darkness, nor the Destruction that wasteth at noon-day."

"CHOLERA" in its early stages is easily curable. When more advanced, is not only difficult to cure but almost defying the power of Medicine.

Preventive measures and prompt attention to the earliest symptoms are chiefly to be relied upon.

The Causes predisposing to "CHOLERA," and therefore to be avoided as much as possible, are—want of Cleanliness of Person,—Intemperance in the use of Spirits—or fermented Liquors—or of Tobacco,—Debauchery, or excess of any kind,—Irregular Habits,—excessive Fatigue,—Sitting in wet Clothes,—or indeed exposure either to wet—cold—damp—or sudden Chills.

The great preventive of "CHOLERA," is—Pure Air and Cleanliness. Every House ought therefore to be kept perfectly clean and thoroughly ventilated. Lime-washing is particularly recommended, and persons whose Work is out of doors should wear a flannel belt round the body, next to the skin.

The symptoms of "CHOLERA," which should act as a warning, are—Looseness of the Bowels or Diarrhœa—Nausea or Sickness—in which stage it is easily curable or preventible. If neglected, the Blue Stage or "ASIATIC CHOLERA" comes on, in which little help is derivable from Medicine.

Let none therefore neglect the slightest signs of Looseness or Diarrhœa, or any other irregularity in the system, as there is a tendency, during the prevalence of "CHOLERA," for all Diseases to merge into this Complaint.

The Guardians are prepared to issue "CERTIFICATES" to the Poor generally, entitling them to Medical Relief gratuitously, should "CHOLERA" break out, or its symptoms prevail in the Neighbourhood. They recommend such persons as cannot afford to pay for Medical attendance to apply forthwith to the Relieving Officer, who will lay the application before the Board. It is important for the Poor to be put in possession of these "CERTIFICATES" before they are actually required.

By order of the Board,

BOARD ROOM, LEYTONSTONE,
29th September, 1848.

S. RICHARDSON,
Clerk.

Cholera poster, West Ham Union, 1848. The instructions, based on a poor medical understanding, did little to prevent the spread of the contagion.

True to their word, the guardians responded to the outbreak with a dismal lack of urgency and purpose. They ignored demands for additional medical staff, provided no nurses, established no hospital or dispensary, and made no provision for lime washing of the affected houses.[73] This neglect, proceeded Gavin, had appalling consequences. In the infamous area of the Old Nichol, Bethnal Green, 147 deaths had occurred in 99 houses, while in Windmill Square, Shoreditch, half the inhabitants perished.[74] Interestingly, Gavin blamed this heavy toll on the pump located nearby, which drew water from a well into which decomposed organic matter had seeped from adjacent cesspits. The point was taken up by Grainger, who noted other instances in London where the removal of a pump had been accompanied by the sudden cessation of further deaths;[75] it was to be another five years, however, before the significance of this observation was fully appreciated.

Cholera again ravaged London over 1853–4, and in its course killed 11,661 Londoners, predominantly those residing south of the river. A large majority of areas experienced fewer deaths than in the previous outbreak, and had lower mortality rates, but in virtually all other respects the epidemic replicated the experience of 1848–9.[76] Rules and regulations for the removal of filth from the streets and the cleansing of houses issued by a reconstituted General Board of Health shortly after the outbreak in September 1853 were ignored with impunity by recalcitrant local authorities. Stepney Union was found to have a great want of proper sewerage and of an adequate supply of water, and great complaints were expressed about the noxious trades. Orders had been issued against one of the guardians, who was found to create a serious nuisance by keeping pigs and collecting dung and night soil. He complied, but in a few days the nuisance was as bad as before. Only under pressure from the Board did the guardians appoint house-to-house visitors and a medical officer to distribute medicine. In Poplar, noxious trades and the accumulation of filth had decimated parts of the population. Removal of nuisances provided only temporary benefits, for the 'real cause of mischief' – the sewerage system and water supply – had not been addressed, and the situation soon deteriorated. The recommendations of district medical officers were treated with contempt.[77]

Greater interest was expressed, however, in the question of the water supply. The Board appointed a Medical Council comprising leading physicians and scientists, including Arnott and Farr, to inquire into the circumstances of the epidemic. Detailed chemical analyses and microscopic examinations were carried out on the water supplied by various companies, but they were inconclusive. '[O]n the whole evidence', their report declared, 'it seems impossible to doubt that that influences, which determine in mass the geographical distribution of cholera in London, belong less to the water then to the air'.[78] The attention of the Committee was attracted by an outbreak in Soho, which was of such severity that special circumstances were suspected. A young doctor, John Snow, had already noted this with interest, and suggest that a contaminated well in Broad Street was responsible.[79] The Committee deliberated on Snow's theory, but sadly determined that 'we see no reason to adopt this belief':

> We do not find it established that the water was contaminated in the manner alleged; not is there before us any sufficient evidence to show, whether inhabitants of the district, drinking from the well, suffered in proportion more than other inhabitants of the district who drank from other sources.[80]

It was not long before Snow was vindicated and the fatal nexus between drinking water and cholera proven. None of this, however, prevented the outbreak of 1866. Once again as the epidemic approached measures were recommended to mitigate its impact. John Simon, who had served on the 1856 Scientific Committee of Inquiry, and was now the Medical Officer of the Privy Council with principal responsibility for applying the Public Health Act, issued recommendations which included the removal of nuisances, a profound suspicion of well water, liberal use of disinfectants, ample ventilation, and lime washing of infected buildings.[81] If these were familiar it was because, although Simon had been persuaded of the critical role of water in the propagation of cholera, he believed that the source of infection could be atmospheric, and thus tended simply to adopt measures that had been seen to be effective in previous epidemics. Few at the time suspected that water companies could be the source. Chemical analysis of waters from the pumps and surface wells of the City, and of the East London and New River Water Companies, proved what most thought, namely, that the latter had far less organic and mineral matter.[82]

And yet when the epidemic of 1866 ravaged across East London, the finger of suspicion pointed to the East London Water Company. 5,973 Londoners perished, many fewer than in 1854, but this time East London was worst affected, accounting for two thirds of all deaths.[83] Apart from Shoreditch, all areas witnessed dramatic increases in numbers and mortality rates.[84] The official report on the epidemic, written by Farr, contained a prodigious amount of statistical information, on the basis of which he put

forward well-informed arguments framed by his expertise in epidemi-
ology. Sanitary authorities had learnt much from the previous outbreaks,
so that when cholera again began to decimate the population of London it
was anticipated that this time it could be confined within narrow limits.
Attention was soon drawn, however, to the unprecedentedly high levels of
mortality in East London and in the industrial centres of West Ham and
Stratford, all of which were provided with water by the East London Water
Company. Four inquiries were subsequently carried out which concluded
rightly, and despite some erroneous medical suppositions, that contaminated water taken by the company from the River Lea and stored in open
reservoirs was responsible.[85] The company launched a spirited defence,
claiming that it had strictly adhered to the requirements of the 1852
Metropolis Water Companies Act. All the water was filtered, and the
reservoirs had long fallen into disuse. But when evidence came to light that
dead eels had been found in water pipes, and foul water taken from the
reservoirs and pumped into the main supply, their lies were exposed and
the case faltered. The Company was later found guilty of supplying
contaminated water, and fined a derisory £200, the maximum permitted
by law.

　　As was so often the case when events in East London prompted the
generosity of the rich, funds set up by the Bishop of London and Mansion
House raised £70,000, including £500 from Victoria herself. This was an
impressive total (equivalent to approximately £3.2m today), but in some
radical circles it represented a betrayal of the poor. An editorial in the
Reynolds's News, for example, expected more from a sovereign who was
kept in luxurious retirement by the state, and expressed outrage that
aristocratic landowners who derived enormous revenue from land
seemed incapable of a 'munificent liberality' towards the poor who
inhabited the slums built thereon.[86] The availability of these funds
provided opportunities for resourceful subterfuges. A Wesleyan missionary,
T.C. Garland, recalled an instance in 1864 when he was called to visit a
victim's family in Ratcliff. He was greeted by a distressed woman whose
husband had been 'taken and dead in six hours', and who now was
anxious to receive money from the Lord Mayor's Fund in order to replace
the bed and mattress on which he had died. Garland's suspicions were
aroused by her demeanour, however, and he resolved to inspect the corpse,
which was laid out with a sheet covering his face. The widow became
agitated, claiming that he might catch cholera and die, but the good
preacher, having lifted the sheet, felt the victim was not quite dead, because
his face was not yet cold.

Pursuing my investigation, I pressed my thumb nail into his face with some force; on which the presumed 'dead man' gave vent to an awful shout, 'Oh, my God! not so hard!' The effect was electric. The woman's tears at once ceased to flow, and she ran downstairs, leaving me alone with her husband, and without thanking me for restoring him to life and vigour.[87]

Having wiped the preparation of flour and whitening from his face, the man was persuaded to pray. Soon afterwards he and his wife fled to another parish.

In the meantime, the authorities of East London itself displayed the same woeful ignorance and resistance to mitigating the suffering of the people as they had during previous epidemics. In no area was this more apparent than in the treatment meted out to medical officers. Many in their ranks were compassionate towards the plight of the poor and committed to wholesale reform, but were forced to operate under extraordinarily trying circumstances. Employed by local boards, they were ill paid, and under constant threat of dismissal if they proved to be too active in pursuit of their duties, particularly if critical of their employers. Annual reports were full of complaints that their advice and recommendations were ignored. Some found the constraints impossible and resigned, such as Dr Rendell, the medical officer for St George-the-Martyr, Southwark, who expressed disgust that he was not allowed to carry out the duties of his office.[88] Mindful of this, we have to exercise a degree of caution in reading the medical officers' reports on the epidemic. When, for example, Thomas Orton, Medical Officer of Health for Limehouse, identified the causes of cholera as 'intemperance in food and drink, feebleness of habits from previous disease or otherwise, fatigue, anxiety, and scantiness of food', or when John Liddle of Whitechapel blamed the susceptibility of the poor on their 'extreme poverty' and their 'crowding together in ill-ventilated rooms', they may simply have been anxious to divert the blame away from their indolent and pitiless local boards.[89] A few medical visitors and nuisance inspectors were appointed by most authorities on paltry salaries. They were routinely recruited from the ranks of ex-sailors or ex-policemen, and were not required to have any knowledge of sanitary matters. At the first sign of a decline in mortality rates, and despite admissions that cholera still lurked 'in a passive state', stringent cuts in sanitary measures were made, and even these were dismissed. In October 1866 Bethnal Green laid off all visitors but one, closed open dispensaries and ceased disinfection of houses, while Mile End Old Town and St George's-in-the-East discontinued visits to suspected cases.[90]

Weale map of East London, 1851. The communications infrastructure was virtually complete; by now the Victoria Dock in West Ham over the River Lea was being constructed, heralding a new phase of industrial development.

It was apparent, however, that a longer-term and infinitely more effective solution to the recurring epidemics had already been set in motion by the Metropolitan Board of Works, and that this would stand as its one lasting monument. The great metropolitan sewer, built by the industrious Joseph Bazalgette, was already well under construction when the epidemic broke. The tragedy was that the works were not yet completed in East London, as a result of which the area continued to suffer from the most damaging consequences of poor accommodation, overcrowding, inadequate sewerage and contaminated water supplies. Furthermore, influential sanitary reformers may have revealed to respectable opinion for the first time the desperate conditions which prevailed, but by drawing parallels between physical environment and moral degeneration their work signalled a worrying shift in how the poor were viewed, so laying the foundations for a powerful mythology about the East End. The creation of 'Outcast London' is the focus of the next chapter.

CHAPTER 6

The Myth of Outcast London, 1800–1900

T OWARDS THE close of the 1880s, a series of events took place in East London which for a short but terrible time persuaded high-minded social commentators that their worst fears had been realized. On 31 August 1888 the body of Mary Ann Nichols was discovered in Bucks Row, Whitechapel. Nichols was a local prostitute and had died from a deep cut to the throat. There was nothing unusual in the violent death of a poor woman, and so the incident created little interest, but when in the ensuing weeks more prostitutes were murdered and mutilated with increasing savagery, a media storm erupted, and the demonic figure of Jack the Ripper was born. Since then, publications on an industrial scale have appeared, most making fanciful claims to identifying the real Ripper. The literature clearly provides gruesome titillation, but there are to my mind more interesting questions that can be addressed about this episode in the history of East London. I therefore wish to consider why Whitechapel was manufactured for the public of the time as a site of gothic horror, depravity and fearful danger, and how this process gave impetus to the myth of outcast London.[1]

It is evident that such imagery was not entirely novel, but drew directly upon the writings of nineteenth-century investigators and evangelical missionaries which expressed with increasing concern what they viewed as the social and moral degradation of the East London poor. Despite their best efforts, however, the poor remained largely unknown and, because of their proximity to the heart of Britain's commercial and imperial power, a threat to the future of nation and empire. This is the context in which we can best understand the apoplectic reaction to the Whitechapel murders.

The nemesis of neglect

As we have seen, Whitechapel had attracted the attention of the authorities from the early moments of its formation. It was one of the centres of Protestant dissent and immigrant settlement, and witnessed a series of riots during the eighteenth century quelled only when the militia was summoned. Most of its inhabitants lived in poverty-stricken courts and alleys, crossed by ill-paved and ill-lit streets, and ravaged by epidemics, or worse still found nightly refuge in the numerous common lodging houses. Overcrowding was exceeded only by that of St George's-in-the-East and Holborn. Such conditions attracted the attention of early sanitary reformers, and mid-nineteenth-century urban travellers, including Watts Phillips and John Hollingshead, who created an image of an alien and depraved cultural landscape (pp. 161–3). And yet, according to the survey carried out by Charles Booth and his co-workers at the time of the murders, the levels of poverty in Whitechapel compared favourably with districts such as Southwark, Greenwich and Bermondsey; indeed, for Booth himself it held a certain fascination:

> The feeling that I have just described – this excitement of life which can accept murder as a dramatic incident, and drunkenness as the buffoonery of the stage – is especially characteristic of Whitechapel. And looked at this way, what a drama it is! Whitechapel is a veritable Tom Tiddler's ground, the eldorado of the East, a gathering together of poor fortune seekers; its streets are full of buying and selling, the poor living with the poor. Here just outside the old city walls, have always lived the Jews, and here they now are in their thousands, both old established and new comers, seeking their livelihood under conditions which seem to suit them on the middle ground between civilization and barbarism.[2]

This was the Whitechapel which witnessed the series of murders of prostitutes in the second half of 1888. Initially, the press showed little interest, for at a time when violent crime was reported to be on the increase such an act was hardly newsworthy. As other murders followed, however, reporters began to detect a gruesome pattern, and grapple with a frightening new phenomenon seemingly beyond rational knowledge. As *The Star* declared after the murder of Nichols:

> Nothing so appalling, so devilish, so inhuman – or, rather, human – as the three Whitechapel crimes has ever happened outside the pages of Poe or De Quincey. The unravelled mystery of 'The Whitechapel Murders' would make a page of detective romance as ghastly as 'The Murders of the Rue Morgue'. The hellish violence and malignity of the crime … resemble in almost every particular the two deeds of darkness which preceded it. Rational motive there appears to be none. The murderer must be a Man Monster …[3]

The *Evening Standard* declared that the murders were of great social rather than literary significance, for they exposed the dangerous presence of a latent savagery among the East London poor. Employing familiar references to empire, it argued that the 'monstrous and wanton brutality … is what we might expect of a race of savages rather than from the most abandoned and most degraded classes in a civilised community', and provides worrying evidence of the wholesale failure of middle-class attempts at reform:

> It is terrible to reflect that at the end of the nineteenth century, after all our efforts, religious, educational, and philanthropic, such revolting and sickening barbarity should still be found in the heart of this great City, and be able to lurk undetected in close contact with all that is most refined, elegant, and cultivated in human society.[4]

The reading public were reminded that events in Whitechapel were strikingly similar to the atrocities of the Indian revolt of 1857, when British subjects were mutilated by alien savages unrestrained by Christian influence. As a letter to the editor of the *City Press* stated, 'thirty years ago one used to read with a shudder of the barbarities practised during the Indian Mutiny upon defenceless women and children; but nothing can be much worse than what had happened here in Christian England'.[5] The very un-Englishness of the crimes diverted attention on to the local immigrant communities, which were subjected to renewed and more intense condemnation. The *Penny Illustrated Paper*, for example, found in East London squalid districts which were the 'hunting grounds of some of the lowest and most degraded types of humanity to be found in any capital. It is there that the dregs of Continental cities deposit themselves'.[6] In a similar vein, the Reverend Tyler of Mile End New Town stated that London now had to fear 'the importation of the scum and depraved characters from all parts of this and other countries … dregs of society coming down … into London and occupying the low lodging houses, had made the centre a very difficult one for the police to deal with'.[7] No doubt the good reverend, like many others, had in mind the recent Jewish immigrants; it was not long before pernicious rumours began to circulate that the Ripper was in fact a Jew who, in obeisance to an obscure blood rite, had sacrificed Gentile prostitutes by cutting their throats.[8]

Towards the end of September 1888 press reports reached a new pitch of excitement. *The Nemesis of Neglect*, an extraordinary cartoon by John Tenniel depicting the Ripper as a knife-wielding phantom stalking the streets of Whitechapel, appeared in *Punch* on 29 September accompanied by a poem on the stygian darkness of East London. On the following day a double murder

The Nemesis of Neglect, 1888. In contrast to most press coverage, the famous Tenniel cartoon suggested that the Ripper murders were the product of the desperate circumstances endured by the poor of East London.

of Elizabeth Stride and Catherine Eddowes was discovered, provoking another wave of press hysteria. *The Star* speculated that this was the work of 'fiendish revenge for fancied wrongs, or the deed of some modern Thug or Sicarius,'[9] and offered a warning of any further failure to heed the plight of the East End:

> Above all, let us impress the moral of this awful business on the consciences and the fears of the West-end. The cry of the East-end is for light – the electric light to flash in the dark corners of its streets and alleys, the magic light of sympathy and hope to flash into the dark corners of wrecked and marred lives. Unless these and other things come, Whitechapel will smash the Empire, and the best thing that can happen to us is for some purified Republic of the West to step in and look after the fragments.

These various observations suggest ways in which Whitechapel – and, by extension, East London – was created as a site of fear, loathing and moral desolation. The events of 1888 served merely to focus and hence greatly intensify the anxieties of respectable opinion about the state of the poor, and the threat they posed to the future of the imperial race. This, I contend, is the real historical significance of the Whitechapel murders. And yet much of the rhetoric had been evident in earlier periods, as a result of which East London came to be seen by all shades of respectable opinion as a site of desperate poverty and criminality. The rubric 'Outcast London' best captured the prevailing sense that this part of the metropolis repre-sented an alien presence, close enough to the City to be a threat to its mate-rial wealth and way of life, and yet remote from its civilizing influences and inquiring gaze. So how did social commentators, notably evangelicals and urban explorers of the nineteenth century, construct this image of East London? What ideas and rhetoric did they draw upon?

Nautical vagabonds

Although a series of public hangings of rioters, and legislation designed to alleviate the suffering of silk weavers, did create a period of relative tran-quillity in the final decades of the eighteenth century, there remained an ever-growing body of unskilled labour and wandering poor who plied their trades outside the City boundary seemingly beyond the reach of guilds and legal authorities. One such group – the unskilled dockworkers congregated in the riverside areas – had been of concern to the West India Merchants Committee for some time; in the troubled decade of the 1790s, as they contemplated the construction of an entirely new dock infrastructure, the merchants decided to act.

The merchants believed that because of lax security in the handling of their ships' cargoes large-scale plunder had taken place, and now operated on such a scale that not only their ability to trade, but the future of London as a great imperial centre, were under threat. At the heart of these concerns was a perceived failure to define and hence prosecute effectively the act of theft; but then the problem was a difficult one to tackle. The appropriation of a small part of the cargo by dock labourers had in many instances been actively encouraged by many employers who considered it as payment in kind, or at least a supplement to cash remuneration.[10] Labourers had regularly been permitted to take sugar, or, more frequently, damaged or dirty goods on condition that they were only for personal use and not for resale. Sweepings of spilt tobacco, coffee and sugar were thus in the eyes of many employers and labourers legitimate sources of income, except that it was widely known that these payments were supported by extensive local networks of dealers and receivers (fences), often publicans and shopkeepers. The distinction between an allowable perquisite and theft was, however, entirely unclear, and therefore subject to contestation, not least in the courts. Old Bailey records are littered with details of cases brought by merchants and wharfingers against dock labourers, not always successfully since the accused could claim in his defence that such perks were an established right. Less defensible, but no less common, were the thefts which occurred from cargoes left on quaysides offering free access to people going about their legitimate and illegitimate business.

In the politically charged decade of the 1790s, when a series of bad harvests pushed up wheat prices to unprecedented levels, and the spectre of the French Revolution haunted the imagination of the metropolitan middle class, the state of the poor and the means of relieving distress through the poor law attracted undue attention. This climate of uncertainty provoked the West India merchants to determine the real extent of their losses through riverside plunder, and to this end they commissioned Patrick Colquhoun to undertake a detailed study of metropolitan crime, and make recommendations on how it could be prevented. The choice was a good one, for as a merchant based in Glasgow, Colquhoun had made his fortune in the Atlantic trade, and, since moving to London in 1789 to represent the interests of Scottish manufacturers, had befriended many influential figures in government, mercantile and evangelical circles.[11] He gained a position as a magistrate in 1792, and in the ensuing years had applied himself assiduously to the practical and moral problems posed by the metropolitan poor, solutions to which he saw principally through Christian philanthropy, as evidenced in the Spitalfields soup kitchen, an initiative in which he played a key role (p. 112).

Out of a desire to make his deliberations known to a wider public, Colquhoun now embarked on a zealous and prolific career as a writer, and met with considerable and lasting success. *A Treatise on the Police of the Metropolis*, which appeared in 1795, mapped out, in its various editions, the extent of metropolitan crime, and made recommendations which led directly to the establishment of the Marine Police Office at Wapping, the precursor of the Metropolitan Police force.[12] In so doing, Colquhoun began to define the urban poor in strikingly novel ways. Whereas previously the London poor had been seen as a motley collection of underworld characters, classified according to the types of fraud and trick used to dupe the bourgeois pedestrian or house-holder, Colquhoun defined them as an endemic and predatory body, organ-ized in confederacies, and operating to defend what they considered customary rights of access to moveable property. And this was a poor that he was able to identify through the application of rational theoretical and statistical inquiry. As he stated in the preface to the 1797 edition, the reader is presented with

> a variety of *evils* of great magnitude … which are not to be found in books, and which, of course, have never been laid before the public through the medium of the press. It may naturally be expected, that such an accumulation of delinquency, systematically detailed, and placed in so prominent a point of view, must excite a considerable degree of astonishment in the minds of those readers who have not been familiar with subjects of this nature.[13]

It is clear from its reception that the book did arouse considerable interest and not a little alarm amongst its readers – and understandably so, for Colquhoun's estimates of losses through criminal activity (most of which we now know were wild exaggerations) were shocking. He reckoned that property to the value of £120m was annually carried in ships, vessels and wagons, and £50m in the form of merchandise, provisions, bank notes and money deposits moved around the metropolis; of this no less than £2m was plundered.

Colquhoun viewed this as a 'melancholy picture of general depravity' created by the 115,000 persons who 'support themselves in and near the metropolis, by pursuits criminal, – illegal – or immoral'.[14] It was not, however, prostitution (with 50,000 prostitutes, by far the largest category of 'criminal') or the extent of petty theft which concerned Colquhoun, but the wholesale plunder of cargoes from the river and quaysides, precisely because he and no doubt the merchant community viewed it as a genuine threat to imperial progress:

> London is not only the grand magazine of the British Empire, but also the general receptacle for the idle and depraved of almost every Country, and certainly from every quarter of the dominions of the Crown; – where the temptations and resources for criminal pleasure – fraud and depredation, as well as for the pursuits of honest industry, almost exceed imagination; since besides being the seat of Government and the centre of fashion, amusements, dissipation, extravagance and folly, it is not only the greatest commercial city in the universe, but perhaps one of the first manufacturing towns that is known to exist.[15]

Here was the real significance of the merchants' vision of criminal depravity. The poor were not unemployed rural labourers plunged into distress because of inefficiencies in the poor law, nor vagabonds who had long been attracted to the back streets of East London, but an international reserve of labour, concentrated in the riverside areas, whose presence was as a canker in the arteries of metropolitan commercial prosperity.

The *Treatise on the Police* went through four editions in two years but ultimately failed in the face of determined opposition against the exercise of 'absolute' power to persuade the government of the urgent necessity of a metropolitan police force. Instead, the Marine Police Office at Wapping was established in 1798, and immediately set about the task of tackling riverside plunder. Early on the office was besieged by a gang of 'half-savage Irish coal heavers' bent on destruction, who dispersed only after Colquhoun read the Riot Act, and the police opened fire, allegedly fatally wounding one of the leaders.[16] But it survived, and there soon followed recognition from the West India merchants that the office had, by protecting property, conferred singular advantages to the commercial interests of the port. Little wonder, therefore, that when in 1797 the merchants wished to understand more about the specific nature of river crime, they turned to Colquhoun. The results of his inquiry were published in *A Treatise on the Commerce and Police of the River Thames* (1800), and sought to reveal the origins and detailed nature of riverside plunder. Colquhoun argued that the problem could be traced back to the habit of smuggling, and had grown during the eighteenth century as the influence of religion and morality receded, with the result that the mass of riverside labourers became contaminated and the evil spread as the commerce of the port expanded.[17] Legislation introduced to check criminal activity had proved ineffective, so that thieves operated with a degree of impunity and in the full knowledge of, indeed with cooperation from, the local community. Together with dissolute coopers, watermen, mud-larks and scuffle hunters, these thieves comprised a criminal fraternity embedded within the local community. This view of an endemic, highly organized and predatory criminal under-class was to frame perspectives on the East London poor throughout the nineteenth century, particularly after 1840, when anxieties over the presence of casual dock labour once again surfaced.

Deliver the outcast and the poor

More effective policing and the construction of secure dock complexes greatly reduced – but never eliminated entirely – the pillage of ships' cargoes along the Thames, and for a while the casual poor of East London slipped from the focus of middle-class observers. As social crises emerged mid-century, more determined attempts were undertaken to dispel the ignorance that surrounded the metropolitan poor. We have seen (Chapter 5) that the epidemics of the 1830s provoked the first studies of the socio-economic conditions of East London, revelations of which helped shape the agenda of sanitary reform, and marked a shift towards an identification of a putative link between squalor and moral degeneration. In the 1840s and 1850s, when Chartism and the Indian revolt of 1857 precipitated a domestic and imperial crisis, evangelical missionaries and urban explorers took up the task of knowing the poor. Since many of these lived and moved amongst the poor, they were the only ones who could legitimately claim to know the impact of poverty, and thus it was through their abundant writings, rather than, say, parliamentary select committees or the national press, that East London came to be seen by respectable sections of Victorian opinion.

Evangelical organizations embarked on an intense phase of missionary work among the metropolitan poor during the 1840s. Driven by a belief that the church had proven ineffective in preventing the moral destitution of the poor, they set about the task of providing Christian precept through the example of good works.[18] Many chose to publish accounts of their experiences – not least to raise funds for missionary work – in which their anxieties about the state of the poor surfaced. In 1850, Thomas Beames, a preacher at St James, Westminster, published *The Rookeries of London*.[19] Based on his experience of ten years' work among the poor, it contemplated why improvements in their conditions had not kept up with those of the higher classes. Pity it is, Beames declared, that the 'close alley, the undrained court, the narrow window, the unpaved footpath, the distant pump, the typhus or the Irish fever should still remind us of what London was once to all – what it still is to the poor'.[20] These rookeries are plague spots, the nurseries of our convicts and outcasts who find refuge therein.Least fortunate are the 'wretched victims of Mammon' such as needlewomen who are forced to shelter in Drury Lane, Saffron Hill, Wapping and Shoreditch, and include many mothers who eke out the rest of their pittance by involuntary prostitution. Is not the 'very name of Christianity forgotten in a land which tolerates such a curse'? If it is then at a time when the flames of revolution spread around Europe, the poor, mindful of neglect, will threaten the Anglo-Saxon race and hence the future of civilization by seeking violent retribution.

This rather alarming prospect was thus predicated on recognition that the poor were an alien presence within, almost a race apart from, the nation. It was a short imaginative step to link this presence to the ever-increasing Irish population which had migrated to London during the famine years of the mid-1840s. This was of particular concern to John Garwood, an Anglican priest who became secretary of the London City Mission. In 1853 he published *The Million Peopled City*, which described the causes of the emigration, the nature of the Irish, and their impact on the religious landscape of the poorer areas where they tended to settle.[21] This was not an altogether unsympathetic account, for Garwood contrasts favourably the 'manliness and honesty' of the English labourer with the 'intellectual acuteness and imaginative glow' of the Irish, and argues that despite the crowded conditions in which they lived they were more virtuous and moral than 'our own poor', and only became corrupted by a long residence in London.[22] They stood condemned, however, by the 'marks of the beast' stamped on them by Popery. A blind faith in their local priest prevented them from being open to argument, and their character thus was debased, worse still they were idle, dirty, had no regard for human laws, and were disloyal to the British government. Wherever the Irish choose to settle – St Giles's, Marylebone, St George's-in-the-East, Wapping, Ratcliff, Southwark and around Commercial Street, Whitechapel – poverty, drunken disturbances, dirt and extreme overcrowding lowered the character of the neighbourhood. Their only hope, Garwood concluded, was to gaze on the streets of the New Jerusalem, and drink of its living fountains. Over time these traits came to define the Irish, and when linked to assumed physical characteristics resulted in the most vicious racial stereotypes.

These perceived threats from an enemy within took on an even greater urgency at a time of imperial crisis. Take, for example, Frederick Meyrick, who in 1858, as the Indian revolt raged along the northern territories of the subcontinent, delivered a series of sermons in London. Under the rubric

'Deliver the outcast and the poor; save them from the hand of the ungodly', he declared that on the streets of London 50,000 outcasts lived and gained their livelihood, all of them as a class 'savages in the midst of civilization, heathens in the heart of Christendom'.[23] This was a population living beyond the healthy restraints of Christianity, and we need look no further than contemporary events in India to learn what the consequences would be if this situation were allowed to continue:

> God gave us the vast empire of India. Millions of souls He committed into the hand of England. They were sunk in debasing superstitions and immoralities, but we would not give them a better religion, or interfere with their wickedness ... And then, when we least expected it, the evil beast within them, which we had not chained by the wholesome restraints of Christian precept and example, rose up, and the demon passions which we had taken no pains to eradicate or repress awoke ...[24]

References in these commentaries to the experience of Ireland, India and the British nation suggest that from mid-century imperial concerns featured powerfully in the attempts of evangelicals to reveal the metropolitan poor and warn of the potent dangers of allowing them to remain beyond the influence of Christian (or, more accurately, Protestant) precepts. Some who had served as missionaries in London and India were drawn into comparisons, like Joseph Mullens, Foreign Secretary of the London Missionary Society, who, on returning to Britain in 1866 from an extensive spell of missionary work in India, reflected on the recent growth of London and Calcutta and the demands this placed on the need for more missionary endeavour, but then turned to the matter of heathenism. Calcutta, he pointed out, had sites of degeneration almost beyond redemption, but even this could not compare with the state of London, for here was a 'real heathenism' which condemned myriads to blackness by crushing hope and purity out of their life.[25] Beyond the heart of religious life in London there was widespread indifference among the intelligent and educated; the darker side of the picture, however, was to be found deep in the East End. See how the Sabbath was observed in 'the New Cut; in Spitalfields; in Rotherhithe; in Ratcliffe Highway; and in Wapping', he despaired, here were vast areas inhabited by the poor sunk in a wretchedness and heathenism which knew no limits:

> There are slums in London, known only to city missionaries and the men who work with them, in which the violence and vice abound to a

degree which cannot be told. But the slums of heathenism go a long way lower. They reach the very horrors of immorality.[26]

Since most evangelicals adhered to a view of the unity of God's creation, there were boundaries to the extent to which they could identify the poor as a race apart. Thus any lines marking divisions were drawn on the basis of perceived departures from Protestant Christianity. Journalists, on the other hand, working in the tradition of urban exploration established by Pierce Egan and Mayhew, were less receptive to ideas about the oneness of the human race, and consequently we can detect in their writings more strident attempts to define divisions along racial lines. Watts Phillips, an acquaintance of Mayhew, published a popular book entitled *The Wild Tribes of London* (1855) containing accounts of visits to districts 'inhabited by those strange and neglected races', in which he employed an extensive repertoire of racial coding. The increasing presence of Jewish immigrants was of particular concern. Petticoat Lane market, for example, is the 'Hebrew quarter', a 'modern Babel' with a 'perfect sea of greasy bargainers, blocking up the thoroughfare'. There is no other place that can compare with the filth of the lane; only in the Ghetto of Rome or the half-Jewish cities of Hamburg and Frankfurt can worse be found. He met at every turn the 'same physiognomy, with its unmistakable indications'. Lest anyone believed that fences were a dying breed, listen to the words of his 'official' friend and guide from the neighbourhood: 'Spitalfields yonder, and Wentworth-street's close at hand – they are all thieves all sides of us. They do the work, and who gets the pull? Why the Jews. And where do we find 'em? Here, of course – here about Petticoat Lane'.[27] He stops and is immediately surrounded by a dozen pair of eyes 'like the vulture, seeing their prey from afar'. On one side is 'a child of Moses, with a portentous squint and a dirty face, the "badge of his tribe" ', on the other a 'Judas Maccabaeus, fierce in aspect, loud of tongue', with 'large eyes and astonished eyelashes, a shock head of hair, and a long ragged beard'.[28] Later Phillips is stopped by a soft voice, and turns to find a

> withered mummy, with toothless gums, and nose and chin in dangerous propinquity. A pair of dark rimmed spectacles sits astride of a nose which stands boldly out, like the prow of a Roman galley; and a dirty nightcap, of uncertain colour, is pulled over a perfect conflagration of red hair.[29]

Along Ratcliff Highway, he finds lascars and Malays congregated around the grog shops, 'quarrelling, of course, writhing their bodies about like snakes, showing equal venom of tongue and double the wickedness of eye possessed by those interesting reptiles'.[30] And near Holborn he recalled courts that swarmed with

> dirty unwashed men, who bear, Cain-like, on every brow a brand that warns you to avoid them – with rude, coarse women, whose wild language, fierce eyes, and strange lascivious gestures strike terror to the spectator's heart. Children … half naked, shaggy-headed little savages, who flock about you, and, with canting phrase and piteous whine, solicit charity for their dying father, – that broad shouldered, burly-looking Milesian, who has just reeled from the tavern-door.[31]

John Hollingshead, a staff member of Dickens's *Household Words*, wrote in similar terms about a street in Spitalfields. Its inhabitants were marked, he claimed, by the 'five great divisions' of 'poverty, ignorance, dirt, immorality and crime', but his account relied more heavily upon the use of now familiar racial and sexual stereotypes:

> Fryingpan Alley … is worse than anything in Whitechapel or Bethnal Green. The rooms are dustbins – everything but dwelling places. The women are masculine in appearance; they stand with coarse, folded arms and knotted hair, and are ready to fight for their castle of filth … Within a few yards of this refuge is New Court, a nest of thieves, filled with thick-lipped, broad-featured, rough-haired women, and hulking, leering men, who stand in knots, tossing for pennies … The faces that peer out of the narrow windows are yellow and repulsive; some are the faces of Jews, some of Irishwomen, and some of sickly-looking infants.[32]

Phillips, Hollingshead and their co-workers may have recognized the multiracial character of the London poor, but their use of pejorative stereotypes reinforced the view that slum districts were inhabited by populations culturally, morally, physically and even biologically alien to the indigenous British. The poor were in effect seen to be an internal orient, a foreign presence at the very heart of the city which, if not revitalized by the immigration of labour from the countryside, would lead to a moral and physical decline threatening the future not only of the metropolis but also of the British empire:

> Every year the manufactures and trade of the country will attract a greater proportion of the population into the larger towns. An actuary

would predict the decade in which the deterioration and waste of the towns shall cease to be adequately sustained by healthy immigration from the country. From that moment the decadence of the British Empire will begin.[33]

Tiger Bay

The 1860s were something of a watershed in the history of East London. A cholera epidemic ravaged through its parishes, and the collapse of staple industries such as silk weaving and shipbuilding – the final nail in the coffin of which was driven in by the collapse of the Overend Gurney financial empire in 1866 – threw tens of thousands on to the labour market, precipitating a series of bread riots. Reforms followed in sanitation, the system of poor relief and housing, but from the early 1870s there remained in the minds of a confident and optimistic middle class the disturbing possibility that these forces of progress might be stifled by the swollen presence of the casual poor.[34] It was at this moment that notions of racial degeneration took hold. Degeneration was a versatile idea; after the publication in 1859 of Darwin's *Origin of Species*, it appeared in the biological sciences, and could readily applied as a means of describing the urban condition. Thus, for example, it was used to explain the pathological presence of the urban poor as a symptom of some degenerative strain within the imperial race, combined with the natural savagery of colonial subjects found amongst their numbers.

The juxtaposition of an indigenous and an alien poor presented for some the most obvious source of degeneration. Drawing on examples from the animal and plant kingdoms, social commentators singled out interracial unions as objects of particular anxiety. Here is Thomas Archer's account of a visit to an opium den in Tiger Bay (Brunswick Street, Wapping):

> A cellar where four lascars roll their yellow and black eyes upon us as they glare silently at each other, and smoke from one bamboo pipe … The two wretched women who are cooking some rice at a scanty fire are English, but so degraded, even below the degradation of such a neighbourhood, that they answer only with ghastly grins and a cringing paucity of words which seem to be borrowed from their companions … Rooms, where dark-skinned, snake-like Hindoos (beggars and tract-sellers by day) live with English and Irish women as their wives, and live, as it would seem, not always so miserably as might be imagined.[35]

Brunswick Street was soon demolished, but the opium den remained the favoured site for urban explorers seeking examples of an internal orient, and was to feature in many of their writings, including, notably, those of James Greenwood. Amongst the generation of urban explorers who followed in the footsteps of Mayhew, Greenwood stood out. A prolific writer, he more than any other defined the genre in the second half of the nineteenth century. In a career spanning forty years, he contributed regularly to periodicals and the national press, and published novels and children's books. As a journalist rather than social investigator (if the distinction can be made), Greenwood approached the poor at a time of social unease, writing accounts which, while demonstrating dramatic power and a degree of empathy with the poor, nonetheless drew heavily on familiar narratives of urban degeneration.

'Everybody,' he declares after an evening's visit, 'has read of Tiger Bay, and the horrors perpetuated there ... of the sanguinary fights of white men with plug-lipped Malays and ear-ringed Africans, with the tigresses who swarm in the "Bay", giving it a name.'[36] Except, that is, a local policeman who when asked for directions says he has never heard of the place, and that it was entirely a fabrication of the newspapers. Greenwood makes his way to the Gunboat tavern at Wapping, and there finds well-dressed and foul-mouthed 'tigresses', all of whom had the 'same short, bull-like throats, the same high cheek bones and deep set eyes, the same low retreating foreheads and straight wide mouths'. What pleasure, he inquires, can a man find in being bullied and robbed by a 'brawny-armed, big-knuckled, wretch, whose breath is pestilence and her language poison'? Where among these creatures is to be found the kindly Moll of Wapping of old?[37]

Later Greenwood, disguised as a labourer, spent a night in the casual ward of a workhouse. The room accommodated approximately thirty. Those asleep appeared as ghastly figures awaiting the coroner; the 'wakeful ones were more dreadful still. Towzled, dirty, villainous, they squatted up in their beds, and smoked foul pipes, and sang snatches of horrible songs, and bandied jokes so obscene as to be absolutely appalling.'[38] Then, much to his horror, he was forced to sleep on a bed of straw stained with blood. His account of the experience, published in the *Pall Mall Gazette*, created a sensation. It was mentioned in parliament. William Hardman, editor of the *Morning Star*, thought it an act of bravery deserving the Victoria Cross, and the pioneering journalist W.H. Stead claimed that it led to poor law reform. One rather less concerned aristocratic lady, on being informed that a journalist had spent the night in the casual ward, replied that she had not realized they were paid so badly.

During the 1870s and 1880s social anxieties about the degenerative influence of the poor on the body of the nation acquired a political dimension. The immediate impulse came from reports of the 1871 Paris Commune which engendered fears that, guided by the example of the Communards, the metropolitan poor would take matters into their own hands and seize London. An anonymous book entitled *Wonderful London* captured the prevailing sense of unease:

> The savage class in question comprises the 'roughs' who infest every one of the hundreds of shady slums and blind alleys that, despite metropolitan improvements, still disgrace the great city. We held up our hands in speechless horror and indignation at the time when the scum and dregs of humanity which clung to the bedraggled skirts of Communism committed such frightful ravages in Paris; but it is certain ... that we have lurking in our undercurrents a horde of ruffianism fully equally to similar feats of carnage, plunder, and incendiarism, should occasion serve.[39]

Expressed here was the fear that despite improvements designed to clear the poor from the streets their numbers had increased, and as a mob they now threatened to break out of the courts and alleys of East London and to annex respectable, bourgeois residential and commercial areas in the City and to the west. Haunted increasingly by the spectre that socialist currents might attract the poor and galvanize them into action, evangelicals and social observers sought ways of knowing the threat, and effectively redefined the casual poor. It is only in this context that we can understand the remarkable reception given to a pamphlet of 8,000 words, first published in 1883. Written by Andrew Mearns, an obscure London City Mission worker operating in East and South London, *The Bitter Cry of Outcast London* had little sociological or literary merit. It had neither the originality of Mayhew nor the flair of Greenwood; it was badly structured and based on a limited survey of housing in Bermondsey, Ratcliff and Shadwell, but it sold in the thousands. Mearns highlighted the gulf which was daily widening between the poor and Christian civilization. At the very centre of our great cities, he argued, lies a 'vast mass of moral corruption, of heart-breaking misery, and absolute godlessness'. The churches did what they could, but it was a thousandth part of what was needed, and in the meantime a 'TERRIBLE FLOOD OF SIN AND MISERY IS GAINING UPON US'.[40] The institution of marriage was not fashionable, incest was common, prostitution rife, and poverty attendant on at best subsistence wages pervasive. Without more

determined action by the church, the political rather than moral consequences would be dire:

> The only check upon communism … is jealousy and not virtue.
> The vilest practices are looked on with the most matter-of-fact indif-
> ference. The low parts of London are the sink into which the filthy and
> abominable from all parts of the country flow. Entire courts are filled
> with thieves, prostitutes and liberated convicts.[41]

Mearns cited the work of George Sims, which was almost certainly the
inspiration for the pamphlet. Working in the tradition of urban travel, Sims
published an influential series of articles throughout the 1880s which
concluded with the same warning:

> This mighty mob of famished, diseased, and filthy helots is getting
> dangerous, physically, morally, politically dangerous. The barriers that
> have kept it back are rotten and giving way, and it may do the State a
> mischief if it be not looked to in time. Its fevers and filth may have
> spread to the homes of the wealthy; its lawless armies may sally forth
> and give us a taste of the lesson the mob has tried to teach now and
> again in Paris, when long years of neglect have done their worst.[42]

It was precisely at this moment that the Whitechapel murders took place.
The response of the press and public to the gruesome events then and now
may appear to be extraordinary, but when placed in the context of how
East London had been represented as a place of degradation, disorder and
threat throughout the nineteenth century, it was merely an intensification
of an older and rather familiar rhetoric and imagery.

Darkest England

In the aftermath of the troubled 1880s, when the immediate sense of panic
created by the Whitechapel murders and the dock strike of 1889 had
receded, attention turned again to the endemic problem of the poor. The
massive survey undertaken by Charles Booth and his co-workers appeared
in seventeen volumes over the years 1889–1902.[43] Provoked by Booth's
determination to challenge claims of the socialist orator Henry Hyndman
that a quarter of Londoners lived in poverty, the survey was the single most
comprehensive and systematic attempt to map the extent and distribution
of the poor. Booth adhered to a vision of social and moral progress, and

proceeded to classify and quantify the poor as a necessary step in introducing reform.[44] He claimed to provide nothing more than a snapshot of
socio-economic conditions, although in later volumes, as he was drawn to
explain the causes of poverty, a more dynamic picture emerged. What
resulted was a more complex understanding of patterns of poverty. Striking
maps of London in which the poverty levels of individual streets were
colour-coded challenged simplistic polarizations between a wealthy West
End and an impoverished East End by demonstrating that pockets of
poverty were to be found in many other districts. Although this was a
disquieting picture, it was not one that Booth believed would threaten
social disorder. In contrast to the more sensational reports of his contemporaries, Booth estimated that the criminal class was a small minority
of the population, and reasoned that the springs of revolution were to
be found among the educated skilled workers, not the casual poor.[45] We
must be careful, however, not to overstate the radical nature of the shift
Booth effected in understanding the metropolitan poor. Although he
seemed reluctant to evoke biological reasoning, his total vision never truly
abandoned ideas of hereditary urban degeneration, racial stereotypes,
demoralization and gender disorder. And even if he contended that
poverty was caused mainly by sickness and lack of employment, and could
therefore be eliminated by moral and social improvement rather than
eugenics, he was prone to employ fashionable, social Darwinist rhetoric on
the survival of the fittest in daily struggles to raise standards of living and
health. Take, for example, his striking passage on the lot of the casual dock
labourer:

> He is at least acclimatized to his surroundings: his mind and body have
> become by a slow process of deterioration adapted to the low form of
> life which he is condemned to live … Apart from work, and away from
> the comfortless and crowded home, neither husband, wife nor chil-
> dren have any alternative to relief except in the monotonous excite-
> ment of the East-end street. Respectability and culture have fled; the
> natural leaders of the working classes have deserted their post; the
> lowest element set the tone of East-end existence. Weary of work, and
> sick with the emptiness of the stomach and mind, the man or woman
> wanders into the street. The sensual laugh, the coarse joke, the brutal
> fight, or the mean and petty cheating of the street bargain are the
> outward sights yielded by society to soothe the inward conditions of
> overstrain or hunger. Alas! for the pitifulness of this ever-recurring
> drama of low life – this long chain of unknowing iniquity, children

linked on to parents, friends to friends, ah, and lovers to lovers – bearing down to that bottomless pit of decaying life.[46]

Other contemporary observers, again drawing upon the genre of travel writing, viewed the problem of urban degeneration in much less ambiguously racial terms, with predictable consequences. In *The Problems of a Great City* (1886), Arnold White identified the problems of London as the 'problems of the race' which needed to be resolved not by private or governmental reform but by a 'moral revolution'. Enlisting Mayhew to the cause of social Darwinism, he argued:

> Compared with the nomadic tribes of tropic countries, where the curse of civilization is unknown, the nomads of London are but miserable savages ... Criminal and pauperised classes with low cerebral development renew their race more rapidly than those of higher nervous natures ... A policy based on relief from funds collected in a hurry, and administered by machinery raised in a night, can be but a temporary policy. The evil grows by what it feeds on.[47]

As part of the moral revolution required, White proposed legislation to sterilize the 'unfittest of the unfit', ban early marriages, control immigration and promote emigration, which with crude eugenicist logic he claimed would accord with the 'inexorable tendencies of our natural law'.[48] William Booth, founder of the Salvation Army on the streets of Whitechapel, adhered to a similar strand of social imperialism. His writings were enormously popular, most notably *In Darkest England and the Way Out*, which was published in 1890 and sold 200,000 copies in the first year.[49] The title, and in part its inspiration, came from Henry Stanley's *In Darkest Africa,* in which the famous explorer recounted an immense area 'where the rays of sunshine never penetrate, where in the dark, dank air, filled with the steam of the heated morass, human beings dwarfed into pygmies and brutalised into cannibals lurk and live and die'.[50] For Booth, the similarities between such savages and the metropolitan poor were only too obvious:

> It is a terrible picture, and one that has engraved itself deep on the heart of civilisation. But while brooding over the awful presentation of life as it exists in the vast African forest, it seemed to me only too vivid a picture of many parts of our own land. As there is a darkest Africa is there not also a darkest England? Civilisation, which can breed its own barbarians, does it not also breed it own pygmies?[51]

Crowds in the abyss

As the century drew to a close, the traditions of evangelical and urban exploration were superseded by the sociological survey and new currents of thought on urban poverty which were shaped by a liberal intelligentsia and fed into the formation of the welfare state. Writers drew heavily upon their nineteenth-century predecessors, but self-consciously saw themselves as a new, modern breed. In this process the poor were redefined; no longer do we see the nomads and tribes which had provided such rich imagery, but in their place the faceless anonymity of the crowd. At a time when the urban poor seemed on the increase, the crowd in the abyss came to represent in a modern society a regressive and irrational presence.

At the vanguard of this liberal intelligentsia stood the figure of Charles Masterman, who in an important collection of articles entitled *The Heart of the Empire* (1901) announced the end of the Victorian era.[52] And yet, modern and broadly sympathetic though their sensibilities were, when Masterman talked of a new city race a familiar language of racial degeneration was evident:

> The second generation of the immigrants has been reared in the courts and crowded ways of the great metropolis, with cramped physical accessories, hot, fretful life, and long hours of sedentary or unhealthy toil. The problem for the coming years is not just the problem of this New Town Type; upon their development and action depend the future progress of the Anglo-Saxon Race, and for the next half-century at least the policy of the British Empire in the world.[53]

A year later Masterman unleashed the full repertoire of anxieties about the existence of the modern crowd. *From the Abyss* (1902) identified this new city race – not the demoralized and destitute poor of the nineteenth century, but the 'dense black masses from the eastern railways [that] have streamed across the bridges from the marshes and desolate places beyond the river'. This is a population of commuters, making their way to work in the City and West End from East London and its suburbs:

> A turbid river of humanity, pent up on the narrow bridge, is pouring into London; aged men in beards and bowlers shambling hastily forward; work girls, mechanics, active boys, neat little clerks in neat little hats shining out conspicuous in the rushing stream ... The abyss is disgorging its denizens for the labour of the day.[54]

This is an unruly population prone to 'bizarre and barbaric revelry'. The press had talked in a 'shamefaced manner about natural ebullitions of patriotism' when clerks had riotously celebrated the relief of Mafeking during the Boer War, but for Masterman these were sinister portents of the 'presence of a new force hitherto unreckoned; the creeping into conscious existence of the quaint and innumerable populations bred in the abyss'. In a remarkable passage of profound pessimism, he then foretells a process of inevitable degeneration:

> Everywhere exuberant, many-featured life, struggling under the tropic sun; a struggle continued ardently year after year, through innumerable succeeding generations. Only always at length the end. Some inexplicable change, slowly, imperceptibly, the torrent of life has overreached itself; the struggle has become too terrific; the vitality is gradually dying. And then, as the whole mass festers in all the gorgeous, wonderful beauty of decay, comes the mangrove – dark-leafed, dank, slippery, unlovely, sign and symbol of the inevitable end. And with the mangrove the black-marsh and the reeking, pestilential mud.[55]

Such visions had purchase, for they attracted wide interest in artistic and literary circles. When early in 1902 Jack London approached Thomas Cook & Son for directions to East London, later to disguise himself as a casual labourer and write up his experiences, he had fully embraced the pessimism of social Darwinism. As a professed socialist, he was seemingly critical of a mighty empire that forced its honest labourers to scavenge the streets for discarded food. But at the same time, he was a believer in white supremacy, and fearful of any potential challenges to the Anglo-Saxon race. In expressing disgust at the threat from the poor of East London, he drew upon the full repertoire of Masterman and his predecessors. The people of the abyss, he observed, are

> the stones the builder rejected. There is no place for them, in the social fabric, while all the forces of society drive them downward till they perish. At the bottom of the Abyss they are all feeble, besotted, and imbecile. If they reproduce, the life is so cheap that perforce it perishes of itself. The work of the world goes on above them, and they do not care to take part in it, nor are they able … The London Abyss is a vast shambles. Year by year, and decade after decade, rural England pours in a flood of vigorous and strong life, that not only does not renew itself, but perishes by the third generation.[56]

Powerful though the myth of outcast London was in the second half of the nineteenth century, it never went unchallenged by the poor and those who had a sympathetic understanding of the difficult circumstances they endured, and so I wish to conclude this chapter by looking briefly at how East Enders themselves viewed the negative portrayals to which they were subjected. No experiences were recorded in print by the poor themselves, since this was a population sustained by oral not literary traditions, but we gain some sense of another, different East London from residents who could put pen to paper. In 1871 an article in *The Graphic* written by a resident of six years who, as part of his 'official duties', was required to visit three nights a week all the 'lowest localities of East London', took issue with the attention given to the area's poverty, misery, drunkenness and other vices. Many people had warned him of the dangers of assault and robbery, but these fears proved groundless, for he never met with a 'mishap of consequence'. The worst experience was his sense of dismay on witnessing the pleasure-seeking 'roughs' – male and female, in the depths of indigence – leaving, in a hideous bacchanalian uproar, the crowded theatres and dancing halls offering cheap entertainment.[57] An account written in 1885 by a 'night nomad' tells of the bonhomie and cheerfulness that existed among the lives of East Londoners. A man would give away his last penny to help pay for the 'doss' of someone who had been without a bed for successive nights.[58] And writing on 'A Whitechapel street', E. Dixon explained that he enjoyed living in the area because the 'very heterogeneous democracy of the East is infinitely more interesting than the *blasé* aristocracy of the West … There is an almost inexhaustible fund of interest in Whitechapel to him who has eyes to see, ears to hear, nostrils not too fastidious, and some sort of sensibility to be touched'.[59] Many priests working in the poor parishes clearly identified with their parishioners and resented ways in which they were popularly portrayed. The Reverend R.H. Haddon of St George's-in-the-East pointed out that

> we who live in [East London] are the constant victims of many amusing misrepresentations … we East-enders owe many a grudge to the journalists, and novelists, and conversationalists, who have written and talked about us without really knowing us.[60]

A similar point was made by Clara Grant, who taught in a charity school by Bow Common, and had genuine insight into the motives of many reporters:

It would seem that novelists and journalists demand vice and squalor when they come down to write us up. They expect evil and seem horribly disappointed if they discover we are not black at all, but only grey ... a rich man, wishing to help our work, induced a big daily paper to send down a journalist to write us up. He said 'it won't do. You're not black enough'. I pointed out that I could not very well work up a murder or two, or put every child in rags and bare feet to rouse interest in us.[61]

The hysteria created by the press during the Whitechapel murders was a particular source of resentment. Even George Sims, who had done much in his writings to create the myth of outcast London, recalled at the time that the inhabitants of Whitechapel were

jealous, and properly jealous, of their local fair name. Whitechapel rose as one man to protest against the atrocities of the Ripper being headlined in the press. 'The Whitechapel Murders'. The indignant Whitechapel folk explained, with much emotion, that the murders were committed in Spitalfields.[62]

At the height of the panic, the Reverend Samuel Barnett, founder of Toynbee Hall in Commercial Street, wrote to *The Times* to remind the public that there were in fact few criminal haunts in the locality. 'The greater part of Whitechapel is as orderly as any part of London', he stated, 'and the life of most of its inhabitants is more moral than that of many whose vices are hidden by greater wealth'.[63] His wife and co-worker at the mission, Henrietta, testified to the virtues of the sort of 'abandoned women' who had been the Ripper's victims. 'Only those who know them personally and intimately, as I did by the hundred, can know the readiness to help, the capacity for sacrifice, the generosity of heart, and the disregard of self that survives all the horrors of their lives.'[64]

The level of indignation that could be roused among the local population is well illustrated by the reception given in July 1901 to an article in the *Daily Mail*. Entitled 'The Worst Street in London', the piece described Dorset Street, Spitalfields, as the 'head centre' of the shifting criminal population of London. This was, claimed the author, because of its numerous lodging houses wherein he found 'depths below the lowest deep'.[65] The article met with a furious response from the residents of Dorset Street and its neighbourhood. A hastily convened meeting attracted such a crowd that the pub room booked for the occasion could not accommodate them. A larger one was therefore booked for five days later; even this proved too small. The bulk of the audience was the local poor, but among them were many employers and priests. They listened attentively as Jack McCarthy in a speech of nearly two hours denounced allegations made in the article:

> Dorset Street, Spitalfields, has sprung into undesired notoriety; here we have a place which boasts of an attempt at murder once a month (a voice said, why, he ought to be smothered) (Lies, wicked lies) and one house a murder in every room (what lies he tells, surely he is the champion at telling 'em), as a rule, policemen go down in pairs, hunger walks prowling in its alleys, and the criminals of tomorrow are being bred there today (cries of lies, where does he get his information from). Now gentlemen, is there *an attempt*? At murder once a month? (no, no, that there a'nt, does he take us for cannibals?).[66]

Other speakers, with the boisterous support of the meeting, declared that the article was entirely false, a gross libel on the body of working people in the area. Such sentiments rarely found their way into print for they had none of the sensationalism that had been so successful in selling newspapers.

At a time when East London was first revealed to a reading public, the myth of outcast London derived its authority from those who could claim to know the poor, but the legacy of the myth long outlived its creators; in one form or another we still inhabit it. And yet the myth was challenged by many within East London itself who were angered by the ways in which they had been represented as a degraded and impoverished race apart. This denial raises a number of important historical questions. If residents of East London responded with such vigour to the demeaning ways in which they were portrayed, what precisely was the changing cultural landscape they inhabited in the course of the nineteenth century? And if the criminal poor who had attracted so much sensationalized attention were only a small minority of the population, what of the majority, namely, the regularly employed and more respectable artisans? These are some of the questions addressed in the following chapter.

CHAPTER 7

From Dissent to Respectability, 1820–1914

FRANCIS PLACE was a master tailor and a leading radical. Writing in 1824 after a tour of inspection of the riverside areas to the east of the Tower with which he was very familiar, he remarked on the considerable improvement in the streets. The great Ratcliff fire of 1794 and construction of the London docks had cleared large areas of miserable hovels, in place of which new brick buildings and wide streets had appeared.[1] Ten years later he pointed to attendant changes in the lives of the inhabitants:

> Forty years ago the working people with very few exceptions were to a great extent, drunken, dirty, immoral and ignorant. He who was the best paid was then the most dissolute. This is not so now … Drunkenness among journeymen, dirtiness, immorality and gross ignorance are not the prevailing vices. Their manners are greatly improved, their morals are mended, their knowledge is considerably extended, and is constantly though slowly increasing … Proofs abound in every direction, in their dress their deportment their language in the reading rooms they frequent, in the book clubs and institutions of which they are members, and the books they possess as their own.[2]

In 1841, the evangelical James Grant also referred to the great moral and intellectual improvements that had taken place in the last few years, progress that he ascribed to mechanics' institutes and the availability of cheap literature. Drunken operatives were now a rare sight, he declared, and the appearance and manners of mechanics greatly surpassed those of twenty years ago. In the meantime, he continued, the mass of the poor remained in a state of destitution and ignorance.[3]

Impressionistic though these contemporary interpretations were, they shared a sense that while the cultural landscape inhabited by the mechanics and artisans of London was being transformed, the poor continued to live beyond the influence of civilizing reform. The assumption that the working class was internally divided by occupation and circumstance into the families of skilled artisans and those of the casual poor was significant.[4] In practice, artisans and casual labourers were situated at the opposite extremes of a fluid continuum between which were located people with different levels of skill and changing economic fortunes (this was particularly so of the nineteenth-century metropolis, as many occupations were deskilled by new forms of capitalist rationalization), but it was evident that divisions did exist among the ranks of working Londoners which influenced how they were seen by themselves and others.

In the aftermath of the industrial revolution, the relative absence of factory production encouraged a corps of elite artisans who were highly sought after, and as a consequence enjoyed high earnings and a large measure of control over their work. Intellectually, morally and economically, they were remote from the army of the unskilled, casual poor whose fate was entirely in the hands of unscrupulous employers. Without security of employment and training, the poor struggled to survive; without education, it is argued, they had few interests or cultural pursuits. Nowhere was this more evident than in the sphere of politics. Artisans were at the heart of the protracted campaigns for workplace rights and political democracy. Trades unionists, Chartists and political reformers came from their ranks. The casual poor, by contrast, had little sense of collective identity and no tradition of collective political struggle. Theirs was a seemingly endless cycle of hardship, relieved on isolated occasions by riots which were little more than vague and primitive expressions of latent hostility offering opportunities for noisy excitement. The defining characteristic of the casual poor, concluded Gareth Stedman Jones, was 'neither their adherence to the left, nor yet their adherence to the right, but rather their rootless volatility'.[5]

This demarcation is useful in helping to explain patterns of political behaviour in nineteenth-century East London, even if the lines are too rigidly drawn: as we have seen, among the casual poor was a large variety of skilled, even professional people who had fallen on hard times. Attempts to capture this changing cultural landscape are fraught with difficulty, since the casual poor in particular created few written records, but if we are prepared to delve beneath the negative imagery of outcast London, there are clues to rich and vibrant traditions. Parliamentary, court and poor law records offer glimpses. We have found details, for example, of riots in the records of the Old Bailey, and learnt of the survival of features of a rural culture on the streets of Whitechapel from a parliamentary select committee on improvement. Outside this official domain, however, there seemed little interest. The poor never attracted the attention of novelists or playwrights, and while guides to London included detailed accounts of churches, historical edifices, West End streets and other elite sites, none explored low-life areas to the east. Towards the close of the Napoleonic wars, when thousands of demobilized soldiers and sailors were thrown on to the streets of London, thereby to swell the numbers of beggars, select committees reported on mendicity and vagrancy (1815) and policing (1816), but the street poor remained remote from their inquiring gaze. It was at this moment, however, that London low life entered into the public imagination, thanks in large part to the remarkable venture of Pierce Egan.

Unsophisticated sons and daughters of nature

Egan was an Irish-born journalist who had migrated to London to live and work in the capital's literary subculture which for the time being survived on the publication of popular romances, criminal biographies, epic tales, and miscellaneous trivia.[6] He soon made a name for himself with the publication of *Boxiana*, which remains one of the finest studies of the sport, but then in 1820 there appeared in serial form *Life in London*, which arguably, when published as a book a year later, more than any other shaped perceptions of the cultural landscape of the nineteenth-century metropolis.[7] It was enlivened by a series of plates etched by George Cruikshank, the outstanding graphic satirist of the day. Armies of colourists were employed in order to keep pace with demand, but even before the final issue was published, shameless imitations were being sold, a practice which was to continue until the end of the century despite Egan's attempts to kill off one of the heroes of the story. Adaptations dominated the London stage of the 1820s; early in 1821 no fewer than five plays based on the characters of the book were performed simultaneously, some of which featured real-life beggars from the streets of London.

The main narrative derived from eighteenth-century travelogues. A country gentleman, Jerry Hawthorn, desirous of experiencing London life, approaches an old friend, Corinthian Tom, who agrees to show him around the more pleasurable sites in the company of Bob Logic. The adventures of the three heroes provide the main thrust of the story, but Egan uses this merely as a device to reveal metropolitan life in all its complexity:

> the grand object of this work is an attempt to portray what is termed
> 'SEEING LIFE' in all its various bearings upon society, from the

high-mettled CORINTHIAN of St. James's, *swaddled* in luxury, down to the *needy* FLUE-FAKER of Wapping, *born without a shirt*, and not a *bit of scran* in his cup to allay his piteous cravings.[8]

Many of the locations and characters visited by the three friends were identifiable to a contemporary readership, and in an extraordinary departure from literary convention included depictions of the metropolitan poor. Thus in addition to accounts of stately homes, auction houses and operas, which had long featured in guides to London, we visit dog fights, boxing matches, the condemned cell at Newgate prison, and riverside taverns, all of which would have been known to Egan. One evening Tom proposed they take up an invitation to see a 'bit of life at the East End of the Town', and make their way to All-Max in the East.[9] This tavern, we are told, required no patronage, for everyone was welcome, 'colour or country considered no obstacle, and dress and address completely out of the question'.[10] Among the clientele were 'lascars, blacks, jack tars, coal-heavers, dustmen and women of colour … all *jigging* together'. There was no thought about birth or distinction, all was '*happiness* – every body free and easy'. 'It is,' said Logic as he turned to Tom, 'the LOWER ORDERS of society who really ENJOY themselves.'

The three heroes were first mistaken for police by these 'unsophisticated sons and daughters of nature', but when a moll stated loud enough to be heard by all that the '*gemmen* had only dropped in for to have a *bit of a spree*, and there was no doubt they *voud* stand a *drap of summut* to make them all *cumfurable*', the suspicions immediately evaporated. After several glasses of max, they join in the festivities. In Cruikshank's illustration of the scene, we find Bob Logic in jovial conversation with Black Sall on one knee, Flashy Nance on the other. Jerry is seen plying the fiddler with drink, while Tom is in conversation with Mrs Mace, the landlord's wife. Later, when Tom and Jerry had finished their revels and were ready to return home, Logic was not to be found. A jack informed them that very likely he had 'taken a voyage to *Africa*, in the *Sally*, or else was out on a cruise with the *Flashy Nance*; but he would have him be aware of *squalls*, as they were not very *sound* in their *rigging*'.[11] Logic was abandoned to his fate.

It would be pleasing to think that this extraordinary celebration of a multiracial, riverside community is reliable, if only as a counterpoint to the condemnation meted out by Patrick Colquhoun (pp. 155–8). Indeed, other studies have pointed to the richness and egalitarianism of the international seafaring community of this period[12] – but perhaps it is more productive to consider in what ways this imagery influenced the way social observers viewed the metropolitan poor during the remainder of the century. Out of the literary subculture inhabited by Egan later emerged two figures who for a time dominated attempts to represent the seamier side of London life. There is no evidence that Charles Dickens or Henry Mayhew ever met Egan, but they were inspired by his work. Egan's knowledge of the diversity of metropolitan life, acquired by walking the streets and frequenting the haunts of London, was imitated and celebrated by Dickens. The characters in the early novels *Sketches by Boz* and *Pickwick Papers* could have come straight out of the pages of *Life in London.*[13]

Mayhew took Egan in a different direction, for as an urban explorer he gave voice to the street poor through an intimate and detailed recording of their experiences. The extraordinary series of letters published in the *Morning Chronicle* and his *London Labour and the London Poor* revealed the struggles of the poor to survive against seemingly overwhelming odds. He may have been unduly harsh in his treatment of, say, what he considered to be the uncivilized elements within the costermonger and dock labour communities, but what prevails is a deep sympathy with the attempts of the poor to make the most of difficult circumstances. His detailed description of costermongers is critical of their preoccupation with the amusements to be found in the beer shop, dance hall and theatre. Card games, skittles, boxing and 'twopenny-hops' are particularly popular pastimes, and yet there is no sense that these are debased forms of recreation; on the contrary, Mayhew points out that some of these are followed also in aristocratic circles. The more prosperous attend the theatre three times a week. A 'most intelligent' coster informed him that love and murder are preferred themes, although in recent years there has been a greater liking for tragedy. Politically, nearly all costers are Chartists. Some remain ignorant of the six points of the charter, but as a body they are greatly influenced by the more intelligent from their ranks who emerge as leaders. They may not recognize the sanctity of marriage, but in good times the vast majority of women are rigidly faithful, and illegitimate children are rare. Children are generally affectionate, and will often perform acts of selfless heroism in order to help keep the household together. Costers approach religion in an entirely instrumental way. Few attend church, but they respect City missionaries because they read to them, visit the sick, and occasionally distribute fruit. The most worrying trait of costers is their lack of education – only one in ten is able to read – but Mayhew is loath to blame the costers themselves for this state of affairs:

> That a class numbering 30,000 should be permitted to remain in a state of brutish ignorance is a national disgrace. If the London costers belong especially to the 'dangerous classes', the danger of such a body

is assuredly an evil of our own creation; for the gratitude of the poor creatures to any one who seeks to give them the least knowledge is almost pathetic.[14]

Similar sentiments can be found in the writings of Grant. A contemporary of Mayhew, and even more prolific, he was a devout Calvinist who straddled the worlds of evangelicalism and journalism. Grant's descriptions of low-life culture reflected the condemnation of fledgling evangelical thought, and yet they were tempered by recognition of the harsh and unjust ways in which the poor were treated. He saw that most notorious edifice of destitution – the workhouse – as a refuge of the 'destitute and indolent of all nations', but at the same time recognized that there was as much variety among its inhabitants as in the streets. The workhouse was a great leveller, and the inmates a 'republican community on a small scale'.[15] The worst cruelties to be seen, he remarked, were perpetrated not by the poor, who were often reluctantly forced to seek refuge therein, but by the inhumane, unnatural and unchristian regulations embedded in the new Poor Law, which merely added to the miseries of the inmates.

Grant was drawn also to those remarkable survivors of a pre-modern, plebeian culture, the London theatres and fairs. Penny gaffs were by far the most frequented form of entertainment; in East London, according to Grant, their numbers swarmed, particularly along the Ratcliff Highway, Commercial Road and Mile End Road.[16] Most were unlicensed, miserable places temporarily set up in stables, sheds and warehouses beyond the reach of the authorities. Their audiences were overwhelmingly the juvenile poor, who had developed a real passion for the tawdry fare on offer, and would go without food rather than miss a twenty-minute performance of *Hamlet*, *Macbeth* or their favourite, *Othello*. Such tragedies, staged as vehicles for horrible murders, were always in great demand. Poor as most of the performers, and even proprietors were, some were assiduous in maintaining standards. Hector Simpson, who owned a theatre in Westminster and a much more profitable penny gaff in Southwark, always demanded that his actors treated the audience with respect, and insisted on repeating scenes if they were performed in a slovenly way.[17] However, Grant concludes, half an hour in such places would convince any respectable person of their immoral tendencies. Some had recently been closed by the authorities but many more should if we were to arrest the corrupting influence they have on the young.

For the same reason, Bow, Stepney and Edmonton fairs had recently been shut down, but the Bartholomew and Greenwich fairs continued.

They were greatly anticipated by the lower classes, at least 100,000 of whom attended on each of the three days of the year when Bartholomew Fair was open, approximately half this number at Greenwich. On offer were innumerable portable theatres, dancing booths, freak shows, kiosks selling food and drink, gambling dens, and displays of animals, little changed in essence from those of a century earlier (Chapter 3). Predictably, for Grant they should be treated with the same opprobrium, since thousands of the youth could trace their physical and moral ruin to attendance at such metropolitan fairs.[18]

Grant later qualified his observations by stating that they had no reference to 'mechanics and artisans as a body', but applied chiefly to those who worked at any job they could find, and often had no work.[19] Suggested here is a separation which had taken place relatively recently. Whilst popular cultural activities deriving from the carnival had originally involved the whole of the community, during repression of what were considered its worst excesses the middling sorts withdrew, but it was not until the eighteenth century that craftsmen began to distance themselves from what were increasingly considered vulgar forms of entertainment and to partake of more rational forms of recreation.

So what distinguished the behaviour of skilled workers? They inhabited for the most part a culture of respectability, self-discipline and learning which required a conscious separation from the world of plebeian pleasures. Place, perhaps expressing the more pronounced sentiments of the culture, declared 'I cannot, like many other men, go to a tavern. I hate taverns and tavern company. I cannot drink, I cannot for any considerable time consent to converse with fools.'[20] Most possessed a powerful desire to preserve their privileged way of life, and were prepared to join organizations and take appropriate industrial action in order to do so. A significant minority were attracted to politics, and, as we shall see, in the aftermath of the French Revolution helped build a radical movement which for a while threatened to destabilize the established order, and later rallied to Chartism which in its struggles for a reformed parliament left an indelible mark on the political landscape of the country.

Worse than Egyptian bondage

Since Edward Thompson's magisterial survey, *The Making of the English Working Class*, we have a better understanding of the regional variations in this culture. While in Manchester, Birmingham, Leeds and other urban centres built around discrete industrial experiences, radicalism could be related directly to the structure of artisan communities, it is more difficult to identify an authentic radicalism in London. London had been at the heart of parliamentary struggles in the seventeenth century, provided the basis of Wilkite agitation for radical reform, and in 1792 gave birth to the London Corresponding Society (LCS). With a membership drawn from a wide range of artisan occupations including silk weavers, tailors, carpenters and bakers, the LCS was arguably the first working-class organization in Britain, and campaigned actively for universal suffrage, mainly through education and propaganda. Towards the end of the century, however, metropolitan radicalism seemed on the retreat, and after government repression curtailed the activities of the LCS the geography of radicalism moved north. All radical leaders had a following in London, and it was London which created and sustained the radical press, but London failed to provide a national focus again until the height of the agitations over the Reform Bill in 1832.

Unlike other manufacturing centres, London displayed a considerable diversity of localized trades, thereby preventing the emergence of an overall leadership; instead leaders sprang up from districts such as Bethnal Green, Lambeth and Southwark who were able to express the grievances of individual trades.[21] East London provided fertile ground for the growth of a radical artisan culture. Silk weavers, shoemakers, shipwrights and tailors were threatened variously by new capitalist rationales leading to deskilling, reduced income and increased provincial competition (Chapter 4), and although deteriorations in work conditions did not automatically engender militant responses, radical platforms clearly appealed to sections of the artisan elite who sought to preserve traditional privileges. At different times and in different places they embarked on embryonic trade union struggle, political activity, social and educational organization, and cooperative endeavour as a means of making their voices heard, and saw no incongruity in so doing.

We have already noted the extraordinary intellectual and social culture promoted and sustained by eighteenth-century Huguenot silk weavers, and a propensity to struggle in defence of their industry, temporarily suspended after the introduction of the Spitalfields Act of 1773. As conditions in the trade deteriorated around 1816, ultra-radicals such as Arthur Thistlewood and James Watson turned to unemployed weavers in the hope of channelling their anger into an uprising against the government, but they met with a muted response, for weavers, mindful of the 1773 Act, retained a faith in constitutional means.[22] A general union of weavers was established in 1823; dedicated to lobbying against attempts to repeal the Act, it refused to

join the fight of other London unions against the Combination Laws, but
when the Act was repealed in 1824, thereby removing protection against
further cuts in income, the union abandoned sectional interests and
widened its terrain of struggle. Against a backdrop of starvation, during
which soup kitchens reappeared on the streets of Spitalfields, and surges in
applications for relief, the weavers shifted awkwardly between political and
industrial struggles to regain a measure of protection against the ravages of
rationalization.[23] They were also prepared to resurrect an older form of
struggle when in 1824 and 1828 weavers rioted on the streets, the latter
incident causing the City to withhold £1,000 from a fund established to
relieve their distress.[24]

This pattern of struggle intensified in the ensuing years. Repeated
attempts were made to regulate wages and introduce tariff protection
through government intervention, and combine with other fledgling
trades unions, notably the National Union of the Working Class (NUWC),
around common causes such as measures to reduce the deleterious impact
of machinery on the livelihood of their members.[25] Frustrated by repeated
failures to attract the support of the government, weavers abandoned more
peaceful means. Late in 1830, a large crowd made up mostly of weavers
attacked the house of the Duke of Wellington and the police watch house
at Covent Garden before marching through the City, there confronting the
police with a barrage of stones.[26] In the meantime, meetings of the NUWC
regularly heard of the desperate state of weavers. One held at the height of
the mortalities in Spitalfields caused by the epidemic of 1832 resolved that
cholera was the best card the privy council had, since it was used to create
terror, hence distracting working people away from the consequences of
bad legislation.[27]

Other staple trades in East London suffered rationalization in the first
half of the nineteenth century (Chapter 4), in response to which skilled
workers formed themselves into organizations – many short-lived – and
embarked on protracted campaigns to defend their livelihoods. The 1820s
witnessed a series of strikes among tailors, shoemakers, shipwrights,
sawyers and carpenters, while the decline continued apace. John Gast led a
strike of Thames shipwrights in 1825, defeat of which left the various
unions weakened and vulnerable to counterattack by employers. At the
Blackwall Yard shipwrights were forced to abandon their union and
commit to join no other.[28] Like weavers, these artisans also combined in
radical struggles on the rights of association, the regulation of wages, use
of machinery, parliamentary reform and tariff protection. Thanks to the
struggles of carpenters, tailors and shoemakers, there were significant

advances in trades unions during the 1830s. Grand Lodges of Operative Tailors and of Operative Cordwainers were established, while the General Union of Carpenters grew rapidly. More symptomatic of a swelling confidence was the move to general unionism, most notably with the formation of the Consolidated Trades Union (CTU), which included among its members twenty-nine artisan trades from London.[29] The CTU promoted sympathetic industrial action among its member trades, but the large majority of strikes organized were unsuccessful.

Self-education went to the very heart of this radical culture. Coffee houses, conventionally thought to be the preferred rendezvous of the metropolitan bourgeoisie, were also established as places of conviviality, advice and discussion by radical artisans, most of whom were simultaneously involved in industrial and political struggles. In 1836, shortly after the demise of the classes organized by the NUWC, a small group of leading radicals including Gast and William Lovett opened the Working Men's Association (WMA) with its own premises and an ambitious daily programme of lectures and discussions. Within a year the association had over a hundred members from trade societies across London, but then faced rivalry – initially friendly, but later more hostile – from the East London Democratic Association (ELDA).[30] At its founding meeting the ELDA declared that, encouraged by the 'brilliant example' of the WMA, they intended to become 'auxiliaries in the cause of justice, and the establishment of truth.'[31] Based in Swan Street, off the Minories, the ELDA thus stood 'to promote the Moral and Political condition of the Working Classes by disseminating the principles propagated by that great philosopher and redeemer of mankind, the Immortal "THOMAS PAINE" '. Accordingly, members paid a subscription of a penny a week to discuss the

> principles of cheap and honest Government, and to adopt such means as may seem expedient to carry out the five grand principles of Radical Reform, viz: 'Universal Suffrage, Vote by Ballot, Annual Parliaments, No Property Qualification, and Equal Representation.'[32]

These principles sprang from the widely held belief among the working class that all their economic ills were due to lack of adequate parliamentary representation. Against a backdrop of the failure of radical agitation over tariff reform, repeal of the Corn Laws and the widespread adoption of labour-saving machinery, and in the belief that political reform would extend suffrage and so enhance their prospects of advance, various shades of radical opinion gathered in the years leading up to the 1832 Reform Act.

This focus on reform led to a revival of metropolitan radicalism, particularly among Spitalfields weavers, who, despite attempts by moderates to limit their demands, talked of a popular uprising. Informants warned the Home Secretary in 1830 that there were no loyal weavers and that their meeting houses were centres of sedition.[33] Hostile demonstrations were staged on the streets of London. On Lord Mayor's Day, 9 November 1830, when the King was due to visit the City, the Home Office received reports that great crowds could be expected with plans to set the City ablaze and kill Wellington and Peel. Thousands marched to different sites around the capital, including the Strand, where half-famished Spitalfields weavers gathered, and in the evening the anticipated fights with the police occurred, but the day passed without serious incident.

The 1832 Act did extend the franchise as radicals had hoped, but overwhelmingly to the ascendant middle classes. Members of the working class were systematically and almost completely excluded. For a time, working-class radicalism, now abandoned by its former allies within the middle class, lacked purpose and direction in the political sphere and so turned its attention to industrial struggle. Only late in the 1830s did political power once again emerge in the radical imagination as the real source of the social and economic oppression of the labouring classes. It was at this moment that Chartism was – perhaps belatedly – born.

At the heart of the Charter were the 'five grand principles of radical reform', together with the demand for payment of MPs, introduced later. This programme successfully galvanized movements around the country into the national Chartist movement. Chartist leaders and the majority of members were artisans, although attempts were occasionally made to broaden its appeal. Avoiding the exclusive respectability of the WMA, for example, the ELDA sought to create a mass organization in support of the Charter, and to that end reached out to the poor of East London, successfully recruiting members from Shoreditch, Stepney and Southwark.[34] Another important, albeit neglected, current in the reform movement was that led by women. In pursuit of Chartist demands, a network of female organizations was established up and down the country. Included among them was the East London Female Patriotic Association, which was formed late in 1838 and could command audiences of 150 at their meetings.[35] Their role, however, seemed a subordinate one in the early stages, since female organizations were generally committed to the support of the activities of male radicals. An address from the Birmingham Female Political Union, for example, congratulated the association for

the noble and patriotic spirit evinced by you in co-operating with your
fathers, brothers, and husbands, in the present struggle to enfranchise
themselves from a state worse than Egyptian bondage … Dear sisters, go
on the great cause in which you have embarked; be not deterred by the
hypocritical cant, that women have no right to interfere with politics.[36]

Despite the significance of the WMA in providing a focus for London
radicalism, its strength had in part been due to a lack of alternatives,
so that when local Chartist movements sprang up its fortunes receded.[37]
London Chartism, like the earlier radical culture, was built by artisans in
local trades, many of which were experiencing profound change brought
by capitalist rationalization. Of all the occupations identified for Chartists
and members of the WMA over the decade 1839–49, shoemakers, tailors,
carpenters, silk weavers and stonemasons stood out, and although we must
caution against a simple-minded equation between Chartist activity and
economic hardship it is perhaps hardly surprising that levels of metropolitan agitation, as revealed by the number of Chartist organizations, were
consistently highest in East London.[38] There were, however, wide fluctuations over time, which can only be understood by looking at how individual trades fared over this period. With the exception of shipwrights,
whose privileges were protected by effective organization and continued
buoyancy in Thames shipbuilding, all of the major trades of East London
were experiencing difficult times, in response to which artisans channelled
grievances into industrial and political action, including Chartism.

The extent to which Spitalfields weavers actively supported the Chartist
movement of the 1830s and 1840s is open to dispute. Perhaps because of
the fickle and changing nature of their struggles, the evidence is seemingly
contradictory. Thus, for example, in 1837 their general union was reconstituted into the United Operative Weavers of London; for a while it published
the *Spitalfields Weavers' Journal*, but according to a contemporary observer
attendance at meetings was poor, largely because of apathy and want of
funds. Throughout the 1840s, however, the union, now the Broad Silk
Hand-Loom Weavers of Spitalfields, had a stable membership of a thousand, who were strongly Chartist.[39] On the other hand, it has been argued
that there is no firm evidence that Spitalfields or Bethnal Green weavers
ever played a part in Chartism. Richard Cray reported to the Chartist
convention of 1839 that weavers

have not been used to Politics being more used to fancy such things as
Birds Dogs and Skittle Playing but that is fast dying away/a great many

are fancyers in flowers In my opinion their wants some good missionary
work among them to teach them Politics.[40]

At the same convention, a 'poor weaver' from Spitalfields wrote a letter
asking for a 'general meeting to be called of all those in the district and
press on them the notion or rather the necessity of organizing themselves
into different bodys'.[41] Through the 1840s, as conditions deteriorated to
the point of wretchedness, the weavers' union adopted as its motto
'Protection to British Industry, Agriculture, and Manufactures', and in
pursuit of this continued to use legitimate channels to press for government intervention.[42]

Shoemakers, who were among the best-organized, suffered a steady
loss of income during the 1840s. Separated geographically between the
West End and the City (including East London), and between makers of
men's and ladies' shoes, the trade societies pursued sectional interests.
Strongest were the societies of aristocratic artisans of the West End, by
comparison with which those of East London, comprising the lowest-paid,
were small and weak. At a meeting of the West End branch in 1842 over a
thousand in attendance adopted the Charter, and resolved to cooperate
with 'all good men' of other trades to secure success. Within a month the
other branches agreed to the same principles, although differences surfaced
over the identity between political and industrial struggles.[43] In an attempt
to overcome sectionalism, the Mutual Assistance Association was formed
at a national conference of shoemakers in 1845, and was joined by the four
branches of the London trade until sectional jealousies again arose, and
amidst charges of corruption they broke away.[44] Amidst a collapse in
demand, when up to a half of London shoemakers found themselves
without work, a Trades' Delegate meeting in 1848 recommended measures
including home colonies, a labour protection board, a graduated property
tax, and the five points of the Charter.[45]

The climax – and denouement – of London Chartism occurred in
1848, a time of revolutionary struggle in France and deepening economic
recession of London trades. Riots erupted in Trafalgar Square and nearby
streets, and on 10 April a crowd, variously estimated between 200,000 and
half a million, gathered on Kennington Common to promote a national
petition in support of the Charter. In a determined attempt to prevent the
occupation of public buildings by demonstrators, the authorities mobilized
tens of thousands of armed police, troops and special constables, barricaded the buildings themselves, and enrolled employees as specials. The
day passed without major incident. During this period of rising tension

East London hosted a series of massive open-air meetings in Bonner's Fields, immediately adjacent to the new Victoria Park, and saw a dramatic increase in the number of Chartist branches.[46] Large assemblies and demonstrations continued, but now the authorities, emboldened by the knowledge that the Kennington Common meeting had not turned into a wholesale attack on the metropolis, met them with violent suppression. Early in June the police launched an assault not only on a peaceful Chartist gathering in Bonner's Fields, but on all others present, and indeed any inhabitants caught within a mile's radius. There followed a series of arrests and subsequent imprisonment of Chartist leaders who had made incendiary speeches at various gatherings, and then, following notice of another meeting to be held at Bonner's Fields, the government banned all assemblies. In anticipation of violent confrontation, the agents of order were again armed and public buildings barricaded. Magistrates clutching the Riot Act were stationed at various locations around East London. The Chartist leader, M'Douall, arrived early at Bonner's Fields, immediately to be confronted by a mass of police armed with cutlasses. On being informed that the proposed demonstrated was illegal and would be resisted, he instructed all under his control to walk away. A ferocious thunderstorm then broke, driving away the lingering crowd of

> ill-favoured and ill-satisfied weavers; larking youngsters and sombre adults; brawny Confederates … ginger-beer men, orange women, children, and that invariable ingredient of an English assemblage, women with children in their arms.[47]

This was effectively the end of the Chartist movement in London. Further arrests of leaders followed; conspiracies of insurrection were hatched, but came to nothing. It was sadly fitting that the final act of the proud tradition of metropolitan radicalism took place in East London, at a site of popular recreation named after the 'Bloody Bishop', scourge of religious reform in a previous age of political turmoil.

A fit subject of national pride

Thirty years elapsed before the working people of East London were again to test their strength in industrial struggle. In the intervening period the industrial landscape had changed irretrievably. Staple trades, most notably silk weaving and shipbuilding, had collapsed; others, including tailoring, shoemaking and furniture, had suffered with ever greater intensity from capitalist rationalization, and now overwhelmingly employed sweated labour.

Unrest had surfaced intermittently. During the harsh winters of 1854, 1860 and 1866, when the docks froze over and poor law officials found it impossible to relieve more than a fraction of the thousands who applied, groups of unemployed attacked and looted the many bakers' shops in Whitechapel.[48] And in 1871 the Labour Protection League was formed, initially among stevedores and wharf workers at the East and West India Docks but later among unskilled dockworkers, who established branches throughout East London. Emboldened by this unprecedented display of organization and a buoyant labour market, the dockworkers struck in support of a pay increase the following year. Joined by permanent staff, the strike spread to other docks, at which point the companies capitulated and conceded most of the increase demanded.[49] A peaceful and ordered victory demonstration attracting in excess of 20,000 converged on Shoreditch Town Hall. In the immediate aftermath of the dock strike, gas stokers employed by the Gaslight and Coke Company at the massive new Beckton Gasworks formed the Amalgamated Society of Gasmen, and embarked on a campaign for shorter working hours. A strike late in 1872 spread to 2,400 stokers throughout London, plunging the metropolis into darkness. Pressure was brought to bear by alarmed authorities for a speedy end to the strike. The company charged the ringleaders with conspiracy, and recruited replacement labour from unemployed riverside workers, scavengers and agricultural labourers. Within a week the strike was broken.[50]

These industrial struggles were significant, not so much because of their success or failure as for what they revealed about the changing nature of workplace relationships in this period. This was a time of economic expansion, based on rising investment in mechanization, employment and productivity, which encouraged the growth of centralized trade unions in older artisan trades and the formation of new unions catering for the interests of semi-skilled and even unskilled sections of the workforce. There was, however, a conscious break from the radical past; leaders repeatedly emphasized to their members the virtues of respectability, good order, legitimacy and defence, in response to which employers adopted a more willing acceptance and understanding of their role.

Gareth Stedman Jones has argued influentially that in the period from 1870 these structural changes effectively transformed metropolitan working-class culture. Towards the end of the century it was apparent that the radical combativity of the early decades had been displaced by a preoccupation with amusement, leisure and sport centred on the family. London trade unions, located as they were in relatively small firms, fared badly in the last quarter of the century, forcing a retreat into sectional interests intended to protect the artisan from both the employer above and threatened incursions from the semi-skilled below. Although forebodings occasionally surfaced about the potential of the poor to wreak havoc in part because of their continued resistance to the civilizing impulses of improvement schemes, and to modes of social and cultural reform brought by evangelical missionaries, the disruptive influences of gin palaces and plebeian recreations such as cock-fighting and ratting had virtually disappeared. The anxieties of respectable opinion were further relieved by the dock strike of 1889, which demonstrated that even when the sections of the poor were organized by leaders avowing socialist thought they remained orderly and well-behaved.[51]

So what were the constituent elements of this culture, and what do they reveal about the cultural landscape of East London in the latter stages of the nineteenth century? This moment has been seen by many as critical to the development of the trades union movement. The strikes of match girls at Bryant and May's East London works in the summer of 1888, of gas workers at Beckton early in 1889, and of dockworkers later that year have gained an exalted place in the history of trades unionism. For the first time, it is argued, bodies of unskilled labour came together to confront powerful employers, so laying the foundations for new unions representing the collective interests of workers apart from the artisan elite. This is, however, only part of a more complex story.

There had been precursors. The strikes of dockworkers and gas stokers in 1872 displayed many of the features of later struggles, and so it is perfectly legitimate to argue that new unionism dates from this earlier period.[52] The Labour Protection League survived the subsequent downturn, although with the loss of dock labourers the union increasingly served the interests of stevedores; a name change in the late 1880s to the Amalgamated Stevedores Labour Protection League merely confirmed the fact. And the enduring, albeit more exclusive, Amalgamated Society of Watermen and Lightermen also arose from the 1872 strike. Both were to play a decisive role in the strike of 1889.

It is also necessary to question the celebrated narratives of the strikes themselves. Take the match girls' struggle, which the Webbs, in a standard account of British trade unionism written nearly a hundred years ago, described in ways that would become very familiar:

The matchgirls' victory turned a new leaf in Trade Union annals. Hitherto success had been in almost exact proportion to the workers' strength. It was a new experience for the weak to succeed because of their very weakness, by means of the intervention of the public. The lesson was not lost on other classes of workers.[53]

The strike was triggered by the dismissal of a worker by Bryant and May, but it expressed deep-seated grievances against starvation wages and conditions of work which, because of the use of phosphorus, were at best unhealthy, at worst deadly. After a period of resolute defiance, and with the active support of Annie Besant, the match workers forced major concessions, including an end to unfair fines and deductions for materials, and the provision of separate rooms for meals, at which point the strike was called off. This picture of young, impoverished women who were prepared to take on a ruthless employer and win is a seductive one; but it has been overplayed. Important though the strike was as an example of what could be achieved by unskilled workers under the leadership of an adroit publicist like Annie Besant, it was isolated and had limited success. A union was formed and run by officers who had little in common with the membership, and functioned as a social and welfare club rather than an industrial trades union. The suggestion that it inspired the wave of industrial struggle that followed is unconvincing; indeed no direct evidence for this has been produced.[54]

Of rather greater significance were the gas workers' struggles. As in 1872, stokers at Beckton took the initiative in launching a determined campaign to improve pay and conditions. The National Union of Gas Workers and General Labourers was formed, and soon attracted gas workers nationwide; remarkably, within six months it had 30,000 members.[55] Early demands for an eight-hour day were conceded by the principal gas companies, but when a contingency of members, buoyed by these successes, attempted to enforce a closed shop the companies resisted. In the ensuing struggle, a decisive and humiliating defeat was inflicted at the South Metropolitan Gasworks, Greenwich, when the company, aided by a large body of police, imported strike-breaking labour in the face of fierce resistance from stokers.

By far the largest of the disputes of the time, however, in terms of the numbers involved and the days of work lost, was the dock strike of 1889. Sparked by a minor dispute over the division of remuneration on a cargo at West India Docks, the strike rapidly spread throughout the London and Royal Docks. The majority of the strikers were unskilled dockworkers who

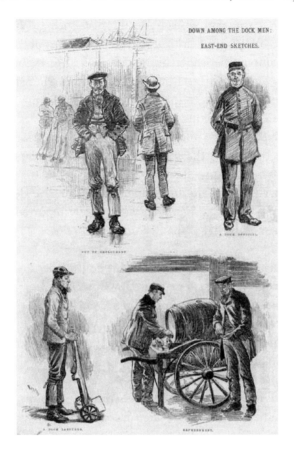

Down among the dock men, 1889. Realistic portrayals of dock workers on the eve of the great dock strike.

spontaneously acted against the conditions they were forced to endure on a daily basis:

> For many years discontent has been sullenly smouldering among the dockers. Employment has been falling. The dock labourer does not, as a rule, reason very deeply about the causes of the change … All he knows is that the waiting at the dock gates had become longer and more hopeless, and that times have been harder and harder, and a vague feeling of injustice has grown up, which has only waited for a spark to burst into a blaze.[56]

The recent gas workers' struggle was an important influence on the strike. Many dock labourers had worked in gas plants and were personally

acquainted with the stokers, while trade unionists such as Will Thorne and
Ben Tillett, who had played a critical role in the conduct of the gas workers'
struggle, were among the leadership of the dock strikers. Indeed, Tillett's
Tea Operatives Union, with its headquarters along the Mile End Road,
converted during the strike to the Dockers' Union, the main body representing the interests of unskilled dock labourers.

Initially, the dock companies stood firm, but then the stevedores came
out, effectively paralysing the industry, and changing the nature of the
struggle. Through skilful use of publicity dockers gained the support of the
public and other unions. The focal points were massive demonstrations
through the streets of London which were widely reported in the press.
Typical were the comments of the Recorder of London:

> The whole history of the world did not afford so wonderful an instance
> of self control on the part of suffering men with starving wives and
> children, and such discretion and forebearance on the part of the
> authorities. It was an instance of cheerful submission to the law which
> was a fit subject of national pride, and would forever do honour to all
> concerned in the matter.[57]

The celebratory, even playful nature of the demonstrations, evidenced in
the conduct of the strikers, bands and decorated floats, and the cheerful
relationships among strikers, the police and the general public, suggest that
the strike more closely resembled a mediaeval carnival than a modern
industrial struggle.[58] Given the inexperience of the metropolitan poor in
such struggles, and the survival of elements of a plebeian culture in their
ranks, this may well be the case.

Because of the discipline and good order displayed on demonstrations
the strike encountered few problems with the police. The support from
East Londoners was to be expected, for this was a struggle conducted in
public by an impoverished industrial community deeply embedded within
the locality. That from the middle classes, no less enthusiastic or generous,
has to be seen in the context of the troubled 1880s. At a time of recession
when levels of unemployment soared, the mid-1880s had witnessed a
series of violent disturbances on the streets of London. Demonstrations of
the unemployed led by the socialist Social Democratic Federation turned
into riots as the poor rampaged through the streets of the West End,
attacking property and carriages they encountered at random. Amidst
rumours that mobs of tens of thousands were preparing to take the City,
shops and property were barricaded, and the police and military turned

out with a fullness of force not seen since the heady days of radicalism. The anticipated attack did not occur, but this provided only temporary relief, for when the dock strike erupted the anxious middle classes looked with horror upon the prospect of a hungry and dispossessed poor, led by social-ists, taking power. These were not the acts, after all, of a maniac selecting victims from among poor women; this was, for the first time in living memory, a famished mob breaking out of the confines of East London which under a socialist leadership had the power to bring down the entire social and political order at a stroke. As such it was a much more imme-diate and direct threat than the Whitechapel murders; little wonder that it was viewed with stupefied alarm by middle-class Londoners. In the event, however, the inflated fears that the casual residuum would combine with socialists to wreak havoc proved unfounded. The sight of peaceful and orderly strikers, cheerfully marching along the main thoroughfares of East London, came as a 'cathartic release' from these profound and deep-seated fears.[59]

With remarkable levels of domestic and international support, and the intervention of Cardinal Manning to broker a settlement, the strike was brought to a successful conclusion. Dockers won a pay increase of 6d per hour (the so-called dockers' tanner), and there were favourable increases for stevedores and lightermen. Sympathetic, even celebratory accounts of the strike began to appear almost immediately – *The Story of the Dockers' Strike* by H. Llewellyn Smith and Vaughan Nash (1889) was the first and remained one of the best accounts – and were sustained later by Sidney and Beatrice Webb in their *History of Trade Unions* (1920).[60] More recently, the centenary history of the Trades Union Congress (1968) described what it saw as the seminal role played by the strike:

> The dockers obtained the major part of what they wanted. A famous victory, which lifted the hearts not only of the London dockers, but of other workers …, all of whom drew their own moral from the story of struggle for the dockers' tanner, and rallied to their own appropriate unions.[61]

In the aftermath of the strike, membership of the unions rose dramatically, but the old sectionalism remained. Compared with the greatly enhanced strength of stevedores and lightermen, the Dockers' Union was organiza-tionally weak. As economic conditions deteriorated in the 1890s, so the gains of 1889 evaporated. Most significantly, the dream of casual labourers to restrict dock work to union members was in tatters, and once again they found themselves isolated and excluded. Even Tom Mann, probably the most able and committed of the dock leaders, expressed his determination

> to eliminate the riff-raff: the wretched wastrels that have disgraced the Docks ... At the end of this week we close our books. The other men at the Dock Gates must clear off; with us there is no room for them; no doubt there are other social movements to provide for them, but our movement is to eliminate them.[62]

Evidenced by this new wave of industrial militancy, the cultural landscape of East London had undergone something of a transformation. Mindful though we must be of the contrasts in militancy and in the ways in which authorities responded between, say, the struggles of the gas workers and the dock labourers, new unionism had as a common aim the organization of sections of the workforce previously thought to be resistant to collective action, and in this it had a marked degree of success. Underpinning this movement was the ascent of semi-skilled occupations attendant on capitalist rationalization and mechanization, partly at the expense of the old artisan elite. Many of these semi-skilled could rely on fairly regular work and therefore income, but there was little to suggest that they inhabited the same powerful tradition of autodidacticism that was integral to the radical culture of the early decades of the century. Unchanged was the continued exclusion of the poor, and the contempt in which they were held.

You would think us respectable

In late-nineteenth-century London, music hall was the most popular entertainment. Although it was to be found in many industrial locations around the country, music hall came to be associated almost exclusively with the metropolis, especially East London. Its origins can be traced to the pubs, cheap theatres, saloons and penny gaffs of the eighteenth and early nineteenth centuries which catered for the tastes of a plebeian public, but then from mid-century it emerged as a distinct and more specialized form in its own right. Music hall expressed the desires and fantasies of an urban working-class culture undergoing change, but was simultaneously shaped by a cohort of entrepreneurs who built the halls and staged performances, and a body of legislation which attempted to place restrictions on their operation.[63] Crucial was the 1843 Theatre Regulation Act,[64] which broke the monopoly of patent theatres granted by the Licensing Act of 1737[65] by allowing other theatres to stage drama on condition that they banned smoking and drinking in their auditoria. So a new dividing line was created between theatres performing 'every Tragedy, Comedy, Farce, Opera, Burletta, Interlude, Melodrama, Pantomime, or *other entertainment of the stage, or any part thereof* under the watchful eye of the Lord Chamberlain, and halls regulated by local authorities where 'public dancing, music, or *other entertainment of the like kind*' could be offered to an audience of smokers and drinkers. The line, however, was bitterly contested, particularly by theatre people who, under increasing threat from the success of the halls, attempted to prevent them straying into the realm of drama.[66]

Programme of the Paragon Theatre, Mile End, 1892. Typical of the more respectable theatres of East London, the Paragon reputedly staged the debut of Charlie Chaplin.

Music hall audiences were thus entertained by a variety of songs, dances, comic acts, tricks, newly imported minstrel shows, and, in some of the larger halls, spectacular tableaux of battle scenes. Halls reflected the social composition of the constituency from which they sprang. Mid-century there were between two and three hundred small halls, most of which operated out of pubs without the appropriate music and dancing licences. Charles Morton, a former publican from East London, signalled a departure when in 1851 he opened the Canterbury Hall in Lambeth. Abandoning what he considered the low and vulgar entertainments offered by the minor halls, Morton offered respectable programmes suitable for family audiences. So popular was the venture that in 1854 he opened a new hall nearby with a capacity of over 1,500 which in its time attracted an aristocratic and middle-class clientele. His example was soon followed by other impresarios, such that by 1866 London had no fewer than thirty-three halls with a similar capacity.[67] As these large halls grew they consolidated their authority over the minor establishments, thereby defining a golden era, familiar images of which remain to the present. No longer part of low-life leisure, music hall was now highly commercial, attracted considerable investment, and paid the top professional performers huge salaries.

East London housed a large number of theatres and music halls catering for a variety of tastes. In 1870, John Douglas, proprietor of the New National Standard Theatre at Bishopsgate, included press reviews in a programme to support his claim that it was not only the 'largest and most magnificent theatre in the world' but also one of eminent respectability. The *Daily Telegraph*, for example, reported that

> The New Standard is undoubtedly the finest theatre in England, if not in Europe, and is steadily acquiring an exalted repute as the house of a higher and more legitimate class of entertainment than the sensational Melo-dramatic spectacles with which audiences of the Theatres in the East and North East London are usually regaled.[68]

Details were given of late trains and omnibuses leaving near the theatre for destinations around London and into Hertfordshire. The programme running from 7 November until further notice opened with an adaptation of *The Vicar of Wakefield*, followed by two tableaux entitled *Estella! The Queen of the Stars*, performed by the New Grand Ballet Fantastique, concluding with a new farce, *A Chapter of Accidents*. Contrasts with the Paragon Theatre of Varieties, Mile End Road, were not immediately apparent. A programme from 1887 claimed that it was the 'grandest palace of amusement in Europe', and reassured the audience that the entertainment offered 'shall be at all times absolutely free from any objectionable features'. Thus it invited 'the Co-operation of the public to this end, and will be obliged to anyone informing them of any suggestive or offensive word or action upon the Stage which may have escaped the notice of the Management'.[69] However, the Paragon offered also a saloon bar 'with all the comforts of a West-End Restaurant', and a programme including The Maxwells, The Wood Family, Brothers Leopold, and Sergt. Simms and his Juvenile Zoauve Troupe. Targeting an audience with what would have been considered less refined taste was McDonald's Music Hall in Hoxton. A programme in November 1866 offered amongst others Pentland & D'Jelim from the Oxford and Canterbury Music Halls, Dick Penny on his mechanical donkey, Paddy Fannon, the greatest impersonator of Irish character, and Bros. Keeling, the Ethiopian Grotesques.[70]

The fluid nature of the boundaries between theatre and music hall is nicely illustrated by the changing fortunes of the Garrick Theatre in Leman Street, Goodman's Fields. The theatre opened in 1830 with standard fare; *House Warming, Or, a few Friends at the Garrick*, in which the managers explained the conduct of the theatre, was followed by a comic ballet entitled *Phantom Lover, Or, the Innkeeper's Daughter*, and a grand musical melodrama, *Friendship, Love & Liberty, Or, the Renegade of Portugal*.[71] Its fortunes soon came under threat from the increasing popularity of music halls, in response to which the Garrick included turns from circuit artistes. A programme from 1880, for example, had *Day After the Wedding* and *The Barber of Bath* combined with Alice Foster, The Elictric (sic) Spark, and The Two Pots (Patty and Cany), Irish Comedians, Vocalists and Dancers.[72] By 1893 the theatre had become the Garrick Music Hall, the 'prettiest bijou music hall in the East End of London'. It now offered only character acts such as Will Dobson, Champion Amateur Clog Dancer, and Will Hawkins, Descriptive Vocalist & Milanese Piper, and of course 'all drinks of the finest quality'.[73]

The question of whether music hall was an authentic expression of working-class culture is a contentious one. For Stedman Jones music hall both reflected and reinforced the trends in the latter stages of the nineteenth century as metropolitan working-class culture was remade, and provides yet further evidence of its fatalism and political scepticism.[74] Artistes sang and joked about trivial pleasures, questioning neither society's inequalities nor British imperial endeavour. Music hall was, he concludes, little more than a culture of consolation, an escape from the realities of working-class life. More recent work has suggested, however, that this explanation provides only a partial picture.[75] We need to recognize that the output of music-hall entertainment was vast, including not only songs but comic acts, dances and a plenitude of the bizarre, grotesque and curious, the expressive potential of which we do not yet understand. Even the songs themselves cannot fully be appreciated simply from their lyrics, for the same song could take on different meanings depending upon the way in which it was performed and how the audience reacted. The swell song, for instance, typified by George Leybourne's *Champagne Charlie*, appealed to the audience using a variety of cultural and stylistic connotations, and was interpreted in ways that were fluid and ambiguous. The songs may have worked by inviting the audience to join in the sense of comic parody, but often they were met with sarcastic remarks and unwanted comparisons between the stage persona and real toffs.[76]

It is important also to ask who made up the audiences in the music halls of East London. It is tempting to assume that after 1843 working-class audiences drifted to music halls, abandoning the theatres to the more respectable elements of society. And yet the divisions between theatre and music hall were not as decisive as this implies; not only did both cater for mixed audiences but they demonstrated wide diversity.[77] Research on East London theatre audiences suggests that they were drawn predominantly from the immediate locality, but hard evidence on their social composition simply does not exist. A series of police reports at the time of deregulation in 1843 claimed that the City of London Theatre attracted people of the neighbourhood, especially weavers, the Standard drew tradesmen, weavers, and artisans and their children, the Effingham in Whitechapel was frequented by local tradesmen and sailors, and the Grecian had audiences of tradesmen, clerks from the City and artisans.[78] Following a visit to the Britannia in 1860, Dickens described the audience as 'mechanics, dock-labourers, costermongers, petty tradesmen, small clerks, milliners, stay-makers, shoe-binders, slop workers, poor workers in a hundred highways and byeways'.[79] Such surveys, however, were descriptive and highly impressionistic, and no doubt reflected the sensibilities of the observers, or an implicit political agenda. It is therefore unlikely that we can identify a specific audience at a theatre, or indeed a generic East London audience; rather, audiences were mixed and varied.[80] This may help to account for the sharply contrasting accounts of visits to the same theatre; it was not merely that the accounts were subjective – the contrasts may indeed have been real enough.

The same arguments apply to music halls in East London, for the evidence is that with the supersession of pub halls by purpose-built establishments there was little distinction between the audiences. And just as theatres catered for different constituencies, so did the halls. East London had no aristocratic variety theatres of the kind to be found in the West End, but it had large music halls attracting respectable sections of the local population, minor halls in the poorer districts attended by working and lower middle classes, and low-life pub halls and saloons with little respect for propriety.[81] When the London City Missionary J.M. Weylland toured a riverside district of East London in 1875 he found more than thirty singing rooms frequented by sailors and their companions, and the criminal classes. 'In these places,' he observed,

> they hear the worst of language, listen to the coarsest of songs, and drink and dance away their time. These rooms are a great attraction to the people I visit, and the good impressions made in the day are frequently obliterated in the evening. There are several 'gaffs' and music halls which profess to be respectable, but bad is the best.[82]

Respectable they may not have been, but most of the small establishments were neither unruly nor licentious. At one such hall, spacious and lavishly decorated, Weylland watched a comic sing about sham swells, sales and goods, finishing with a verse describing the sham House of Commons. He was followed by 'The Hypocrite' who performed a parody upon the Bible to riotous applause. The manager feigned admonishment of the performer under the watchful eye of Weylland, but then turned to him and added that if 'you saw the amusements down Ratcliff, you would think us respectable'.[83] James Greenwood, prolific chronicler of the metropolitan poor, spent an evening at a Whitechapel gaff and there saw a performance of a new play, *Gentleman Jack, or the Game of High Toby*, featuring real horses and a carriage. Since the actors could utter no words for fear of falling foul of the authorities, the whole of the dialogue was sung. The horses were old and subdued, but they were greeted enthusiastically, as were the songs, by an audience of young costers and their female partners, who at appropriate moments threw small coins on the stage to be eagerly retrieved by the performers.[84]

It is almost certainly the case that the poorest had no access to most of the larger and more respectable halls, simply because of the price of entry, but all other sections, including large numbers of juveniles and women, were to be found amongst the cheapest seats in their galleries. Given this, any argument that music halls reflected a new metropolitan working-class culture dominated by skilled and semi-skilled workers is open to qualification. The larger halls of East London might have offered respectable programmes, but even here, if by so doing they did express an authentic working-class culture, it was highly mediated by the impresarios who financed, organized and staged the performances, and the licensing authorities who strove to enforce public safety and maintain a sense of decency and decorum. As a form of entertainment, respectable music halls provided no more of an insight into the culture of East London than does the soap opera *EastEnders* today. Arguably, the saloons and small halls, less troubled by respectability and audiences, did reflect the cultural sensibilities of East London, but only those which were survivals of a bawdy plebeian world now increasingly under threat from the gospel of improvement and mass culture.

The ambiguities of music hall were perhaps most evident in one of its lasting creations, namely, the figure of the cockney. As a term used to describe a native of London, the cockney had been around for a very long time.[85] Some have detected the cockney in costermongers, who had been a troublesome presence in London since the twelfth century, and in Shakespeare's comedies, but the vital link to East London, or, more accurately, to the east of the City, was first made at the beginning of the seventeenth century when writers identified the true cockney as one born within the sound of Bow Bells (St Mary-le-Bow in Cheapside). With the publication of Johnson's *Dictionary* the reputation of the cockney was secured. Drawing upon citations from Shakespeare, Johnson defined the cockney as a 'native of London, by way of contempt' and 'any effeminate, ignorant, low, mean, despicable citizen'.

Pierce Egan's celebration of metropolitan low life and its use of cant which Johnson had found so vulgar may not have been specifically about East London itself, but in the pages of *Life in London* the cockney enjoyed something of a reprieve. Mayhew and Dickens rarely employed the term, and yet many of their characters embodied what were seen as essential cockney qualities. Around the mid-nineteenth century, attendant on the rise of mass consumption and extension of the franchise, the cockney was transformed into a comic figure of sham gentility. And here the music hall played a critical role in marginalizing the darker and more threatening aspects of the character. Star performers including Alfred Vance and George Leybourne depicted sartorially elegant young cockneys with absurd pretensions to equality. This archetype was further developed in the pages of *Punch*, particularly with the character of E.J. Milliken's 'Arry, a commercial clerk who feebly attempted to copy the style and manners of his superiors.

The most popular site of leisure remained the local public house, many of which were enticingly brilliant spectacles for those wandering along dark and forbidding streets. One temperance reformer who made his way along the Ratcliff Highway on the Sabbath could hardly refrain from expressing wonder at the sight of its gin palaces before remembering the clientele they served:

> at one place I saw a revolving light with many burners playing most beautifully over the door of the painted charnel-house: at another, about fifty or sixty jets, in one lantern, were throwing out their capricious and fitful, but brilliant gleams, as if from branches of a shrub. And over the doors of a third house were no less than THREE enormous lamps, with corresponding lights, illuminating the whole street to a considerable distance. They were in full glare on this Sunday evening; and through the doors of these infernal dens of drunkenness and mischief, crowds of miserable wretches were pouring in, that they might drink and die.[86]

The correspondent was not alone, for Highway attracted undue attention from all shades of temperance reform. On entering the Ship's Cabin, the itinerant Rev. Weylland encountered a scene little changed from Pierce Egan's All-Max in the East over fifty years previously. The pub was a small room, crowded with sailors and labourers of the 'lowest class', and at least forty women, with seats and tables around the perimeter, leaving the centre free for dancing. On cue a fiddler scrapes a lively tune; in an instant the room is transformed by the 'rapid twirling and odd ungraceful movements' of the dancers, and the ear assailed with oaths and blasphemies.[87] James Greenwood also recounted a visit to the pubs of the neighbourhood. At the Gunboat in Wapping he found a melancholy barn with dirty walls and a floor bespattered with saliva, attended in great numbers by 'tigresses', well dressed but 'ten times bolder and more foul mouthed than in more respectable establishments.[88] Sailors of the merchant service sat swilling beer, gin and rum, handing over their hard-earned money to the muscular tigresses, danced, or watched the entertainment, which included clog-hornpiping and comic singing. Little wonder that Archbishop Manning could inform a prohibitionist meeting in 1871 that 'there is not a sin which the imagination of man can conceive which is not rife in that north Bank of the river Thames'.[89]

Such sensational reports boosted the assault upon the consumption of alcohol among the working class in the second half of the nineteenth century, so that divisions which had first appeared early in the century, when radicals resolved that sobriety benefited their cause, were by the end firmly established. Thus while labourers continued to frequent pubs, the respectable working class either abstained or, in keeping with the domestication of leisure, chose to drink at home. And yet the role of the pub in working-class culture was changing. Many of the large coaching inns which had acted as staging posts or termini for travellers to the metropolis were badly hit by the coming of the railways, which provided faster alternative routes and station hotels for those needing overnight accommodation.[90] Pubs were much less vulnerable, for they continued to cater to the various needs of labourers, and here their siting was vital. Many were located along the main thoroughfares. In 1899 Charles Booth counted no fewer than forty-eight pubs along the Whitechapel Road between Commercial Street and Stepney Green, that is, one every thirty-eight yards. Similar patterns were evident in streets leading up to the docks or major factories. Such pubs were convenient stopping points for labourers walking to work or returning home in the evening. Others were to be found on street corners, natural focal points for working-class street life, where warm and convivial surroundings encouraged relaxed social exchange.

Without wishing to understate the continuing problems associated with the consumption of alcohol, here also were signs of significant improvement since the gin-soaked decades of the eighteenth century. Breweries transformed the interiors of their pubs by providing large bars where customers were encouraged to stand while drinking rather than sit and become steadily drunk. And pubs were not merely – or even chiefly – places where alcohol was consumed. Quite apart from an atmosphere of conviviality, a warmth unavailable to many at home, and a temporary refuge from life's daily tribulations, pubs sold decent food, provided a variety of entertainment, and remained an important exchange of labour and stolen goods. Connections between sport and pubs were particularly strong. Able to trade upon their fame and connections, many retired boxers and footballers became landlords. In other respects, and in ways which further encouraged the exodus of artisans, the days when the London Corresponding Society, early trades unions and Chartists regularly met in pubs faded with the decline of radicalism, although some pubs continued the tradition established by Huguenots a hundred years earlier by hosting friendly societies.[91]

Recent research on the food culture of East London in the late nineteenth century has confronted myths of outcast London by demonstrating that in the domestic sphere East Londoners proved sophisticated and resourceful.[92] Challenging widely held beliefs that families of the labouring poor were malnourished she argued that mothers in particular were knowledgeable about food and resourceful in providing their families with wholesome, regular and nourishing meals. Indeed, the importance of food was suggested by the extent to which it determined the ordering of domestic space and the lives of working-class women more generally. The kitchen was the critical site, for here not only was food prepared and consumed, but since it was the only room constantly to be heated by the fireplace or cooker the kitchen served as the centre of family life. Its cleanliness and general appearance were therefore a source of considerable pride and a marker of a sense of working-class respectability. Main meals regularly included fish, meat and vegetables. Substantial yet tasty stews were popular, followed by a pudding such as rice pudding or bread-and-butter pudding to provide a plain, inexpensive yet wholesome meal. Occasionally, for a treat, or if the mother was too busy, the family ate out in one of the numerous eating places in East London, most notably the pie and mash shops which provided highly nutritious meals of stewed eels served with mashed potato and 'liquor' (a parsley sauce), fish and chip shops, cafés and local pubs. The purchase of food required the same measure of resourcefulness. Most was available from street stalls but a smart shopper knew where the best deals were to be found at what time of the week, even the day. Striking a friendly relationship with a grocer or butcher always helped since he might well slip into the shopping bag an extra item of food.

This culture of food was underpinned by an extensive knowledge of its preparation and nutritional value. This knowledge was passed on from generation to generation, but also acquired through more formal lessons at school and later cookery lessons offered to adults. After 1878 school cookery lessons were compulsory for girls, and yet evidence suggests that most in East London participated willingly, choosing to attend further classes once they left. Most school lessons were run under the auspices of the National Training School for Cookery, which provided teachers qualified in cookery and maintained high standards in their many centres. At the turn of the century nearly a hundred such centres operated in East London, offering clean, well-lit and well-equipped surroundings for the lessons. Working-class girls were instructed in plain cooking, very much along the lines of what already took place in their households; the recipes may have been quick and easy but they had the merit of being nutritious and affordable. Success as a pupil demanded intellectual engagement and diligent application. Such education went beyond compulsory lessons, for many young women on leaving school attended cookery demonstrations on weekday evenings, and other free demonstrations and public exhibitions held in various museums which tended to encourage an interest in more exotic fare. Articles promoting cooking skills now appeared regularly in the press.

The various and complex dimensions of food culture in East London together created and maintained a distinct working-class respectability. Women may have had no choice in taking on this role, but they took obvious pride in – and were judged by – their ability to feed their families well on what for many were limited budgets, time and space. Further, this responsibility demanded a range of knowledges and skills which simply cannot be gainsaid. The organization of domestic space and time, purchase of food on a daily basis, and preparation of wholesome and tasty meals went to the very core of women's identity as working-class mothers and wives, from which they derived a vital sense of respect and pride within the family and from the wider community. The males of the family were able to bask in the reflected glory.

The want of interest and culture

Overall, there were few areas of working-class life and leisure in late-nineteenth-century East London which suggested a cultural degeneration, naivety or barrenness. Despite this, the activities organized for local people by the middle class, rather than by local people themselves, were more likely to meet with the approval of respectable opinion. Nowhere was this more apparent than in the university settlement movement. The movement attracted scores of middle-class Christians – many of whom had been educated at public schools and Oxbridge – as volunteers in the struggle against what they perceived as the social and moral desolation of East London. They shared a deep suspicion of, even hostility to, previous attempts to ameliorate the poor, especially those organized around public relief, and determined instead to effect reform though moral regeneration. It is all too easy to criticize the motives of settlement workers in seeking to do 'their bit' for the poor of East London, and yet amongst them could be counted a cadre of remarkable individuals who worked, lived and died among the self-same poor. Samuel and Henrietta Barnett at Toynbee Hall, Whitechapel, Scott Holland at Oxford House, Bethnal Green, and Percy Alden at Mansfield House, West Ham, and many others, sacrificed their time and often their well-being to fulfil their vision of Christian duty by doing good works, and in so doing provided many local people with opportunities for self-development which otherwise would have been denied.

Thanks to the biography of Samuel Barnett written by his wife some years after his death we have a detailed record of the origins of Toynbee Hall and its work among the poor.[93] In 1873 the Barnetts had moved to St Jude's Church in Whitechapel – at the time empty and unused – and they later recalled the conditions they encountered:

> the whole parish was covered with a network of courts and alleys. None of the courts had roads. In some the houses were three stories high and hardly six feet apart, the sanitary accommodation beings pits in the cellars; in other courts the houses were lower, wooden and dilapidated, a standpipe at the end providing the only water … In these homes people lived in whom it was hard to see the likeness of the divine. If men worked at all it was as casual labourers, enjoying the sense of gambling which the uncertainty of obtaining work gave. But usually they did not work; they stole, or received stolen goods, they hawked, begged, cadged, lived on each other with generous discrimination, drank, gambled, fought, and when they became well known to the police, moved on to another neighbourhood.[94]

They brought a particular vision of the work required to ameliorate such degradation which was based on a searing critique of existing measures to relieve the poor. Following the pioneering work of the Spitalfields Benevolent Association, the relief of metropolitan poverty in the nineteenth century had centred on the work of the many agencies and societies which in various ways had sought to offer material aid in forms that the Barnetts found wasteful and ineffective. The Metropolitan Visiting and Relief Association (1843), the Parochial Mission Women Fund (1860), the Society for the Relief of Distress (1860) and others pursued their endeavours through exaggerated publicity, and in complete ignorance of each other's activities. More damaging, however, was the influence over the poor themselves, who were encouraged to beg, lie about their circumstances, cadge instead of work, and consider any relief from the rich as fair game.[95] Soon after moving to St Jude's, Samuel Barnett laid out an alternative strategy:

> If one sentence could explain the principle of our work, it is that we aim at decreasing not suffering but sin. Too often has the East End been described as if its inhabitants were pressed down by poverty, and

every spiritual effort for its reformation has been supported by means
which aim to reduce suffering. In my eyes, the pain which belongs to
the winter cold is not so terrible as the drunkenness with which the
summer heat seems to fill our streets, and the want of clothes does not
so loudly call for remedy as the want of interest and culture.[96]

It was a strategy which determined Barnett's course of action, even though
it resulted in a calculated cold-heartedness to suffering. Henrietta recalled
an incident which well illustrated her husband's seeming indifference:

> On a freezing night, with the north wind tearing down Commercial
> Street, human brothers, and worse still, human sisters slept on the
> clean hearth-stoned Vicarage steps, and one dared not give them
> fourpence for the doss-house bunk, or even twopence for the rope
> lean-to. If we had only been poor it might have been easier, but to
> possess money and to have to withhold it! – The 'principles' made life
> difficult, but Mr. Barnett never wavered.[97]

Samuel also served on a small committee responsible for distributing
charity to relieve suffering among the poor. He acted harshly, often refusing
applications on the grounds that it was in the suppliants' own interests.[98]
Occasionally, in response, the vicarage was attacked, forcing him to escape
through the church and call for the police; in the longer term, he never
shook off his reputation as an enemy of the poor. The Barnetts admired
British rule in India, and their ideal of service drew inspiration from what
they saw as the pursuit of truth and justice demonstrated on a daily basis
by colonial administrators purely out of a sense of duty. Abandoning all
previous notions tainted by imperial greed and ambition, here was a
professional and knowledgeable elite acting without prejudice to provide
good governance and wise counsel to an alien peoples.[99] There thus
followed a vigorous campaign to provide local people with the opportunities to raise themselves from cultural poverty by participating in what the
Barnetts considered meaningful forms of artistic and educational activity.
For a decade they toiled with little success to create a slum parish linked to
social and cultural institutions, but with the completion of Toynbee Hall in
1884 they had a focus for the work free from the constraints imposed by
St Jude's.[100] With the support of like-minded men, this 'university settlement' (Barnett coined the term) could be a real force in enriching the lives
of the poor. Despite charges that the Barnetts were sailing close to
socialism, the support was forthcoming. Indeed, a roll call of those who

came to be associated with the work of Toynbee Hall includes those in the vanguard of a liberal intelligentsia, some of whom were to lay the foundations of social reform culminating in the establishment of the British welfare state. Charles Masterman, R.H. Tawney, E.J. Urwick, Herbert Llewellyn Smith, William Beveridge, Arthur Sidgwick and Clement Attlee – to name a few – committed their energies to Toynbee Hall, securing its rightful place in the history of the settlement movement.

The Barnetts enthusiastically supported the public libraries movement, seeing librarians as missionaries spreading the light of knowledge. In 1888 a students' library was built in Toynbee Hall with just under 4,000 volumes, the large majority of which were non-fiction. By 1892, 21,000 people visited annually. Samuel also energetically campaigned for the adoption of a Whitechapel library under the 1890 Public Libraries Act. Like so many other libraries in East London, this was part-funded by the philanthropist Passmore Edwards; when it opened in 1892, Samuel talked of the dangers of ignorance, and the friendship from books that was so absent among the poor.[101] From a series of art exhibitions at Toynbee Hall and St Jude's developed the idea of a permanent space, and the Whitechapel Art Gallery was founded in 1901, again financed by Passmore Edwards, and with Samuel as chair of the Board of Trustees. Regular series of classes were organized, many given by leading social theorists of the day, including Beatrice Webb and Frederick Rogers, clubs were established, such as the Toynbee Travellers Club and Inquirers Club, and Toynbee Hall played host to many prominent social and political figures, including Charles Booth during his work on the survey, the Central Strike Committee of the 1889 dock strike, Octavia Hill and William Morris.

The Barnetts, however, were not without their critics, and in 1884, just as Toynbee Hall was opening, a group of men at Keble College, Oxford, founded the rival Oxford House in Bethnal Green. Keble had recently been created to preserve conservative Anglo-Catholic ideals now under threat from the admission of nonconformists as undergraduates, and yet from its ranks sprang the same desire to confront the poverty of East London – except that the founders of Oxford House were deeply suspicious of the creeping socialism of the Barnetts' vision, and wished to have none of their broad-church appeal. Restricted to Oxford men who were prepared, even keen, to live the life of a Christian ascetic of old, Oxford House was small and Spartan, but arguably it, rather than Toynbee Hall, provided the model for the numerous university settlements based on a single religious denomination which were subsequently founded in East London and its neighbourhoods.[102] Whether or not these settlements were successful in elevating the poor from their material and cultural deprivation is open to question; that they intervened through the large variety of classes and sports, theatre, reading, health, holiday and recreation clubs on offer is not.[103] This is perhaps the nub. Despite the prodigious efforts of the Barnetts, church attendance among the East End poor did not increase. Perhaps Samuel's past record on relief persuaded them that his god was cruel and merciless; perhaps they took what they wanted from what the Barnetts offered, and left the rest.

The late nineteenth century also witnessed the birth of the public libraries movement. Prior to the creation of metropolitan borough councils in 1899, responsibility for public libraries rested in the hands of vestries, most of which, out of a sense of civic duty, recognized the need for them but were unwilling to commit funding from the rates to provide adequate facilities. Contemplating rows of empty shelves, the first public librarians from the late 1880s therefore resorted to sending begging letters to philanthropists and charitable institutions. Even with limited stocks, the libraries proved hugely popular, and came to occupy a place at the heart of the literary and intellectual life of working-class communities.[104] Small reading rooms attracted 500 visitors daily; registered borrowers were numbered in their thousands.[105] Within this context we can understand something of the historical significance of the Bishopsgate Institute, a charitable educational centre located at the western boundary of East London adjacent to the City, which opened on 1 January 1895. The founder was the Reverend William Rogers, rector of St Botolph's Church nearby. As someone who had been to Eton and Balliol College, Oxford, and had subsequently worked for social reform among the slums of East London, Rogers fits the mould of a university settlement worker, except that he passionately believed in the value of non-sectarian education and rational recreation, even refusing to allow hymns or sacred music at the opening ceremony. Purpose-built, the Institute had reference and lending libraries, a reading room, and a large hall for public lectures, concerts and exhibitions. The charitable foundation was financially secure, providing the library with much better resources than those found in rate-assisted public libraries. Within the first three months of opening over a quarter of a million people had made use of the library's facilities, and 10,000 had registered as borrowers; by September the list stood at 12,000, at which point the governors decided to close it.[106]

The popularity of libraries and more formal classes suggests that at a time of profound educational deprivation elements of an autodidactic working-class culture which had been integral to radicalism survived in

East London throughout the nineteenth century. Apart from the Bishopsgate Institute, the mechanics institutes, where skilled labourers attended classes to enhance work-based knowledge and skill, and countless examples of individual passions for learning, the People's Palace, Mile End, stood out.[107] It was originally planned early in the 1880s as a centre for technical education. The inspiration is sometimes seen as Walter Besant's 1882 novel *All Sorts and Conditions of Men*, in which one of the central characters has a prophetic vision of a 'Palace of Delights' to uplift the souls of East Londoners.[108] It is more likely, however, that Besant, who was a skilled propagandist, used the novel's popularity to promote the scheme. With a bequest from the Beaumont Trust, the patronage of the Queen and numerous of the metropolitan elite, and five acres of land donated by the Drapers' Company close to an old Sephardic Jewish cemetery along the Mile End Road, work began in the summer of 1886 on what was misleadingly described as the University of the East-end. Victoria formally opened the Queen's Hall in May 1887, and laid the foundation stone for the East London Technical College.[109] Besant's efforts were recognized at the occasion when he was presented to the Queen. A year later the octagon Library, described at the time as the largest of its class in England, and the extensive technical schools were opened.

At its peak in the 1890s the Palace provided recreation and scientific and technical instruction to approximately 8,000 apprentices and workers who had proved the brightest elementary school pupils. Thereafter, competition from the London School Board drastically affected enrolment, and encouraged the Palace to raise its level of instruction. By the turn of the century it offered degrees of the University of London, and it was incorporated in 1834 as Queen Mary College, inclusion of 'East London' in the title being considered a deterrent to future recruitment.

Changes in the cultural landscape of East London during the nineteenth century were broadly underpinned by the impact of capitalist rationalization on the social composition of the workforce, and the commercialization of leisure. A radical political culture sustained by powerful artisan communities of shipwrights, tailors, silk weavers and shoemakers, and deriving strength from a profound belief in self-improvement, was dismantled as their trades and industries were exposed to provincial competition and the systematic loss of skilled work. There followed decades of relative tranquillity when, with the exception of occasional and isolated strikes, the tradition of political unrest was abandoned. Late in the 1880s it resurfaced, not as a radical movement, but in the form of industrial struggles around new unionism involving for the most part semi-skilled and unskilled sections of the working population, particularly in the docks and gasworks.

There may well be something to the argument, therefore, that the working-class culture of the East End was remade in the course of the nineteenth century, but we must caution against too convenient a distinction between an early radical culture that sustained Chartism and militant industrial struggles, and a later commercial culture that in expressing working-class sentiment represented a turn to amusement, leisure and hospitality. What is apparent is that at no point during the nineteenth century was East London the desolate and threatening cultural landscape described in the sensational images conjured up by the myth of outcast London.

By the end of the century the cultural boundaries of East London were redrawn as the population, seeking to escape overcrowding or driven out by clearance schemes, began to migrate eastwards beyond the River Lea. Into the spaces vacated moved another migrant population. Jews fleeing persecution in Eastern Europe found refuge in Whitechapel and its neighbourhoods, which thus became the centre of a rather enclosed and defensive culture sustained by sweated trades, but one nonetheless which possessed extraordinary vitality and richness. These matters are the subject of the next chapter.

CHAPTER 8

Migrants and Sweaters, 1860–1914

I N THE second half of the nineteenth century the demise of staple
industries, combined with cyclical depressions, forced large numbers
of workers on to the casual labour market in East London, creating a
vast reservoir of people prepared to take almost any job on offer. Many
found their way into one of the sweated trades, which were weathering the
storms from provincial and foreign competition, in part because of the
abundant supplies of cheap labour they could exploit. So evident was this
shift that perspectives of the East London economy in this period were
dominated by images of tailoring, footwear and furniture, popularly
understood to be at the core of the sweating system. While these arguments
have weight, they tell only part of a more complicated story.

The so-called sweated trades, however, had a longer history. Structural
changes promoted by capitalist rationalization in the early decades of the
century had created small workshops in which groups of itinerant craftsmen
and women worked long hours on discrete tasks for meagre rates of pay to
produce for a market increasingly attracted to cheaper, mass-produced
commodities. These processes were intensified by the limited introduction
of mechanization and the collapse of staple industries. In the first of a
series of important inquiries into the sweating system of East London, John
Burnett carefully described the changes which had taken place. Defining
the system as one in which subcontractors (sweaters) employed people to
work in small workshops or houses to complete a contract, he observed
that the scale of the operation varied; while the vast majority of workshops
held fewer than twenty workers, some existed with up to one hundred, at
which point they approximated to a factory system with superior conditions of employment.[1]

Burnett's inquiry presaged a wave of official anxiety about the sweating
system and its effects on the poor conditions of work endured by its labour
force. Given that these conditions were no worse than those experienced

by the bulk of casual labour for most of the century, and sweated trades provided employment for less than a fifth of the total workforce, this concern seemed misplaced – except that sweating was inexorably linked to Jewish immigration, and the problems it created for indigenous labourers.

A tenantless factory

By all accounts Samuel Gurney was a shrewd but benevolent man. Born into a Quaker banking family of Norwich, he began work at fourteen in the counting house of his brother-in-law Joseph Fry. Wealth acquired from the family firm and his father-in-law enabled him in 1807 to join and assume control of a City banking business recently founded by Thomas Richardson and John Overend. Exploiting the niche market of buying and selling bills of exchange at a discount, the firm of Overend, Gurney & Co. expanded rapidly to become the greatest discounting house in the world. Much of its success depended upon an unimpeachable reputation which derived largely from the steadying influence of Samuel and his involvement in a wide range of philanthropic concerns. After his death in 1856, the firm decided to consolidate its portfolio by undertaking investments in a wide range of activities, including shipbuilding, grain, ironware and railways, many of which proved risky. By 1861 Overend Gurney was in crisis. Strategies for recovery were ill-judged and ineffectual; the final act was to convert to a limited-liability company in 1865, but by then the firm was bankrupt, a fact that the directors had conveniently failed to mention in the prospectus, and for which they were later put on trial. An independent committee appointed to scrutinize the books found the firm was rotten. No help from the City was forthcoming, and Overend Gurney collapsed in the summer of 1866.[2]

In the troubled economic climate of the 1860s bank failure was unexceptional, but Overend Gurney was a financial giant, and its fall had considerable repercussions throughout the City and in neighbouring East London. The crash brought down the Bank of London, the Consolidated Bank, the Agra and Masterman's Bank and others which had unwisely opted to deposit their reserves with Overend Gurney in the hope of higher returns. Businesses, such as that of the great contractors Samuel Morton Peto and Edward Betts, which had been responsible for much of the rail and dock development in East London, went bankrupt. The most telling casualties, however, were the London shipbuilding yards, into which Overend Gurney had poured considerable amounts of money.[3] It is tempting to see 1866 as a decisive moment in the fortunes of the

1 The first plate in William Hogarth's moral fable of 1747, *Industry and Idleness*, shows Tom Idle and Francis Goodchild at work as apprentice Spitalfields silk weavers. The master weaver hovers in the doorway ready to strike.

2 L.P. Boitard's *The Imports of Great Britain from France* shows goods being unloaded at a London wharf in 1757. The ready access of bustling crowds to valuable cargoes invited theft, while in the background stands the Tower of London and what contemporary observers accurately described as a forest of ships' masts.

3 John Wilkes is pulled into the City by enthusiastic supporters after his election victory at Brentford in 1768.

4 A group of dock labourers awaiting the call to work, 1855. By this time, the use of casual labour was widespread, promoting anxieties about an improvident and degraded workforce.

5 A depiction of an opium den, *c*. 1880; through popular writings the opium den had come to represent the symbolic site of a racially degenerate Chinese community thought to congregate around Bluegate Fields, Limehouse.

6 The Abbey Mills Pumping Station on the Northern Outfall Sewer in West Ham, built in 1868 and still standing as a lavishly ornate reminder of Joseph Bazalgette's great sewage scheme, which eradicated cholera from the lives of Londoners.

7 Petticoat Lane market derives its name from the secondhand clothes sold there from as early as the sixteenth century. Held each Sunday along Middlesex Street, it continues to attract large crowds.

8 Match girls from the Bryant and May factory who in 1888 organised a successful strike against the appalling conditions they were forced to endure.

9 The 1876 plans for the proposed East London Synagogue in Stepney Green. With its Moorish architecture it was an influential centre of Jewish life and included amongst its members the Rothschild family. It was sold in 1987, and converted into smart flats, although some of its original features remain.

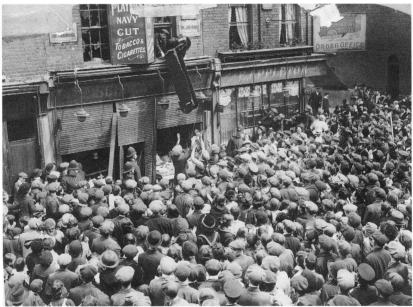

10 In the frenzied climate created by the sinking of the *Lusitania* in 1915, East London crowds gather as a shop with a German-sounding name is ransacked while the police stand by. The attacks were indiscriminate; some premises were owned by families with sons fighting in the British army.

11 The matriarchs of the Lewis and Sims families gather in Jersey Road, Plaistow to celebrate the Silver Jubilee of George V in 1935 while the men stand by.

12 George V is driven through the streets of East London in 1935 pursued by children, few of whom would have previously seen a Rolls Royce, let alone a king. Royal visits to the area were particularly evident at times of perceived social unease.

13 September 1940. Three children sit in front of what remains of a bombed building in East London. The bewilderment on their faces may have been staged, but it would not be long before East Londoners came to appreciate the full horrors of the Blitz.

14 The new sweaters? South Asian workers in the clothing trade, Brick Lane, 1978.

industries of East London, a time when heavy, capital-intensive firms were driven out of existence, leaving the way open to small-scale, labour-intensive manufacturers. It is more likely, however, that the crash accelerated trends that had been apparent since earlier in the century. Thames shipbuilding had already entered into protracted decline by 1866, and the forces of capitalist rationalization had begun to set the seal on the area's industrial development by encouraging small workshops employing poorly paid, semi-skilled workforces to produce finished goods for a growing consumer market (Chapter 4).

Local shipbuilders were therefore amongst the first to experience the full force of the crisis. Although the advent of iron and steam placed many yards at a disadvantage compared with those of the north, the Crimean and American Civil Wars had swelled their order books, and Overend Gurney had injected large amounts of capital which had temporarily headed off the inevitable decline. By 1866, however, Thames shipbuilding was in a parlous state; surviving on speculative orders, it could do nothing to withstand the crash, and sank into a deep recession from which it never recovered. For a contemporary observer it marked the end of a glorious tradition:

[A] mournful scene of desolation greets a visitor to the once famous yards of Green, Wigram, Somes, Young ... the great works and factories at Millwall, once occupied by Scott Russell, are dismantled and closed, the machinery sold, the factory tenantless, and the building yard – the birthplace of the *Great Eastern* – a grass-grown waste. The adjoining yards of Mare & Co., and The London Engineering Co., are in the same conditions as Scott Russell's yard ... At the Thames Ironworks ... I saw the double screw monitor *Magdala* and two casement ironclads for the Sultan of Turkey, but not one merchant steamer ... this establishment like those higher up the river, seems to be doomed. The prosperity of London as a shipbuilding port is at an end, and no one here looks for a revival of the business.[4]

The human costs were severe. In a worsening climate, 27,000 shipbuilding workers were unemployed at the end of November 1866; by January it was estimated that in Poplar alone 30,000 of them were receiving relief. Other industries fared no better. Building and railway construction, which had enjoyed a period of unprecedented expansion, came to a sudden halt, throwing out of work the large workforces which had been taken on.[5]

Silk weaving and the docks may not have been affected directly by the financial crisis but here too were staple industries of East London which had origins traceable to a pre-industrial era and were undergoing protracted decline. Mid-century, the contraction of silk weaving had greatly reduced the number of local weavers, but then any hope of a revival was dashed by the 1860 Cobden Treaty, which effectively opened up the market to foreign – in particular, French – competition. Whereas previously French rivalry was feared because of the finer workmanship of their weavers, now it seemed that the English were equally, if not more, skilled but refused to accept the low wages for which the French were prepared to work. By the late 1880s the number of weavers had fallen to 1,260. They remained a 'capable and industrious people' with the 'natural good taste characteristic of the French Huguenot', but this was an ageing population working on borrowed time.[6]

From the moment when the dock companies lost the privileges of monopoly control over the movement of foreign trade their fortunes deteriorated (Chapter 4). The companies found to their cost that despite increased trade the competition for lucrative income from dutiable goods requiring bonded accommodation was subject to intense competition; put simply, there were too many warehouses chasing too few goods, particularly after completion of the technologically advanced Victoria Dock in 1855 and the Millwall Dock in 1868. After 1870 further losses to trade led to significant falls in profits. A direct route was opened to the continent, thereby strengthening foreign competition. Goods destined for Europe which had formerly been unloaded into dockside warehouses were now transferred straight from ocean-going vessels into continental boats. And the construction of the Albert Dock in 1880 and Tilbury Dock in 1886 further depleted the tonnage of cargoes landed upriver. In the decade 1877–87 tonnages unloaded in all the London docks fell from 2,171,732 to 1,598,146; of the individual docks, only St Katharine's experienced an increase.[7] In order to maintain dividends, the companies imposed economies by taking on fewer labourers for more irregular hours.[8] Beatrice Potter estimated that in Tower Hamlets only 10,000 casual labourers were employed, principally in the docks, and 1,000 permanent labourers who, with steady income, chose to live at some distance from the docks in the outlying districts of Hackney and West Ham.[9] Industries dependent upon the London docks were necessarily affected not only by this decline but also by cheaper technology. Sack making and cooperage, she observed, were virtually obsolete; sugar was now handled in bags rather than casks, and sacks were provided by the massive jute mills of Dundee.[10]

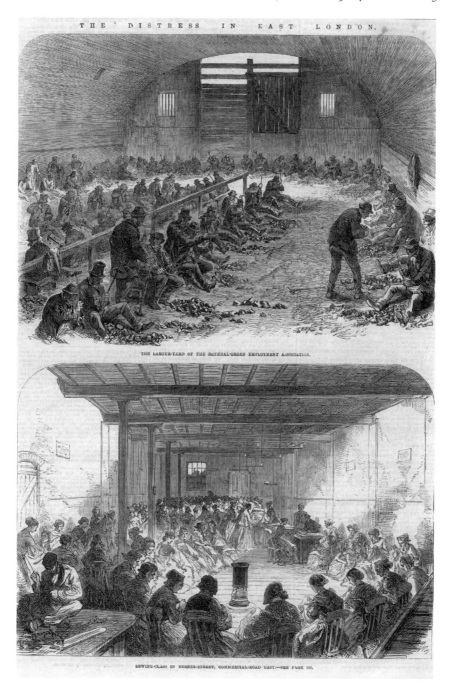

THE DISTRESS IN EAST LONDON.

THE LABOUR-YARD OF THE BETHNAL-GREEN EMPLOYMENT ASSOCIATION.

SEWING-CLASS IN BERNER-STREET, COMMERCIAL-ROAD EAST.—SEE PAGE 101.

Distress in Bethnal Green, 1868: the sort of work and conditions offered to East Londoners seeking relief from distress.

What else can I do?

It was against this background that the sweating system took a stranglehold of important sections of the economy of East London. In one form or another, this system had existed for over fifty years, for it offered obvious advantages, particularly for tailoring. Initially, the subcontractor was spared the expense of renting workshop accommodation, and relieved of the responsibilities of constantly supervising the workforce, while the workers could enjoy a degree of control over the work undertaken and performed. The increase of cheap labour, the introduction of machinery and the growing importance of cheaper, ready-made clothing transformed the situation. The demand for cheap clothes forced out many of the old-fashioned tailors, to be replaced by a range of workers undertaking specific tasks defined by a rigid division of labour. Since the necessary skills could easily be acquired, the labour market became flooded with unskilled male and female workers seeking entry into the trade, many of whom were taken on by sweaters. This process was hastened by the introduction of the sewing machine and the band-saw, which enabled the skilled tasks of sewing and cutting to be taken on by workers with little training, and of the small hand-held spokeshave in shoemaking, which prepared parts usually cut by a skilled knifer.

Contemporary observers considered sweated trades an anachronism, a troublesome survivor of a pre-industrial age which in time would be super-seded by the forward march of the more progressive factory system.[11] This particular narrative of industrialization helps to explain why the industrial landscape of nineteenth-century East London was seen to be distinct and peculiar. In certain important respects, however, this is a misleading picture. The fact that small workshops used relatively primitive technology, and employed labour in small units under harsh conditions, does not mean that they were backward. On the contrary, such workshops not only survived but prospered because they were innovative responses to high rents, an abundance of cheap labour and fluctuating demands. Put simply, workshop production was a more efficient alternative to factory organization.[12] Measured by output per person, London's clothing industry was the largest and most efficient of all the regional centres, and no less than forty-five per cent more than that of Leeds – the next largest centre – where factory production prevailed. This was due partly to the sheer exploitation of workshop labour, but workshops were also much better suited to coping with rapid and unpredictable shifts in demand. Low-capital investment in expensive machinery, combined with a workforce possessing discrete but finely tuned skills in the production process, provided workshops with the flexibility to switch lines of production at short notice and with minimum disruption.

Changes in consumer demand had underpinned the rise of the sweating system. In the second half of the nineteenth century large populations of male urban workers enjoyed real increases in disposable income, and could as a result afford inexpensive clothing as a preferable alternative to bespoke garments which over time had passed from hand to hand, gradually filtering down through the social ranks. Working-class women also found new, fashionable outfits within their reach. The development of a mass market for footwear similarly provided the working-class consumer with access to a wide range of products. And yet it was not merely a question of demand; without the ability of the sweating system to supply such clothing cheaply the consumer revolution would not have happened.

In the troubled decade of the 1880s, when recession forced many on to the casual labour market, public attention was drawn to the sweating system as the source of every hardship and social malaise in the lives of the working people of East London. Following the report of Burnett, the system was subject to detailed scrutiny by Charles Booth's great survey and an exhaustive investigation by a select committee of the House of Lords.[13] Although Booth submitted evidence to the select committee, he remained somewhat detached from, and sceptical of, its deliberations. While not denying the extent of serious social evils in East London, he rightly concluded that no single industrial system was to blame; rather there were many with their own particular faults. Within the clothing trade, for example, sweating occurred when wholesale manufacturers abdicated their responsibility as employers by issuing a contract to a middleman who hired people to do the work. Such subcontracts were most often to be found in shoemaking, where several distinct processes of manufacture were involved.[14] Although sweated industries took different forms, they all operated out of an imperative to minimize costs by abusing the contract system, and in so doing further oppressed the lives of the poor and vulnerable. Rather unhelpfully, Arnold White (about whom, more later) went as far as to say that sweating described any system of labour which ground the faces of the poor.[15]

The sweated industries of East London were normally identified as tailoring, shoemaking and furniture manufacture; Booth's arguments suggest that this focus was too narrow. Many other industries combined long working hours in dangerous and unsanitary conditions with poor wages. Important evidence submitted to the select committee by Ben Tillett, secretary of the Dock Labourers' Union, indicated that in all essentials the docks operated a sweated system.[16] Sixteen years previously the

DISTRESS IN THE EAST OF LONDON: THE SPITALFIELDS SOUP KITCHEN.—SEE PAGE 218.

Spitalfields soup kitchen, c. 1870. The first soup kitchen was opened in Spitalfields in the late eighteenth century. This picture conveys well the industrial scale of the production necessary.

dock companies determined to introduce contract labour as a means of avoiding responsibilities imposed by the Employers' Liability Act, and simultaneously reduce their overheads. The consequences had been dramatic. Most of the work now undertaken was by contract, a process facilitated by the great variety of tasks performed. Under this system, for example, the landing of goods, warehousing, loading of barges, and the subsequent weighing, marking, sampling and delivery of goods were all done by different classes of workmen under different contracts. Thus dock companies sublet the loading and unloading of ships to an army of subcontractors, many of whom sublet further. In the majority of cases, such subletting went through three hands, but often as many as seven were involved. At each stage the rate was reduced, so that while the principal contractor might, for example, be awarded 1s 8d per hour the last in the chain – the poor unfortunate who actually did the manual work – earned no more than 4d. This was a system made possible by the vast pool of casual labour on which the docks, like other sweated industries, could draw; indeed, one of the defining features of the East London economy as a whole was an inter-dependency based on the ready exchange of casual labour. As Tillett observed, in the winter months large numbers of men in the building, tailoring and bootmaking trades, costermongers and mechanics swelled the ranks at the dock gates, prepared to accept anything on offer.

As in other industries the contract system had led to a sharp deteriora-tion in the conditions of dock labourers. The contract prices had fallen by more than half since they were first introduced, and while this had not been accompanied by a corresponding decrease in hourly rates of pay, the amount of work gained by an ordinary dock labourer had plunged from an average of ten months per year to less than five. The increasing use of machinery had largely been responsible for this. Hydraulic lifting gear for unloading had replaced the manual labour of large numbers of dock-workers; a vessel of 5,000 tons could now be discharged in less time than one of 500 tons twenty years earlier. Overall, the growing pool of casual labour, seasonality and shorter, more irregular employment had forced approximately 100,000 to depend in part upon dock work in East London.

The system of casual labour also shaped female employment in late-nineteenth-century East London. Domestic service still provided most jobs for the single women who dominated the female labour force; for the wives of casual labourers, however, many of whom were compelled to work in order to supplement the family income, sweated trades, particu-larly those based on home work, provided the only opportunities.[17] Thus many wives continued to labour long and hard with their children to manufacture a range of cheap household items, including matchboxes, brushes, artificial flowers and sacks. In return for this, they received piti-fully low incomes. It was reported at the Sweated Industry Exhibition of 1906, for example, that matchbox makers were paid tuppence farthing (approximately 1p) per gross, the same as they had received over forty years earlier.

Sweating workshops could be found in provincial centres of manufac-ture such as Leeds, Leicester and Northampton where they existed alongside larger factories, but in East London small workshops were prevalent. They may have been a rational and innovative response to market conditions, but the human costs were high, for this was also an exploitative and abusive system. Witnesses to the House of Lords Select Committee on Sweating testified that since Public Health and Factory Regulation Acts governing work conditions, including hours, ventilation and sanitation, could be ignored, either because strict enforcement was impossible or because they did not apply to domestic spaces, in which much of the work was done, the statutory eight-hour day with time for meals rarely obtained. Work started at 6am; men normally worked sixteen hours and women fourteen, with the hour for dinner and half-hour for tea deducted. Occasionally when large contracts had to be completed quickly, men were required to work thirty-six-hour shifts.[18] For a normal week's labour a quick worker made an average of 15s, a slow one 12s – hardly enough to maintain a large family. So claimed Samuel Wildman, a boot finisher who had migrated to East London ten years previously, when the same work could command wages of at least 25s.[19] Similar stories of long hours and falling wages were recounted by a host of other witnesses.[20]

The introduction of machinery impacted on earnings in complex ways. The sewing machine, for example, undercut the role of many skilled workers, while workshops offered some of the unskilled an opportunity to acquire a measure of skill and more regular employment.[21] The ready acquisition of requisite skills even enabled many without the practical experience of a skilled worker to become masters in their own right, although they remained forever vulnerable to downturns in demand.

Burnett estimated that two thousand sweaters operated in East London; of these, two thirds were unknown to the authorities and could therefore also disregard factory and workshop regulations, and continued to employ people in the worst possible conditions.[22] A graphic account of what was seen to be a typical workshop, with all of the familiar racial undertones, was submitted by Herbert Evans, an assistant inspector of factories, to the Royal Commission on Alien Immigration:

> The taskmaster and sweater is an unprincipled, loathsome individual, whose tyrannical methods and disposition are only equalled by his complete ignorance and open defiance of everything that is moral and humane. He is usually found in a basement or garret, concealed from the outside world altogether. His workshop reeks with foul smells; the atmosphere is loaded with human vitiation; the combustion from burning refuse and the emission of sickly fumes from cheap oil lamps and other implements of work, and from the process of manufacture, together with the absence of natural light, make this particular class of workshop a positive danger to the community. Here the alien is imprisoned day and night, and kept at work in a semi-nude state for a starvation allowance. Family and all sleep in the same room. A few women are employed. The effect of this is found in the anaemic and lifeless state of the workers.[23]

In 'The Tailor', the poet Joseph Leftwich described vividly the toll taken on the human mind and, ultimately, life by the sweating system:

> Have you ever heard that a tailor was ill?
> I mean a real tailor, who stitches until
> He feels that the needle goes right through his head
> And he crawls with his stitching away to his bed.
>
> No, indeed not, for the tailor sits cross-legged like a Turk,
> And he stitches, until he drops dead at his work.[24]

Unenviable though the reputation of the sweater was, many of the smaller ones were victims of the same exploitative system. The fifty-six-year-old Isaac Wolf had a workshop of about ten foot square at Brunswick Street, Whitechapel. When interviewed he was busy with an order of sleeved waistcoats for railway porters on which he worked together with his daughter, who was paid 4s per week, and two male machinists earning 3s daily. Burnett reckoned on this basis that his earnings were 'very small indeed'. 'What else can I do?' asked Wolf plaintively in broken English. 'I'm a poor broken-down old man, nobody else will employ me.'[25] Next door Nathan Rees was working on an order for postmen's tunics from 7am to 10pm, with a presser who earned 4s 6d daily and a machinist earning 5s. His weekly earnings were approximately 10s 9d. And Charles Solomon, a master boot finisher, employed three men during busy periods for up to eighteen hours a day. This was made possible by deskilling, brought about by the introduction of the spokeshave some sixteen years earlier, but his work conditions had not improved; he now worked the same hours, and after paying for overheads, including rent, fuel, grinding, ink and tools, earned the same as his workmen.[26]

Beatrice Potter went so far as to suggest that the sweater was a theatrical figure. He is pictured in the comic and sensational press 'sauntering about his workshop with his hands in his pockets, with a cigar in his mouth, and with the East End equivalent to an orchid in his button hole'.[27] The workshop over which he presides reeks of the smell of the thirty or forty workers huddled closely together. The real picture, she claimed, was rather less picturesque. The average master offered regular employment to fewer than ten persons in conditions which were comfortable and secure, and worked on the premises as hard as any of his employees for a precarious and uncertain livelihood.

Reliable data on those engaged in sweated trades do not exist, although we can gain a sense of perspective from the numbers identified in particular industries which appear in the censuses. The number of workers in the London clothing industry as a whole increased from 186,000 (representing 8.5 per cent of the employed population) in 1871 to 269,000 (12.4 per cent) in 1911.[28] These aggregate data, however, disguise significant variations in the fortunes and regional concentrations of dressmaking, tailoring, boot- and shoemaking and shirtmaking. Dressmaking and tailoring maintained their share of the workforce while boot- and shoemaking fell by over a half, and shirtmaking by over a third. Overall the proportion of female workers remained constant at approximately two thirds, but individual trades showed marked variations. Dressmaking remained exclusively the preserve of women, while those in tailoring increased from about a third to a half; in boot- and shoemaking the proportion remained constant at approximately a fifth, while the proportion of women in shirtmaking fell from 84 per cent to 72 per cent.[29]

The demography of clothing production changed over this period. In 1861 the highest concentrations of male workers were to be found in the west and central districts, reflecting the importance of the fashionable bespoke and City ready-made businesses. By 1891 the east possessed by far the highest number and proportion of male workers in the clothing, wood and furniture, and boot and shoe trades; similarly, while the number of female workers was highest in all but clothing, even here the proportion was the highest in London.[30] We can assume that the large majority of these workers in East London were employed in sweated workshops, and so estimate roughly the aggregate numbers. In 1861, there were approximately 25,000 male and 26,000 female workers in East London; by 1891 the numbers had risen to 43,000 and 35,000 respectively. To put these figures in perspective, in 1891 the total engaged in sweated trades in East London was 15 per cent of all those employed.

The question therefore arises: if the numbers in sweated trades comprised less than a sixth of the workforce, why was such extraordinary attention devoted to the problem in the 1880s? Sweating had attracted the indignation of earlier social commentators. Mayhew devoted the majority of his *Morning Chronicle* letters to sweated labourers; Christian socialists, such as Charles Kingsley in his novel *Alton Locke*, expressed outrage at the conditions of sweated labourers; and Thomas Hood's poem 'Song of the Shirt' created a sensation when printed in the 1843 Christmas edition of *Punch*. The number of trades affected by sweating had increased, particularly in the last quarter of the century, and this intensified the concern with the social evils that were seen to be associated with the system, but what becomes clear from the various inquiries which were conducted in the 1880s is an overriding interest in Jewish immigration, the perceived urgency of which underpinned the deliberations of all the investigations undertaken.

Problems of a great city

The origins of sweated trades predated the large waves of Jewish migration and settlement in East London, and so there was nothing intrinsically Jewish about the system. And while the majority of Jews who migrated in the latter stages of the century found such work, they tended to be concentrated in particular trades, notably clothing; they never dominated sweated trades as a whole. Little in the literature of the time suggested this was the case. Burnett's report on sweated trades, for example, opens with a brief account of the subdivision of labour before moving on to what he considers the crucial issue:

> The learning of any one of these branches is, naturally, so much easier than the acquisition of the whole trade that immense numbers of people of both sexes and of all ages have rushed into the cheap tailoring trade as the readiest means of finding employment. The result of this entry into the trade has been an enormously overcrowded labour market, and a consequently fierce competition among the workers themselves with all the attendant evils of such a state of things. Under any circumstances, this condition of affairs would have been fraught with misery for most of those engaged in such work, but matters have been rendered infinitely worse to the native workers during the last few years by an enormous influx of pauper foreigners from other European nations. These aliens have been chiefly German and Russian Jews, and there can be no doubt that the result has been to flood the labour market of East London with cheap labour to such an extent as to reduce thousands of native workers to the verge of destitution.[31]

Thousands of Jews arrive here in a state of pauperism, he proceeds, unable to speak English and with no knowledge of a trade. This 'patient submissive race' is thus forced to take work at lower rates of pay than 'native' workers, degrading all those employed in the industry. A large proportion of the Jews who seek work are female, many of whom are driven on to the streets by the continued influx of others, thereby presenting the Jewish authorities with a problem previously unknown within the community.

Beatrice Potter may have helped to debunk popular images of the East London sweater, but her study of home work in the tailoring trade bemoaned the increasing presence of Jewish workers attendant on the rise of the wholesale houses. The inadequate accommodation, long hours of work and irregular employment of home work had been wrought into a system by the Jews, many of whom were skilled and well paid, and turned out superior-quality clothes by their standards, but similar in most respects to the work of inferior English tailors. However, eighty per cent of East London trade, she claimed, was produced in sweated workshops where small Jewish masters were able to gain control, not through merit but rather the play of racial characteristics:

> [T]wo circumstances tend to an indefinite multiplication of small masters in the Jewish coat trade, competing vigorously with each other, not only for the work of the shops, but for the services of the most skilled hands: the ease with which a man becomes master, coupled with the strongest impelling motive of the Jewish race – the love of *profit* as distinct from other form [sic] of money-earning.[32]

Such endeavour enabled Jewish contractors and workers to ascend the social scale. Were they alone the object of inquiry, none would be needed. The real victims, Potter concluded, were the 'mongrel' population which surrounded the Jewish community, the worthless who grasped at the jobs left by Jews, earning a pittance which even a recent migrant would have despised in the hope of better prospects.

A concern with Jewish settlement dominated the first report of the Lords' inquiry into the London trades. The first witness heard was Morris Stephany, Secretary to the Jewish Board of Guardians, and the majority who followed professed a knowledge of the Jewish community. What emerges from the evidence is a familiar picture of poor Jewish migrants from Russia, Poland and Germany attracted to East London by the promise of work. Destitute, they approached relatives, synagogues and finally the Board of Guardians for assistance. Accustomed to living in primitive accommodation, witnesses testified, the migrants had few of the decencies of domestic life such as cleanliness, though they retained for the most part a strong sense of morality. Their only employment was to be found in the sweated trades, in particular clothing, which they now dominated. Because of the daily struggle to survive, powerful antagonisms had grown between established workers and 'greeners', that is, recent migrants who belonged to no union and were willing to undercut work rates and take on work during times of strikes.

Arnold White, a radical who had become a vigorous campaigner against immigration, was an influential witness. He displayed a detailed knowledge of the sweating system, and was vociferous in its condemnation. His evidence was framed, however, by the sorts of crude eugenicist arguments which had been elaborated in his popular book *The Problems of a Great City*.[33] Masters, he claimed, were compelled to employ more men than they wished and at lower wages by the introduction of machinery which had enabled greeners to learn the necessary skills with great facility.[34] This influx of pauper labour, the great increase of which after 1880 coincided with an intensification of the evils of the sweating system, had inflicted a disproportionate amount of harm on native workers by driving down their conditions of work. Poor foreigners were therefore responsible for the sweating system because they encouraged masters to impose longer hours and lower wages; and so, without any further measure, a ban on further immigration would put an end to it. We owe justice and humanity to our own people, he concluded, before foreigners, no matter how industrious or intelligent they are, or how desperate the circumstances which forced them to leave their homes in the first instance.

The fragility of White's arguments was later exposed when he was forced to admit that sweating was also practised by Christians on Christians, but he had made a compelling case which found popular support, even within the established Jewish community.[35] Many of the Jewish witnesses, either those engaged in the trades or those associated with institutions such as the Jewish Board of Guardians, may have disputed the detail – the destitution of greeners on arrival, the extent of exploitation by masters, the numbers who returned having been unable to find work – but none challenged the main thrust of White's evidence or denied the desirability of restricting further immigration.[36] The Lords' committee, no doubt mindful of the complexity of the contradictory evidence submitted, refused to apportion blame, concluding its exhaustive inquiry with bland and timid recommendations to strengthen the roles of the factory inspectorate and sanitary authorities, and encourage technical education among the workforce.[37] When compared with the sensational nature of the evidence this was something of an anti-climax, and did nothing to mitigate the evils of the trade or of a rising tide of anti-semitism.

Prior to the large-scale influx of poor Jews, there had been a long history of anti-semitism directed towards the Anglo-Jewry community, in part because of the positions of wealth and power its members occupied. In the 1880s, the focus shifted to Jewish immigrants, as evidenced in the official inquiries undertaken, and, more importantly, in various publications. The principal activists were understandably committed to making their views known to a wide audience, and in doing so they articulated issues of broad concern. White's *The Problems of a Great City* proposed solutions to the immigrant threat based on eugenicist arguments, and included measures to control the fecundity of the poor, limit immigration, and promote emigration to Britain's colonies.[38] W.H. Wilkins' *The Alien Invasion* (1892) followed similar arguments in declaring that thousands of London labourers had been pauperized by the loss of their jobs, and young English women had fallen into destitution and prostitution because foreigners were willing to work for such low wages, while Major Evans-Gordon's *The Alien Immigrant* (1903) argued from first-hand experience of a tour of Russia that immigrants were not only damaging to the interests of English workers but need not have emigrated in the first place because their conditions in eastern Europe were much better than they had claimed. None of these authors was unambiguously anti-semitic. Evans-Gordon went out of his way to attack the persecutions of Jews he witnessed in Russia, and supported Zionist aspirations for a separate state of Israel.[39] White praised the beneficence of Anglo-Jews who had assimilated into English culture, and their unimpeachable loyalty to the nation. Each professed that their overwhelming concerns were with the deteriorating conditions of the English poor, and it was only in this context that immigration was raised as an issue. High levels of foreign immigration would attract their opprobrium no matter what the origins of the migrants – except, of course, that whenever they spoke of the demoralizing effects of immigration it was the Jews they had in mind.

For many members of the beleaguered working class in East London these arguments made eminent sense. 'There is no feeling against foreigners as foreigners,' said Charles Freak of the Boot and Shoemakers Union in 1890, 'only when they work against our interest by taking a reduced price.'[40] Expressing a putative solidarity with the indigenous poor of East London, trade unions up and down the country supported resolutions critical of the deleterious effects of alien immigration on the interests of their members. Union leaders, including John Burns and Ben Tillett, who had played such a decisive role in struggles around new unionism a few years previously, were amongst the most vocal.

A peculiar people

So what was the impact of Jewish immigration on East London? As we have seen, there had been a small Sephardic Jewish presence in London since the seventeenth century, but in the early decades of the nineteenth larger numbers of Ashkenazi Jews began to settle. By 1850 the London Jewish community numbered approximately 18,000, two thirds of whom resided in the eastern wards of the City or in Whitechapel, where many were engaged in the second-hand clothing trade or peddling a variety of wares. There had been a Jewish-owned fruit market at Duke's Place, Aldgate, until it was superseded by the new Covent Garden market in the 1830s, after which many Jewish hawkers made a precarious living by peddling brushes made with pig bristles imported from Poland, pencils and cheap household items.[41] Through the decline of older markets and coaching inns, and anti-semitism in other parts of London, Jewish traders were forced to congregate around Middlesex Street (or Petticoat Lane market, as it was better known), which by the 1860s became a specialist market in second-hand clothing.[42] A significant Jewish middle class managed to escape these daily struggles for survival through the wholesale import and manufacture of pencils, cigars, foreign curios, fruit, jewellery and clothing. Salmon & Gluckstein, for example, operating initially from the Whitechapel Road in 1873, became highly successful cigarette manufacturers, later founding the chain of Lyons' teahouses. Many of these families followed the example of their indigenous predecessors and moved out of East London at the first available opportunity.

This Jewish community sought assimilation and therefore tended to be anglicized. To take one important example, the Jewish Working Men's Club was established with the banker Samuel Montagu as president in 1874.[43] It occupied an old public house in Aldgate purchased by Montagu and let out free of rent for the first year. The club's success was immediate. 1,400 joined, and though many soon drifted away, leaving a regular membership of 700, this gradually increased, reaching a peak of 1,500 in 1887. It was affiliated to the national Working Men's Club and Institute Union, and, with the active and enthusiastic support of the *Jewish Chronicle*, organized an ambitious programme of activities, including lectures, debates, concerts and sporting fixtures. Over time, and paralleling the experience of other working men's clubs, the educational part of its programme declined, so that by the time the club closed in 1912, it was almost exclusively recreational.

The survival of this community of traders, labourers and manufacturers serves to remind us that the Jewish East End of the late nineteenth century was not built upon the sweating system alone, even though a large majority of Jewish settlers from the 1870s sought employment in the small sweated workshops. Through natural increases and immigration from eastern Europe the Jewish community of East London increased to 30,000 by 1882, but then swelled dramatically, largely as a result of the settlement of Russians and Russian Poles, whose numbers in London soared from approximately 9,000 in 1881 to 27,000 in 1891 and 63,000 in 1911.[44] Much of this increase is conventionally attributed to the series of pogroms waged against Jews in Russia, particularly in 1882, 1891–2 and 1903–6, when persecution coincided with higher levels of emigration, but there were deeper underlying causes of the demographic changes.[45] None of the witnesses to the Lords' Committee on sweating spoke directly of such violence; instead, stories were heard of lives rendered increasingly impossible by systematic repression. Typical was that of Mayer Feilweil, who two weeks previously had arrived in London from Odessa:

> When I came to Kieff I found my mother was turned out. Then I registered myself at one of the police agencies, and I told them that I had been sent to Kieff. Then I asked the serjeant or the chief inspector where I could go in the town, and he told me I must not live there; I said, 'Why must I not live here; I am a soldier.' He said, 'Soldiers are not worth anything in this town, you must go.' … Then I went to Radywill, where I found my mother. When I came there I found out they had turned my mother out from that place as well, so I returned to Odessa. Then I found my mother and wife there; but, as I could not support my wife, I could not live with her. When I left the army they took everything away from me, and I walked about in a ragged condition.[46]

In desperation, Feilweil's mother collected money and sent him to London, where he would not be persecuted so ruthlessly. He travelled with his brother overland, working where they could, until reaching Whitechapel, where they stayed with friends. Among other migrants, Samuel Wildman came to London because he could not make a living as a teacher in Hungary, and Solomon Rosenberg, who had settled in 1870, argued that greeners favoured the greater sense of freedom offered by London.[47] Overall, what promoted Jewish emigration from Russia in the last decades of the nineteenth century was the slow development of the agrarian economy, government restrictions and the early stages of state-managed industrialization, from which Jews were largely excluded.

Burnett's claim that the majority of the migrant population lacked knowledge of a trade was inaccurate. The very exclusion of Jews from the professions and the civil service in Russia forced them into trade and commerce, in particular tailoring, shoemaking, baking and slaughtering, which, according to a census carried out in 1897, accounted for up to 40 per cent of the Jewish population in some areas.[48] With such backgrounds, and the operation of exclusions through blatant prejudice from many East London docks, factories, shipyards and engineering plants, it comes as no surprise that 70 per cent of the migrants found employment in the sweated trades of East London, the vast majority settling in the relatively small area of Whitechapel and surrounding districts, thereby creating what at the time and ever since was described colourfully as a ghetto.[49] The degree of residential concentration was indeed remarkable. A map of East London compiled by Russell and Lewis shows graphically that a large majority of the Jewish population lived in a circle formed around Bishopsgate to the west, Bethnal Green Road to the north, the London Hospital to the east and Cable Street to the south. Practically all of the streets in this circle were occupied wholly or overwhelmingly by Jews.[50] As part of the Booth survey, Hubert Llewellyn Smith contributed a not entirely unsympathetic study of immigration in which he singled out the significance of the area:

> London is the great centre in England of the foreign resident population, and Whitechapel is the great centre of the foreign population of London. It is not the least interesting of the features that makes the Whitechapel Road the most varied and interesting in England, that amid the crowds that jostle each other on the pavement, or gather in eager groups round the flaring lights of the costermonger's barrow, the fancy shows, and the shooting salons of the great trunk artery of East London, the observant wanderer may note the high cheek-bones and thickened lips of the Russian or Polish Jew, the darker complexion and unmistakable nose of his Austrian co-religionist ...[51]

Why Whitechapel? Quite apart from its proximity to sweated trades, Whitechapel had a striking similarity to the homes left by migrants, with the same small and dirty stores, dingy workshops, exhausted, pallid faces wandering narrow streets, and Yiddish as the principal means of communication. When the fictional character Mottel Paysi arrived in East London, he found familiar food and goods in the shops, and an environment which was 'just as muddy as at home. And it smells as bad. Sometimes even worse. We were delighted with Whitechapel.'[52] Over time, Whitechapel came to occupy an almost mythical status in the long history of Jewish migration and settlement; as the poet Avram Stencl later recalled:

Pumbedita, Cordova, Cracow, Amsterdam,
Vilna, Lublin, Berditchev and Volozhin,
Your names will always be sacred,
Places where Jews have been.

And sacred is Whitechapel,
It is numbered with our Jewish towns,
Holy, holy, holy
Are your bombed stones.

If we ever have to leave Whitechapel,
As other Jewish towns we left,
Its soul will remain a part of us,
Woven into us, woof and weft.[53]

Most Jewish accommodation was not the decrepit and pestilential houses found in the worst slum areas of East London, but larger dwellings – such as those originally built by Huguenot weavers in Spitalfields – which were once respectable, but now exhibited all the signs of a decayed gentility.[54] The houses were multiply occupied by families and small workshops; rents were inflated, making the Jewish quarter a profitable enterprise for the landlords.

Jewish tailors, c. 1900. A picture which contrasts somewhat with images of sweated labour thought to be typical of the clothing industry.

Whitechapel thus became one of the most densely occupied areas in London, raising in the minds of the medical profession many of the old anxieties about disease and contagion. In 1884 the foremost medical journal, the *Lancet*, commissioned a study of what it described as a 'Polish colony of Jew Tailors' in Whitechapel, visiting large numbers of their homes and workshops.[55] Against a background of declining population in Whitechapel as a whole, the parish of Christ Church, Spitalfields, where most Jews resided, had seen an increase. Since no houses had been built to accommodate them (indeed, some houses had recently been demolished), serious problems of overcrowding in particular streets ensued. Shepherd's Buildings, for example, a large block of thirty-nine tenements erected three years earlier, had 150 occupants. Some of the rooms were so dark that candles were needed, even in the middle of the day. In Booth Street was a similar block with 230 rooms occupied by 700; here toilets were so neglected they were removed to the outside yard, a move that prompted the inhabitants to throw the soil out of the window rather than descend the stairs and brave the cold. Workshops were found generally to be grossly overcrowded, ill-ventilated and -lit, and unsanitary. Although the conditions described were little different from those in other slum areas of East London, the authors could hardly resist the temptation to link the existence of such conditions to race. The report concluded that 'all the difficulties attached to the question of the housing of the poor are aggravated by the special habits of this peculiar people'. Modest though the study was, and familiar though its details were to become with the inquiries into the sweating system and immigration, it was the first to reveal the desperate conditions in which members of the Jewish community lived.[56]

Whitechapel also provided a defensible space within an alien and often hostile environment in which Jewish culture and an important sense of collective identity could be sustained. This created an isolation from the host community which was viewed unfavourably by contemporary observers. In a survey of the Jewish community conducted under the auspices of Toynbee Hall, C. Russell advised that the Jewish community was a state within a state, and 'so long as the Jews remain an isolated and peculiar people, self centred in their organisation, and fundamentally alien in their ideas and aims, the rapid growth of their community can hardly be regarded with complete satisfaction'.[57] A large variety of institutions were established which, although never immune to the authority of British law and custom, reinforced this sense of isolation. Two played a key role in the political and social affairs of the community. The Jewish Board of Deputies, founded in 1760 and recognized by the British state as a body representative of all Jews in England, administered religious law within the Jewish community. Under the auspices of the Chief Rabbi, it had the power to arbitrate in family quarrels and labour disputes, thereby avoiding the shameful spectacle of Jews contesting Jews in English courts of law, and to register marriages.[58] The Jewish Board of Guardians, on the other hand, originally established as a voluntary institution in 1859 to provide relief to destitute Jews in London along the lines of, but completely independent from, its English counterpart, had by the end of the century assumed a much wider responsibility. It lent sewing machines to tailors and provided apprenticeships in a large variety of trades, offered personal loans without interest, organized work rooms in which girls were taught the skills of dressmaking, assisted persons wishing to emigrate to the USA or British colonies, improved the sanitary condition of poor Jews by putting moral pressure on the landlords, and arranged for women to visit the homes of the poor offering advice and support wherever necessary, expenditure on which greatly exceeded the amounts given in direct relief.[59]

For the majority of the Jewish community synagogues and chevras were the principal sites of cultural practice. Organized along ethnic lines, they tended to reflect and sustain divisions within the community. The first synagogue was built at Duke's Place in the City around 1690, followed soon after by the earliest remaining synagogue, Bevis Marks in Houndsditch, built in 1701 for the Spanish and Portuguese Sephardic community, and the Dutch Ashkenazim synagogue in Sandy's Row, first opened as a chapel in 1766 and becoming a synagogue in 1854. These had large congregations and constituted orthodoxy within the Jewish community. The immigration of eastern European Jews in the second half of the nineteenth century, however, led to a considerable increase in smaller synagogues. By the end of the century no fewer than twenty-seven of the thirty-one small synagogues brought together within the London Federation of Synagogues were located in East London, ranging in size from Sandys Row Synagogue, with a membership of 318, to Konin Synagogue, Spitalfields, with a membership of 45.[60] These small synagogues, or chevras, were at the very core of the poorer Jewish communities. Many were of temporary construction; hidden in small alleys or back yards, and named after the places in Russia or Poland from which their members had originated, they were not merely places of worship but a means of recreating a sense of a shared experience among exiled communities. Many had benefit clubs for times of death and sickness, and ran sessions for the study of the sacred books of the Talmud. Beatrice Potter movingly relates a visit to a chevra in a long wooden building, the entrance to which was littered with household debris. During the service she imagines herself in a 'far-off Eastern land', and then as worship ends steps out, 'stifled by the heat and dazed by the strange contrast of the old-world memories of a majestic religion and the squalid vulgarity of an East End slum'.[61]

Few institutions exerted as much influence on the Jewish community as the friendly societies, which with a steady membership of 15,000 at the turn of the century far exceeded the numerical strength and stability of trades unions. Although the origins of the societies were traceable to Huguenot settlers, they had emerged during the nineteenth century as an integral part of indigenous English working-class life. In providing a degree of financial security at times of sickness, distress or death on better terms than those offered by insurance companies, and a congenial social environment built around conviviality, friendship and collective identity, reinforced by ritual and regalia, the societies had an obvious appeal to Jewish immigrants, and many of the Grand Masters held high status within the broader community. The first and best known was the Order Achei Brith, founded in 1888 with a membership of 2,800 distributed across thirty lodges, and a capital fund of over £7,000, followed by the Grand Order of Israel, the intriguingly titled Hebrew Order of Druids, and the Ancient Order of Maccabæans which was devoted to the cause of Zionism. Some societies bore the names of Russian and Polish towns from which their founders and many of their members came. Of these the Cracow Jewish Friendly Society, with a membership of 379, was the most significant, but there were lesser ones named after Warsaw, Plotsk, Radom and Witebsk.[62]

Voluntary Jewish schools were established early on to provide education for the fortunate few. With origins as a Talmud Torah of the Bevis Marks synagogue in the eighteenth century, dedicated to the study of Jewish religious law, the Jewish Free School moved in 1822 to Bell Lane, Spitalfields, where it flourished. Under the benign influence of the Rothschild family, which appeared to regard the school as its own charity, it successfully fused elements of Judaism with anglicized elementary education. After the 1870 Education Act all teachers in the school were certificated, and although classes were large, requiring rote learning, the quality of education produced some outstanding scholars, including Israel Zangwill and Selig Brodetsky. At the end of the nineteenth century over 4,000 pupils were on the rolls, making it the largest Jewish school in Europe. Among smaller schools were the Spanish and Portuguese School, with 350 pupils, and the Stepney Jewish School by the Green, with 400, founded in 1863 by the Adler family in an attempt to attract Jews away from Whitechapel. After 1870, however, with the increased control of the state over schooling, hard distinctions between Jewish and state schools tended to disappear; instead, the sixteen state schools in the Whitechapel area at the end of the century were effectively controlled by members of the Jewish community and provided an anglicized Jewish education.[63] Dismayed by the trend towards secular education, many parents sought religious education for their children elsewhere. Classes sprang up to cater to their needs, in particular, khadorim, most of which were held in sparse, unsanitary rooms in private homes. They offered roughly a dozen pupils religious education for a few hours per week for a fee of between 6d and 1s 6d; by 1891, 250 khadorim operated in East London. This was paralleled by a dramatic growth in the Talmud Torah, even though constrained by a shortage of funds and opposition from Anglo-Jewish reformers.[64]

In many respects similar to the refugee Huguenots of a hundred years earlier, the Jewish community brought a powerful cultural heritage which blossomed on the streets of East London. Take, for example, its literary culture, which may have been erratic and diffuse, but possessed a seemingly unbounded energy. Despite the pioneering work of Lloyd Gartner over fifty years ago, we understand little of the significance of this literature and how it impacted on Jewish identity and cohesion. In all of its manifestations, this was a hybrid literature. European Judaism in the nineteenth century nurtured new generations of writers who, whether in Hebrew or Yiddish, created a distinctly Western literature by borrowing from different genres and expanding the range of subjects beyond the religious. In so doing, it held up a mirror to Jewish life and sought to develop a modern, enlightened society.[65] The London-based *Jewish Chronicle*, first published in 1841, appeared in English and remained the most important expression of the Anglo-Jewish community nationally. It had limited relevance, however, for those Jewish communities who could speak no English or thought it a compromise too far.

Here we need to be sensitive to the profound divisions which existed, in particular between Hebrew- and Yiddish-speaking sections. The blossoming of Hebrew literature owed nothing to the Jewish community in England. Largely through the enterprise of Isaac Suwalsky working out of his little flat in Whitechapel, *HaYehudi* (The Jew) appeared weekly from 1897 until his death in 1913, but it lacked the milieu necessary to maintain circulation and quality – the Hebrew-speaking audience was minute, and even within that there was resistance to use of a secular Hebrew. Fiction suffered the same fate. Also working in isolation, Joseph Brenner printed and distributed *HaMe'orer* (The Awakener) during 1904–8 as a personal vehicle for his plays and short stories, which, while often revolutionary in tone, were located spiritually in Jewish Eastern Europe. Even Ahad HaAm, one of the pre-eminent Hebrew scholars, was unable to sustain the creative brilliance of his time in Odessa during the fifteen years he spent in London.

A part of humanity

Similar problems beset Yiddish culture borne by the new wave of immigration from Eastern Europe. It possessed a sense of inferiority, nurtured in part by Hebrew speakers who considered it – and the community from which it sprang – incapable of expressing elevated thought, and its writers struggled in vain to find receptive audiences. Their only success was in the emergent currents of Jewish socialism and anarchism, which cared little for Hebraic tradition but were attracted to translations of contemporary Western literature. The immigrant community was sizable enough to sustain a Yiddish newspaper press. Before 1890 at least five Yiddish newspapers were launched in London; none survived a year, but by the turn of the century a variety of papers, from the socialist *Poilishe Yidl* to the sensational *Idisher Telefon* and religiously orthodox *HaZofeh*, managed a degree of stability.

Although few of the Jews migrating to London inherited traditions of organized workplace struggle, among their number were intellectuals whose activities had formed the bedrock of the underground resistance to Tsarist persecution. The experience of wage labour in London, and frustrated hopes of a better life, enticed many of the new migrants to turn to the promise of social revolution, anarchism and trades unionism.[66] Without the tradition of struggle or intellectual inquiry that had shaped the formation of the English working class, and in the face of deep hostility from the indigenous rank and file who considered Jewish workers unskilled, uneducated and foreign, there was little hope of organizing campaigns on common platforms; instead, Jewish trades unions and political organizations in the first decades remained independent and distinct. The first stirrings of Jewish political unrest occurred in London during the 1870s, when Lewis Smith, a refugee who had fought in the Paris Commune of 1871, formed a short-lived union of Lithuanian Tailors, and Aaron Lieberman, who had been a leading figure in the revolutionary circles of Vilna before fleeing from the Russian police, made his way to Whitechapel, where he immersed himself in socialist agitation. In 1876 he and nine others founded the Agudah Hasozialistim Chaverim (Jewish Socialist Union). Lieberman was appointed secretary and drafted its manifesto in both Hebrew and Yiddish; its intellectual underpinnings in European socialism were evident:

The system, everywhere, is no more than oppression and injustice; the capitalists, the rulers and their satellites, have usurped all men's rights for their own profit and through the power of money have made workers their slaves. As long as there is private ownership, economic misery will not cease. As long as men are divided into nations and classes, there will be no peace between them. And as long as the clergy hold dominion over their emotions, there will be religious strife ... While we Jews are a part of humanity, we cannot achieve personal liberation except through that of all men. The emancipation of all mankind from oppression and slavery can only be brought about by the workers themselves, in their united efforts to wage war against their exploiters; first to destroy the existing order and then to replace it by workers' control, justice, freedom and the brotherhood of man.[67]

The Union held weekly meetings, attended by up to forty people, at which a range of international issues were discussed, organized public meetings and propaganda in order to expose the sufferings of Jewish workers, published a socialist journal, *HaEmet*, and made rather optimistic overtures to other bodies of workers in pursuit of united action. Doctrinal differences weakened the Union, however, so that when it faced the inevitable backlash from within sections of the Jewish community its fate was sealed. Meetings were disrupted by members of the orthodox community who accused the socialists of being missionaries intent on converting Jews; in this they had full support from the *Jewish Chronicle*.[68] Opposition to Lieberman's leadership escalated; in December 1876, he suddenly departed for Germany, and the Union collapsed. It had lasted less than a year.[69]

And yet the foundations of a radical Jewish culture had been laid – even if it took time to come to fruition. Eight years followed the demise of the Union before the first Yiddish socialist periodical appeared. Published weekly from a small office in Whitechapel, the *Poilishe Yidl* (The Little Polish Jew) – soon changed to *Die Tsukunft* (The Future) – was the child of Morris Winchevsky, a talented writer with a steady job in a bank, and his friend E.W. Rabbinowitz. Written in a popular style and laced with humour, it sought to expose the conditions under which the Jewish community laboured and lived, holding sweaters, wealthy Anglo-Jews, capitalists, politicians in government and anti-semitism, and occasionally Jews themselves, responsible for vices such as gambling. Here, for example, Winchevsky describes how the labour market operates within tailoring:

So when you come to London, on a Sabbath take a stroll to the well known … *chazar mark* and you will see masters (you can distinguish them by their fat bellies!) scuttling about like a plague of mice between poverty stricken workers [calling], 'Jack, are you a machiner? John! I need a presser. Jim! I need a hand!' This is how they address the workers – not as a whole man, but by his hand, foot, etc … eventually you will discern a belly grab an arm just as a wolf seizes a lamb. As for those unfortunates who are left without a master, they gaze with baleful eyes which could consume belly and hands together.[70]

Within a year Winchevsky had split from Rabbinowitz over the direction of the newspaper and decided that the time had come for an openly socialist periodical. Encouraged by the active support of radical circles, *Arbeiter Freind* (Workers' Friend), first appeared in 1885 with the aim of spreading 'true socialism among Jewish workers', and to this end proposed a united front of all socialists against capitalism.[71] This 'true socialism', however, was never made clear, for while Jewish radicals were united in opposition to the capitalist order and Judaism they were deeply divided on the question of how they should be overthrown. The views of social democrats, revolutionary socialists and anarchists were all given space in the newspaper; in time, these divisions became insurmountable and the radical culture degenerated into factional strife. Also in 1885 the International Workingmen's Educational Club was founded, and immediately took over responsibility for the newspaper, which it transformed into a popular vernacular weekly. Occupying premises in Berner Street off the Commercial Road in Whitechapel, the club served as a base for the socialist and trade union movements, and as a rendezvous for radicals from across Europe. True to its name, it offered a varied programme of activities, including lectures, plays, concerts and classes on a range of subjects, most notably English.[72]

This radical Jewish culture, however, had little success in promoting struggles in the industrial sphere. The structure of the sweated labour market effectively militated against combined forms of industrial action. In addition to the casual nature of employment, it was apparent long before large-scale Jewish immigration that small workforces and an intense division of labour presented considerable barriers to a common struggle for reform. And yet there were instances when combined action temporarily overcame them. When the London tailors regrouped to form the London Operative Tailors Protective Association in 1866 it sought to recruit sweated workers and so monitor wages and conditions. A strike of that year met with initial success when wage increases were secured for its members. Further success followed in 1867 when the union agreed a joint programme of defence and action with the national Amalgamated Society of Tailors, but now the master tailors, fearing the growing strength of tailors, retaliated by drawing up an alternative scale of remuneration, so precipitating a strike and lockout which lasted for six months. A small group of Jewish tailors from Whitechapel supported the strike and set up a branch of the union, but when leaders of the strike were found guilty of conspiracy after a trial at the Old Bailey, and London tailors accused the AST of betrayal, the unity which had made recent successes possible crumbled, and London tailors, having accepted defeat, entered into a period of disorganization.[73]

Fortunes revived briefly in 1872, when the unions patched up their differences. In the belief that the wages and conditions of all tailors were related to those of the most exploited sweated labour, and that it was necessary to exercise a degree of control over entry to the trade, the London section determined to organize the whole workforce, starting with an East London branch of Jewish workers, who as an incentive were offered 'trade' memberships, relieving them of payments for sick and funeral benefits. Particular attention was paid to women, who were considered the principal source of cheap labour in the clothing trades, and with the active intervention of the Women's Trades Union League a number of branches were established, including one in East London. The AST, however, refused to admit women members on the grounds that they would swamp the labour market; without that national focus, women's unions remained small and insular.

If the growth of Jewish trades unions in the 1880s owed something to *Arbeiter Freind* it was because the paper's commitment to the promotion of independent organization coincided with the structural changes which affected the wider labour movement of the 1880s. 1889 is generally viewed as the climax of the Jewish trades union movement in London when, after a few small and spontaneous strikes among tailors, 10,000 unexpectedly took strike action in the summer months. There were few links between Jewish struggles and those organized by sections of the indigenous working class – the cultural and language barriers were simply too powerful to surmount – and so any coincidence with similar struggles of dock and gas workers suggested that the tailors were swept along by the same phase of militancy which mobilized sections of the indigenous unskilled labour force previously resistant to united action.[74]

Whatever the origins of the 1889 dock strike, it provided a massive boost to the flagging fortunes of Jewish organized labour. Early in the year there were portentous signs of trouble. In March, a request from a committee of the Jewish unemployed to the Chief Rabbi, and old antagonist, Dr Hermann Adler, that he give a Sabbath sermon on the evils of sweating and unemployment, was declined. Sweating, he professed, was better than hunger; if it meant overwork then he and his congregation were also victims. Such provocation incensed the radicals of the Berner Street Club, who reacted by organizing a march to the Great Synagogue in pursuit of work and an eight-hour day. On the morning of 16 March approximately 2,000 gathered outside the club before setting off for the synagogue. The *East London Advertiser*, not known for its sympathy towards Jewish migrants, expressed surprise that 'Hebrews', normally a 'peaceful and industrious folk', should join such a demonstration, and proceeded to describe the crowd,

> headed by a German brass band and a repulsive looking black and white banner, bearing the words 'JEWISH UNEMPLOYED AND SWEATERS' VICTIMS'. They proceeded to Duke Street. A more abject and miserable set of men it would have been impossible to have seen anywhere. Ill clad, dirty, unwashed, haggard and ragged, they looked in the bright sunlight, a picture of abject misery.[75]

More temperate, the *Jewish Chronicle* also pointed to the unprecedented nature of the event, seeing it as an expression of a smouldering hostility that the Jewish poor felt against the Chief Rabbi and the established community he represented. A resolution written in English and Hebrew declared that 'In consequence of the indifference of the rich Jews in not telling us, through the Chief Rabbi, how to improve our miserable condition, we clearly see that they are unwilling to assist us in ameliorating our position; we, therefore, call upon our fellow workmen not to depend upon the rich classes, but to organise in a strong body to strike for the abolition of the capitalist ruling.'[76] It was not long before this resolve was acted on as strikes began to take place in some of the large clothing firms. A committee of 'London tailors and sweaters victims' was convened which adroitly exploited the revelations coming out of the Lords inquiry into sweating. Describing them as a disgrace, the committee expressed the hope that recommendations would follow to improve the conditions of sweated tailors, but since the Commission was not due to meet again for some months, decided to join the struggle of the unskilled poor and called for a general strike of London tailors.[77]

By September 10,000 tailors in 120 shops had heeded the call. In many respects, the subsequent conduct of the strike was remarkably similar to the struggle being waged by dockworkers. Demands for a twelve-hour day, meals off the premises, wages at trade union rates and no outwork after working hours on all government contracts were modest enough, and tended to reflect the moderate temperament of the strike committee. The strike had the enthusiastic support of the Berner Street Club and *Arbeiter Freind*, which brought out a special edition and continued to carry news of the struggle to the Jewish community. Peaceable demonstrations took place in East London which helped to attract public sympathy for the plight of sweated workers. Contributions from unions flowed into the strikers' fund, supplemented by personal donations from prominent Anglo-Jews, including the local MP Sir Samuel Montagu and financier Lord Rothschild. Even the *Jewish Chronicle* welcomed the struggle to improve the condition of 'foreign tailors', although it questioned the advisability of strikers placing themselves in the hands of 'men conspicuously associated with Socialistic movements'.[78] After five weeks of exhausting campaigning, and following the personal intervention of Montagu, who by organizing a joint meeting between strikers and master tailors at the Berner Street Club outmanoeuvred the socialists, a settlement was reached which accepted most of the original demands, and the strikers returned to work on 6 October.[79]

For a while the contagious spirit of militancy prevailed. A series of meetings held at Berner Street accepted the need to amalgamate unions into a single federation capable of sustained collective action. To this end, 4,000 Jewish workers gathered in December at the Great Assembly Hall, Mile End, to hear the likes of Tom Mann, Ben Tillett and Charles Mowbray, together with a host of Yiddish speakers, and unanimously vote for the inauguration of the East London Federation of Labour Unions. And the following year witnessed a large strike of boot and shoe workers, and another of tailors against the refusal of some masters to adhere to the agreement of 1889. The changing currents of the labour market, however, were against further success. Nothing could be done to counter the debilitating influence of seasonality, and a new wave of immigration during 1890 threw more Jews on to the tender mercies of the market for sweated labour, effectively undermining the recent hard-won gains. The rush of enthusiasm to join a union soon ebbed; by 1892 *Arbeiter Freind* estimated that of 30,000 immigrant Jewish workers, fewer than 1,200 were members of a union.[80]

A loss of confidence, combined with recognition that the struggle to organize Jewish workers was going to be a long and difficult one, hardened the divisions between socialists and anarchists. The Berner Street Club staged a struggle between the anarchist Knights of Liberty, socialist Proletariat, and social democratic Forward from which the anarchists emerged triumphant. In April they took over control of the club and of *Arbeiter Freind*, both of which immediately entered into decline. Jewish anarchism, however, was not quite finished. In 1898 the remarkable Rudolph Rocker arrived in London and took over as editor of *Arbeiter Freind*, even though he could not then speak Yiddish. A German Gentile, widely read and travelled, fluent in several languages, Rocker was to bring a richness and rigour not only to the anarchist movement but to Yiddish culture as a whole. He transformed *Arbeiter Freind*, which became the most popular Yiddish radical newspaper, reaching a peak circulation of 5,000 copies in 1905, and was instrumental in opening the Workers' Friend Club at an old Methodist church in Jubilee Street, which in the promotion of education and social activity surpassed Toynbee Hall.[81] Rocker insisted that the doors of the club were open to everyone. In its stage productions, and series of lectures on literature, music and politics (even on day trips to Epping Forest Rocker would provide a lecture), the club introduced the members of the immigrant community to European culture, dramatically expanding their mental horizons, and laying the foundations for the vital literary culture of East End Jewry. In recalling his early experience as a protégé of Rocker, Sam Dreen captured the excitement which must have been shared by many others:

> He acquainted us with Tolstoy and Dostoevsky, Ibsen and Strindberg and Maeterlinck, with Leonardo da Vinci, Michaelangelo and Rembrandt. And with our great Yiddish writers, Mendele, Peretz, Sholem Aleichem, An-Ski, Reisen and Asch. This German *goy* had a thorough command of Yiddish ... He was one of those who stood at the cradle of modern Yiddish literature. He taught us history, philosophy, science, theatre, painting, music and acquainted us with the work of Marx and Proudhon, Bakunin, and Kropotkin, who was his close friend. He was *our* teacher.[82]

For many this intellectual ferment became part of a way of life. The workshop in which Hymie Fagan worked was a 'university'. Here he was introduced to the writings of Jack London and Upton Sinclair, and participated in passionate debates about the canon of European literature, including the works of Tolstoy, Gorky, Zola and France.[83] Rocker continued to promote this extraordinary programme of political and cultural enrichment until 1914, when he was arrested and interned as a German alien; the suppression of *Arbeiter Freind* and the forced closure of the Club followed. In these years around the turn of the century, however, the socialists fared poorly. A new monthly, *Fraye Velt* (Free World), was launched in May 1891, but despite including many of Winchevsky's best poems it published only nine issues; most were sold in North America, which was fast emerging as the new centre of gravity of the movement. In 1907 their numbers within the immigrant community were no more than 200. Attempts were made to unite dwindling socialist factions, but following the departure of most of the leaders for America Jewish socialism in London petered out.

The late nineteenth century has often been identified as a turning point in the history of East London. Staple industries such as silk weaving and shipbuilding, which had underpinned the growth of its workforce since the early modern period, finally succumbed to the logic of the market and entered into a period, of rapid terminal decline. Many of their workers were thrown on to the casual labour market to seek employment in the expansive sweated trades. From the 1880s the market was augmented by large numbers of Jewish labourers who had sought refuge in East London from persecution in eastern Europe, and the sweating system came to symbolize the economy of the area. From its numbers sprang political and literary traditions which indelibly printed their mark on the course of the history of East London, especially when the decline of Jewish radicalism before the First World War encouraged trade unionists and political activists to throw in their lot with the resurgent indigenous labour movement. The rise of labour is examined in the next chapter, but before that we need to look briefly at the remarkable exodus from the familiar East London to the fast industrializing area of West Ham, wherein new unionism and labour representation first took root.

CHAPTER 9

The Ascent of Labour, 1880–1920

EAST LONDON had always been overcrowded. Restricted boundaries, building restrictions, population increases, a poor communication infrastructure and a large reservoir of labourers in need of accommodation close to the sources of employment encouraged highly congested living and working conditions. Towards the close of the nineteenth century, these pressures reached a point at which the area seemed no longer able to contain its population, and the centre of gravity of East London shifted further to the east. Were this part of the trend to occupy yet more open fields, as had housing development when it marched inexorably past the Mile End Road towards Bow and the River Lea, then the matter would have little historical interest; but large numbers of East Londoners were now crossing the ancient boundary of the River Lea to settle in West Ham, then undergoing spectacular industrial growth. The fact that the growth of West Ham was determined by the same commercial and imperial interests as East London, and that its population largely comprised people who had migrated from the inner East End, suggests that over this period the boundaries of East London shifted eastwards to incorporate West Ham.

This exodus thus posed significant questions not only about the precise location of East London but also about the nature of industry and politics thought to characterize the area. Not only was the industrial landscape of West Ham distinctive, but also it created a remarkable political culture. In contrast to earlier patterns of industrial settlement in East London, West Ham attracted firms employing not hundreds but thousands of labourers. This solid industrial base provided the foundation for the growth of powerful trades unions which in turn revived an interest in the question of labour representation. In giving birth to new unionism and independent labour representation, West Ham led East London and then the country as a whole into the modern political era.

Now filled to excess

It is impossible to determine precisely how many persons were displaced by the construction of railways, new thoroughfares and slum clearance schemes during the middle decades of the nineteenth century; Gareth Stedman Jones estimates that across central London during the years 1830–80 they numbered in excess of 100,000.[1] Holborn, the City, St Marylebone and Westminster were most affected by improvement schemes, no doubt contributing to a continuous loss of population from the centre after it peaked in 1871.[2] East London, however, tells a different story. After 1861 the population dipped slightly until 1881, but then increased steadily to 1911, at which time the area had over 100,000 more residents than fifty years earlier.[3] Over 1871–81 the poorest and most overcrowded areas of East London lost population through emigration, due largely to the 'demolitions of dwellings, partly to give place to model blocks, partly for commercial purposes, as in the case of the district near the Mint'.[4] Those who remained competed for the diminished supply of accommodation, so that in 1881, despite emigration, the parishes of Whitechapel, St George's-in-the-East and Holborn had the highest levels of overcrowding in the whole of London.[5]

This process of clearance was to continue with increased intensity when the full impact of the Artisans' and Labourers' Dwellings Act (1875) was felt, particularly in Whitechapel. Under the act, which was designed to provide decent accommodation for the labouring population, large swathes of slum property were cleared. One of the most zealous in implementing the full force of the act was the Rev. Samuel Barnett, who as an influential member of the Whitechapel Board of Guardians had looked with moral disfavour on the area around Flower and Dean Street, and resolved to clear it. By 1883 the houses considered most unfit for human habitation had been demolished, eradicating what seemed as much as half of the parish of St Jude's.[6] Even though this represented only a fraction of what the disappointed Barnett had envisaged, his policy as a guardian merely added to his unwelcome reputation as an avowed enemy of the East End slum – a reputation that created deep resentment in the minds of many local residents, and one that came to haunt his work in Toynbee Hall.

Telling also was the continued exodus of the middle classes, made possible by an improved railway service. Late in the century, the *Methodist Observer* had good cause to lament the decline of congregations in East London. Fifty years earlier, it commented, there had been large chapels in Spitalfields, Whitechapel, Limehouse, Bow and Poplar filled with congregations of well-to-do people. In recent years, however, the altered condition of the districts and better means of travel had led to a general emigration of the prosperous, leaving the chapels 'empty and blighted with poverty'.[7]

There followed a period of massive reconstruction, when the great model blocks of Brunswick, Wentworth, Rothschild, George Yard, Lolesworth and College Buildings were completed, and subsequently occupied, not by the displaced poor, but by miscellaneous artisans and their families who could afford to pay the rent on a regular basis. This rebuilding programme coincided with the first large wave of Jewish immigration into the area; indeed, in some respects the increased presence of Jews actually prompted the construction of these model dwellings, since the indigenous Jewish community was encouraged to take responsibility for the well-being of the new immigrant settlers.

This provided the context for the construction of Rothschild Buildings on the small, notorious area between Flower and Dean Street and Thrawl Street, which had been cleared under the powers of the 1875 Act.[8] The moving force was Nathan Rothschild, head of one of the richest dynasties within Anglo-Jewry, who as chair of an inquiry commission set up by the United Synagogue in 1885 had recognized the need for a model dwelling along the lines already adopted by several charitable housing organizations, and was willing to back the idea with his own money. He bought the vacant site from the Metropolitan Board of Works for £7,000, and the Charlotte de Rothschild Buildings were completed in 1887 to provide accommodation for approximately two hundred families.[9] Monolithic as a prison it may have been, closer in appearance to a warehouse than a dwelling, but Rothschild Buildings actually provided the space for a vibrant and close-knit Jewish community to live in cleaner and more comfortable surroundings than the overcrowded tenements from which many had come.

This period of construction coincided with an expansion of residential areas eastwards to the River Lea, and a revival of the economy, thereby reversing – albeit temporarily – the decline in the population of East London. Running counter to this trend was the spectacular growth of West Ham. Situated on the opposite banks of the River Lea, beyond the administrative boundary of London, West Ham was undergoing industrialization and urbanization at speeds unprecedented in metropolitan history; Llewellyn Smith recognized early on that its population increase was being fuelled by emigration from East London. He attributed the fall in the population of London between 1871 and 1881 in part to

Peabody's Building, Spitalfields, 1866: an early and imposing example of the tenements constructed by philanthropists as a means of alleviating the chronic problem of working-class housing.

> contact with the country and other parts of London which may be a surprise to many, though scarcely perhaps to those who are aware of the extent of the overflow from the congested districts in the centre towards the newer suburban districts such as West Ham. It is difficult adequately to study East London as a centre of absorption or dispersion without constantly keeping before our minds the fact that the most rapid growth has taken place in districts such as this which industrially are part of London, but are not included in the Metropolitan area.[10]

These observations have to be taken seriously, for the emergence of West Ham did alter radically the demographic contours of East London; even more so, it transformed the industrial and political landscape.

London over the border

The ancient parish of West Ham was situated in Essex.[11] It had a rural economy, with small settlements at Stratford, Plaistow and West Ham. Fields and market gardens were devoted to produce for the London market, while the southern part, being below the high-water mark of the Thames, was subject to constant flooding and therefore used to pasture cattle. In 1851 its population was 19,000; in all respects it was a fairly typical parish with its share of wealth and poverty. And yet by the end of the century it had emerged as the industrial heartland of the metropolis with a population of over a quarter of a million.[12] This staggering increase in population was fed by migration from the metropolis. During the years 1851–1910 approximately 180,000 people crossed the River Lea, the vast majority of whom sought refuge from the overcrowded and slum-ridden areas of East London. Bethnal Green, Stepney, Mile End and Poplar experienced considerable net losses of population from migration. For most migrants the move to 'London over the border' was physically and mentally comfortable; there they found familiar surroundings and jobs which drew upon acquired skills.[13] And yet West Ham seemed an unlikely site for industrial development. Even as late as 1874, when Henry Tate bought land on which to build his Silvertown sugar refinery, his nephew asked:

Is this man really sane?
He's bought up a marsh and a gasworks
At least seven miles out of town
We'll either go down with swamp fever
Or the whole ruddy workforce will drown.[14]

Despite such unpromising remoteness in the minds of some, the transformation of West Ham owed everything to its proximity to London, and access to good river and rail communication. In the early decades of the century chemical and silk- and calico-printing industries had been able to exploit clean and ample water supplied by the River Lea, and the relatively lax legislation controlling noxious industries encouraged the siting of slaughterhouses and processing of animal refuse. The point was made in 1857 by Henry Morley in an article entitled 'Londoners over the border', published in Charles Dickens' *Household Words*:

London does not end at the limits assigned to it by those acts of parliament which take thought for the health of Londoners. More suburbs shoot up, while official ink is drying. Really, there is no limit to London; but the law must needs assign bounds; and, by the law, there is one suburb on the border of Essex marshes which is quite cut off from the comforts of the Metropolitan Buildings Act; – in fact, it lies just without its boundaries, and therefore is chosen as a place of refuge for offensive

West Ham, c. 1870. The Victoria Dock was now complete, and the area on the verge of massive and rapid industrial growth, fed by an exodus of labour from East London.

trade establishments turned out of town, – those of oil-boilers, gut-spinners, varnish-makers, printers ink-makers and the like.[15]

But these offensive trades were eclipsed by developments made possible initially by the completion in 1839 of the Eastern Counties Railway Company line, which was then extended to the Thames, effectively opening up the southern reaches of West Ham. Events followed quickly. Contractors now floated the Victoria Dock Company and set about the construction of docks to accommodate the new breed of steam ships. Completed in 1855, the Victoria Dock spanned the parishes of West and East Ham, and provided a massive boost to the industrialization of the area, not least by making available abundant supplies of cheap coal. The narrow strip of land between the dock and the Thames now possessed such locational advantages that a host of large firms were persuaded to settle. The India Rubber, Gutta Percha and Telegraph Company, the Gas Light and Coke Company, Tate & Lyle, Burt, Boulton and Haywood and others all relied on coal and access to the river, either to import raw materials or to export finished goods. Nearby the Thames Ironworks and Shipbuilding Company in Canning Town benefited from the same advantages and entered into a period of growth at a time when Thames shipbuilding was in terminal decline. To the north of the parish, Stratford was chosen as the site for the Eastern Counties Railway locomotive works, and attracted sizable firms including the West Ham Gas plant, the Leather Cloth factory and the Three Mills Distillery.

Until recently, it has been something of an orthodoxy to argue that unlike the great industrial conurbations of the Midlands and the north, London was not begat of the industrial revolution, and therefore remained tied to relatively small-scale workshops employing fewer than twenty-five persons until late in the nineteenth century (pp. 48–50). The notion that London was immune to the influence of industrialization, however, is without foundation. In exploring the development of East London industries, we have seen that nineteenth-century modernization fostered the rise of sweated trades. And we can identify examples of foundries and shipyards which employed hundreds of people. Consider, though, figures on the workforces of industries that emerged in West Ham. At their height in the decades around 1900, the Great Eastern Locomotive Works at Stratford employed 7,000, the Thames Ironworks in Canning Town 6,000, and Beckton Gasworks 10,000.[16] At a time increasingly dominated by small-scale production attendant on the terminal decline of staple industries such as shipbuilding and silk weaving, these data point to a very different metropolitan experience – one suggesting that London did after all have an 'industrial revolution' of its own.

West Ham, 1935. At its zenith, West Ham had a population in excess of a quarter of a million and was the industrial heartland of the metropolis.

The working men's party

This experience underpinned an extraordinary culture which redefined the politics of labour representation. The idea of popular representation was not new – Chartism, after all, had promoted universal suffrage in the 1830s and 1840s – but it was not until 1885 that we can begin to speak of an adult suffrage which embraced significant sections of the male working class, and to claim that elected members of parliament represented real constituencies. The 1884 Representation of the People Act followed the great reform acts of 1832 and 1867 by extending the franchise to all adult males owning or occupying premises worth at least £10 per annum, and the 1885 Redistribution of Seats Act introduced constituencies of approximately equal population, thus abolishing pocket boroughs and ensuring that urban centres had adequate representation. While this was far from universal suffrage – women were still denied the vote – the franchise now extended to approximately 60 per cent of adult males.[17]

These reforms redefined the electorate of East London. In practice, any man over twenty-one who was regularly employed and therefore could afford rent on decent accommodation had the vote; thus nearly 90 per cent of those in the various constituencies qualified as a householder or occupier, that is, owned a property worth £10 per annum or, much likelier, was a tenant therein for at least a year.[18] In most instances, however, only the head of a working-class family, or the principal occupant, was entitled to vote. These measures were deliberately framed to exclude the poor, who were considered too feckless to make rational political judgements; not only did they occupy inferior accommodation, but also applications for poor relief resulted in automatic disqualification, and any move in search of work required a year's residence before regaining the right to vote. In practice, these exclusions were rarely enforced conscientiously. The 1883 electoral register for the ward containing the notorious slum Old Nichol, on the western edge of Bethnal Green, contained 473 voters who had not appeared in the 1882 register. Of these 276 had not lived in the borough for the full year required by the 1884 Act. And when in 1890 Conservatives in Bethnal Green determined to purge the register by objecting to 2,000 entries in the south-west division alone, the majority subsequently excluded were poor relief beneficiaries, the overseers claiming that they had insufficient time to look closely into the matter of eligibility.[19] Notwithstanding such failures to apply a rigid calculus to the electoral registers, the acts enforced significant class-based exclusions. In the early 1890s less than a quarter of the male population of Tower Hamlets had the vote; of the total, approximately half the population was over twenty years of age, so we can say with some confidence that half of the adult male population was denied the vote.[20]

The number of constituencies, however, more equitably reflected the large population of East London. Whereas previously Tower Hamlets and Hackney had two members each, now they both had seven.[21] These new electorates more closely reflected the social composition of their localities. In the North ward of St George's-in-the-East, labourers made up 29 per cent of the electorate, artisans 26 per cent, professionals 4.5 per cent, the remainder comprising mainly retail, transport and home workers. In the comparatively comfortable ward of Mile End East, on the other hand, labourers comprised 12 per cent of the electoral register, artisans 30 per cent, and professionals 23 per cent.[22]

How, then, did East London vote in general elections after 1885? The data point to such a complex picture it is difficult to draw out any general lessons about the voting behaviour.[23] For the most part they dispute any easy and convenient relationship between social composition and political allegiance. Mile End, which was the wealthiest constituency, with the highest proportion of white-collar and professional residents, and Stepney, with its significant pockets of considerable wealth, voted consistently Conservative over this period, while the relatively poor constituencies of Poplar, Bethnal Green SW and Whitechapel voted overwhelmingly Liberal. And yet other desperately poor areas, including Limehouse and St George's-in-the-East, fluctuated between Liberal and Conservative. What this suggests is that any relationship between class and voting was highly mediated by the play of local factors. Turnouts were high by today's standards; in 1895, for example, they varied between 68 per cent in Whitechapel and a remarkable 82 per cent in St George's, but because the electorate was small the winning margins in most elections were less than a thousand votes, making the results susceptible to relatively small swings in local opinion.

Any relationship between levels of poverty in East London and the Liberal vote over this period seemed tenuous – quite apart from the fact that the poorest were not enfranchised, dispossession was not the harbinger of a more radical politics.[24] The experience of the Jewish community in East London points to the significance of race in patterns of electoral behaviour, but again in ways that are far from straightforward. The fact that Whitechapel voted consistently Liberal may suggest that immigrant Jews were politically progressive, but it is more likely the case that the local MP, Samuel Montagu, and the Federation of Synagogues, of which he was president, skilfully created a political power base built on his personal prestige. Few though Jews were on the electoral register, they may have been enough to guarantee Liberal success. In other parts of East London, where the Jewish electorate were part of the rich and influential Anglo-Jewish community which resolutely voted Conservative, the results were much more ambiguous. And how the presence of the community provoked anti-alien sentiment which was then translated into the vote can be assessed with no greater reliability.

In the meantime, remarkable political events stirred in neighbouring West Ham. The growth of new unionism in the 1880s had owed much to the organization of gasworkers at the Beckton Gasworks and dockworkers in the Victoria and Albert Docks. The employers' counter-offensive during and in the immediate aftermath of the 1889 strikes had led to a period of retrenchment when labourers forfeited hard-won gains and unions lost much of their membership. From this position of industrial fragility rather than strength, unions turned to politics in the hope that with representatives of labour in parliament and local administrative bodies their interests might be better served than they had been by the Liberal Party. Thus it was argued that though the Liberal Party had been able to secure the traditional allegiance of labour activists on the basis of progressive policies such as state education and extension of the franchise, and though the trades unions had sponsored working-class MPs who were effectively affiliated to the radical wing of the party, by refusing to countenance reform leading to real improvement in the lives of working people the party had forfeited their support. Some years before the formation of a distinct Labour Party in 1906, those seeking independent representation were affiliated to a variety of organizations. In addition to the unions, there were co-operative societies, friendly societies, disaffected Liberal radicals, Irish nationalists, members of the Marxist Social Democratic Federation, and the influential Independent Labour Party. The alliances were uneasy, although most seemed able to agree that as a minimum programme labour activists should strive to build upon the gains of Liberalism by extending political democracy, improving the lot of the working class through government intervention in areas such as wage rates, hours, and promoting public ownership, and launching ethical assaults on capitalism and the free market. As a first step, they needed to increase labour representation. As Will Thorne, the Beckton gas stoker who had led the formation of the Gas Workers' and General Labourers' Union in 1889, suggested at the anniversary celebrations in 1892:

> The Gas Workers' Union had spent £20,000 on strikes to maintain an eight-hour day. It would have been better to spend £5,000 in supporting twenty five labour candidates so that they could get by law what they

failed to get by organization … The future policy for trade unionists would be to get control of public institutions and, through them, bring about the amelioration of social conditions.[25]

This strategy in West Ham was to result in the election in 1892 of the first independent labour member MP and in 1898 of the first labour council in British electoral history.[26] The story, however, had unexpected twists. West Ham had two constituencies in 1885, both of which returned Liberal candidates in the election of that year, only to be wiped out by the Tories in the following year, when the well-known local grandee Major Banes defeated Joseph Leicester, president of the Glass Bottle Makers' Union, in the south, and Forest Fulton defeated E.R. Cook, a local employer with Liberal sympathies, in the north, largely because of superior organization and canvassing. Stunned into action, the South West Ham Liberal Association expressed dismay that the constituency was represented by a Tory while the vast majority of its members were pronounced 'radicals'. The members set about organizing a united front. The first step was to invite a self-made, wealthy local accountant and advanced Liberal, Hume Webster, to stand at the next election.[27] But the antagonisms between Liberals and more radical elements were not yet eradicated, and so the rival South West Ham Radical Association, unhappy with Hume's credentials, presented Spencer Curwen, heir to a long tradition of radical nonconformity, as an alternative candidate.

Webster did his cause no harm when he contributed generously to the strike funds in 1889. Curwen, sensing his chances had receded, resigned early in 1890 in the hope that a genuine labour representative would come forward. The Radical Association sought a replacement, but the first two people approached declined on the grounds that the Liberal vote would be split; the third, Keir Hardie, had no such reservations. Hardie was a former coalminer from Ayrshire who after a period as a miners' leader devoted himself to the cause of labour representation. On adoption as an independent labour candidate in West Ham, he set out his programme of independent labour representation:

[T]hey had nothing to hope for from either the Liberal or Conservative parties, and therefore a new party had become a necessity. Unless the working men formed a party belonging neither to the Liberals nor to the Tories it must continue to be the plaything of parties in the future as it had in the past … The Labor [sic] party of the future must take advantage of every opportunity which could serve to advance the interests of the working classes in this country.[28]

VOTE FOR

Home Rule.

Democratic
Government.

Justice to Labour

No Monopoly.

No Landlordism

Temperance
Reform.

Healthy Homes.

Fair Rents.

Eight-Hour Day.

Work for the
Unemployed.

KEIR HARDIE.

Keir Hardie election poster, 1892. Such slogans guaranteed a broad level of support for Hardie, although his successful candidature was made possible only with the suicide of the rival Liberal candidate.

These were momentous words, heralding as they did a new phase in the history of political struggle. They were not greeted with popular approbation, however, for Liberals were understandably indignant at Hardie's threat to political unity, but he enjoyed the enthusiastic backing of influential trade unionists who were now committed to parliamentary representation. Had both Webster and Hardy run, there can be little doubt that the Liberal/radical vote would have split, allowing the Tory candidate victory. Early in 1892, however, the drama reached a new pitch as Webster unexpectedly committed suicide, apparently because he faced financial ruin when a risk venture involving a South American racehorse failed. History sometimes turns on such moments, for the way was suddenly clear for Hardie to run unopposed by local Liberals. By presenting himself as the 'Labor, Liberal, Radical, temperance, Home Rule and Nonconformist candidate' he successfully overcame residual hostility, and in the election of July 1892 was returned as MP for West Ham South.

Hardie's election as the first independent labour MP, some years before the foundation of the Labour Party itself, had rightly been seen as a milestone in the history of labour politics, but we must be careful not to treat it as the harbinger of a new age, after which things were never quite the same again. Although Hardie secured the support of local unions his victory was built on a fragile alliance among different sections of Liberal support which were attracted to his temperance and evangelism rather than his union militancy. In parliament, he campaigned tirelessly for state intervention to deal with the rising problem of unemployment, and the need for labour representation, but in so doing neglected his constituency. In the 1895 election he was heavily defeated by Major Banes – a result that has been attributed to Hardie's poor electioneering and the loss of the Irish temperance vote, but in fact most sections of his original support were disenchanted with broken pledges.[29] The loss of the nonconformist vote – estimated to be 3,000 in West Ham South – was crucial, as was the desertion of skilled workers who had formed the backbone of the old Liberal–Labour constituency.[30]

The hope expressed by Thorne, Hardie and John Burns that the phoenix of labour representation would arise from the ashes of new unionism was not realized, at least not in its bold totality. Hardie had failed, but the sphere of municipal politics offered an alternative terrain, particularly in West Ham, where the achievement of borough status in 1886 had provided a genuine focus of civic pride for many sections of the community. In 1894 the West Ham Socialist and Labor Council was founded with the aim of proposing suitable candidates at local elections. Of the nine labour candidates selected that year, only Thorne was returned in a largely apathetic election. A leader in the local press commented not entirely unfavourably on his victory:

> [H]e has been returned not because but in spite of his Socialistic opinions … Whatever we may think of the Socialist Scheme we must admit that its adherents are in earnest, that they feel themselves the depositaries of a plan which will benefit the world. The large majority of the people in West Ham think their plan wrong; obviously then the attempt must be made to convert the majority, if it be possible.[31]

This was good advice – which went unheeded. Hardie, Thorne and their followers believed that early successes were due to a heightened political consciousness among the electorate, and so they simply needed to present an advanced political programme to maintain the momentum. Only slowly did they come to recognize the importance of electioneering, in particular, updating the register and door-to-door canvassing, but from that recognition the success of labour candidates grew steadily. In the 1897 election three labour candidates were returned for Canning Town ward; at Plaistow two others followed. The leader in the local press was emphatic about the reasons for the defeat of tried and trusted councillors:

> It is certainly surprising that four of the outgoing councillors who sought re-election and two others who have been councillors should have failed … That they should have befallen people who have deserved so well of the burgesses, and who in some cases are very popular is a striking proof of the extreme importance of electioneering work. The lesson is scarcely likely to be lost. The socialist party in the borough evidently learnt this lesson before the election.[32]

In the campaign of the following year socialists worked strenuously: 'week after week, month after month, without cease and without lassitude, they have put their views by word of mouth before the electors', observed the local press.[33] After a comparatively heavy poll, enough labour candidates were returned to provide them with an overall majority on the council – the first in British municipal history. The local press greeted the victory with a guarded enthusiasm, placing hope that the enterprise of labour members would overcome years of Liberal inertia:

> [T]he Labor Party is well led and well officered; there is no reason to suppose that it will throw away its present strong position by inconsiderable rashness. It will propose – and doubtless with some success – some things from which more timid spirits will shrink. It may be tempted into enterprises beyond its strength. The danger of that, however, is not so great as some of the burgesses seem to imagine … There may be an eagerness, a spirit of adventure, which are not without some risks; but there is also a power of judging the relation of ends and means.[34]

Again, however, we must be cautious not to read too much into this victory by seeing it as the first step in the triumphal ascent of the Labour Party. Although the dominant group campaigned and acted under the rubric of the party, it was actually an uneasy alliance of members of the Social Democratic Federation and Independent Labour Party, augmented by support from Christian socialists of the settlement movement and Irish nationalists, which did not stand the test of time. The labour group embarked on an ambitious programme of progressive reform, including street widening, new schools and public health centres, and the public control and supply of electricity, tramways and housing. At first the programme was viewed by the electorate as a responsible use of municipal power, but ratepayer interests, united in the Municipal Alliance, grew increasingly restive about the levels of expenditure and the 'crude experiments in Socialism for the benefit of the Socialists at the Ratepayers' Expense'.[35] Unable to overcome its structural vulnerability, the labour group lost ground, and in 1900 it was voted out of power, not to regain it for another ten years.

The first cost on all human life

In the period leading to the First World War the Labour Party in East London had little electoral support and no coherent identity. The party itself was formally constituted in 1906 but had neither the will nor authority to determine the electoral strategies of local parties. This led to a considerable diversity in the programmes and tactics adopted in municipal and parliamentary campaigns.[36] The war completely transformed this political landscape. Take, for example, the parliamentary sphere. Over the years 1900–1910 Conservatives steadily lost ground to Liberals, such that by the December 1910 election East London boroughs had only one Conservative MP in Mile End, and two Labour MPs in West Ham South and Bow and Bromley; the rest were Liberal. By 1922 Labour dominated with eight MPs, followed by three Liberals and two Tories, and by 1924 Labour had eleven, Tories two and Liberals one. How are we to account for this transformation?

In the early years of the interwar period the Labour Party had a much greater confidence and strength than in 1914. Whether the experience of war contributed to this rise, however, remains a contentious issue.[37] There was little to suggest that the conditions of prewar East London necessarily offered fertile ground for the advance of the party. Only in West Ham and Poplar had the active intervention of trades unions led to small but significant gains in parliamentary and municipal elections, but even here success was fragile.

The war took a massive toll of human life and affected deeply the nation's collective psyche. The battlefields of France and Flanders may have witnessed the worst of the carnage, but poor areas like East London had their share of suffering. The Rev. William Lax, who worked at the Wesleyan Mission in Poplar for more than a quarter of a century, recalled that the war 'added to the miseries of life in the East End. For one reason, an unusually large proportion of the men had gone, and the casualties were terrible. Every street had its war shrine and its Roll of Honour.[38] For another, East London was subjected to aerial bombing. Compared with the Blitz, the damage was slight, but the effect of unprecedented nightly raids on the population was traumatic:

> On mischief bent, enemy aircraft followed the gleaming waters of the Thames, and never a visitation to the Metropolis but Zeppelins, Taubes, or Gothas hovered like devouring hawks above our humble roofs. Fear of these horrid visitants accounted for the nightly thronging of dug-outs, tunnels, basements – indeed, anywhere out of danger – by thousands of terrified women pushing rickety prams containing children, blankets, pillows and food, and strong men carrying sick and infirm folk. Such sights burnt themselves into the memory.[39]

One incident conveyed something of the terror. Just before noon, a Poplar housewife, Mrs Barge, heard the familiar drone of an aircraft engine and rushed to the front door, only to be met with the wild cries of a neighbour opposite beseeching her to go back inside. Retreating behind a half-closed door, she looked up and saw eight Gothas at low altitude. Suddenly she heard a bomb fall with devastating force, followed by screams from a distraught woman who was there in the street carrying a baby. Another bomb fell, tearing off doors and window frames; ceilings collapsed. The woman fell and the baby lay motionless on the ground. Mrs Barge ran out to help. She discovered the baby was dead, and the woman dying from ghastly wounds, but before she could carry her off to safety another bomb fell. Mrs Barge lived just long enough to be taken to hospital by an ambulance crew.[40]

The most devastating wartime disaster, however, had nothing to do with enemy action. Early in 1917 the Brunner-Mond munitions factory in Silvertown exploded, killing seventy-four, injuring nearly a thousand, and laying waste to factories and houses in the immediate vicinity. It was the worst explosion ever seen in London, and yet it could have been much worse, as one of the more fortunate workers later recalled:

> There were not more than 40 people on the premises, the day shift having gone … I was at work in the office when I heard women shrieking. I came down to the door and saw the high explosive building thoroughly afire. Somehow, providentially, I was able to get away without a scratch, though others going along the road were

knocked down beside me by flying missiles hurled in all directions by
the explosion. The force of the explosion seemed to take a curious
zig-zag course, and it must have missed me, though I could not
have been more than 200 yards away. My first thought, when I saw
the whole plant aflame, was 'This is the end of all things for me'. All
I was clearly conscious of was a rain of heavy things falling in front
of me.[41]

Worried about the possibility of sabotage, the Home Office immediately
appointed a committee to determine the cause of the explosion. Its secret
report pointed to the probability of human error; no mention was made of
the madness of locating a high explosive TNT plant in a densely crowded
working-class area.[42]

The real impact of the war, however, was felt by families plunged yet
further into poverty by the conscription of their male wage-earners. The
remarkable Sylvia Pankhurst, who had established the radical East London
Federation of Suffragettes in 1913, was deeply moved by the distress she
witnessed from her house in Mile End in the early years of the conflict:

> Up and down the Old Ford Road under my windows, women were wont
> to hurry past, pushing the battered old perambulators of children, or
> packing cases on wheels, laden with garments for the factories. Now,
> with their little conveyances all empty, they lingered hopeless … Women
> gathered about our door asking for 'Sylvia'. They had followed and fought
> with her in the hectic Suffragette struggles; they turned to her now in
> these hours of desperate hardship; poor, wan, white-faced mothers,
> clasping their wasted babies, whose pain-filled eyes seemed older than
> their own. Their breasts gone dry, they had no milk to give their infants,
> no food for their elder children, no money for the landlord.[43]

Seeing the faith these families placed in her as a 'sacred charge', Pankhurst
embarked on a determined campaign to provide relief from their suffering,
not in the form of charitable donations but rather in practical, community-
based initiatives. Over the ensuing months she established an employment
bureau, regular free clinics, centres offering advice to those pleading for
assistance from the guardians, landlords and trade unions, and she distributed free milk, organized a toy factory and ran a school.

The desperation witnessed by Pankhurst, however, was not the whole
story, for the war also brought real benefits to East London. The switch to
wartime production temporarily provided close to full employment in

some areas. Within a year of the outset, government contracts were providing a measure of unprecedented stability to many industries. The London tailoring trade had increased by 60 per cent to meet the demand for uniforms and boots, food industries were working at capacity, carpenters found ready employment in the production of tables, chairs and army huts, the docks were so congested that a call for additional dock labour was sent to Southampton, and complaints were voiced that the footways under the Thames to the Royal Arsenal could not cope with the pedestrian traffic to and from East and West Ham.[44] Steady employment led to real increases in the standard of living; teachers remarked on how well-fed – and hence better-behaved – their pupils were.

Some Jewish trades experienced unprecedented prosperity, on the crest of which their workers embarked on spending sprees. Complaints by residents of Clapton Common soon appeared in the local press that exuberant groups of smart Jewish youths from the East End were disturbing the tranquillity of the neighbourhood.[45] Unsurprisingly, those on the margins of legitimate business also prospered. The memoirs of Arthur Harding, a notorious villain from Bethnal Green, recall that his sister did particularly well as a money-lender and credit clothier because her clients were now earning regular money and could come to her more often.[46] And yet there was significant change neither to the industrial structure of East London nor to its workforce, mainly because many men worked in protected industries, including munitions, transport and the docks, thus avoiding conscription. Workshop production remained largely intact, and the system of casual labour, although improved, was never eliminated.

What did change, thereby opening up new opportunities for local activists, was the intervention of the state and local government into vital areas of people's lives. Measures pioneered by organizations including the Women's Cooperative Guild and the East London Federation of Suffragettes persuaded the Labour Party that it could harness patriotic sentiment, and at the same time resist ratepayer charges of collectivism and extravagance in implementing a truly progressive programme of social reform.[47] Immediately after the war this programme was boosted by extension of the franchise. By abolishing property qualifications for men over twenty-one, and enfranchising women over thirty, the 1918 Representation of the People Act effectively tripled the electorate. This expanded electoral base greatly facilitated alliances of working-class activists to capitalize upon opportunities that had opened up during the war to take a greater measure of control of local institutions. These activists used councils and boards of guardians to advance the interests of labour in ways that owed little to trade union organization.

This helps to explain why the most spectacular advances of Labour in East London occurred in areas dominated by workshop production and casual labour, and although unions also made advances in these areas, their success was dependent upon political intervention to, say, enforce minimum wage levels or agreements between employers and their workforces. Thus in the docks, transport and the clothing trades labourers resorted increasingly to political rather than industrial solutions as a means of alleviating low pay and irregular employment, while the unemployed turned with a sense of entitlement to the boards of guardians. For some prominent local activists such work was integral to their ideals of social transformation. Clement Attlee, who had been a settlement worker at Toynbee Hall and was now the first Labour mayor of Stepney, declared that 'municipal work is part of the means of changing the basis of society from profit-making to Life', while George Lansbury referred to fellow councillors at Poplar as 'all clear class-conscious socialists working together, using the whole machinery of local government and Parliament for the transformation of Capitalist Society into Socialism'.[48]

Nowhere was this more evident than in West Ham, where the party witnessed an extraordinary growth during the war and into the interwar period. Given the relatively small numbers of party members, however, it is clear that the ascent to power was built upon foundations laid by its active supporters, most notably, the cooperative movement and local trades unions. The great industrial centres of Manchester, Leeds, Bradford and the like had given birth to cooperation in the mid-nineteenth century and sustained its dramatic rise to prominence in the lives of so many working-class people. Cooperation was built around the simple idea that the working class had everything to gain from organizing its own retail system, particularly in the sale of food, which led to the founding of the Co-operative Wholesale Society.

London, lacking a coherent and organized labour presence, resisted the influence of cooperation, with two significant exceptions. In 1860 a group of railwaymen at the Eastern Counties Railway works at Stratford founded the Stratford Cooperative Society. Following amalgamation with small societies in West Ham it could claim a membership of 13,000 at the turn of the century; along with the Royal Arsenal Cooperative Society (22,000), similarly built around a stable and skilled labour force, it was the only one in the metropolitan area which could rival the traditional strongholds of cooperation in the north. Expansion continued, so that with the formation of the London Cooperative Society, based at Stratford, membership stood at over 100,000; by the end of the interwar period the LCS, having taken over all the smaller London societies, had nearly 800,000 members, and was the largest cooperative society in the world.[49]

From the outset cooperation was a political movement; formal involvement, however, was considered unnecessary, even harmful, since cooperation successfully attracted a variety of political opinion. That changed towards the end of the nineteenth century as significant sections – no doubt inspired by the example of trade unions – flirted with the idea of representation, although it was not until 1917 that the Cooperative Congress, furious at the treatment meted out by government control over the food supply to the detriment of their trading interests, voted overwhelmingly to use their considerable resources to help secure direct representation at the parliamentary and municipal levels. The case was put well by the Parliamentary Correspondent of the *Cooperative News* on the eve of the conference:

> Co-operators cannot expect to protect themselves against the threatened attack of the opposing forces without carefully preparing a united plan of campaign, in the same way that the Labour Party has mobilised its battalions … The Labour Party had become a power in the land owing to its having at its back a large mass of the voting strength of the country. Until the cooperative electorate is similarly organised we shall remain in a state of political impotency. Our political weakness is our opponents' strength.[50]

Although the paramount desire to retain political independence prevented formal affiliation to the Labour Party, cooperators campaigned actively with trade unionists and party members on common causes throughout the war. Arguably of more importance in East London, however, were the exploits of a remarkable group of women from the Women's Cooperative Guild. Founded in 1883, the guild shared a common intellectual heritage with the broader cooperative movement but possessed a jealously guarded independence which enabled it to work outside the political boundaries of routine cooperative practice. Under the leadership of Margaret Llewellyn Davies from 1889 to 1921, the membership grew to over 50,000, by which time the guild was a national force in campaigns around minimum wages, female representation on public bodies such as boards of guardians, and reform in the lives of married women.

On the outbreak of war, the guild focused its considerable energies on child and maternity welfare. In a speech to the 1915 Congress, the president, Mrs Barton, laid down an ambitious and radical agenda:

While men have been destroying life, women have been building up a system that will diminish suffering and save life. We pay the first cost on all human life. We shall not rest satisfied until every mother can take advantage of all that medical science can offer, which means that every town and village must have its maternity centre.[51]

This intervention was of particular significance in areas such as East London with chronically high infant and maternal death rates. In West Ham, for example, the guild campaigned to overcome the meagre facilities by enlisting the support of the Public Health Committee in developing the Plaistow Maternity Hospital, by far the largest provider of maternity care in the south of the borough since it was first opened in 1889. More influential in promoting reform was the Canning Town Health Society. Originally established in 1906 to improve local health by offering advice, investigating sanitary conditions and promoting improvement, the society had set up a baby-visiting committee, organized an anti-TB exhibition in 1911 attended by over 30,000 people, and opened a depot to provide unadulterated milk to mothers of young children. Under the forceful guidance of guildswomen Rebecca Cheetham and Edith Kerrison at the outbreak of war, funding was secured from the Local Government Board and the Board of Education, and directed to improving infant welfare. In the last year of the war regular classes on cooking and infant care were held, nearly 3,000 consultations took place, and two and a half tons of dried milk were distributed to necessitous mothers.

By exposing the failures of the government to address this area of public health, such initiatives hastened the introduction of the 1918 Maternity and Child Welfare Act. This required local authorities to set up maternity and child welfare committees, and made grants available for home helps, food for expectant and nursing mothers and children under five, and crèches and day nurseries, all of which bore the unmistakable stamp of guild thought and practice. Throughout the 1920s guild members served on the West Ham committee, and encouraged a dramatic expansion of local provision for mothers and infants, over time reducing the infant mortality rate to below the national average. Due recognition was given to these achievements by the local electorate, in particular the women enfranchised in 1918. The Labour Party may have been able to capitalize by capturing the female vote, but its success was built on the shoulders of guildswomen who did most to spread the Labour gospel of women as healthy and responsible mothers.[52]

First things first

The trades union movement played a crucial role in Labour's rise to power in East London. The stability of employment created by wartime production provided propitious conditions for union growth, as a result of which the number of trade unionists practically doubled, and unions emerged with a new-found confidence in their strength.[53] Julia Bush has identified this power as the single most important factor in the success of the party, since unions provided organization, finance and a channel for the political expression of an enlarged working-class electorate: 'post-war Labour victories,' she writes, 'were to be built around a solid core of union support, tempered and taught by wartime experience.'[54] The problem is that this confidence in union strength did not translate readily into political action; indeed, the course of the war exposed real fissures within the labour movement. Take, for example, attitudes towards the war, which impinged on virtually all spheres of union activity. The majority of union leaders and rank-and-file members fully supported the war effort out of a sense of patriotism. Against them were disaffected members of socialist organizations, including the British Socialist Party, Independent Labour Party and Herald League, who looked with horror on the sacrifices made by working-class men in pursuit of what was a capitalist war. Relatively few in number, they were unable to found a mass anti-war movement, choosing instead to put aside sectional differences and campaign on common objectives. The War Emergency Workers National Committee, set up at the beginning of the war to protect the interests of workers against profiteering, attracted the active support of pro- and anti-war factions in East London, and played a decisive role in securing better representation on poor law and distress committees, and in campaigning against increases in the price of food.[55] In truth there was a middle ground on which both factions could meet. Will Thorne, MP, founder member and leader of the National Union of Gasworkers and patriot, declared that the patriotism of West Ham unionists would not prevent them from taking a strong political stance on questions of relief, while few socialists opposed to the war were prepared to undermine the war effort by leading damaging strikes.

Only in the latter stages of the war did unions embark on industrial militancy. From 1917 the unions made considerable gains in membership, thereby enhancing their political authority and helping to lay the foundations for the victories of the Labour Party that were to follow. It was not merely that unions successfully negotiated major pay increases for their members at the Beckton Gasworks, Tate & Lyle's sugar refinery, the creosote works of Burt, Boulton and Haywood and a host of smaller plants, nor that their leaders were now courted on the national stage by government ministers, but that union members and bodies such as trade councils had come to recognize the real value of municipal politics, and thus decided to consolidate their power in local affairs. As the end of the war drew near, union branches resolved to bolster their political funds and exercise a decisive influence over the selection of Labour candidates at the next elections; these included Walter Devenay of the Dockers' Union at Mile End, and Will Thorne and Jack Jones of the Gasworkers' Union at Plaistow and Silvertown respectively.[56]

The 1918 election proved something of a disappointment to Labour, with only Thorne and Jones returned from East London boroughs; the other seats went to coalition candidates. But lessons were learnt on the vital importance of unity. With the cessation of hostilities Labour leaders discarded the patriotic card, and in a new climate of reconciliation attempted to heal the rifts that had opened up between themselves and radical, anti-war elements. Thorne was in the forefront:

> In days gone by there had been little differences between the members of the party on the war policy, but the war was now over and they wanted to unite all their forces ... One of the most important questions they had to consider was that of public health, including housing. Education was also a big question and a lot of money would have to be spent on it.[57]

In the West Ham municipal election of November 1919 – the first for six years – Labour won eight of the nine wards contested, giving them control of thirty of the forty-eight seats on the council. It was a control that was never subsequently forfeited. This success owed much to Labour's recognition of the need for unity and effective electioneering, but it was union backing which proved a necessary if not entirely sufficient condition. Three unions dominated the industrial and political landscape of West Ham in this period – the National Union of Railwaymen (NUR), National Union of Gasworkers and General Labourers (NUGW), and the Transport and General Workers Union (TGWU) – each of which had grown dramatically during the war. The NUR had a history of promoting labour representation and was among the first to sponsor candidates. Prior to the 1918 election it reaffirmed its commitment to the Labour Party, resolved to redouble its efforts to link up with the cooperative movement, and was prepared to back any pledges with generous contributions. The NUR had six branches in West Ham with a total membership peaking at over 8,000 in 1919. The two branches in Stratford were by far the most important; not only did they contain the bulk of the members – over 5,000 in 1919 – but they were dominated by skilled artisans employed at the locomotive works who were steeped in a tradition of political involvement. None was more active than Tom Kirk, a signalman in the West Ham branch who had been elected to the council in 1910, and had proved a staunch ally of Thorne during the political turmoil of the war. On the eve of the 1919 election, he reported on progress in terms that revealed much of the incipient jingoism of the local labour movement:

> Every ounce of our energy, enthusiasm and native resourcefulness was put into the South West Ham contest … In spite of the intriguing Bolsheviks, spirit-rapping pacifists, temperance cranks, Liberals and Tories, on Saturday Will Thorne and Jack Jones will head our poll. Thus endeth a strenuous year. Our motto for the New Year: 'First things first'. Britain for the British.[58]

The measure of this success has to be tempered by the recognition that no Labour candidate ran in Stratford and a Tory was returned. Kirk argued with some justification that the sectionalism of elite railway workers had for years held back the advance of the local Labour Party, for they had voted solidly against Labour in municipal elections on the grounds that 'the dustman, the road sweeper, the carman, and the scavenger were accorded by the corporation a social status and economic standing superior to the ordinary working-class ratepayer'.[59]

We have already encountered the electoral activities of the NUGW, particularly in support of its general secretary Will Thorne. Along with the NUR and miners' union, it had pioneered labour representation at national and local levels, as a result of which in the period leading to the war it had four MPs and was well represented on municipal authorities. Membership of the NUGW increased tenfold over the years 1910–18, in part because its doors were opened to recruitment of women workers, which paved the way for amalgamation with the National Federation of Women Workers in 1919. Membership in West Ham reached nearly 8,500 in 1921, the vast majority of whom were in either the West Ham or Canning Town branches. The attendant financial stability provided opportunities to increase sponsorship of Labour candidates; in the 1918 election, for example, the union granted expenses of over £3,000 to eight candidates, five of whom were returned. Less was forthcoming in municipal elections, but it was sufficient in West Ham to encourage members to stand; after that of 1923 the NUGW could claim twelve of the forty-seven Labour councillors.

When the TGWU was formed in 1922 from an amalgamation of transport unions – by far the largest of which was the Dockers' Union – it could claim nearly 7,500 members in West Ham branches. The union had also benefited from a considerable increase in numbers during the war, many of whom were women recruited from munitions and light engineering factories. Representing unskilled and semi-skilled labour with no tradition of political involvement, the union's stance had been largely apathetic, but in the immediate postwar period it resolved to back candidates from amongst its higher officers. The general secretary, Ben Tillett, who on a patriotic ticket had been elected in a by-election at North Salford in 1917, was the union's only MP. Aided by union funding of £2,500, he was re-elected in 1918 along with James Wignall at the Forest of Dean, while Ernest Bevin was defeated at Bristol and Walter Devenay at Mile End, where he had been adopted after failing to be nominated for Silvertown. On the formation of the TGWU, and when Bevin had successfully ousted Tillett as general secretary, the union broadly supported the aims of the Labour Party but tended to subordinate political activity to industrial struggle.

The experience of West Ham in the immediate postwar period suggests that even when unions were strong there was no easy identity between unionism and politics. The three major unions adopted the programme of the Labour Party and financed candidates, but they held different views on the efficacy of work in the political sphere. Whatever these differences, almost without exception the figures who were instrumental in promoting labour representation in the locality came from the ranks of trade unionists. At times of crisis they could and did call upon the considerable weight of union support in order to salvage their careers. In this respect, unions provided ballast in the unsettled political climate of East London during the interwar period. In the early years of the interwar period, the Labour Party was able to build on this success to dominate the municipal sphere in East London boroughs. Its authority, however, was never secure, for, as we shall now see, as recession took hold and levels of unemployment soared, the local labour movement faced its sternest challenge.

CHAPTER 10

Recession, Mass Culture and the Entrepreneurial Spirit, 1920–1939

T HE FIRST World War reversed the fortunes of the industries of East London. In promoting production geared towards prosecution of the war, many firms were able to offer employment to most who wished to work, with palpable improvements in the living conditions of local families. And it was during this period that the local Labour parties began to consolidate their power by involving themselves directly in the day-to-day struggles of people to cope with wartime conditions.

The interwar depression hit East London hard. Local industries failed to respond adequately to the new economic realities, thereby exposing longer-term structural weaknesses which had previously been masked by piecemeal reform. The docks, for example, had suffered from a declining share of world trade for decades, in response to which the companies had introduced mechanization and a degree of rationalization, but the system of casualization and work practices which had emerged from the mid-nineteenth century remained intact. Levels of local unemployment increased steadily, plunging families further into poverty. The conditions may not have been as desperate as those revealed by Booth forty years earlier, but the depth and extent of deprivation experienced by East London rivalled that of any region of the country similarly affected by industrial decline. It was against this backdrop that particular patterns of political activity emerged as East London became the site of some of the most important struggles against unemployment.

The largest part of unbroken depression

Since the late Victorian years, the process of mechanization had accelerated so that industries now employed machines of ever-growing complexity in mass production, thereby rendering obsolete old skills, intensifying the division of labour, and opening up new opportunities for women in the labour force.[1] The extent of mechanization was uneven across the economy and hence the regions. Engineering and woodworking witnessed greater use of electric-powered automatic machinery, particularly in larger plants which could justify the heavy initial capital expenditure. Many of the small workshops found in East London, on the other hand, made little use of such machinery; ship repairing, clothing, and boot and shoe production thus remained tied to practices which had emerged in the second half of the nineteenth century. And while the introduction of lifting gear, electric trucks and mechanical devices for loading and unloading coal and grain had relieved dock labourers of hard physical toil, dock work continued in much the same way as it had for the previous fifty years.

Against this background, those employed in the industries of East London operated at a disadvantage. Although clothing had earlier been mechanized with the adoption of the sewing machine and band-saw, production was dominated by a system of subcontracting in which small workshops carried out specialized tasks. This had attracted the opprobrium of the Lords inquiry into the sweating system, but by the early years of the twentieth century it was more generally recognized that the system had been responsible for significant advances in production. Herbert Evans, a highly experienced factory inspector in Stepney, observed as early as 1903:

> a general improvement in trade co-existent with the East End indus-tries intensified the demand for spacious workshops. I have no knowl-edge of native labour suffering by this evolution. I do not know of a single case during the past eight years ... where any native labour has been displaced either by pressure for a dwelling or by any kind of substituted labour – not a single case where the native has been displaced by an alien ... The new trades or developments of trade have been due solely to foreign labour, and the increase in productive capacity has been due in the same degree to the same persons. The districts have benefited as much materially as the workers ... and the money-earning capacity of the districts affected by this question of alien immigration has trebled during the past eight years. This is almost wholly due to the extension of manufacturing works producing articles of daily use, the demand increasing gradually.[2]

The emergence of multiple tailoring stores and departmental stores, which in part displaced the large independent warehouses of the nineteenth century, reinforced this tendency, as a result of which East London consoli-dated its position as most important centre of clothing production over the next thirty years. In 1931, for example, clothing employed a quarter of the working population of the Borough of Stepney.[3] In spheres of women's work, notably millinery and dressmaking, the factory system became established which, by effectively eliminating home work, provided regular work. More assiduous factory inspections required by the Trade Boards Acts of 1909 and 1918 led to a general improvement in working conditions. Changed also was the distribution of the trade; following the path of outward Jewish migration from Whitechapel, and an improved transport infrastructure, the trade spread to the neighbouring districts of Stepney, Bethnal Green, Stoke Newington and Hackney.[4]

The furniture trade of nineteenth-century East London, concentrated in Shoreditch and Bethnal Green, was also bedevilled by subcontracting, deskilling and the downward pressure on wages. The early decades of the twentieth century witnessed continued growth as many of the workshops found more spacious and cheaper premises in neighbouring Hackney, so that while numbers employed in London hovered around 26,000 during the years 1881–1921, those in East London increased by fifty per cent to 13,000.[5] Although there were signs that production increasingly took place in larger factories equipped with machinery for the burgeoning wholesale market, the sweating system had continued in the smaller trade workshops which congregated in East London, where the legacy and influence of Jewish workers continued unchanged.[6]

Largely because of the area's seafaring past and the continued importance of the docks, transport remained a major employer. The structure of the sector, however, was undergoing transformation. The populations of seamen that had given Wapping, Ratcliff and Limehouse such reproachful reputations in the nineteenth century had migrated to the new dock areas down-river, leaving at most 8,000, approximately 1,000 of whom were lascars, that is, foreign seamen, mostly from India. The London docks themselves were experiencing difficult times. After the opening of the Suez Canal in 1869 and the subsequent extension of cable systems which encouraged direct shipments to continental ports, London began to lose its status as a world port. With the creation of the Port of London Authority (PLA) in 1908, all London docks were placed under a single management; although this provided much-needed rationalization, the authority of the PLA was compromised by the fact that the influential wharfingers retained their historic rights to deliver and collect goods in the docks without charge, and remained outside its control. Furthermore, the promise that the wretched system of casual labour would be eradicated by better management of demand was never realized, and so the casual reservoir survived more or less intact. It survived because of the age-old problem of seasonal fluctuations in the demand for labour. In 1929 the average daily number of casual dock labourers taken on was approximately 14,000, but on certain days of high demand the number increased to 17,000 or conversely dropped to 11,000.[7] Immediately after the war the Shaw Court of Inquiry, set up to resolve a long-running dispute over conditions of dock labour, voiced concerns that had been repeated for at least fifty years:

> The Court is of the opinion that labour frequently or constantly under-employed is injurious to the interests of the workers, the ports and the public, and that it is discreditable to society. It undermines all security, and is apt to undermine all self-respect on the workers' part. It is only among those who have sunk very far and whom the system itself may have demoralised, that it can be accepted as a working substitute for steady and assured employment. In one sense it is a convenience to authorities and employers, whose requirements are at the mercy of storms and tides and unforeseen casualties, to have a reservoir of unemployment which can be readily tapped as the need emerges for a labour supply. If men were merely the spare parts of an industrial machine, this callous reckoning might be appropriate; but society will not tolerate much longer the continuance of the employment of human beings along those lines. The system of casualisation must, if possible, be torn up by the roots. It is wrong.[8]

The inquiry recommended a system of registration, and the principle of maintenance of unemployed casual labour, but because of opposition from employers and unions they were not fully implemented, and so casualization of dock labour continued. The numbers subsequently registered on the scheme far exceeded those required, and yet excluded many who were actually employed in the docks on a regular basis through the two hundred calling-on places where casual labourers scrambled for any work available on the day.

Throughout the 1920s the tonnage of vessels unloading at the Port of London increased, and yet the numbers employed fell steadily. This was attributed to advances in the size and capabilities of cranes and extensive use of conveyors of every kind, the introduction of piecework requiring fewer men, and the trend to unload cargoes directly into barges or on to quaysides, effectively dispensing with warehousing facilities.[9] Ancillary industries also fared badly. By the twentieth century, cooperage and the sailcloth industry in East London were in terminal decline due to the

Royal Docks, c. 1930. The George V Dock had been opened in 1922, and the docks were clearly busy, but their days were numbered.

availability of new materials and machine production. Thirteen cooperages survived in Stepney into the 1930s, employing approximately 130, mostly old and highly-skilled since the young, it was said, were no longer willing to serve the arduous apprenticeships.[10]

Of the remaining groups, the most significant numerically were those employed in domestic service and commerce, representing 8 and 12 per cent respectively of the occupied population of Stepney Borough in 1931. It is impossible to determine precisely how many of these actually worked in East London, but with an improved transport system it is reasonable to suggest that many in the growing commercial and financial sector commuted on a daily basis to take up white-collar jobs in the offices and institutions of the City. London women had an aversion to domestic service, which in part explains the protracted decline since the previous century, particularly since new opportunities for female labour presented themselves.[11]

By the mid-1920s it was also clear that the extraordinary industrial growth of West Ham was at an end. The considerable advantages offered by the area which had encouraged industrial settlement from the late nineteenth century were to stifle the ability of firms to adapt to the conditions found in the transformed economic environment of the interwar period. It was not merely that by the end of the war few suitable sites remained to attract new industry, but also that established firms continued to benefit from their location. The road and rail infrastructure was extended, the George V Dock was completed in 1922, and, following pioneering development of the supply of electricity by West Ham Corporation, power was made available at rates cheaper than in other metropolitan areas. All this encouraged a certain complacency and reluctance to meet the challenges from new industrial developments, as a result of which West Ham entered into a period of stagnation and protracted decline.[12]

The occupational structure of interwar West Ham, which was determined by the previous phase of rapid growth, proved vulnerable to the recession. Badly affected were ship repairing, and the river, dock, gas, chemical and electricity industries, which employed proportionately higher numbers in West Ham than in the rest of London, while the more buoyant sectors of vehicles, banking and insurance, personal services and public administration were under-represented. Factory and dock areas to the south were dominated by the families of unskilled and semi-skilled manual workers, who were also to be found around the industries located in Plaistow and Stratford. They were cruelly exposed to the economic recession, and there was little that local agencies could do to break the downward spiral of underemployment, overcrowding and deprivation which many districts encountered.

In sharp contrast to these experiences, interwar London benefited greatly from the development of new industries, shielding its population from the worst effects of the depression. Vehicle production, light and electrical engineering, and the manufacture of foodstuffs were among them, and they sprang up not across the metropolis as a whole but in the two great manufacturing zones which had been untouched by the reach of nineteenth-century industrialization. By the 1930s the Lea Valley zone, stretching from Stratford to Tottenham and Edmonton, employed approximately 40,000 people in engineering, clothing, furniture, stationery and vehicles, while the West Middlesex zone, covering the areas around Hendon, Wembley, Acton and Brentford, employed 75,000, in engineering, chemicals, vehicles, food processing, stationery and wood products.[13] That some of these were survivals from a previous industrial age, that the fundamental distinction between a West End craft industry and an East End wholesale remained, and that Park Royal – the most important of the new industrial areas – was dominated by small-scale plants suggests that the distinction between 'old' and 'new' industries was not clear-cut, but the important point here is that this development did little to promote the fortunes of East London; on the contrary, by encouraging the migration of the more expansive firms from older industrial areas, it weakened further the ability of East London to recover from the depression.

The consequences of the failure of East London industries to respond to new economic challenges were disastrous. The *New Survey of London Life and Labour* concluded that the condition of most Londoners had improved over the past forty years because of the steady increases in real incomes and the decline of sweating, and that poverty was approximately a third of the level recorded by the Booth survey. The most acute problem now faced was that of underemployment.[14] Because of the unreliability of the data on levels of unemployment, this is a topic that needs to be handled with caution, but it does seem clear that London fared comparatively well during the depression, the percentage of its unemployed numbering less than half the national average. Underemployment persisted, however, in industries relying on casual labour or short-term engagements, and these tended to be concentrated in East London, especially in the dock, ship-repair, clothing, furniture and building industries.[15] Levels of unemployment were correspondingly high. In 1927, for example, 6.5 per cent of the working population of London were unemployed, compared with 13.2 per cent in Poplar, the worst affected of the old East London boroughs, and 19.0 per cent in West Ham. Over the next five years, as the recession deepened, these increased to 12.2, 18.2 and 27.5 respectively.[16]

Unsurprisingly, such levels of unemployment were linked directly to the poverty experienced by East Londoners, plunging many families into conditions redolent of the nineteenth century. During a week in 1929 when a survey was taken, it was estimated that the worst afflicted boroughs were Poplar and Stepney, where nearly 20 per cent of the families were living in poverty. They were followed closely by Bethnal Green, Shoreditch and West Ham, so that five of the worst six London boroughs were located in East London.[17] And in ways which also remind us of a previous age, distinct pockets of poverty continued to blight the social landscape and attract notorious reputations. The area in Limehouse known to Charles Booth as the Fenian Barracks, a slum in Canning Town between the North Woolwich railway and the River Lea, and another in Stratford between the Great Eastern railway and a branch of the river were among the enclaves which had remained isolated by physical boundaries, and were inhabited largely by congested populations of the casual poor. Occasionally, the

blight spread out to embrace an entire district, as with the old seafaring
centres of Wapping, Shadwell and Limehouse:

> South of Commercial Road East is a region of mean streets and alleys,
> dating from the eighteenth and nineteenth centuries, fringed by ware-
> houses, docks and wharves on the riverside. There has been some
> clearance of slums, but overcrowding and poverty are still character-
> istic of this region, the worst parts being Gill Street, Limehouse, and its
> immediate neighbourhood where Chinese and other Asiatics abound,
> and Stepney Causeway ... A considerable proportion of the common
> lodging-house population of London is focused in the borough.[18]

Poverty was not always a legacy of past neglect. One of the worst areas was
to be found by the riverside in West Ham, which seventy years previously
had been open marshland:

> The southern area (Canning Town) is the abode of workers at the
> docks, gas works and sugar refineries, marmalade and rubber facto-
> ries: there is also a fleeting population of seafaring men of various
> races who help to provide a livelihood for the keepers of numerous
> common lodging houses ... Poverty and overcrowding are character-
> istic of the greater part of the Canning Town and Silvertown areas,
> which make up what is perhaps the largest part of unbroken depres-
> sion in East London.[19]

How did East Londoners respond to the problems of unemployment and
poverty which affected their lives so egregiously? One option was simply to
get out. Faced with the dogged persistence of wretched slums, and rising
expectations of 'homes fit for heroes', the London County Council (LCC)
embarked on an ambitious programme of housebuilding which created a
series of cottage estates encircling the capital.[20] During the interwar years,
250,000 Londoners were rehoused in the suburbs, approximately 100,000
on the Becontree Estate in Dagenham.

Built over the years 1921–34, Becontree was by far the largest public
housing scheme of the time. It was an idealistic project to provide decent
accommodation, principally for the people of East London, on a site
unlikely to provoke a wave of middle-class anxiety about the movement to
their neighbourhood of thousands of undesirables, but long before completion it attracted hostile comment from other quarters. In 1930, Henrietta
Barnett, for example, ever mindful of the importance of bringing classes

together, condemned the 'huge and dreary building schemes such as Dagenham where 90,000 of the same class are housed in what must be annoying monotony'. Others spoke of an 'isolated waste' and a 'vast dormitory desert'.[21]

There was something to these criticisms. Although the estate was initially planned as a mix of housing sizes with differential rents for different classes, the process was rushed, with little regard to the matter of building a community, or indeed whether this was at all possible in a predominantly working-class area with no sense of history or identity. Leisure activities provided by churches or community associations with little money proved unpopular; instead, tenants preferred domestic activities, including gardening on allotments, DIY and listening to the wireless. Nor was the scheme successful in ameliorating the conditions of the poor; rents were generally higher than in East London so that the tenants – as in the philanthropic building schemes of the late nineteenth century – tended to be part of an economic elite who paid a higher proportion on rent. Among the tenants identified in the 1931 Census were artisans, transport workers, office clerks, policemen and shop assistants. What this suggests is that the anticipated benefits offered by construction of the giant Ford plant at Dagenham in the early 1930s were never fully realized, and so many tenants travelled early each morning on the packed workmen's trains to Whitechapel and Moorgate.[22]

For some, the additional cost of travel to jobs in inner London, and the social strains such travel created, proved too heavy a burden, and they were forced to resort to age-old strategies of pawning goods or taking in lodgers. When these failed, many returned to the areas of East London they had previously inhabited, leaving empty houses.[23] Indeed, the turnover of houses was very high; between 1932 and 1934 there were 6,300 new lettings, but almost 5,000 vacancies, making it virtually impossible to establish a stable population on the estate.[24] And yet it was evident that for some Becontree provided a once-in-a-lifetime opportunity to acquire their own modern house remote from the squalor of East London. Grace Foakes moved from East London to Becontree in 1932. 'We were overjoyed,' she later recalled, 'at being given our own house, complete with garden. The plans we made were as fantastic as they were impossible, for to us this was paradise compared to what we had left behind.'[25]

For those who were left behind to face continued economic depression, apathy was always an option, but many occupying the political spectrum from the far left to the far right chose to fight against perceived injustices, as a result of which interwar East London became an important battlefield.

In a constitutional manner

During the 1920s political struggles developed in response to rising levels of unemployment. Trades unions proved singularly apathetic; a brief period of industrial militancy in the immediate aftermath of the war was followed by a retreat into sectional interests when unions were concerned narrowly with the protection of their own members' interests. Rather, following the strategy developed during the war of intervening politically in the apparatus of the local state, members of local councils and boards of guardians demonstrated a preparedness to take a stance against perceived injustices, and here the Labour strongholds of Poplar and West Ham assumed a particular significance.

In the local election of 1919 Labour members won control of the Poplar Borough Council. George Lansbury, pacifist, Christian and socialist, was chosen as the mayor. Succeeding the rather unspectacular mayoralty of William Lax, Lansbury seemed the obvious choice; for thirty years he had fought on behalf of the poor, and before the war had been one of the two Labour MPs, only to resign on the grounds that the party's support for the enfranchisement of women was at best weak. As part of an ambitious programme of reform, not unlike that of West Ham's first Labour council over twenty years earlier, Poplar councillors developed a borough-owned electricity undertaking, extended maternity and infant welfare provision, opened public libraries and established public health schemes to combat the scourge of tuberculosis.[26]

As the economic recession descended, and ever larger queues of unemployed appeared outside the offices of the Board of Guardians, the focus shifted. Late in 1920 the council prepared details of a large public works scheme to provide employment, on the understanding that the cost of £31,000 would be met by the government. Unconvinced that the jobs would go to ex-servicemen, however, the government reneged on its decision. Angry council meetings took place from which emerged a renewed determination to take the matter further. Early in 1921 Poplar Council took the fateful decision to challenge the whole system of metropolitan rating. Under existing arrangements, boroughs and poor law unions were required to levy their own rates. It was an inequitable system, for it effectively penalized the poorer ones by forcing them to levy higher rates to cover the cost of relief than the rich ones where little poverty prevailed. Labour councillors at Poplar contended that since poverty was a problem for the metropolis as a whole the costs of relief should be shared, and resolved that until rates were equalized Poplar would refuse to levy rates required by the various London-wide bodies, including the LCC, Metropolitan Water Board and Metropolitan Police.

In July thirty-six offending councillors were served writs by the LCC, and summonsed to appear in court to answer the charge of contempt. Proceedings of the trial were followed closely by other poor boroughs which had a vested interest in the outcome, although it was never really in doubt. The councillors were given fourteen days to levy the rates; failure to do so would result in imprisonment. They remained defiant, however, and then one by one were rounded up and sent to Brixton or to Holloway, where they suffered the privations and humiliations of prison life until their release six weeks later. While they were in prison, public support grew, and there was a real threat that other East London boroughs would follow the example of Poplar. Stepney and Bethnal Green passed resolutions to withhold the levy unless the prisoners were released; the same in Shoreditch was defeated by a single vote, but in Hackney, where Herbert Morrison was mayor, a similar resolution was heavily defeated.[27]

March in support of Poplar councillors, 1921. Demanding equalization of the rates throughout the metropolis, the council had refused to levy rates, an act of defiance that ended with their imprisonment.

Morrison, Secretary of the London Labour Party, looked with increasing consternation on the course of events. He decided the tactics of Poplar were ill-judged and would bring the whole party into disrepute if the fiasco was allowed to continue, jeopardizing his ambition of winning control of the LCC. He therefore approached the Prime Minister, Lloyd George, who agreed to Morrison's attempting to broker a deal on equalization of the rates with the Minister of Health, Sir Alfred Mond, so paving the way for the eventual release of the councillors. It was a move greeted with universal relief, particularly by a government now highly inconvenienced and embarrassed by the whole affair. The London conference which met to scrutinize the details of equalization failed to come up with a solution, largely because of hostility from richer boroughs; instead, it decided that by pooling the costs of poor relief across the metropolis, the politically sensitive focus would be deflected from the boroughs to the guardians. In practical terms, this meant that the rates of the poorest poor law unions fell dramatically. Poplar, Woolwich, Bethnal Green, Limehouse and Bermondsey were all granted considerable reductions, while the richest had modest increases.[28]

Celebrations of this putative victory were short-lived. Almost immediately after the reductions in rates were secured, they began to rise as the recession deepened. In 1922–3, average rates for London boroughs were nearly forty per cent higher than in 1919–20.[29] And the struggles of Poplar had failed to galvanize popular support from the labour movement; indeed, they drove a wedge between Morrison's London Labour Party, which sought to dissociate itself entirely, and the more radical elements within the party. The outcome was a disastrous showing in the municipal elections of November 1922, when Labour lost control of several of the poorer boroughs, including Stepney and Hackney.

Something of the spirit of Poplar, however, was subsequently resurrected in West Ham.[30] At the time, a meeting of the influential West Ham Trades Council considered the advisability of the Labour-controlled council supporting the Poplar struggle but decided that to take a stand would be impractical since it would merely increase the borough's obligations. As levels of local unemployment began to climb steeply, the unemployed, no doubt mindful of the example of Poplar, sought redress for their grievances at the door of the West Ham Poor Law Union by demanding increased scales of relief. In order to secure these they needed to overcome the resistance of those moderate guardians who represented the boroughs of East Ham, Leyton and Wanstead in the Union – not an easy task when the Union was outside the metropolitan boundary and therefore excluded from the benefits of the Common Poor Fund, making it vulnerable to high levels of expenditure.[31] Initially, the guardians resisted on the grounds that ratepayers could ill afford the burden they were already carrying, but at a meeting in September 1921, lobbied by 5,000 unemployed, they agreed to increase relief on condition that it was sanctioned by Mond. Numerous re-enactments of these scenes occurred in the ensuing weeks. By late October the moderate elements, caught between Union finances on the edge of bankruptcy and fears of the unemployed resorting to riots on the streets of West Ham, proposed to replace monetary relief with grants to cover rent and supplies of food. It was a move designed to force the government to recognize that it had some responsibility for relief of the unemployed, but Mond had refused to give financial assistance in the past and was unlikely to give in to renewed pressure.

Nonetheless, the problem for the government and many of the poor law unions was that the unemployed were now a force to be reckoned with. Gone were the days when pathetic groups of ex-servicemen stood passively on street corners begging for money, or joined makeshift bands to play for cinema queues in all sorts of weather. As the numbers of unemployed climbed in 1921, so the somewhat spontaneous and uncoordinated struggles of the unemployed were given a sense of organization and militancy by the London District Council of the Unemployed (LDCU) and the National Unemployed Workers Movement (NUWM), both of which were led by members of the newly formed Communist Party. Wal Hannington, a skilled engineer, was the best known.[32] Dismayed by the tactics of ex-servicemen, he laid down a manifesto for a new programme of action based on demands for full maintenance at trade union rates of pay, and the restitution of trade with Russia as a means of providing work.[33] Deputations from the LDCU pressed these demands at poor law meetings. Initially, the unemployed showed restraint, but when met continually with indifference their attitudes became openly strident. At a meeting of the West Ham guardians in February 1922, for example, a deputation warned:

> We are going to be more audacious than we have been in the past. This is the last time we are coming to you in a constitutional manner ... The longer the [guardians] continued to delay, the more they would drive these men to desperation. You will be sorry if, through your inactivity in the near future, these men take to looting shops and helping themselves ... If all the unemployed had been of the same political mind as himself he would have taken the same action as was taken at Poplar and locked the doors; but as the deputation had no mandate from the men to take that drastic step it was not done.[34]

An editorial in the local press argued that if the self-styled 'militant section' looked to emulating the example of Poplar, they were misguided. The unemployed needed to understand that the guardians were their best friends and that their real grievance was with the government, against which any 'unconstitutional methods' should be directed.[35] A similar deputation was refused a hearing at the next meeting; when the assembled unemployed marched back to Stratford fights broke out with the police, and the ringleaders were arrested for obstruction.

So-called communists

Unemployment levels in East London during the early interwar years reached their peak in 1921, after which they gradually declined. At the same time the cost of living fell by approximately a third, which, with scales of relief kept constant, meant real increases in their value. Militant appeals no longer had the same purchase among the unemployed, and the scenes witnessed in West Ham were not repeated. Although this eased the most acute pressure on the guardians, it was no solution to the chronic problem of expenditure and rising levels of debt, and so interest again turned to government. A conference took place in June 1922 of so-called necessitous areas, namely, the 200 constituencies which suffered undue hardship because of the high levels of expenditure on relief they were forced to meet. It resolved to send a deputation to Lloyd George with a case put together by Thomas Smith, Clerk to the West Ham Guardians, for immediate financial aid. In the belief that the government had already distributed £80m in benefits, and that unemployment was now falling, Lloyd George remained impassive.

In the meantime the debts mounted; by April 1924 the West Ham Union owed the government £1.25m, more than double the figure for Poplar, the next highest. Hope now resided in the first Labour government, which had recently taken office, but it proved no more responsive to the plight of necessitous areas. Then later in 1924, following a vigorous campaign conducted by a united front between the local Labour Party and the NUWM, Labour members took control of the guardians. It was a decisive act which ultimately brought the crisis to a head. For the Labour group was determined to reform the machinery of poor relief; the first steps were to reinstate May Day holidays and to introduce compulsory membership of trade unions for guardian employees and coal allowances for those on relief, although it did stop short of increasing scales of relief. Throughout 1925, the Minister of Health, Neville Chamberlain, met deputations from the guardians and agreed to further loans, but on condition that the guardians reduce scales of relief. At first they agreed, but a large, animated meeting of the unemployed took place at which established labour leaders Will Thorne and Jack Jones were howled down and refused a hearing. Immediately after the General Strike of May 1926, during which an additional £80,000 was paid in relief, the guardians found themselves £2.5m in debt, and approached the ministry for a further loan of £425,000. This time Chamberlain demanded drastic reductions in relief, far exceeding previous conditions. The guardians refused, and then in an unprecedented move against representational democracy, and on the back of legislation rushed through parliament, the government superseded the guardians, appointing in their place a committee of three headed by Sir Alfred Woodgate. Draconian cuts in relief followed.[36] Thomas Kirk, a leading Labour councillor, promptly sought to deflect any blame for the attendant suffering imposed on poor families:

> Whatever the mistakes the Labour Guardians made in their fight against the Government, the local unemployed leaders must take the blame. Their public utterances and private intrigues were carefully and deliberately calculated to bring the Labour Guardians into contempt … I assert that the private spite of a handful of 'so-called communists' against such men as Thorne, Jones and Killip is more responsible for the present Guardians' situation, disenfranchisement of the people, and the suffering of the wives and children of the unemployed which the 25 per cent reduction of the scale of relief has involved, than any other cause.[37]

There were signs of resistance early on, but without the active support of the NUWM, enfeebled by the imprisonment of its leaders, they soon faded, and for the three years the committee was in power it operated without hindrance. All boards of guardians were abolished in 1929, Public Assistance Committees assuming responsibility for the administration of relief. Reverberations from this defeat reached into the 1930s as levels of unemployment in West Ham again climbed sharply. Demonstrations of the unemployed occurred, occasionally provoking isolated acts of violence, but they lacked the scale and intensity of those previously witnessed around the old board of guardians. Nationally, many of the unemployed from the worst-hit areas now took to the road. The hunger marches may have evoked sympathy, and continue among the most iconic images of the interwar years, but they serve to remind us that by then the unemployed had accepted defeat.

The confusion of words

The interwar period has been seen as a watershed in popular culture, a time when the emergence of mass culture heralded a decisive break with the past.[38] The course of entertainment and the arts was no longer determined by the civilizing mission of a middle-class, cultural elite, but rather by a desire to reach the broad masses. The mass media in particular experienced extraordinary growth. Although the beginnings of a popular cinema were evident before the First World War, it was in the 1920s, largely under the hegemony of Hollywood, that it became an essential part of the lives of countless people. Of less significance, but vital nonetheless, was radio broadcasting, which, unknown in 1918, could in 1939 reach directly into approximately nine million homes where it provided company for even the poorest. Radio, and to a lesser extent the gramophone, which remained beyond the reach of many, revolutionized the production and consumption of music by bringing it into the living rooms of the entire nation. Sport also was transformed by the course of cultural modernization. Popular forms such as football, boxing and cricket could all trace their origins to plebeian entertainment, but from the latter stages of the nineteenth century were disciplined by sets of rules and the exigencies of commercialization.

How did East Londoners respond to these changes? Here was a population with a long history of enjoying themselves, often pursuing forms of entertainment that fell foul of the authorities. How did people who had enthusiastically attended cheap theatrical performances, music halls and public houses take to the technological sophistication of mass culture, particularly at a time of economic hardship?

That the transformation in popular culture happened at a time of economic recession may at first sight seem odd, but these novel entertainments were cheap, and since the end of the nineteenth century real incomes had increased at the same time as working hours had fallen. The review of 'Life and Leisure' undertaken as part of the *New Survey of London Life and Labour* commented on the notable increase in daily leisure and holidays.[39] It was not merely a question of quantity, however, for alongside the greater facility for leisure were significant changes in the type of entertainment on offer. Amusements and recreations were now provided for audiences, it was argued, which were largely passive. Cinema had taken the place of music hall, and had greatly diminished the part occupied by the pub in the lives of working-class families. In 1911 there were 94 cinemas in London, seating approximately 55,000 persons; by 1931 this had increased to 258 with a capacity of 344,000 seats, indicating not only a strong growth in their number but equally a dramatic increase in their size.

Popular though cinema was, its growth had been uneven. Moving pictures originally appeared as novel entertainments either in music halls and theatres or in church rooms, shops and halls adapted for the purpose, but the technology and art of making pictures were primitive. The short newsreels and crude melodramas and farces were of poor technical quality; projected images shook and there were constant breaks in transmission. With the outbreak of the war in 1914, a boom was heralded by advances in cinema technology and art. Productions like *Intolerance* and *Birth of a Nation* demonstrated its real potential. Then in 1915 Charlie Chaplin, a music hall performer who had made his stage debut at the Paragon at Mile End, burst on to the screen.[40]

It was apparent before 1914 that cinema was a force to be reckoned with in East London. Music halls, purpose-built picture theatres and religious buildings were converted to cinemas. In Bethnal Green, for example, the Foresters' Music Hall along the Cambridge Road became a cinema in 1910, and lasted until 1960, at which point it had a capacity of 1,000. Sebright's Music Hall in Coate Street was converted to a cinema in 1914, but survived only until 1927, when flats were built on the site. In 1911 the Adelphi Chapel in the Hackney Road was converted to a cinema, named the Hackney Grand Central, which operated until the 1930s.[41] In West Ham, before purpose-built cinemas appeared in 1909, films were shown in converted shops and factories. During the First World War, their popular appeal soared so that by 1921 at least twenty cinemas were to be found in West Ham with capacities ranging from the 400 of Rathbone Street Cinema in Canning Town to the Queens Cinema, Forest Gate, and the Grand Cinema, Canning Town, each with 1,500 seats. By the end of the 1920s, the Premier, Carlton, Broadway and Rex cinemas had been built, each with capacities of approximately 3,000. Prices of admission started at 4d, making cinemas accessible to all but the very poor, and weekly attendances exceeded 120,000.[42] A settlement worker at Mansfield House in Plaistow reflected on the nature of this new phenomenon:

> Though the cinema as a social factor is but beginning to operate, it has already outstripped in popularity and influence every other form of entertainment ... It is more readily intelligible to the slightly educated, unimaginative millions. The highly educated have been trained to create mental pictures under the stimulus of language. But words rather confuse than illumine the untrained mind.[43]

If we look beyond the rather elitist sentiments, this may help to explain the appeal of cinema to working-class audiences. The narratives, characterizations and spectacle offered by film were accessible to a non-literate culture in ways the printed text was not. And audiences quickly developed a skill in reading films beyond the competence of previous generations. Stanley Reed, born in Plaistow, later to become Director of the British Film Institute, found that films made for schools were simply oblivious to this intelligence, for they were:

> pedestrian, underestimating the sophistication of the thirties generation of children from their experience of commercial cinema and much greater than that of most of their parents and teachers. This curious reversal of roles had been brought home to me by the difficulty on those rare occasions when [my father] went to the cinema in the following the plot of the film; it all went too fast he complained.[44]

We must therefore be cautious in dismissing cinema-going as a passive activity, and audiences as mindless and inert consumers. Films extended the mental horizons of their audiences by developing new forms of visual and verbal communication. And people attended the cinema not merely to watch a film. Programmes were long and varied, including typically two films (an A and a B), a newsreel, cartoons, a stage performance, and an organ recital in the interval. And the larger cinemas being built were veritable palaces, offering warmth, dazzling spectacle and comfort to people who for the most part inhabited dim and meagre accommodation. Courting couples found their own uses for the facilities.

The rise of the cinema reconfigured the cultural trends of late-nineteenth-century East London. Its relationship to the changing fortunes of music hall and theatre is a complex one, and so their decline cannot be attributed to cinema alone, but over a comparatively short period of time cinemas captured music hall audiences, in part because in terms of performers, staging and narratives there were significant continuities between the two. Theatres survived, largely because middle-class audiences held up, but the low-life theatres and penny gaffs of the nineteenth century departed for ever. Hardest hit by the inexorable rise of cinema, however, were the pubs and the consumption of alcohol. From the time of the Booth survey, drunkenness fell steadily and consistently; between 1913 and 1932, for example, annual convictions for drunkenness in the Metropolitan Police area dropped from 85 to 15 per thousand of the population, and although this was due partly to improvements introduced towards the end of the nineteenth century, cinema was able to draw large sections of the population which otherwise would have spent their evenings drinking in pubs.

Despite (perhaps because of) the closeness of kinship networks within the local community, it was important for most families to have a space which was their own, and which could be symbolically claimed by the simple act of shutting the front door.[45] People were therefore reluctant to invite one another to their homes, but in the pub friends met to gossip, exchange information and put the world to rights in a relaxed atmosphere.[46] Many pubs also made efforts to improve conditions by providing better seating and music, and to cater for different clientele in public and saloon bars. The economic role of pubs, however, was no longer important. Some selling and buying of goods (often stolen) took place, and bookmakers operated, but the hiring and firing of labour was rarely practised.

By the 1920s it was apparent that an even smaller section of the population frequented the pub on a regular basis, the most notable decline being among the young, who, instead of spending leisure time in the pub or hanging around street corners, went to the cinema.[47] Women of all ages were less likely to be found in pubs, not merely because of rival attractions available but also because the wireless provided a degree of sociability and pleasantness to otherwise drab surroundings.

A four-minute mile

It was the time also when sport came of age. East London had a long tradition of proletarian sport. Boxing, football, horse-racing and running had attracted considerable levels of support from early in the eighteenth century. All emerged from popular recreations embedded within working-class culture, and provided a few with the opportunity of riches either through betting, which was intimately associated with sport, or from purses won in fights and races. Serious, talented and professional sportsmen thus appeared from time to time whose exploits compare favourably to more recent stars. Take, for example, James Parrott, a costermonger, who completed the mile from Goswell Road to Shoreditch Church in under four minutes on 9 May 1770, that is, nearly two hundred years before Roger Bannister's famous run.[48] Sceptics should note that in the late eighteenth century time and distance could be measured accurately, and the fact that some races attracted huge wagers suggests people had a keen interest in ensuring that this was the case.[49] The codification of sport which took place under the watchful eyes of Victorian public schools, allied to the promotion of the amateur ideal, relegated professional sportsmen and sportswomen to the margins, and airbrushed their achievements from the records. By 1914, professional running, or pedestrianism, had virtually ceased.

Boxing and dog racing also had their origins in plebeian culture, but were not subject to appropriation by social elites in the same way. Boxing, or, more accurately, bouts of brawling between unequal opponents, often under the influence of alcohol, had been a feature of the big London fairs since mediaeval times. With the suppression of fairs, boxing was declared a public nuisance in 1743; thereafter, in an attempt to avoid the unwelcome attention of magistrates and the police, contests were staged in makeshift rings erected in the fields and commons at the edge of the metropolis, including the marshland areas of West Ham. Clandestine they might have been, and yet the matches were able to attract audiences of thousands from all sections of society.[50] Bare-knuckle prize fighters themselves were drawn overwhelmingly from the working class. Butchers, paviours, coal heavers, bakers, bargemen and carmen were numbered among those who developed boxing into a sport, success at which relied increasingly on the use of skill instead of brute strength. The best of them could make small fortunes, and gain enormous prestige within the community, indeed nationally, thus offering a way out of poverty and obscurity. A purse of a thousand guineas or more was not uncommon.

For reasons which are not entirely clear, East London produced no outstanding boxers in this period. Typical, it seems, was the Spitalfields weaver, Wasdale, who with his considerable size and weight had gained such a reputation in the locality as a serious fighter that he risked twenty guineas against the celebrated Irish boxer Jack O'Donnel, only to be wretchedly defeated in three rounds. There were, however, some notable exceptions, all from the Jewish community. Daniel Mendoza, born in Aldgate in 1764 of a Sephardim family, was generally regarded as the most complete boxer of his time, repeatedly defeating opponents of much greater size and weight, before retiring to become publican of the Lord Nelson in Whitechapel, dying in penury in 1836. And there was Samuel Elias, better known as Dutch Sam, born in Petticoat Lane in 1775, who despite his small stature had a reputation as the hardest of hitters, and was able to retire from boxing undefeated. Although these and other lesser Jewish boxers were subjected to prejudice, they helped to dispel the popular belief that Jews were a timid and defenceless people.

The association with boxing continued into the modern era. University settlements and boys' clubs provided opportunities for young hopefuls. At the Repton, Fairbairn, Docklands Settlement and other clubs keen to channel the energies of East End youth into disciplined and controlled

combat, free boxing lessons were made available. Some were enthusiastically taken up by members of immigrant communities intent on defending
themselves against racial violence. Again a clutch of outstanding boxers
sprang from the Jewish community, this time headed by Kid Lewis, welterweight champion of the world from 1915 to 1917, and Kid Berg, light
welterweight champion in the early 1930s. There was, however, one notable
fighter from the indigenous population of East London, namely, Bombardier
Billy Wells, born in Cable Street, Stepney, in 1889, who became British and
British Empire heavyweight champion from 1911 to 1919.[51]

By this time, the rules of modern professional boxing had been laid
down, and the sport was governed under the watchful eye of the National
Sporting Club, and yet it never relinquished the long association with
gambling. Indeed, in areas such as East London, boxing provided profitable opportunities for criminal elements which increasingly patronized the
numerous halls where minor contests among the several thousand professional fighters were staged for small purses. One former patron recalled
fights at Shoreditch Town Hall:

> There was always 'nobbins' [coins thrown into the ring after a good
> fight]. You would always see a great fight. The word got around.
> This was the place to go if you wanna see a real scrap. It was like a
> cockpit ... You'd get people come out of the West End. Show business
> people, they've always been closely involved with boxing ... The
> villains? They were definitely at the ringside, no doubt about that, and
> everyone seemed to know it.[52]

More so than boxing, dog racing and speedway remained peculiarly working-
class sports. With origins in hare coursing, greyhound racing was introduced
in the 1920s, initially at the Belle Vue stadium, Manchester, and White City
and Walthamstow stadiums in London, after which 'going to the dogs'
rapidly gained huge popular support, almost entirely because of the opportunities offered for betting. In 1927 5.5 million people attended racing tracks,
13.5 in 1928, and, at its peak in 1945, 50 million, by which time there were
77 tracks, 17 of which were in London, and the total amount wagered
rivalled that spent on horse-racing.[53] Regular patrons took great interest in
the form of the dogs, following their fortunes from one meeting to another,
and studying forecasts included in most of the national dailies, including the
Communist Party's *Daily Worker*. Others were happy to bet on a whim. In
London it was possible to attend racing every night of the week except
Sunday. Charles Dimont's amusing if patronizing account of a visit to a

London meeting describes a week in the life of regular punters Sid and his
fiancée. Every night they must have something to do. Mondays and Fridays
they go to the cinema, Wednesday is football pools evening, Sundays they
dance, and on Thursdays and Saturdays – their favourite nights – they go to
the dogs, where they get a thrill from the chance of making money.[54]

Speedway racing was imported from Australia in 1928 and quickly
attracted large crowds. London had five tracks at Clapton, Wembley,
Crystal Palace, Wimbledon and West Ham in 1933, offering racing one
evening each week. Total attendance was just over one and a quarter
million people, the large majority of which comprised local young women
who were attracted more by the excitement of the spectacle rather than
betting, which remained low-key, or as family members of the riders.[55]
Tuesday evenings at the stadium in Prince Regent Lane, Custom House,
regularly attracted crowds in excess of 50,000 in the 1930s to watch the
exploits of Tiger Stevenson, Bluey Wikinson, Eric Chitty and Tommy
Croombs, local heroes of the West Ham Speedway Team.[56]

In terms of both participation and spectatorship, the most popular
national sport by far was association football. Like other sports, football
can be traced back to the plebeian culture of the Middle Ages, but in the
course of the nineteenth century it was appropriated by public schools,
which established regular teams and divested the game of unruly and
violent aspects by providing rules, later to be codified by the Football
Association in 1863. In part through a desire to address contemporary
concern over the poor physical condition of working-class children,
schoolboy football associations worked vigorously to promote the game on
the school curriculum, and slowly but steadily its social base shifted away
from the public schools.[57]

And yet the impact of football on metropolitan leisure pursuits was
muted. Professional teams emerged from the industrial heartlands of the
north and Midlands which challenged the dominance of the public
schools. Football came late to London; when the first league was formed in
1885 no London club featured, nor did it until the Woolwich Arsenal
joined in 1893, to be followed by Chelsea and Clapton Orient in 1905. The
interwar years witnessed a sharp rise in attendance. While in 1910 there
had been only five professional clubs in London with an average weekly
attendance of 84,000, by 1921 there were eleven with an attendance of
217,000.[58] Despite this growth, East London was never able to sustain an
elite club. The three largest clubs in the area had originally been formed
from works teams with financial support from employers. Millwall was
born in 1885 from J.T. Morton's Cannery on the Isle of Dogs, the Woolwich

Arsenal in 1886 from the Royal Arsenal, and West Ham in 1900 from the Thames Ironworks and Shipbuilding Company. By the 1920s, when the fortunes of metropolitan football looked more favourable, both Millwall and the Arsenal had been forced to migrate elsewhere in search of less remote locations. West Ham eventually settled at Upton Park on the border between West and East Ham in 1904, since when it has acted as a nursery for English football talent, and famously reached the first FA cup final to be played at the new Wembley Stadium in 1923, only to be defeated by Bolton Wanderers. Success at the highest level of the league or in Europe, however, has eluded the club. In the meantime, the other East London club, Leyton Orient, founded as Clapton Orient in 1898, and with its ground in Walthamstow, has languished in the lower divisions of the football league.

On the make

There is good reason to think of crime as part of the cultural landscape of East London. The pursuit of ill-gotten gain was always an option for those who found it difficult to make ends meet. Given the privations witnessed in the interwar period, we might reasonably suppose that East London emerged as the centre of metropolitan criminal activity; the reality was, however, that there was no necessary relationship between poverty and crime. 'The fact is,' concluded Llewellyn Smith, 'that persons with vicious and criminal propensities are found in all economic strata, being marked off from the rest of the community by character and temperament rather than by degree of material well being.'[59] And there was no evidence from the official statistics that as the recession bit crime had increased in London.[60] Contemporary observers scrutinized these statistics and proposed, as had many more impressionistic ones in the past, that reductions in crime were symptomatic of the gospel of improvement in the metropolis. The *New Survey of London Life and Labour*, for example, decided that although the volume of crime was the 'net resultant of a large number of inter-acting causes and influences, whose separate effects cannot be disentangled by statistical methods', it was clear that much had been done to reduce crime by such organizations as the boys' clubs, borstals for young offenders, and the introduction of the probation system.[61]

The data furnished no information on the size or geographical specificity of the criminal population; indeed, so many difficulties attended such calculations that most commentators shied away from them.[62] There remained the tacit acceptance, however, that London was the natural home of the criminal population, and East London was the headquarters. To understand why this was the case we need briefly to revisit aspects of the more distant history of the area. From the time of its formation and recognition as a distinct part of the metropolis, East London had attracted worrying glances from the authorities. Beyond the reach of metropolitan authorities and the cognitive boundaries of the City itself, little was known of its population apart from the somewhat rarefied domains of the wealthy elite. What was known suggested a somewhat lawless and dissident populace. This image of a criminal underclass, organized, predatory and woven into the fabric of the local community, haunted views of the East London poor throughout the nineteenth century.

This mythical imagery may have shed more light on the nature of respectable opinion than on East End culture, but all myths are built on some essential truth. The people of East London in the nineteenth century did experience acts of violence; they were occasional and probably no more frequent or intense than those witnessed in other poor areas of the metropolis. There was, however, a distinct culture which operated at the permeable boundary between the legal and the criminal. This culture was encapsulated in the spiv, a figure who lived on his wits but was prepared to transgress if the potential rewards were big enough. He shunned the discipline required by wage labour to follow the promise of independence. Sartorial display, attitude and verbal dexterity were at the core of a sense of identity which was looked on with affection if not admiration by others within the community. With a smile on his face he attempted to cheat and trick anyone thought gullible enough to fall for his wiles. To his credit, violence was never used; the gains were relatively small, so his victims rarely suffered apart from a sense of dented pride. In any case, he calculated, they probably deserved what they got for allowing themselves to be duped.[63]

The spiv was the most recognizable entrepreneur in the sizable twilight economy of London as a whole, East London in particular. But he was not alone, for this hidden economy was lubricated also by the exploits of petit bourgeois operators attempting to establish legitimate businesses, informal networks of individuals seeking to augment their incomes by making deals, villains unloading their ill-gotten gains, petty traders peddling varieties of cheap merchandise, and even those in regular employment making a bit on the side. 'On the fiddle', 'on the make', 'doing the business', 'wheeling and dealing', 'ducking and diving' captured something of this opportunistic entrepreneurial culture in which capitalist business ethics and commercial protocols were adapted to the requirements of a working class located within the peculiar economic structure of East London.[64] Somewhat removed from the civilizing influences of the middle class and the discipline of the factory, successive generations of sharp and manipulative East Enders thus survived in part through a powerful sense of independence, and the pursuit of individual endeavour, often in collusion with members of the police who were only too familiar with the entrepreneurs and the ethos they inhabited.

When Dick Hobbs returned to East London to conduct research on this entrepreneurial culture, he discovered that everyone was 'at it', and some more than most.[65] But then he moved in a particular milieu which, pervasive though it was, could not be held to represent the whole of the East End. Many would simply have not entertained such exploits. At the other end of the spectrum were the full-time, hard-core villains, the majority of whom had served apprenticeships as entrepreneurs before turning professional. They inhabited a dark and violent underworld and, although in a small minority, exercised a considerable influence over the lives and imaginations of the communities in which they operated.

The autobiography of Arthur Harding, compiled by Raphael Samuel from taped interviews over a six-year period, provides remarkable insights into the criminal underworld of East London.[66] Harding was born in 1886 on the site of the Old Nichol, one of the most notorious of the criminal slums of the nineteenth century, the streets of which were coloured in black and blue by Charles Booth.[67] Early on he was introduced to its entrepreneurial culture:

> The children of the Nichol would hang about the High Street seeing if they could fiddle something off the stalls. If they could pinch anything, they'd pinch it. If they had anything over they'd sell it to the neighbours … Twos and threes used to do it together, sometimes more than that. If an owner had three or four kids hanging around his stall, he'd got to keep an eye on what was happening under them, to know what was going on. Girls and all used to be at it. They were very nimble. Anything they could lay their hands on.[68]

Most stallholders were unwilling to prevent such predation by invoking the law; either they sympathized with the plight of hungry children, or they decided it was better to lose a little than cause trouble. Shopkeepers had to keep an eye on the small items hanging outside, particularly when boys like Harding with sharp penknives wandered by. Closer to home, Harding's mother purloined clothes from church sales on a regular basis, arguing with admirable logic that they had been sent to the church to be given away, not to be sold in order to provide the rector with another bottle of whisky.

At the age of nine Harding was forced out of home when it became too cramped, and following a brief spell of sleeping rough was sent to a Barnardo's home for three years. Truanting from school he then earned money by selling around the pubs, and for a while his family's future looked brighter, but his mother's drinking problem drained their income, plunging them back into destitution. Harding found a series of short-lived jobs in cabinet-making, glass-blowing and clothing, and served for a time in the army before they discovered he was under-age. He began to associate with a group of boys in Brick Lane, learning from more experienced thieves who hung out in the pubs and coffee houses how to lift goods from the slow-moving carts passing by. Early in 1902 he was apprehended while 'giving a hand', convicted at Worship Street magistrates' court, and sentenced to twelve months' hard labour in Wormwood Scrubs – it was to be the first of many imprisonments.[69] A fellow inmate – 'a real bloody villain, a complete criminal' – taught Harding the art of pickpocketing. On his release, Harding formed a gang operating in the markets of Whitechapel and Petticoat Lane, and later teamed up with local Jewish boys who were so smartly dressed and innocent-looking that few suspected they were skilled pickpockets operating around the country.

The environment in which Harding matured recalled descriptions of the criminal enclaves of an earlier age. 'Brick Lane was a hotbed of villainy,' he recounted:

> Women paraded up and down the streets, took the men to their 'doubles' and sold themselves for a few pence. Thieves hung about the corner of the street, waiting, like Mr Micawber, for something to turn up. In the back alleys there was garrotting – some of the brides would lumber a seaman while he was drunk and then he would be dropped – 'stringing someone up' was the slang phrase for it.[70]

And the villains resembled tragic characters from a theatrical production of a gothic horror. China Bob, of Jewish extraction, was a wild animal who carried a small hatchet in his coat pocket, terrorizing the local population. His body was riddled with scars and half-healed cuts when found one morning in a gutter of Commercial Street. No one was charged with his murder; no one cared. Spud Murphy was another of the 'half-mad loafers'. He had served in the mercantile marine, and then lived off the earnings of local prostitutes, several of whom he murdered before the law caught up with him, and he was hanged at Pentonville.[71] The women were no better. Biddy the Chiver had a notorious reputation with a knife, terrorizing local prostitutes into paying her money. She married a man who beat her, until found with another woman, at which point Biddy stabbed him to death. She was given three years in Holloway on the grounds of diminished responsibility, but died before completing her sentence.[72] Many of these small-time villains died thus, or on the fields of France and Ireland in conflicts they never understood.

Harding was one that survived. Over time, in part because he could read, in part because of his impressive physique and fighting skills, he gained a reputation from Clerkenwell to the Elephant and Castle as someone to be reckoned with. He bought his first gun at the bottom of Brick Lane in 1904, and although he claimed it was for protection, it enhanced his persona. After a spell of wrongful imprisonment, he became vicious, taking on and beating many of the other 'terrors'. The police gave him a wide berth until 1911, when his nemesis, Chief Inspector Fred Wensley, laid an ambush for him and his gang. Five were taken into custody and subsequently imprisoned, effectively breaking up the gang. Harding later married, decided to go straight, and, fearing for the future of his children, moved out of Bethnal Green to the more respectable Leyton.

Social banditry

In retrospect, despite his long record of imprisonment, crime and violence, Harding is best understood as an East End entrepreneur and petty thief rather than a professional or habitual criminal. He encountered gangs including the Titanic, Hoxton, Old Nichol and the Coons, and for a time led the notorious Vendettas, but by his own admission they were more hooligan than criminal. The professional gangs of the East End underworld operated at a different level. Their origins are obscure. Outlaw bands were a common feature of pre-industrial landscapes around the world. In Japan, Italy, Germany, Spain and Russia, for example, bandit gangs, based largely upon kinship networks, sought to establish and maintain power over their rivals in long-standing and bloody feuds. Many of the bandit gangs, however, were manifestations of peasant rebellions against the rich landlords and merchants who had disrupted their traditional ways of life. As in the legend of Robin Hood, these gangs were often provided with protection by villagers, not only because their members sprang from these very communities but also because they gained a reputation for robbing the rich to give to the poor.[73] In Britain, with the passing of the feudal order, social banditry disappeared; no such movement was again witnessed after the sixteenth century. Instead, banditry resurfaced in the ascendant urban centres as criminal gangs inhabiting dark and unknown underworlds.[74] As the greatest centre of wealth, London remained the favoured target, but with more effective policing in the nineteenth century, gangs found it increasingly difficult to operate and therefore tended to die out. Towards the end of the century they reappeared, not as a revival of an indigenous tradition but out of the various immigrant communities, which had brought their own criminal fraternities tied together by powerful ethnic and regional – even tribal – loyalties, thus suggesting the profound continuities between pre-industrial banditry and modern urban ganglands. Their victims were powerless shopkeepers and publicans to whom they offered protection at a price, and those myriad entrepreneurs who operated at the boundaries of legality and were less likely to seek help from the police. 'Keepers of shady restaurants, runners of gambling dens, landlords of houses of resort, street bookmakers,' declared Wensley, 'and other people on the fringe of the underworld were among those peculiarly open to trouble.'[75] And he should know.

There were a number of immigrant gangs which fought over manorial rights in East London during the early decades of the twentieth century. The forty-strong Russian Jewish Bessarabians were based in Whitechapel, where they exercised a reign of terror over the local community. Previous experience of collective struggle against the Tsarist police defined the ways in which they operated, and help to explain why the Jewish shopkeepers upon whom they preyed were so reluctant to turn to the authorities for assistance.[76] Their main rivals were the Odessian gang, with which a constant state of war existed until a series of convictions for robbery and assault, and the emigration of some of their members to America in order to avoid prosecution, curbed their power, reducing them to thugs hired to break up anarchist meetings. The Grizzard gang, led by Joseph 'Kemmy' Grizzard, was probably involved in every major burglary committed in Edwardian London. Working from his office in Hatton Gardens or house in East London, Grizzard was recognized not only as the biggest receiver of stolen goods, but the mastermind behind the most spectacular jewellery robberies, for which he recruited the most skilled villains in the business.[77] The law eventually caught up with him, and in 1913 Grizzard received a sentence of seven years. A police report at the time suggests why he was wanted so badly:

He is a diamond merchant by trade, but has no established business premises. He does undoubtedly do a little business, but the greater portion of his time is taken up by organising crimes, and buying and disposing of stolen property. Much has been heard of him during the past fifteen years as having been connected with many serious crimes.

A large number of statements made by prisoners are in our possession showing that they have disposed of property to him, but unfortunately we have been unable to prosecute for lack of corroborative evidence.[78]

Prison life took its toll on Grizzard but did nothing to prevent further fraudulent activity on his release. When again arrested and sentenced in 1923, he was found to have advanced tuberculosis and diabetes, and died later that year aged fifty-seven.

Finally, mention should be made of Brilliant Chang and Yasukichi Miyagawa, heads of the largest drug empires, employing hundreds of dealers and runners. Having been sent to England from China by his wealthy father in 1913, Chang opened a restaurant in Regent Street from which he entered the world of drug trafficking, later moving to Limehouse, where abundant supplies of cocaine and opium were available to be sold on to his rich clients in the West End. The police eventually caught up with him in 1924; following an imprisonment of over a year, he was deported. The police noted a dramatic fall in prosecutions for drug dealing.[79] Miyagawa assumed the role of a dosser, shuffling along the gutters of East London in threadbare clothes, no doubt to deflect public attention from the fact that he had made a large fortune from importing and exporting sizable quantities of morphine and heroin. After drugs were discovered during a police raid on his premises in 1923, Miyagawa was sentenced to four years, and then deported back to Japan.[80] It was the beginning of the end of Limehouse as an epicentre of the opium trade.

The mixed fortunes of these gangs were to inspire rather than deter organized criminal activity in the decades which followed. As immigrant communities were assimilated the presence of their exclusive gangs declined, to be replaced by home-grown bands which operated more freely across ethnic lines. The career of Jack Spot exemplified this. Born of Polish Jewish parents in Whitechapel, Spot started as a small-time criminal in protection rackets around Petticoat Lane, and bookmaking. After eliminating the opposition, he became the self-styled King of Aldgate, but it was during the rise of fascism in East London that he secured a reputation as a protector of the Jewish community and was sentenced to six months' imprisonment for grievous bodily harm on a blackshirt.[81] Like a Jewish godfather, or a Robin Hood of the East End, as he was called, Spot found his services in great demand from Jews around the country whose businesses suffered from anti-semitism, and yet simultaneously he expanded his criminal empire by moving into the club scene of the West End, often by teaming up with other gang leaders, most notably Billy Hill.

Looting, the black market, gambling and pilfering from the workplace provided abundant opportunities for criminal endeavour during the Second World War. In the immediate aftermath, a number of home-grown criminal gangs emerged or consolidated their power. The Watney Streeters remained in control of the docks, while local gangs ruled over the criminal landscapes of Whitechapel, Upton Park, Poplar and Hoxton. The most notorious, and best remembered, however, was that of the Kray twins, Ronnie and Reggie, the structure and operation of which came closest to those of the gang syndicates found in the United States. They were born into a poor family in Bethnal Green in 1933. Strict authority was exercised by their grandfather, Jimmy Lee, who had been a promising flyweight, and yet from their school days the twins seemed to attract trouble. For a time they were amateur boxers, later turning to petty and then more serious crime. Through military discipline and planning, a sophisticated network of connections and information, and use of savage violence resulting in numerous murders, they established a fearsome criminal empire which moved beyond London into international markets.[82] The murders, however, led eventually to the Krays' conviction and life imprisonment. Ronnie died from a heart attack in 1995, Reggie from cancer in 2000, having been released on compassionate grounds a few weeks earlier. Their funerals were well-attended and lavish occasions. Like most gangland bosses they were ultimately tragic figures. Paranoid schizophrenia, bisexuality, sadism, fantasy, an obsession with weapons and a great admiration for Hitler have retrospectively been offered as explanations of the twins' behaviour, and yet their reputation as loving sons and local benefactors remains undimmed.

While East London had demonstrated a rather ambiguous relationship with the forces of modernization, it could not escape them in their most destructive guise. As we shall see in the next chapter, East London witnessed a dramatic rise of fascism in the interwar period before its German counterpart launched the Blitz and laid waste to the material and cultural environment of the area.

CHAPTER 11

Fascism and War, 1920–1945

O NE EVENING in the 1930s Phil Piratin, a Stepney communist, attended a fascist meeting in Limehouse addressed by Oswald Mosley:

> I went along to this meeting, made myself inconspicuous, and watched to see the support which Mosley had. When the meeting ended there was to be a march to Victoria Park Square, Bethnal Green, another of Mosley's strongholds. I was curious to see who and what kind of people would march. The fascist band moved off, and behind them about fifty thugs in blackshirt uniform. Then came the people. About 1,500 men, women (some with babies in their arms), and youngsters marched behind Mosley's banner. I knew some of these people, some of the men wore trade-union badges. This had a terrific effect on my attitude to the problem, and I went back to Stepney branch committee determined to fight this.[1]

The issue of particular interest in Piratin's account – and the one which clearly shocked him – was the ability of fascism in East London to attract ordinary working-class people. This was not a movement made up exclusively of fanatics in military uniform; it embraced also large numbers of local residents, some of whom were known to him and yet saw no incongruity between membership of a trade union and marching behind a fascist banner. This chapter begins by exploring this seeming paradox and unravelling some of the myths which have surrounded fascist activity in East London.

Some rough hands

The putative link between unemployment and fascism in East London, combined with the view that fascists ruthlessly and successfully exploited anti-semitic sentiment, has contributed to something of an orthodoxy about the interwar period. There can be little doubt of the importance of the area to the fascist movement, in particular the rise to prominence in the 1930s of Oswald Mosley's British Union of Fascists (BUF). Estimates vary, but it seems likely that between late 1935 and late 1938 the active membership of the BUF in London was between 3,000 and 3,600, no less than 70–80 per cent of which was located in East London branches.[2] Incautious attempts to explain this by focusing on the desperate poverty of East London and the continued presence of a large Jewish population fail to capture adequately a rather complex situation.

The ideology of British fascism was neither monolithic nor a pale reflection of continental thinking.[3] At its heart was a profound distrust of economic and political liberalism. Fascists opposed what they saw as the anarchy of unfettered capitalism; the interwar recession was accordingly blamed on a blind allegiance to the principles of laissez-faire, and the social disorder on a parliamentary democracy which had sown the seeds of class antagonisms. Evoking a native tradition, fascists professed admiration for the way in which the Tudor state had forged national integration through authoritarian, centralized government, and found inspiration in writers like the nineteenth-century philosopher Thomas Carlyle who had stood against what they saw as the sordid materialism of liberal economics, and had argued for the merits of authoritarian leadership. The answer to contemporary problems of internal disintegration had therefore to be sought in national regeneration based on a spirit of harmony instilled by military discipline. Here the ideas of social Darwinism had a powerful appeal, for regeneration was conceived in terms of the evolution of more advanced forms of biological existence, in part through the elimination of degenerative strains found among the poor and certain foreign populations.

This might suggest that the anti-semitism which gained momentum as waves of poor Jews migrated to East London in the late nineteenth century would be enthusiastically adopted by fascist currents, but not so, at least not for some time. The economic and moral anxieties around sweated trades which had surfaced in the 1880s identified Jewish immigrants as a particular object of concern (Chapter 8). The failure of the Lords' Committee on Sweated Trades to lay down firm recommendations prompted Arnold White, who had been one of the most vigorous witnesses, to found and finance the Association for Preventing the Immigration of Destitute Aliens.[4] The society was fronted by several peers of the realm, and included among its members well-meaning philanthropists such as the MP for Poplar, Sidney Buxton, but in effect was run by White and his anti-alien partner W.H. Wilkins. With the aim of 'organizing and directing public opinion, as a preliminary to an attempt to obtain legislative enactment', the society planned a series of public meetings in East London but was singularly unsuccessful in overcoming popular inertia. No local MPs, borough councillors or trade union officials were recruited to the Executive Committee, and by 1892 the Association was wound up.

Other organizations proclaiming similar causes, such as the Navy League (1895) and National Service League (1901), came and went, but then in 1901 the British Brothers' League was founded by Major William Evans-Gordon, who in a pernicious climate of xenophobia and nationalism created by the Boer War had recently been elected as a Conservative MP for Stepney on a platform opposing further alien immigration. An experienced army officer who had been responsible for famine relief in north-west India, Evans-Gordon brought energy and discipline to the task of building the League from the ranks of East Londoners. Encouraged by the packed attendance at the first meeting in Stepney, the League organized a series of rallies, one of which saw 4,000 crammed into the People's Palace in Mile End, with many others turned away at the door.[5] In ways which anticipated the BUF, meetings were 'stewarded' by hefty labourers who were placed strategically around the room, ejecting any among the audience who dared to protest against the proceedings. A petition supporting a ban on immigration collected 45,000 signatures from East London alone, and rallies were held in other locations, although the area remained at the core of the League's activities. In 1903 the Immigration Reform Association was established; with 125 MPs and a number of East London clergy amongst its members, the Association was intended to liaise between parliament and popular opinion in order to hasten the passage of legislation curbing immigration. The Aliens Act was subsequently passed two years later.

With the passage of the 1905 Act, however, and the recovery of the economy from the depression of the 1890s, anti-immigration sentiment faded. So did the numbers of immigrants, not, however, because of defects in the act and its implementation, but despite them. When war broke out in 1914 the figure of the alien was resurrected, this time as a threat to national security rather than national well-being. The Aliens Restriction Act and the Defence of the Realm Act, hurriedly passed through parliament, required all aliens to register, severely restricted their movements, and gave the Home Secretary powers to exclude, intern or deport suspect aliens. These measures severely affected the movement and employment of foreigners, most particularly Germans, who were the obvious target, but many suffered at the hands of ordinary people dispensing what they viewed as rough justice. Ugly acts of xenophobia were committed against Germans, or people with German-sounding names, virtually from the commencement of hostilities. Some local papers reporting attacks initially sympathized with the plight of the victims:

> A well known German butcher in Stratford has since the outbreak of war, closed his business and gone away. Several German tradesmen have had demonstrations outside their shops, which have been closed. Many of them are highly respected citizens carrying on a useful and legitimate business. They probably deplore the present state of affairs as much as anyone, and it is unsportsmanlike and alien to the British institution of fair play to harass them in this matter. Several German tradesmen have adopted the precaution of displaying the Union Jacks, and it is to be hoped the emblem at any rate will suffice to shield them from wanton acts of irresponsible people.[6]

As hostilities intensified, the violence became more extreme. After the sinking of the *Lusitania* in 1915, shops in West Ham owned by butchers and bakers suspected of being German were smashed and their entire contents removed as thousands gathered around.[7] The riots lasted three days, causing damage estimated at £100,000. Since much of this was done by drunken crowds on binges of indiscriminate looting, it is quite possible that xenophobia was rather less significant than the opportunities offered for personal gain at little risk to themselves.

Many of the victims were Jews, who made up a sizable proportion of the German population in London, but overall the effect of the war on Jews was more oblique. The *Jewish Chronicle*, which previously had taken a pacifist line, displayed an enthusiastic patriotism once war broke out, and vigorous efforts were made to encourage enlistment.[8] At first the call met with considerable success as young Jewish men flocked to the recruiting stations in East London, but after this initial wave of enthusiasm enlistment among Jews virtually dried up. Quite apart from the fear of military discipline instilled by experience of serving in the Tsar's army, the war was of no concern to the majority of East End Jews, and even if they did enlist, the exigencies of war would force them to compromise or abandon their religious customs. Instead, young Jews with new-found prosperity were seen enjoying themselves on the streets, to the obvious consternation of the indigenous local population. An embittered *East London Observer* published editorials condemning the Jewish war effort, and included letters from disgruntled locals, including one sent anonymously, purportedly by a Stepney councillor:

Since the war began I can honestly say that I have not come across a dozen Jewish soldiers. I have been told in many quarters that they are earning heaps of money in consequence of the shortage of men. If this is so, it is a despicable advantage to take, and the sooner it is brought to an end by conscription the better.[9]

Attitudes towards the war, and the detailed scrutiny to which Jews were subjected, widened fissures within the Jewish community, and between it and the host nation. Sections of the community clearly benefited from the war, but in disputes over vital issues including conscription, Sunday trading, poor relief and food controls Jews lost out, and the quality of their life deteriorated. War thus provided the context for revisiting, rehearsing and selectively playing out the complex strands of anti-semitic ideology; when fascist organizations sprang up in the years which followed, the lessons were not forgotten.

From 1922, the periodical *The Patriot* soon established itself as the main vehicle for anti-semitic propaganda. Drawing upon conspiracy myths, it argued that since British imperial interests had for years been under attack from secret Jewish societies and Jewish Bolsheviks with the active assistance of Germany, it was necessary to eliminate their influence by bolstering the laws on immigration and naturalization.[10] The first explicitly fascist organization in Britain, the British Fascists, was founded in the following year by the wayward figure of Miss Rotha Lintorn-Orman. Its members were mostly war veterans who adopted a programme similarly committed to the purge of Jews from public life, and the eradication of their influence on the financial, political and cultural life of the nation, but it lacked direction and organization, finally collapsing in 1935 with the rise to prominence of the British Union of Fascists.

No smoke without fire

The BUF was founded by Mosley in 1932 and was soon established as a significant political force in East London by attracting members from across the class spectrum. The unskilled and poorly educated, trade unionists, Catholics, small traders, shopkeepers and the lower middle class all sought solutions to perceived grievances in fascism. This is what surprised Phil Piratin when he attended a fascist meeting in Limehouse, and completely changed his thinking on ways in which the problem could be tackled:

The case which a minority of us put up in Stepney was that while we would fight Mosley's thugs, where did we get by fighting the people?

We should ask ourselves: 'Why are these ordinary working-class folk (it was too easy to call them *lumpen*) supporting Mosley?' Obviously, because Mosley's appeal struck a chord. There were certain latent anti-Semitic prejudices, it is true, but above all these people, like most in East London, were living miserable, squalid lives.[11]

For many contemporary observers like Piratin the rise of British fascism in the 1930s was linked closely to the privations caused by unemployment and the failure of political parties to offer realistic solutions. Two of the most perceptive writers, G.D.H. and Margaret Cole, in a 1937 survey of interwar Britain, looked with anxiety on the threat of fascism, and concluded:

Men turn Fascist when they have lost faith in the continuance of the conditions under which they have managed to find a tolerable accommodation with life. They turn Fascist out of a desire to do something where inaction seems to threaten them with disaster, and out of a strong desire to preserve the superiority which they have hitherto possessed – in fact, or at least fancied themselves to possess – over the groups and classes lower down the social scale.[12]

It is evident that the Coles considered unemployment the principal threat. '[F]or a large section of the unemployed,' they concluded, 'the existing conditions involve not only continuous mental suffering and deterioration, but also bodily privation.' And then with some menace they warned:

It may be 'cheap' in the short run to keep the unemployed on a low diet. It may diminish the immediate risks of social revolution or radical uprising. But in the long run it is not cheap, or good insurance. For in the long run misery is apt to take its bloody revenge.[13]

The leader of the NUWM, Wal Hannington, also considered the threat of fascism that year, particularly in areas of the country worst affected by unemployment. So far, he warned,

The Fascist Party finds very little support at present amongst the workers in the Distressed Areas, but if those workers on a mass scale are ever allowed to lose faith in the strength of working-class organisation we shall see Fascism sweep through those areas like a prairie fire, in the same way that it has swept through the ranks of the unemployed in Germany.[14]

We cannot afford to be complaisant, Hannington concluded, for the great mass of the unemployed remain unorganized. British fascists 'know where they are going', and at a time when the Labour Party and Trades Union Congress have failed to provide resolute leadership, will exploit the situation by promising jobs with decent wages, and an end to the use of the unpopular means test, by which families' savings and income levels were minutely examined before they could qualify for any financial help.

Piratin rather downplayed the role of anti-semitism, and more recently it has been argued that Mosley was not rabidly anti-semitic, but merely cynically exploited the situation in East London to boost the party during the difficult months of 1934.[15] Some light can be shed on this, not from the view that overall East London provided fertile ground for the BUF, but from the fact that responses varied from one area to another.[16] In the whole of East London and its surrounding areas, Hackney and Stoke Newington demonstrated the strongest and most enduring support for the BUF. By the 1930s the Jewish exodus to these boroughs from the old areas of settlement had gathered pace, as a result of which they now contained high concentrations of Jewish families, many ultra-orthodox. Local residents complained that Jewish workshops disturbed the tranquillity of Hackney's streets, and traders disrupted the peace of the Sabbath, forcing many of the indigenous population to move out.[17] And yet this sense of loss of a mythical urban arcadia was not necessarily translated into open hostility against the Jewish workers themselves. As one Hackney BUF official declared:

[W]e believed that the Jew had his place in the country if he was prepared to be honest and patriotic … and work for the benefit of the country and not for the benefit of the big Jew. It's the big Jew that caused all the trouble. As Oswald Mosley always said, we've got nothing against the small Jew. Nothing against the Jew who wants to be a patriot. And wants to respect … loyalty over religion.[18]

Simultaneously, and without any appreciation of the contradictions posed, other East London fascists singled out economic rather than cultural faultlines:

[A]s he [Mosley] attacked the system … he was coming up with Jews all the time … [I]n the East End of London, where I lived, the Jews were hated for a good reason. There's no smoke without fire, you know. And they flogged the, er … unemployment market. I mean, I was young myself and I had mates that were in the furniture trade, polishing trade. It was terrible.[19]

Neighbouring Shoreditch had many fewer Jewish families than Hackney, and yet fascist attacks on Jews and their property there were more intense. Part of the explanation for this may lie in the territorial awareness of a largely indigenous resident population which had a history of suspicion of outsiders, but important also was the racial radicalism of the leadership of the Shoreditch branch of the BUF, which represented the physical-force wing of popular fascism. It actively recruited local thugs, the most notorious of whom was 'Dixie' Deans, a pugilist and casual labourer who, in addition to boxing professionally, trained local Mosleyites. His services proved invaluable:

> [The BUF] always used to send the vans down to Shoreditch. [They] used to go to Tottenham Western corner on a Sunday night, all the Reds would be up there ... about half a dozen of them would get out, go 'bang bang' ... You had 'Dixie' Deans, 'Jimmy' Doyle, all good scrappers. See, we had some rough hands. And, 'course, so that's why Shoreditch got a bad name.[20]

BUF branches at Limehouse, Whitechapel and Bethnal Green similarly prospered following campaigns based on the politics of exclusion, augmented by a deep resentment of the record of socialists on local councils. Only in Poplar and West Ham did the BUF meet with little success, largely because of the endurance of labour traditions established in earlier struggles.

Thus although fascism gained a particular momentum in East London in the interwar years, which has been interpreted as a visceral response to unemployment and a large Jewish presence, its success owed more to its ability to articulate some of the genuine and imagined grievances of ordinary people. Any analysis is further complicated by the recognition that events on an international level could also exert a decisive influence. Some Catholics, appalled at the murder of Catholic priests by republicans in the Spanish Civil War, joined the BUF, and there was broad enthusiasm for Hitler's attempts to rebuild Germany. Women were attracted by Mosley's commitment to peace, an espoused programme of equality, and the opportunities the BUF offered for active participation in a political cause.[21] For others, the charisma of Mosley and the trappings of militarism were sufficient reasons to join. Uniformed marches and rallies provided a sense of collective identity and solidarity which some, like this member from Limehouse, remember to this day with unbridled affection:

It meant everything to me. A sort of goal that we wanted to reach. It just became our existence really. We used to look forward to everything ... Those were the happiest days of my life. We had a spirit of comradeship that we very seldom get.[22]

Why, then, after a period of spectacular growth, did the BUF eventually fail in East London? For many, the turning point was the battle of Cable Street, which has since attained a mythical status. As a provocative show of strength, Mosley planned a march from the Tower along Cable Street in Shadwell via Gardiner's Corner at the top of Whitechapel High Street. Despite anticipated trouble, the Home Secretary refused to ban the march, which accordingly went ahead with a strong police escort. Along Cable Street the marchers encountered barricades and determined resistance, organized mainly by communists. A series of running street battles ensued during which the fascists were routed, never again to recover their strength in the East End.

Cable Street riots, 1936. Anti-fascist demonstrators flee from a barricade erected in Cable Street, pursued not by members of Mosley's British Union of Fascists but by the police.

It is a heroic story, but sadly in almost every respect an inaccurate one. In the days leading up the proposed march, anti-fascist forces were deeply divided on the question of tactics.[23] Initially, the Communist Party, which had planned a rally in Trafalgar Square that same day to show support for the Spanish Republic, advised its members to cancel the rally and mobilize resistance to the BUF march. Mass mobilization was also supported by the Independent Labour Party, but the Labour Party itself advised East Londoners to stay away on the grounds that any potential disturbance would merely serve to attract more fascists. On the day, large crowds of anti-fascists gathered at Gardiner's Corner and in Royal Mint Street. A large police presence sought to maintain order by cordoning off side streets, and pushing crowds down Cable Street where they could be controlled more effectively. When Mosley eventually turned up, he was informed by the Police Commissioner that because of the threat of serious disorder the march could not proceed, at which point the fascists were escorted away from the area by the police. In the meantime, the police attempted to dismantle barricades built by anti-fascists in Cable Street. They were met with determined resistance, which for a time was successful, but the police returned with reinforcements, and after numerous brutal baton charges managed to clear the area. It was the action of the police, not the BUF, which created disorder, and inflicted the worst of the damage to persons and property.[24]

Far from driving fascists from the streets, Cable Street seemed to provoke a renewed determination in their ranks. There followed a series of propaganda rallies around East London attended by thousands, and in the three weeks following 4 October the London Command of the BUF nearly doubled its membership.[25] This was merely a temporary resurgence, however, for in 1936 the government introduced the Public Order Act, which, by banning the wearing of military uniforms in public, and requiring police consent for political rallies, undercut the emotive appeal of the fascists. In East London, the communists strengthened their electoral support by working effectively with tenants' organizations, many of which had previously been attracted to the BUF. Support for the BUF further haemorrhaged with the worsening international situation, and finally ceased with the outbreak of war, when Mosley and many of his followers were interned under the emergency regulations.

After a period of awkward calm following the declaration of war with Germany, many English cities were subjected to mass bombing raids, none more so than the industrial and communications hub that was East London. The Blitz devastated the lives and physical environment of the people of Stepney and West Ham, and changed forever the face of some of its most deprived areas. Hitler, it was popularly noted, achieved more in a few weeks than had town planners over decades.

More than flesh and blood can stand

Nobody knew what to expect on 7 September 1940 when the first bombs of the Blitz fell on London. Previous incidences of the bombing of civilian populations provided unreliable guidance on the likely casualties. During the First World War bombing raids had claimed the lives of 1,239 Britons, a relatively small number, but sufficiently high to unleash wild speculation on the potential damage of future conflicts. In 1924, the Air Staff estimated that in any new war 300 tons of high-explosive bombs would be dropped on Britain in the first twenty-four hours.[26] Each bomb would claim fifty casualties, a third of which would prove fatal. At about the same time, the military historian and theorist J.F.C. Fuller painted an apocalyptic vision of the effect of such bombing on London:

> London for a few days will be one vast raving Bedlam, the hospitals will be stormed, traffic will cease, the homeless will shriek for help, the City will be in Pandemonium. What of the Government in Westminster? It will be swept away by an avalanche of terror. The enemy will dictate his terms which will be grasped like a straw by a drowning man.[27]

Following the example of the Spanish Civil War, when German planes strafed the town of Guernica, estimates of British civilian casualties in the event of war with Germany soared. By 1937, the Imperial Defence Committee alarmingly forecast 1.8 million in the first two months of bombing, the majority of whom would suffer from insanity. The Home Office computed that 20m square feet of seasoned timber would be needed each month to construct coffins. Since this was an impossible target, plans were laid to bury the dead in mass graves with lime.[28] Happily, these figures proved to be gross overestimates. In July and August 1940, Bristol, Birmingham, London and Liverpool were bombed with the loss of 'only' 1,336 lives. Any sense of relief that the nightmarish predictions were unfounded was temporary, for when London was then subjected to intense and systematic bombing of the Blitz for fifty-six consecutive nights (barring one when the weather was bad), it must have seemed that the merchants of doom had been right after all.

Hitler was intent on ending the war by striking at the metropolitan heartland. East London bore the brunt of the attacks as the docks, factories, gasworks and warehouses were targeted by incendiary bombs. On hearing the first wave of approaching aircraft, eighteen-year-old Len Jones stepped outside his house in Poplar and looked up at the sky:

> That afternoon, around five o'clock, I went outside the house, I'd heard the aircraft and it was very exciting, because the first formations were coming over without any bombs dropping, but very, very majestic; terrific. And I had no thought that they were actually bombers. Then from that point on I was well aware, because the bombs began to fall, and shrapnel was going along King Street, dancing off the cobbles. Then the real impetus came, in so far as the suction and the compression from the high explosive blasts just pulled you and pushed you, and the whole of this atmosphere was turbulating so hard that, after an explosion of a nearby bomb, you could actually feel your eyeballs being sucked out.[29]

This sense of excitement was shared by other young East Enders. 'I have never before seen such a sight in my life,' recalled Leslie Jerman, who at the time was living with his large family in East Ham. 'I had had no experience of air-raids and felt no fear. It was somewhat thrilling.'[30] And Bryan Forbes, ejected from the Forest Gate Odeon during an air raid, joined groups on the pavement outside 'watching pattern after pattern of sun-silvered Dorniers winging high overhead'.[31] Any sense of novelty at German technological wizardry was soon dispelled by the carnage and remorseless discomfort which became part of the routine of daily life for East Enders. On the first day 430 civilians were killed, 1,600 seriously wounded, and thousands made homeless. These totals were to be repeated time and again, so establishing a grim pattern of human destruction which touched practically everybody in East London directly. Even those fortunate enough to escape serious injury witnessed scenes that would stay with them for the rest of their lives. After the second attack, Len Jones surveyed the damage; it was clear by then that his initial excitement had been displaced by a profound sense of shock:

> I went out to see how our house was, and when I got there the front door was lying back, and the glass of the windows had fallen in, and I could see the house had virtually disappeared. Inside, everything was blown to pieces, you could see it all by the red glow reflecting from the

Dorniers over West Ham, 1940. A famous image of German bombers on a raid, with West Ham stadium clearly visible.

fires that were raging outside. Then I looked out the back and suddenly I realized that where my father's shed and workshop used to be, was just a pile of rubble, bricks. Then I saw two bodies, two heads sticking up, I recognized one head in particular; it was a Chinese man, Mr Say, he had one eye closed, and then I began to realize that he was dead.[32]

People took to the air-raid shelters in their tens of thousands each night. The conditions they encountered were appalling, but at least the shelters provided a modicum of safety. Quite apart from the unsanitary conditions, and sheer boredom and inconvenience, a decent night's sleep was virtually impossible; the most that could be hoped for was a few hours after the all-clear had been sounded around dawn. A week into the Blitz, Mollie Panter-Downes recorded her impressions for readers of the *New Yorker*:

For Londoners, there are no longer such things as good nights; there are only bad nights, worse nights and better nights. Hardly anyone has slept at all in the past week. The sirens go off at approximately the same time every evening, and in the poorer districts, queues of people carrying blankets, thermos flasks, and babies begin to form quite early outside the air-raid shelters … After a few of these nights, sleep of a kind comes from complete exhaustion. The amazing part of it is the cheerfulness and fortitude with which ordinary individuals are doing their jobs under nerve-wracking conditions. Girls who have taken twice the usual time to get to work look worn when they arrive, but their faces are nicely made up and they bring you a cup of tea or sell you a hat as chirpy as ever ... As for breaking civilian morale, the high explosives that rained death and destruction on the capital this week were futile.[33]

This picture of a cheerful resilience soon entered into myth, and the figure of the cockney who was seemingly untroubled by the constant presence of death became something of a folk hero.[34] So complete was the transformation after the comic persona of the nineteenth century that the cockney was recreated as a national talisman, in particular by the countless anecdotes which were circulated of wise-cracking cockneys with an unshakable defiance and a determination to carry on regardless. At a time of great peril, this image may have served well to boost morale, but it was partial, for amongst the acts of extraordinary courage, selflessness and stoicism displayed by many in the East End were less public stories of how panic and terror were fuelling a profound social discontent. It could not have been otherwise, for here was a civilian population attempting to respond to, and make sense of, a collective trauma never before experienced in human history, and no matter how determined the attempts to maintain a semblance of normality, people were ever close to breaking point. For a minority, the experience of continual bombardment was more than they could take. 'It's me nerves,' cried a middle-aged woman, 'they're all used up, there's nothing left of me strength like I had at the start.' A working-class woman of sixty conveyed a sense of the deepening horror: 'It's the dread, I can't tell you the dread, every night it's worse.' Evidence of a builder revealed great distress at the deterioration in his wife's state of mind. 'It's getting more than flesh and blood can stand,' he declared, 'it just cannot be endured, night after night like this. My wife, I've got to get her out of it, she's like a mad woman ... as soon as the siren goes.' And an observer provided a harrowing account of a young woman caught up in the mayhem:

> During the day she keeps saying 'I can't bear the night, I can't bear the night. Anything like this shouldn't be allowed.' As it grew dark, her state became worse. Eventually she was trembling so much she could hardly talk. She ran upstairs to the lavatory three times in half an hour. Finally when the warning came, she urinated on the spot and burst into tears.[35]

Shelters may have provided a degree of safety, but as an extraordinary report by an investigator for Mass Observation revealed, this did not prevent an emotional climate which verged on collective hysteria.[36] On the first night of mass bombing, approximately thirty-five people took refuge in a street shelter at Smithy Street, Stepney. At 8.15 p.m. the shelter was shaken by a bomb. A woman screams, 'My house! It come on my house! My house is blown to bits!' Three more colossal crashes follow. Women scream, and huddle together, waiting for more with drawn breath. People begin to shout at one another. 'Stop leaning against that wall, you bloody fool!' screams a twenty-five-year-old woman to a girl. 'Like a bleeding lot of children! Get off it, you bastard … do you hear? Come off it … my God, we're all going mad!' An ARP helper tries to start a song. 'Shut your bleedin' row!' shouts an old man. 'We've got enough noise without you.' A few people manage to sleep around midnight, only to be woken every time a bomb falls nearby. Two men argue about the last incident (bombs often seemed to be much nearer than they actually were). A girl cries, 'I wish they'd bloody well stop talking and let me sleep! They talk such rot … such rot it is! That man, listen to him … he's got such a horrible voice! Tell him I said he's to stop, he's got a horrible voice.' A neighbour tries to calm her. 'No,' she screams, 'it's no good! I'm ill! I think I'm going to die!' The all-clear sounds at 4.30 a.m. It is greeted with relief until the first people to leave the shelter catch sight of the damage; screaming and weeping, they call for absent relatives. One man has a fit; another vomits.

These emotional traumas were intensified by lack of sleep, which was often identified by Londoners as the single biggest problem. Over time, some grew accustomed to the nightly bombing, but never adjusted to the poor quality of sleep; as one female civil servant recorded, 'It's not the bombs I'm scared of any more, it's the weariness … trying to work and concentrate with your eyes sticking out of your head like hat-pins, after being up all night. I'd die in my sleep, happily, if only I *could* sleep.'[37] The wholly inadequate response of public authorities to the crisis merely compounded the distress and sheer inconvenience of the profound disruptions caused to people's lives. It was not only that officials were rarely up to the task, or even that amidst the labyrinthine network of organizations people simply did not know where to turn, but that because of the apocalyptic visions of the prewar period, authorities had given priority to the disposal of the dead rather than provision for the needs of the homeless, tired, confused and hungry. An unpublished report compiled by Mass Observation from interviews at the time inquired into how well public and voluntary organizations of East London stood up to the massive trial posed by the first weeks of the Blitz.[38] Almost immediately after the first air raid, and before any official scheme was in place, a mass evacuation of local people occurred. Most went to stay with friends and relatives in the country or other parts of London, those with work returning every day, but there were many desperate families who loaded their belongings on to carts, barrows and prams (anything to hand), and headed off to the country with no particular destination in mind. Within the first fortnight, it was reckoned over half the population had moved out, leaving behind deserted streets and empty churches. The supplies of gas and electricity failed; it took weeks to restore gas, making it impossible for most to cook a meal. Lyons' tea shop next to Whitechapel Station managed to boil kettles on improvised stoves for the long queues which formed outside, but could offer only salads by way of sustenance.

Enough of my sort

A diet of salad was not the worst that residents had to endure. For those rendered homeless, the problems of finding alternative accommodation were considerable. Official schemes were established to provide rest centres and then billets for those whose homes had been completely destroyed. Little was done for the much larger numbers whose homes were partially uninhabitable, for those made temporarily homeless by, say, an unexploded bomb in the vicinity, or for people who simply were too frightened to stay in their (undamaged) homes at night. But the Public Assistance Committee of the London County Council, which had responsibility for providing centres for the homeless, had been given a pitiful £2,000 prior to the Blitz to equip them, and for their administration were forced to use their own staff working on twenty-four-hour shifts. The wartime correspondent Ritchie Calder described the conditions he found in one of the East London centres:

> It was appalling. Bare and bleak, with the homeless huddled on the floor, it had no protection except brown paper strips on the windows. The windows were large, and mothers had spent the night before crouched on all fours above their sleeping children, to shelter them from flying glass. The alternative (it was the official arrangement) was to go out into the raids which had rendered them homeless a few hours before and find a proper shelter under arches some streets away. I saw a 'rest room' – intended to give peace and quiet to the sick and ailing, or the aged, or the exhausted children. It was unfurnished.[39]

Little information was provided on the whereabouts of the centres. Indeed, because the Local Information Committee was provided with no staff by the Ministry of Information it simply did not function throughout the Blitz. Sites designated as bulletin boards remained empty. Most information was therefore passed by word of mouth. The People's Palace along the Mile End Road soon became widely known as the chief centre, in part because it acquired a reputation for providing better food than most, and was deluged by tired and hungry people. Regulations stipulated that centres were open only to the genuinely homeless, but in practice these were impossible to enforce.

Initially, local authorities had the responsibility to find billets for those in rest centres, but the planning had been seriously neglected, with the result that they were overwhelmed by the thousands made homeless in 1940. Stepney council had no power to requisition accommodation outside the borough, and so, after a period of great confusion, turned to the Public Assistance Committee of the LCC, which became a clearing house for the whole of London, providing accommodation in the Greater London area wherever it could persuade other boroughs to requisition billets for dispossessed East Londoners. Occasionally these billets were so dirty, uncomfortable or no less safe from bombing that people chose to return to Stepney to take their chances in familiar surroundings.

In neighbouring West Ham the situation was even worse. On the afternoon of 9 September, South Hallsville School in Canning Town overflowed with families from Silvertown and Tidal Basin made homeless by the previous nights' bombings. Warnings about the vulnerability of the school to attack had been ignored because the Council had nowhere else to put the refugees; in any case, the coaches booked to take them to safe billets were due at 3pm. They did not arrive; apparently, the drivers had misheard the garbled message and headed to Camden Town instead. Late in the evening, the coaches found the school, but just as the homeless were boarding the sirens went, and so it was decided to postpone their evacuation until the next day. That night the school suffered a direct hit. Nearly four hundred were killed, most of them women and children. It was the single biggest civilian disaster of the war.[40]

Those who had lost everything and needed emergency support or compensation after the war were required to approach the Assistance Board, but after three weeks none of the appropriate forms was to be found in Stepney. In practice, the scheme faltered in the face of unanticipated demand, and the great difficulties in assessing genuine claims; by the end of September it had effectively broken down. The story of one Stepney man was typical of the personal costs of the chaos which ensued:

I been bombed out. That's my house, that heap of rubbish. I been 48 hours trying to get someone to do something about it. Can't get money, can't get my furniture out (what's left of it), I've only got the clothes I stand up in. I went to the Food Centre at the People's Palace – they hadn't got no grub. They sent me to the district centre for rationing down Barnes St. They could do nothing. They sent me down East India Dock Rd. to the U.A.B. [Unemployed Assistance Board]. The U.A.B. told me it was a case for the P.A.C., so I saw them, but no go … I got fed up. Asked 'em if somebody couldn't make up their minds where I really ought to go. They ordered me out of the office, said they had enough of my sort coming in all day, demanding this or that. The neighbours give me food – I have to rely on the neighbours.[41]

Ultimately, it seemed that, as in all crises, the poor relied on their own for survival. The thousands made unemployed by the bombing fared no better. Labour Exchanges could not cope with the demand for benefits. Such was the length of queues which formed outside the exchange off Commercial Road that in order to sign on it was necessary to stand in line at least half an hour before it opened. Even then there was no guarantee. Exchanges shut promptly with every siren warning, so disrupting the service, and causing some of the unemployed to stand in the queue all day without being seen. These humiliations created deep resentment. Exchange staff could run for cover, but nobody in the queue moved for fear of losing their place. Fights broke out when people were seen to jump the queue, and the police generally struggled to maintain order.

Schemes for the evacuation of children were similarly ill-prepared. Limited arrangements were made for children under five to be taken with their mothers to stay with friends or relatives outside London, which were then hurriedly extended with the onset of mass bombing to cover unaccompanied children of any age to safe accommodation wherever people could be persuaded to take them in. Parents were required to sign an undertaking that they would not bring their children back, but the decision to evacuate a child was heart-rending for people inhabiting a culture of close familial networks, and many evacuated children who failed to adjust to the new surroundings, or were billeted with families who reacted with disgust to their appearance and habits, returned home. Typical was the experience of Doreen Holloway, who along with her brother was picked out by a lady from a group of evacuated children assembled in Binfield village hall. They rarely saw the lady of what seemed an enormous house again; instead, they were put under the care of two servants who treated them as outcasts, making them sleep outside the kitchen on sacks filled with straw, and forbidding them to play in the garden. Alice Golder recalls travelling with her family from their uninhabitable house in East London to Finchley, where the lady of the house refused them entry until informed by the billeting officer that she had a legal obligation to do so. They were provided with no cooking facilities, and were not welcome in the house during the day, and so sat in a local park eating sandwiches or walking around to keep warm.[42] For Molly Matthews and her sister, the whole experience was so unpleasant she wrote to her parents in Canning Town threatening to walk home:

> So consequently we had a letter saying that they would be down that weekend. When they came, they arrived in a taxi. Now I presume it must have taken the best part of their savings, if not all ... So the taxi arrived and the delight, the joy. Then we left and I came home. And I'd rather have faced at home the bombing and things than go back there.[43]

By the end of 1939, more than half of the 750,000 people evacuated from London had decided to return, and even later, when the initial shock of mass bombing had receded, the numbers evacuated remained well below government expectations. At the end of September 1940, only 20,000 unaccompanied London schoolchildren out of a total of 500,000 had been evacuated.

The public sites providing refuge for those who chose or were forced to remain in East London were scandalously neglected. Tube stations were originally closed as shelters but public pressure, often in the form of direct action, opened them up, and the platforms housing sleeping families became one of the most iconic wartime images. People headed for the most convenient of the deeper stations – residents of Whitechapel to Piccadilly Circus and Leicester Square, of Mile End to Liverpool Street and Bank. Large public shelters were provided in the bowels of commercial premises such as the London, Midland and Southend Railway goods station along the Commercial Road, and the breweries of Mann, Crossman and Charrington along the Whitechapel and Mile End roads. Some small basements were also made available by local authorities.

The largest and most notorious of these was the LMS goods station, which somehow acquired the name Tilbury. It was a massive underground warehouse, 300 yards long and 50 yards wide, occupied at night by carts and lorries, and up to 15,000 desperate local people, including a working girl who described well some of the tensions that emerged from the trying conditions:

The structure is colossal, mainly of platforms and arches. The brick is so old, the place so filthy and decrepit, that it would be difficult for the best of artists to convey its ugliness on paper. By 7.30 p.m. each evening, every available bit of floor-space is taken up. Deck chairs, stools, seats, pillows – people lying on everything, everywhere. When you get over the shock of seeing so many sprawling people, you are overcome with the smell of humanity and dirt. Dirt abounds everywhere. The floors are never swept and are filthy. People are sleeping on piles of rubbish ... Everyone there was working class. The shelter is near the dock area, and near the coloured quarters. Mostly Cockneys, but also many Jews and Indians ... Race feeling is very marked – not so much between Cockneys and Jews, as between White and Black. In fact, the presence of considerable coloured elements was responsible for drawing Cockney and Jew together.[44]

Members of the Stepney Tenants' Defence League, many of whom were communists, were particularly active in giving information and advice to beleaguered residents. Under the slogan 'Stay in Stepney and stand by the people', they organized shelter committees and campaigned to help improve the dreadful conditions found in places like the Tilbury. One of their stunts was reported around the world. Incensed by the contrast between shelters provided for the rich and for the poor at the height of the Blitz, they gathered a group of seventy, including women and children, marched on the Savoy Hotel and made their way to the shelter, where they found freshly painted cubicles with linen bedding, and a ready supply of deckchairs and armchairs. The manager called the police, but when they were informed that any attempt to evict the women and children would be fiercely resisted, he backed down and decided instead to ignore the intruders. In the meantime, the waiters, who were greatly amused by the incident, agreed to supply pots of tea and slices of bread and butter at prices charged in Lyons' teahouses.[45]

The human cost borne by East Londoners during the Blitz was such that for a time the government feared social disorder. Daily reports from a variety of observers around London were commissioned by a Ministry of Information mindful of the need to monitor the mood of the people and identify potential problems. Unsurprisingly, the individual accounts were impressionistic and contradictory, and therefore of little value. One report of 9 September, for example, pointed to the rise of anti-semitism, largely because Jews, in a desire to save themselves, had shown little consideration for others. It concluded that the situation could become extremely serious, and recommended that plans for evacuation be carried out 'with all speed'.[46] On the following day it was reported from East London:

> Increased tension everywhere and when siren goes people run madly for shelter with white faces. Contact spending time in West Ham reports loyalty and confidence in ultimate issue unquenched but nerves worn down to a fine point. Conditions of living now almost impossible … Class feeling growing because of worse destruction in working class areas; anti-Semitism growing in districts where large proportion of Jews reside owing to their taking places in public shelters early in the day.[47]

Familiar anecdotes of the cheerful resilience of East Londoners during the Blitz tell only part of the whole story. Few accounts were written at the time by the people who suffered the most; what we have are observations of predominantly middle-class investigators which give some insight into the prevailing temper. While there can be no doubt of the courage and determination displayed in the face of terrible trials, there were darker moments when hysteria, defeatism, crime and racism surfaced. We may never know how significant a problem this was, or precisely how many people were close to breakdown, but in the eyes of the Home Office there was a real threat of social disorder. Perhaps this helps to explain why there were so many royal visits to the devastated East End, and why the emblematic figure of the resolute cockney was served up for public consumption.

The Blitz suddenly ended on 10 May 1941, and Hitler turned his attention to the invasion of Russia. This might have signalled the end of the most destructive phase of the war for the people of East London, but bombing raids continued, often in retaliation for those inflicted by the RAF on German cities. On the evening of 3 March 1943, warning sirens sounded, and a large crowd of people rushed to take shelter in Bethnal Green underground station. The entrance was narrow, steep and dimly lit. Nearby in Victoria Park a newly erected anti-aircraft battery of rockets opened fire with a deafening roar. Fearing a bomb had fallen, the crowd surged forward. A woman carrying a baby slipped and fell at the bottom of the steps, and hundreds followed. In the ensuing confusion, 173 people were crushed to death, 62 of them children. An inquiry was undertaken which blamed the tragedy on the behaviour of the crowd, but its publication was delayed because the government believed it would give undue prominence to the incident and lead to further raids.

In a final desperate act early in 1944 London was again subjected to aerial attack, this time by V1 and V2 rockets, which because of their unpredictability and explosive power were feared as much as any bombing during the Blitz. In the belief that London faced a crisis which after five years of unremitting hardship its people might not be as well able to confront, the Cabinet quickly put into operation plans for evacuation, this time with rather more success. By the end of August more than a million mothers, children, elderly people and homeless families had left London for billets in the country.[48]

Fatalities in London from enemy action during the war numbered just under 30,000, two-thirds of them occurring in the weeks of the Blitz.[49] After the initial period of chaos and confusion, official organizations did manage to put their house in order, so that in the relatively quiet months when mass aerial bombing had virtually ceased and services were no longer under severe pressure, the people of East London were provided with the support they demanded and deserved.

The physical destruction was massive. Figures are unreliable and estimates vary wildly but in London roughly 100,000 houses had been destroyed or damaged beyond repair, and about a million damaged. Overall, therefore, 80 per cent of the housing stock had suffered damage to some degree, a fifth of which were uninhabitable. In a list compiled by the LCC showing the percentage of vacant and war-damaged areas in each borough, the City was worst hit (30 per cent), followed by Stepney (22 per cent), Shoreditch (20 per cent) and Poplar (18 per cent).[50] Large areas of Stepney, Poplar and neighbouring West Ham were laid waste. Stepney and West Ham lost approximately a third of their housing stock either through outright destruction or severe damage; along the Beckton Road near the docks in Canning Town the proportion rose to nearly a half, and reached an astonishing 85 per cent in Tidal Basin at the western end of the Victoria Dock.[51] Many of the houses damaged beyond repair had been demolished during the war, leaving large gaps in terraced streets.

The loss of industrial floor space was relatively small; office space, wharfage and warehousing suffered more, but with a total loss of approximately 12 per cent of the total, the situation was nowhere near as bad as had been anticipated. Given that East London was targeted because of its importance as a centre of manufacturing and communications, it was hardly surprising that many workshops and factories had been forced to close or move elsewhere, while the docks and central markets experienced dramatic losses of trade. This picture of wholesale destruction, however, needs to be seen alongside the record of those businesses that were able to continue, or even thrive on wartime contracts. Badger's Engineering was heavily engaged in engine repairs and the construction of landing craft for the Admiralty and, when hostilities ceased, in the conversion of vessels to peacetime use. George Cartwright, timber merchant, made tent pegs and basket bottoms for the services. The coal merchants Fardell & Sons helped maintain essential supplies to local industries, and used its vehicles to help victims of the Blitz move their belongings, while White's joinery manufacturers was busy with war damage repairs.[52]

In the climate of postwar optimism, many businesses were able to grasp the opportunity to rebuild their damaged premises and local businesses while East Londoners confronted the challenge of the massive destruction which had obliterated their neighbourhoods. In the following chapter, we consider the impact of this on the long-term economic decline of the area, and on the extraordinary growth of multiracial East London.

CHAPTER 12

Postwar Decline and the Rise of the Cosmopolis, 1945–

I N THE optimism of the immediate postwar years, many local firms, including those which had been badly damaged, used the opportunity to rebuild. Thomas Ide's famous Ratcliff Glassworks, for example, which had been so badly damaged that production ceased, was totally rebuilt and modernized after the war, the premises now extending well past the original seventeenth-century boundaries. Charrington brewery lost an eighth of its houses in the war, but by the 1950s was strong enough to acquire three large independent breweries. In addition to the revival in the fortunes of traditional firms, new industries such as plastics were attracted. An impressionistic picture at the time taken from a bus ride along Bethnal Green Road conveyed something of the vitality of the local economy:

> You do not have to live in Bethnal Green, you only have to take a bus down the main street, to notice that this is a place of many industries. You pass tailors' workshops, furniture makers, Kearley & Tonge's food warehouse, and near to Allen & Hanbury's big factory. The borough has by itself a more diversified economy than some countries. But the borough has no frontiers: it belongs to the economy which stretches down both banks of the Thames … As the older industries have declined, the economy of Bethnal Green has merged ever more closely into the wider economy of the East End.[1]

Even when people were made redundant, there was a good chance that other work would be found within easy travelling distance from their homes. Integration into the wider economy also helped to sustain many of the older and larger industries. Viewed from the 1960s, the economy of East London seemed reasonably healthy. Among the important firms still operating in the area were Allen & Hanbury pharmaceuticals, Allison's flour mills, Bryant & May matchmakers, Fraser & Sons boilermakers, Tate & Lyle sugar refiners, and of course the docks.

The challenge of providing decent housing to those whose lives had been disrupted by the war was also met with a sense of optimism. Immediately after the war, the government ordered that emergency repairs to the housing stock be carried out under the control of local authorities rather than through the initiatives of individual householders, so that the thousands living in temporary and inadequate accommodation would suffer no longer than necessary. The LCC turned to the task of repairing those which could be salvaged, and in January 1945 the London Repairs Executive, which had been established at the height of the bombing from V2 rockets, reported that of the 719,300 houses targeted for repair over the winter, no fewer than 368,230 houses had been repaired and 'made tolerably comfortable' (although it was later admitted that the degree of comfort was low). Approximately 130,000 men were employed on the work, supplemented by 4,700 servicemen and 225 American soldiers.[2] By July 1945 the total exceeded one million, with substantial progress also on houses considered uninhabitable.[3] By the end of the year, the work was complete.

The real challenge, however, was rebuilding as attention turned to the question of what was to be done with areas which had been bombed to the ground. An army of planners approached the task armed with visionary zeal and the necessary authority. The 1944 Town and Country Planning Act empowered local authorities, including the LCC, to purchase compulsorily areas which had been destroyed, and to develop them or sell them off to private developers for approved schemes. East London was given priority as the LCC took the first steps in rebuilding the southern parts of Stepney and Poplar. Ambitious plans estimated that the work would take thirty years at a cost of £45m, part of which would be recouped from leasing land to private developers. This, however, was not merely a response to bomb damage – many other areas of London could legitimately claim priority – but an unprecedented opportunity to deal with the obsolete, overcrowded and unsanitary housing, the unhealthy mix of residential housing and industry, and the lack of open space which had blighted the lives of so many East Enders.[4] Thus, under plans laid down by the LCC in 1946, large areas of East London that had been virtually obliterated were physically reconstructed by clearing whole streets and erecting in their place a mix of semi-detached dwellings, tall blocks of flats and low-rise maisonettes. The badly damaged area in Poplar around Chrisp Street market, for example, was transformed into the Lansbury and Robin Hood Gardens estates as part of the largest development scheme in Britain.

Boroughs outside the immediate domain of the LCC had to rely on their own resources. In West Ham the borough architect's department took responsibility for building the Keir Hardie Estate out of the devastation of Tidal Basin. The moment was captured wonderfully in a 1948 documentary by Stanley Reed entitled *Neighbourhood 15*.[5] Tidal Basin had long been in need of redevelopment. It had been a highly congested area scarred by a scattering of industries amidst residential accommodation, and with narrow streets through which heavy lorries rumbled on their way to and from the docks. Tidal Basin was laid waste during the war, and now resembled a vast bomb site. Large open spaces existed where houses had been flattened and then cleared. Weeds grew up from the cracks in the old concrete foundations of houses and roads. Amidst piles of rubble stood the ruins of charred houses, many fenced off to prevent the access of playful children or supported unsteadily by wooden props.

A reconstruction committee had been appointed as early as 1941 and immediately singled out Tidal Basin as a priority. Hundreds of temporary huts and bungalows were erected to house those who had been bombed out, but at the end of war, with the return of thousands of evacuated civilians and demobilized service men and women, a more radical solution was required. This was to take the form of the Keir Hardie Estate which came optimistically to symbolize a new West Ham. The size of a new town, with its own facilities and forty acres of open space when previously there had been none, the estate was an ambitious project. The first house was occupied in April 1947. By 1948, 350 more houses had been completed, and families were moving in at the rate of 600 per month.

The estate, which has survived to the present, represented a solution of sorts to the urgent problems faced by the borough in the immediate postwar years. Rather less successful were the plans that followed for the estates dominated by high-rise blocks of flats. So bad was the publicity that such estates came to attract, particularly after the Ronan Point tragedy of 1968, when the corner of a newly constructed high-rise block in Canning Town collapsed like a pack of cards, killing four residents, that it is difficult to appreciate the intense optimism that informed the initial planning. The architecture was heavily influenced by the modernism of the Russian constructivists and the Bauhaus School, which were thought of as the vanguard of social progress.[6] High-rise blocks in particular would allow the sort of public space for walks and gardens which the old East End lacked, segregate housing from industry, and provide well-designed and up-to-date accommodation. This was a new world created by physical reconstruction. All this was to no avail. In a climate of economic recession,

Collapse of Ronan Point tower on the Keir Hardie Estate, Canning Town, 1968. This tragedy marked the beginning of the end of high-rise tower blocks, which had been such an important feature of postwar housing developments.

with few local facilities, and without hope of re-creating neighbourhood life, the estates rapidly degenerated into soulless no-go areas occupied only by those who had no other choice of accommodation.

Seemed like paradise

In the meantime Sir Patrick Abercrombie, who had been appointed during the war to prepare ambitious plans to address long-recognized problems such as traffic congestion and overcrowding, published the *County of London Plan* in 1943 and the *Greater London Plan* the following year. Together, they proposed the rigid enforcement of a green belt around London, beyond which a ring of satellite towns, including Harlow, Stevenage and Basildon, would be constructed to house the overspill population. In the event, neither scheme was adopted by the LCC, but they did prepare the ground for its own County of London Development Plan (1951), which recommended rather more modest proposals for demographic decentralization along lines tried and tested in the interwar years by estates such as Becontree.[7] These plans tended to follow rather than dictate the course of events, for it was apparent to most that one of the most significant consequences of wartime destruction was the net exodus of the population from East London. In the longer term, however, planning did come into its own as the easterly migration of families to metropolitan Essex gained momentum.

The effect of this exodus on population levels was dramatic. The population of Bethnal Green was already declining in the 1930s, but in the years from 1939 to 1941 when the Blitz occurred it fell sharply from 90,000 to 47,000. There was a partial recovery to 60,000 in 1948 following the return of the evacuees, but as more estates were built the population again began to shrink. Between 1931 and 1951, Bethnal Green lost 54,000 people, 40,000 of whom can be accounted for by the exodus to LCC estates.[8] Similarly, the return of 46,000 people to West Ham in the eighteen months after the war did not reverse the protracted decline in population since the peak of 1925. New housing schemes provided many with the opportunity of escaping the devastated and poverty-ridden streets of East London, although the exciting prospect of a new house with modern facilities was unexpectedly mitigated by a profound sense of loss of community and neighbourhood. One estate at Debden, built in the immediate aftermath of the war, was the subject of a study which has since come to be recognized as a classic account of the social and cultural consequences of this migration.

Family and Kinship in East London was part of a project launched by Michael Young and Peter Willmott at the Institute of Community Studies to assess how schemes of postwar reconstruction impacted on the lives of working-class families. The Debden estate, situated in the Essex countryside approximately twenty miles from Bethnal Green, was typical of the estates constructed by the LCC in this period. In an attempt to learn from past mistakes, the estate was designed to mix different types of houses but each was adjacent to a road, fenced off, and had a small flower garden at the front, and a larger vegetable garden to the rear. In every respect the conditions were a sharp contrast to those of Bethnal Green. The book therefore investigated how the move to 'Greenleigh' affected the familial and kinship relationships which were such a vital part of the community in Bethnal Green, where the Institute was based.

Confronting conventional anthropological wisdom that the extensive family structures of pre-modern society had been dismantled by the

Industrial Revolution, giving rise to the privatized, nuclear family, and sociological wisdom that such modern working-class families were to be held responsible for much of the social malaise of the 1950s, the researchers found that in East London kinship systems were still very much alive. And by and large they functioned well. Husbands were neither absentee nor irresponsible, but happily shared domestic duties and child care with their wives. Because of fewer children, longer lives, more domestic space, shorter working hours and less arduous work, families were under far less stress than even fifty years earlier. The mass media in the form of the popular press, cinema, the radio and increasingly television had disseminated new ideas to local people, creating novel aspirations and ideals.

Although some couples lived with their parents, the majority chose rather to live nearby. A half of all married men and 59 per cent of married women had parents living in the borough.[9] Wider kinship networks were similarly striking. In a typical local street with 59 households, 38 had relatives in at least one other. Contact with members of the extended family was thus frequent, and while this did create tensions and jealousies, bonds of mutual support and obligation were generally strong. This was particularly evident when working mothers relied on relatives for child care. Such networks were locked into powerful identities of locality, many of which had been passed down by previous generations. Mr Townsend liked the area of Bethnal Green near Victoria Park where he lived, and stressed that he was not talking of 'Brick Lane or that end'. And Mr Gould, who on marrying had moved near his wife's parents in Bow, confided that he would prefer to be back in Bethnal Green: 'In Bethnal Green we had good neighbours, better than those in Bow I can tell you.' Mrs Gould, on the other hand, was more content, although she did affirm that she would not like to move on the other side of the (Regent's) Canal – 'it's different there'.[10] For some, places beyond Bethnal Green were another world. A few women never ventured outside the borough except for an occasional trip to the 'Other [West] End', or to Southend, where they felt rather isolated and strange.

Why, therefore, did so many people choose to move to the estate at Debden? A few were relieved to escape from claustrophobic family attachments, but for the majority their own new house surrounded by open country, providing space, a bathroom with hot and cold water, a kitchen with a proper cooker and a lounge with a coal grate, was the simple and obvious attraction. To Mrs Sandeman, who left behind two mice-infested rooms, Debden 'seemed like paradise'. And Mrs Young and her husband were delighted at the prospect that they no longer had to share a toilet with four other families, or go up and down the stairs for water.[11] Others were

only too well aware that the new surroundings were better for their children, many of whom had been sickly, and this overrode any desire to
return to Bethnal Green.

This desire was palpable. Compared with the intimacy of the streets of
East London, Debden was quiet, lonely and remote. The busy and supportive
social life became a distant memory, shopping amidst the glass, chromium
and tiles was a lonely experience for people who could remember the bustle
and mess of the local market, evenings were spent around the television,
and neighbours were unfriendly, keeping very much to themselves. Given
this, it was unsurprising that initially a quarter of the families chose to
return, and although over time this figure gradually fell, the numbers who
made day trips to the East End to shop and see their families increased.
Writ large, the move represented an acceleration of tendencies that were
already apparent within the culture of East London. The majority of men
now chose to spend money on the home and children rather than on
drink. Take, for example, Mr Morrow, who used to have £3 for himself in
Bethnal Green, most of which was spent in the local boozer he frequented
every night. 'In Greenleigh it's different. What I used to give to the publican
goes into the home,' he explained. Together with the loss of contact with
friends and relations, these changes shifted the centre of gravity to the
confines of the home, where everybody lived in a world of their own.[12]
Here too the legacy of powerful localisms created in East London were
apparent. Families from Bethnal Green simply did not mix with those from
Bow or Hackney. They may have had shared histories of deprivation, even
work, but they had grown up in different neighbourhoods with distinct
senses of place.

The privatization of leisure, social isolation and changing patterns of
expenditure encouraged an increasing preoccupation with status and
possession. Notions of respectability were now tied to the economic
fortunes of individual households rather than roles assumed within wider
kinship networks, and the more successful a family was, the more it
guarded its privileged status against incursions from others whom they
looked on with disdain:

> People are not very friendly here. It's the same on all the estates.
> They've nothing else to do when they've finished work except watch
> you. It's all jealousy. They're afraid you'll get a penny more than they
> have. In London people have other things to occupy their minds. Here
> when they've done their work they've nothing else to do. They're at the
> window and they notice everything.[13]

The lessons to be drawn from the study were evident. Better by far for planners to provide new or refurbished homes in established working-class communities than to attempt with bricks and mortar to build new estates where the very sinews of community life were absent and had little chance of being created afresh. The problem was, however, that many areas of East London were so badly damaged it simply was not possible to salvage viable levels of housing. In retrospect, Young and Willmott also drew too boldly the lines separating what they saw as the warm sociability and mutual support integral to working-class culture in East London, and the rather bleak and anonymous landscape of the Debden estate, but, at the time and since, the study acted as a necessary corrective to those who viewed East End working-class families as dysfunctional and pathological. Furthermore, its influence has been revived in recent years, as East Londoners have again been swept along by remarkable demographic shifts. In the thirty years which elapsed after the study, the borough of Tower Hamlets lost nearly half of its population, Newham a third.[14]

This has been largely due to what has come to be known as the cockney diaspora, that is, the continued movement of people from East London eastward along the Thames estuary in Essex until Southend-on-Sea is reached, at which point the migrants come up against an impassable barrier. What has prompted this outward migration, and how have East Londoners viewed their new neighbourhoods in south Essex, ask recent researchers? Well, these questions and many of the answers to them are straight out of *Family and Kinship*. The need for better and affordable housing has continued to play a critical role in decisions made by many families, but what is novel is that this is intertwined with a wish to enhance social position by removing themselves from what they consider rough and undesirable areas with high immigrant populations.[15] The notion of 'white flight', therefore, has come to refer to the migration of an indigenous, overwhelmingly white population from East London to predominantly white suburban areas such as Romford, Thurrock and Basildon, prompted in part by concern over socio-economic deprivation, crime and drugs, which are seen to be associated with immigrant groups. The benign conditions of order, tranquillity and cleanliness perceived in the suburbs assuaged these anxieties, and provided spaces in which to re-create a 'real' East End of pie and mash shops, markets and football supporters' clubs.

The convenient distinction between East London and the suburbs, however, has been complicated by socio-economic decline and the eastward migration of immigrant communities. Essex suburbs can no longer provide upward mobility to aspirant families, and are becoming increasingly socially heterogeneous because of the eastward migration of black and Asian families, and the settlement of asylum seekers. Perhaps this is just a little too much of the real East London from which many cockneys sought to escape.

London's Harlem

How has the ethnic landscape of East London changed in recent years? Given that East London has always attracted migrant communities, is there anything distinctive about recent patterns of immigration? Much has been written about the migration of people to Britain in the postwar, postcolonial years. Because of its centrality in the nation's imagination, and the fact that disproportionately high levels of immigrants were drawn to its streets, London has been of particular interest.[16] In a skilful review of what he terms the most significant event in the history of London since the Norman Conquest, Jerry White has recently surveyed the remarkable events that transformed London into one of the world's great cosmopolitan cities.[17] Early in the 1950s as few as one in twenty Londoners was foreign-born, and only a fraction of them had originated from the corners of the empire. Thus while Poles, Germans and Russians living in London totalled over 100,000 in a city of 8 million, Caribbeans numbered less than 4,000, with far fewer from the Indian subcontinent and other parts of the world. Forty years later there were 1.35 million black Londoners, accounting for one in five of the population. Of these, over 500,000 described themselves as black (predominantly Caribbean and African), and nearly 700,000 as Asian (predominantly Indian, Pakistani and Chinese).[18]

With its long history as a refuge for immigrant communities, East London possessed a large population of peoples with foreign origins. Many of the Russians and Germans counted in 1951, for example, would have been there as a direct result of the earlier waves of Jewish immigration, and heirs to the Chinese community established around the turn of the century continued to live in the riverside areas of Stepney.[19] But it was the first black immigrants who settled in the immediate postwar years who are of particular interest here. In the early 1950s the number of Africans and Caribbeans in East London was probably little more than at earlier periods in its history, and very much lower than those of earlier Huguenot, Irish and Jewish settlers.[20] Little wonder, therefore, that their experience was largely ignored by contemporary studies, despite the fact that the problems they encountered presaged the troubled arena of race relations in the ensuing decades.[21]

Black seamen had landed in East London ever since it emerged as a major maritime centre. Along with Asian lascars, they were vital to the crews of British shipping but since they possessed few rights, and ship owners felt under no obligation to provide for them once they reached London, many were simply abandoned and had to fend for themselves until a return passage could be found. Dismayed by the plight of Asian seamen found wandering on the streets of London, and more particularly by the 'foul atmosphere of human depravity in which these Orientals live', the Rev. Joseph Salter of the Baptist Missionary Society embarked on an ambitious programme of missionary work which included the founding of the Strangers' Home for Asiatics, Africans and South Sea Islanders in 1857.[22] Located in Limehouse along the West India Dock Road, and financed by Maharaja Dulip Singh, the home was the first of its kind to provide accommodation for black and Asian seamen.[23] Other lascar missions followed, most notably the Coloured Men's Institute in Canning Town, established by the inspirational Kamal Chunchie in 1926 under the aegis of the Wesleyan Methodist Missionary Society, which ministered to the physical and social welfare, rather than spiritual needs, of the local black population until his death in 1953.[24]

During the war many of the black settlers were evacuated to other parts of London. Those who remained campaigned against prejudice in the allocation of accommodation in air-raid shelters, police harassment and the lack of leisure facilities, in response to which the Colonial Office opened a hostel for colonial subjects in Whitechapel.[25] They chose to socialize with members of the small Pakistani, Arab and Maltese communities who ran the busy cafés-cum-lodging houses around Cable Street thought to be at the centre of prostitution, gambling and profitable sidelines in the sale of cigarettes, alcohol, nylons and drugs. Such was the concern felt by the local clergy and social workers that they commissioned a survey of the area in 1943.[26] The report described the experience of the black population in terms that were to become only too familiar in the ensuing decades. It claimed that approximately 400 black settlers lived in the area, half of whom were Indian, nearly a third African, and less than a tenth Caribbean. These were supplemented by a transient population of seamen and US black troops totalling 300. Despite their relatively low numbers, myths spread that Cable Street was full of black residents, and for a time Stepney was known in the national press as London's Harlem. For those seeking work, even if they were well qualified, only unskilled and semi-skilled occupations were available. A large majority of Africans and Caribbeans were employed as labourers, porters and stokers, with much lower numbers in the more skilled work of the clothing, building and woodworking trades. Sikhs in Stepney, numbering no more than a hundred, were self-employed as pedlars and fortune tellers, from which considerable sums of money were made. Low incomes, poor housing stock and racism conspired also to prevent access to decent accommodation. The homes of black residents thus generally comprised

> one or two poorly furnished rooms in dilapidated and overcrowded houses in one of the back streets … A few are more fortunate in having flats in the older blocks of building in the area, but even if the family should want good housing accommodation they are unlikely to obtain it as most of the landlords of the better type of property do not want coloured men as tenants. This is chiefly due to the fact that the coloured man, in the minds of the landlords, is connected with promiscuous living in the neighbourhood; investigation has shown that a very large percentage of coloured men in the area are living promiscuous lives while some of the white women with children consort with other men while their husbands or unmarried partners are away at sea.[27]

This view of the black population was largely supported by the investigation. In the absence of recreational facilities the cafés became local clubs where men and women congregated to chat for hours over a single cup of tea. There was no legal marriage in 27 per cent of the families headed by a black male. White women who entered into relationships with black men were inferior types of prostitutes and runaways from deprived northern cities who had 'little moral sense'; most were ostracized by the local population. The half-caste children of these relationships were neglected – no fewer than twenty-three had been taken into care by the LCC because of domestic turmoil or desertion of the mother.

Racial tensions mounted as concern over the behaviour of black immigrants continued to escalate in the immediate postwar years. Complaints were made to the council that black immigrants accosted white women of any age walking along Cable Street, and committed indecent acts in the alleys and bombed buildings. A petition signed by 1,200 persons and presented to the borough council protested at the 'grave moral and physical danger' which existed in the area of Cable Street, brought about by the 'excessive numbers of cafés open at a late hour, and the disgusting conditions in the public houses'.[28] No reference was made to immigrants in the wording, but it was obvious to everyone who was being targeted. On being asked to sign, people inquired 'Oh, you've come about the petition to get rid of the blacks?', and in one instance a signatory declared that he would organize a hundred men to march along Cable Street, and warn anyone in the cafés and pubs that if they were found there again the following evening they would be 'dealt with'. Irresponsible reports appeared in the national press. 'Seamen all over the world know of Cable Street,' commented one, 'and, if their tastes lie in that way, make for it as soon as their ships dock. Some of them are coloured boys just off their first ship. A few months ago they were still half naked in the bush.'[29] To its credit, however, the council refused to contemplate action against the immigrant population, and interest in the matter waned for the moment.

In the late 1950s, when the matter of prostitution increasingly attracted parliamentary concern, Cable Street again surfaced as a site of moral panic. The focal point was the campaign led by the Christian socialist and tireless reformer Edith Ramsay, who, following a series of articles in the national press, came to be dubbed 'Florence Nightingale of the Brothels' and 'Stepney's Vice-Fighter No. 1'. In July 1957 she also led groups of Stepney housewives to lobby MPs on the conditions of the area. Tactically, however, it was a delicate issue, for while wishing to publicize the plight of the young women drawn into prostitution, Ramsay was determined to prevent unsympathetic observers turning the whole issue into one of race, specifically, the potentially incendiary matter of black men consorting with white women.[30] In the meantime, Barney Borman, a Communist member of Stepney Council, led a deputation to the Home Office to impress on the minister that the problem had to be tackled by the clearance of slums and provision of decent accommodation rather than persecution of the immigrant population. Because of the interest raised in the area, the experience of Stepney was instrumental in framing the 1959 Street Offences Act, which sought to remove prostitutes from the streets, and in the longer term influenced the deliberations of the Wolfenden Committee of Homosexuality and Prostitution.

Cable Street was also a harbinger of the cosmopolitanism evident along so many London streets today. It contained Maltese, Somali, Greek and Pakistani cafés, an Italian restaurant, Jewish and English shops, a French-owned general store, an Arab and a Trinidadian hairdresser, a dyer and cleaner run by Guianese, and a variety of lodging houses catering for different nationalities. Sadly, we know little of how well these various communities mixed, but it seems that despite exposure to racial sentiment from what was probably a sizable minority of the indigenous population, and an institutional racism which damaged their opportunities for decent employment, accommodation and education, immigrant settlers managed – as always – to adapt to the new and alien environment. In 1949, an African student, Derek Bamuta, carried out a brief investigation into their experiences, and left a vivid impression of his meeting with one such group:

> I became friendly with four Indian lads who had come over as ship's cooks and seemed to enjoy their life immensely; it was divided between attending cinema shows, walking about the streets looking for girls, and smoking Indian hemp. A fellow Indian owned a dilapidated four-roomed house; he sublet one room with two double beds to my friends for £2 per week. If one of them brought in a woman the others had to sit on the door-step or stand at the street corner. There was an adapted gas ring on which they cooked all their meals. The house was probably condemned and the sanitary arrangements were filthy, nevertheless, they gave me the impression that their living conditions were far better than in India.[31]

The winding up of the British empire from the late 1950s prompted dramatic increases in the migration of colonial and former colonial peoples to London. As was so often the case, distinct settlement patterns were forged by communities seeking forms of collective support. Thus while Caribbeans were widely dispersed, reflecting in part the desire among different island communities to live separately, Brixton and Stockwell soon gained reputations as epicentres of black settlement and culture. Cypriots later congregated in Stoke Newington and Harringay, and the Chinese in Soho and Limehouse, but it was the powerful waves of migration of Indians and Pakistanis from the 1960s which created the largest imprint on the ethnic landscape of the capital.[32] A Bengali presence in East London can in all certainty be traced back to the eighteenth century, when as skilled seamen they were employed as lascars by the East India Company, or were brought over as servants by Indian Army officers. A sizable settler community existed after the First World War when some of the thousands of seamen brought over to replace British sailors who had enlisted decided to stay on in Britain; many married white women. Several boarding houses, restaurants and cafés run by Bengalis were established in Canning Town, Stepney and Whitechapel, while others moved into tailoring workshops, where they were welcomed by Jewish owners.[33] In the interwar years, the lure of London enticed seamen to jump ship and head for Aldgate in the knowledge that someone would help them to find work and accommodation. Shah Abdul Qureshi was one of them:

I had one or two addresses, but they were wrongly written, they were not correct, and when I showed them to anyone they didn't know. I was very much disappointed, didn't know what to do. At the time I cannot go back to my ship, because I have come here to stay … I suddenly saw a young man, about twenty five, very dark looking … he spoke to me in Sylhet dialect … I was so very glad, I held him, embraced him. I said, 'By good luck, at last I have found someone who can help me.' He said, 'You have come from the boat?' I said, 'Yes.' He said, 'Come with me, I will give you shelter, I live in Mr. Munshi's house.'[34]

Mothosir Ali had also worked as a seaman on passages between Calcutta and Tilbury during the 1930s. Following mistreatment at the hands of a sarong (chargehand of lascars) on the SS *Mohoth*, he decided to desert when the ship reached Tilbury, and made his way to East London. Like many Sylheti men at the time, he found work in a Jewish tailor shop on menial tasks, earning seven or eight shillings for a six-day week until war broke out, at which point he returned to sea, working in the engine room of the troop carrier *City of Rangoon*.[35]

On gaining independence in 1947 India was partitioned. East Bengal became part of the newly created Pakistan. During the 1950s and 1960s the small numbers of Pakistanis identified in Stepney were therefore overwhelmingly from Bengal; only after seceding from Pakistan in 1971 to form the independent state of Bangladesh did this community come to identify itself as Bangladeshi. From that moment, the South Asian community in East London grew exponentially.[36]

Stinks of foreign cooking

The South Asian diaspora was complex, and here the briefest details must suffice. Pakistanis and Sikhs from the Punjab, who had first migrated to Britain at the beginning of the twentieth century, now started to settle in larger numbers. The Sikh community later grew dramatically following the expulsion of Indians from East Africa in the 1970s. The majority of these peoples who found their way to London chose to settle in Southall, but there was a significant presence also in East London. It was the scale and rapidity of Bangladeshi settlement, however, which marked it out as one of the most remarkable episodes in the postwar history of the area.[37]

A large majority of Bengali migrants originated in the Sylhet district, which as an important tea-growing province of Assam during the Raj had already established vital links with Britain. Near enough to Calcutta, it had

Muslims at the East London Mosque, many of them soldiers and merchant seamen, celebrate Eid ul-Fitr, 1941

also been the source of many lascars on British ships. With partition in 1947, however, the province was incorporated into East Pakistan, and the link with Calcutta broke. The uncertainty of future employment combined with fear of involvement in the bloodshed on the streets of Calcutta that came with partition persuaded many to stay in East London, where they found employment in restaurants and the clothing trade. Immigration legislation introduced during the 1960s curbed the numbers, but after a devastating cyclone in 1970 which ravaged East Pakistan, and the great loss of life caused by the war of independence in the following year, many of the married men who had settled decided to bring over their wives and children. Aided by kinship networks which spanned the continents, the Bangladeshi community thus continued to grow steadily. By 2001, the population of those born in Bangladesh was fifteen times the size of the next largest foreign-born population, that from the Caribbean; overall, Bangladeshis comprised a third of the population of Tower Hamlets. And although they were to be found in all parts of the borough, particular concentrations existed in the older inner areas such as Spitalfields and Banglatown (as the Brick Lane area was now called), where no less than 62 per cent of the population stated their religion as Muslim, compared with 18 per cent Christian.[38]

In ways which resembled previous migrant experience in East London, the Bangladeshi community asserted its own strong sense of collective identity, often in response to a hostile environment.[39] Self-help organizations sprang up in the 1950s, the most important of which, the Bangladeshi Welfare Association, survives to the present. Many Bengalis were actively involved in the movement for independence led by the Awami League, and in 1970 founded the UK branch of the League with its headquarters at the Dilchad restaurant in Spitalfields. But it was in the 1970s and 1980s that the community really consolidated its political presence with an extended series of campaigns against unemployment, homelessness and racism, organized by a large variety of groups, including the Bengali Housing Action Group and the Federation of Bangladeshi Youth Organisations. Faced with continued discrimination, and the racially motivated murder of three Bengalis in East London during the 1970s, activists forged alliances with others outside the community, and began to involve themselves in municipal and national politics, in part as a means of gaining access to vital funding. In 1982 the first of many Bengalis was elected to Tower Hamlets Council.

It was in the aftermath of these events that Michael Young and his co-workers returned to the area forty years after the publication of *Family and Kinship in East London*. In marked contrast to this early study, which had completely effaced the issue, it was now clear to the researchers that 'the problem of ethnic conflict could not be avoided', and so they embarked on a detailed investigation involving a series of interviews with the people affected.[40] In the past, they proposed, no doubt with the experience of Irish and Jewish immigration in mind, conflict between the indigenous population and new settlers had been created by competition for work. Although this was still a factor, the struggle over access to welfare, housing and education was now decisive. At the core of the conflict was a profound unease among the indigenous white community about how the good, equitable society forged after the war had been dismantled by well-meaning but ill-informed policies, particularly in housing. In extending the rights of citizenship to Bangladeshi settlers, priority was now decided on the basis of need rather than, as it had been in the past, on the basis of claims to membership of the community. Put simply, by demonstrating need, settlers had been able to jump to the front of the housing lists, leapfrogging over those who had waited patiently while they slowly worked their way to the front.

Much to the authors' initial surprise, the most hostile racist sentiment against Bangladeshis was expressed by the local white granny – the archetypal East End mother who had featured so prominently as the heroine in

Family and Kinship. One interview contained a typical, visceral response from a granny to the perceived loss of this world:

> You have to lock your door where you never used to. My partner ran a local pub for fifty years. You relied on people in the street and doors were open and people sat on the doorsteps until late at night. The neighbours are not like they were – but mine are good! There are too many stinks of foreign cooking. You can say I'm racist if you like. The lifts are filthy because of their spitting and urine, and they leave rubbish everywhere … The flats used to be beautiful, and the windows clean. It's heartbreaking really now as it's so filthy … There's too much noise now all night – with their shouting and running about. The kids run amok in the park and tread on plants.[41]

Occasionally, the sense of loss of entitlement earned over the years, and of a certain betrayal by the British government after years of hardship and self-sacrifice during and since the war, came over. One part-time school cleaner in her late sixties confessed:

> You find that most people who lived in Bethnal Green have moved out. They're not getting anything like a fair deal. Me and my husband don't get a farthing off anyone. We only get our pension … But I was in the post office the other day. It was packed in there and most of them was Bengali. They wasn't just going up with one book but with eight or nine books and they were sending the money back to their country. And of course it caused a riot. People were saying, 'Look at so-and-so; I bet he hasn't done a day's work here. I bet if there was a war they'd all go back to their own country.'[42]

Powerful though such perspectives on the Bangladeshi community are in the minds of indigenous East Enders they amount to little more than racial stereotyping. Forgotten is the long service that many Bengalis gave to the British empire, the poverty and alienation experienced by settlers, the thrift exercised enabling them to send money from their meagre resources to relatives in Bangladesh, and the complete lack of evidence that their families received preferential treatment from local social services. Indeed, the irony is that in many respects Bangladeshi families resemble those remembered fondly by grannies from the 1950s. The same extended kinship networks, offering mutual support and with a strong sense of collective identity, prevail, and far from the view that women are passive victims of a religiously based male oppression, Bangladeshi mothers are determinedly matriarchal, exercising firm control over their families. One young woman visiting Bangladesh for the first time was surprised to discover:

> Women are very, very strong in Bangladesh … It is to do with economic power, with money and with providing for your family and things … Men are lumbered down with one thing, their business or their land. Women are involved with anything, virtually everything. They don't go out; when I was there I did not see women go off and help their husbands in the fieldwork. But I saw that women are very strong in the household and with managing money within the household.[43]

Migration to East London did little to prevent the transmission of these practices to the next generation:

> With my parents, my father has to bring his money and give it to my mother. It's the same with my aunt. My uncle at the end of the week will give his money to her … in my family it is not just with my mother and father, but it's my brother-in-law and sister too. When his parents were in Bangladesh, he'd bring his money to my sister for her to keep.[44]

Like *Family and Kinship* from which it drew inspiration, the study has drawn divisions too neatly and conveniently, this time between the indigenous white and Bangladeshi communities. Even before the interviews were completed it was apparent that the area was undergoing dramatic change as large numbers of Bangladeshis, following the route taken by so many migrant settlers communities in the past, moved eastwards, no doubt on their way to metropolitan Essex. Spaces vacated have been filled by other migrants, most notably Somalis and East Europeans, whose presence, if recognized, would complicate the picture. And the narrative is rather too close to that of the 1950s; what prevails here is a sense of decent, cosy working-class community assailed by the impersonal forces of an unthinking state, when we need a rather more nuanced view of how the response of East Enders can be seen as part of a longer story of immigrant settlement, and how their distinct sense of identity has been thrown into confusion by the arrival of people who had previously been colonized by the British.

The history of immigration to West Ham provides an interesting counterpoint to that of the older East End. As we have seen, because of the

lateness of its industrial development and remoteness from London, there
had been little experience of overseas settlement apart from the Irish poor
prior to the mid-nineteenth century. The remarkable growth of industry
from that point attracted significant numbers of Germans and Lithuanians,
many of whom brought specialist skills in chemical manufacturing and
glass-blowing, and the presence of the docks encouraged a sizable population of lascars in Canning Town. A Jewish community was later established, not by migrants from Eastern Europe but, in a pattern that was to
be repeated time and again by other communities, by the exodus from
Whitechapel and Bethnal Green. Morris Granditer opened a menswear
shop in Canning Town as early as 1910, to be followed by various businesses of other Jewish families. By 1923 the Jewish community was sufficiently well established to build the Canning Town Synagogue. A large and
prosperous Jewish community settled in the residential area of Forest
Gate, building the West Ham Synagogue in 1928 to accommodate over a
thousand worshippers.[45]

The Blitz dispersed much of the black community near the docks, but
postwar migration led to a dramatic increase in the Caribbean and later
Asian populations. At the time, few moved directly to West Ham; rather
they were initially attracted by the demand for cheap labour advertised by
London Transport and the Post Office around London, or by factories,
mills and foundries in the Midlands and north, only later to be lured by the
prospect of the relatively high wages offered by firms such as Ford and
Standard Telephones & Cables.[46] The Asian experience was comparable.
Early postwar Gujurati and Punjabi settlers in the north and clothing
workers in Stepney later migrated to West Ham, where they established a
large community around Green Street, which was greatly augmented by
families expelled from East Africa during the 1970s.

Many of these families were subjected to personal and institutional
racism during the 1960s, 1970s and 1980s. Numerous incidents were
recorded of stabbings and beatings of immigrants, and petrol-bomb attacks
on their homes. Serious also was the systematic denial of equal opportunities in employment, housing and education. Industries to which black
workers had been actively recruited operated forms of discrimination
preventing their recruitment to the higher positions. Elsewhere, they were
forced to take the least attractive jobs, often when they were vastly over-
qualified. Former graduates, teachers, managers and army officers thus
found themselves working as unskilled labourers on night shifts or in factories with appalling health and safety standards. Ford in Dagenham had a
good record of recruiting black workers, such that in 1979 they represented

over a third of the workforce. Few were employed as skilled labourers, however, the foremen were overwhelmingly white, and the unions refused to take up legitimate grievances around harassment and the sorts of discrimination that denied black workers promotion.[47] They could expect little solidarity from other workers. On the contrary, in April 1968 a large contingency of dockers from East London had marched with Smithfield meat porters in support of the anti-immigration rhetoric of Enoch Powell's infamous 'rivers of blood' speech delivered a few days earlier, and this despite the fact that because of the restricted recruitment practices there were virtually no black workers in the docks or markets.

In this climate of fear, fascist organizations again resurfaced. Mosley's paper *Action* called for work within the unions, and was prominent in organizing the dockers' march. The newly formed National Front also saw the importance and potential gains of union agitation. It established a broad foothold in Canning Town largely from campaigns on the politically sensitive issue of housing, and recruited actively at the ground of West Ham Football Club, where racist chants and hooligan behaviour were commonplace. On a ticket of repatriation the NF had some electoral success. In the local election of 1974 it polled 29 per cent of the vote in Hudson's Ward and 25 per cent in Canning Town, while in the general election a few months later the NF had its greatest success with 5,000 votes.

And yet from the 1980s Tower Hamlets and Newham witnessed a remarkable reversal of the postwar decline in population. From the low point in 1981 of 140,000, the population of Tower Hamlets reached 220,500 in 2008, while that of Newham rose from 209,000 to 249,500 in the same period.[48] Most of this increase was due to the expansion of existing ethnic communities such as the Bangladeshi, and arrival of new ones, notably, Somali, Vietnamese, Ethiopian, African and Eastern European. Critical to this expansion has been the settlement of refugees and asylum seekers as once again East London provided sanctuary for persecuted minority populations from around the world. In the early 1990s it was estimated that 12,000 foreign-born refugees resided in Tower Hamlets and 9,000 in Newham. Somalis and Tamils fleeing civil strife comprised the largest groups, with significant numbers also from Uganda, Zaire, Angola, Kurdistan and Eastern Europe.[49] In the meantime, as Sikh, Pakistani and Hindu families who had previously settled in Newham migrated out to less deprived areas such as Ilford, South Woodford and Chadwell Heath, so they were replaced by Bangladeshi and Tamil populations from Tower Hamlets following the same demographic trajectories as their predecessors. These two boroughs, with the possible exception of Brent, have the most culturally diverse populations

in Britain, and the highest proportions of non-white people, while the
outer boroughs of Redbridge, and Barking and Dagenham, remain overwhelmingly white.[50]

The crown of Father Thames

In ways which were causally related, the rise of immigrant communities
coincided with a sharp decline in the economic fortunes of East London.
After a brief postwar resurgence, when many firms turned enthusiastically
to the challenge of rebuilding, the local economy entered into a protracted
industrial decline from which it has never recovered. No single factor was
responsible. The war had driven businesses away; some found favourable
locations elsewhere and stayed, some returned to East London where they
found shattered infrastructures. While the bombs fell, the Barlow
Commission on the Distribution of Industry and the Abercrombie Greater
London Plan applied themselves to the task of reducing the population of
London by encouraging the outward migration of industry and the construction of a series of satellite towns beyond the green belt, and by discouraging
the peacetime settlement of new industries.[51] These were followed by the
1951 County of London Development Plan, which, mindful of the lack of
open space in much of the capital, sought to tackle its greatest industrial
concentration by the Thames adjoining the Lea. The planners were encouraged by signs of postwar losses in manufacturing employment, particularly
in Stepney and Poplar, and set about further reductions as a means of
releasing land for public housing and open space. So successful were these
various initiatives that by the late 1960s the Greater London Council (GLC)
warned that the decline in the population was depriving London disproportionately of the young, skilled and educated, leaving it with the burden of
the old, poor and unskilled, and if the trend were not reversed London's
economic vitality would be fatally weakened.[52]

The industries of East London, however, belonged to a different age
and in many respects were living on borrowed time. Created largely in the
eighteenth and nineteenth centuries, they had proven resistant to the
exigencies of twentieth-century modernization. West Ham had reached its
peak in the 1920s, after which it entered into a period of industrial stagnation and decline, while Tower Hamlets clung tenaciously to small-scale
manufacturing firms. Both experienced levels of unemployment quite
uncharacteristic of the region as a whole. Bombs, planners and a postwar
climate of deindustrialization merely accelerated the downward trend, with
the inevitable toll on once vibrant industries. The story of S.W. Silver & Son

was emblematic. Silver's started in Greenwich as a waterproof clothing factory early in the nineteenth century. Mid-century it moved across the river to West Ham, where it diversified into a wide range of insulating materials, particularly for the buoyant telegraph cable industry. Reformed as the India Rubber, Gutta Percha and Telegraph Works, it occupied over twenty-three acres, employed close to 4,000, was for decades the largest manufacturing ratepayer in West Ham, and gave its name to the area of Silvertown. By the 1920s, however, it faced financial difficulties and was taken over by the British Goodrich Rubber Co., which reorganized the plant on a smaller scale. It suffered heavy bombing during the war, but survived until the 1960s, when it was finally closed, and the land sold for redevelopment.

Ford, Standard Telephones & Cables, Tate & Lyle, and a host of smaller concerns also either closed or cut back production at this time. In the period 1965–75, East London lost 24,000 jobs in traditional manufacturing industries. As always, the areas worst hit were those that had been built around local industries. In 1966 over half of 7,000 employed residents of Canning Town worked in the local manufacturing plants. Of the 3,000 jobs shed by Tate & Lyle in 1967, approximately 550 were those of Canning Town residents. Further closures followed over the next ten years, by which time half the area's working population had been made redundant.[53]

The closure of the docks was seismic in its impact on local communities. The docks had been at the heart of the maritime culture of Stepney since ancient times, and their great development early in the nineteenth century was the ultimate symbol of commercial and imperial modernization. All this was lost in the course of the 1970s and 1980s. It was not merely that jobs went, and communities were dismantled; the myths of dockland culture which had been created and sustained from one generation to another now existed only in memory. Again, it is difficult to identify a single factor held to be responsible; pressed hard, many might well claim that containerization killed off the upper docks. And yet the docks rarely realized their operating potential. For much of the time since their construction, economic viability had been hard hit by outdated work practices, failures to adopt new technologies, their sheer number, and the growing threat from continental ports. Only through mergers, the ruthless exploitation of dock labour, and the absence of a practicable alternative did the companies survive for as long as they did. In the immediate postwar period, the docks enjoyed something of a resurgence, with the port handling record tonnages of goods and accommodating record levels of shipping. The future must have looked bright. A small history of the docks written by the eminent English historian Sir Arthur Bryant to mark the fifty years of the Port of London Authority (PLA) in 1959 described the docks as heir to a glorious tradition of British ingenuity and endeavour.[54] The 'greatest port in the world' comprised docks which were engineering marvels. The Victoria Dock, for example, now 'modernized out of recognition and the most up-to-date in equipment', had mechanized berths for the discharge and delivery of chilled beef, and seven floating pneumatic grain elevators, each capable of unloading 300 tons per hour. In all, the Royal Docks had 211 electric cranes, the sight of which was 'one of the wonders of the modern industrial world. Here is "the principal centre of London's commerce and the brightest jewel in the crown of Father Thames" '.[55] And yet within the space of twenty years these selfsame docks would be idle, the ships departed never to return, and the warehouses empty, awaiting demolition.

Amidst Bryant's celebration of the contemporary port were hints of the future. His peregrination of the docks began at Tilbury, twenty-six miles down-river from London Bridge. The docks here had been greatly developed since being taken over by the PLA in 1909, and now occupied a site of over a hundred acres, with four miles of quays, deep-water berths capable of accommodating large vessels, and an impressive passenger terminal through which over a quarter of a million travellers passed annually. Of critical importance was the road transport infrastructure. Before the war twelve per cent of the cargo was removed by road; today the figure stood at seventy per cent.[56] The significance of this transformation gradually unfolded. 1962–3 was a high point of port trade; thenceforth it declined sharply, in part because of Britain's poor economic performance, in part because continental ports were quick to exploit the logistical revolution brought about by containerization. Only gradually did the PLA come to recognize this by opening Britain's first ocean container-ship terminal at Tilbury in 1968. Within a year it was found that seven container berths could handle nearly ninety per cent of the traffic of the upper port. Virtually at a stroke, containerization and the total lack of a road infrastructure rendered the older docks obsolete, and in order to cut costs St Katharine's, London and East India Docks were closed, followed shortly by the Surrey Docks. The effect on the workforce was dramatic; in the years 1955–1975 the numbers employed fell from 31,000 to just under 10,000. The losses suffered by ancillary trades were rather greater. For a time the PLA retained the hope that the West India and Millwall Docks on the Isle of Dogs, and the Royal Docks in West and East Ham could be salvaged through continued investment and rationalization, but upper dock trade continued to fall, and over 1980–81 these too were abandoned.

Whether under different circumstances the upper port could have been transformed into going concerns is sadly academic. The historian Jerry White has a point in arguing that the actions of the dockworkers over the years 1966–81 finally nailed the coffin of such hopes. The protracted and farcical series of unofficial strikes by dockworkers, drivers and seamen did incalculable damage to any future prospects, leaving the PLA with no choice but to move remaining trade downstream.[57] This struggle, however, was not merely about the livelihood of dockworkers; they believed (as did the miners just a few years later) that the whole way of life of a historic community was being threatened by a myopic authority and an intransigent Conservative government which simply did not care.

Shady Dickens areas

Their worst fears were realized in the aftermath of dock closures with the redevelopment of what became known as London Docklands. As early as 1971 the Secretary of State, Peter Walker, made clear that Docklands provided a unique opportunity to transform a riverside area close to the City, but since the task was beyond the imagination, experience and powers of local government it required the robust intervention of central government.[58] The consultants Travers Morgan were commissioned to assess the potential for comprehensive redevelopment by identifying a 'number of separate options so as to provide data, information, and various possibilities from which a decision can finally be made.'[59] The 1973 report proposed water parks, office development, sports and equestrian centres, golf courses and mixed housing which would attract 100,000 new people to the area. Unsurprisingly, it created deep resentment among local residents, who claimed they had not been consulted, and led directly to the formation of the Joint Docklands Action Group by union and Labour Party activists, and the Docklands Joint Committee comprising representatives from the GLC and five local boroughs. Both groups launched opposition to the report and urged an entirely different approach to the redevelopment, but progress was stalled over the next decade by political machinations until in 1979 the newly elected Conservative government under Margaret Thatcher announced the setting up of the London Docklands Development Corporation (LDDC).

With a remit to do anything necessary to promote regeneration, the LDDC was soon viewed as an all-powerful body capable of riding roughshod over local planning regimes, and of dismissing consultation, particularly with local communities, although traditional responsibilities for housing, health and education remained with the boroughs of Tower

Hamlets, Newham and Southwark. Initially, while publicly expressing opposition to the LDDC, representatives from the boroughs adopted a more pragmatic stance by deciding that their best course of action was to work with the new reality as a means of achieving what they could for their local communities. Within a year relations had been sundered. The local elections of 1982 saw decisive shifts to the left and the return to power of Labour Party activists who were committed to outright opposition to what was seen as an ideologically motivated attempt to wrest control of Docklands from elected councils, and who therefore refused to cooperate further with the LDDC.

Undeterred, the LDDC embarked on what was initially a fairly modest programme of regeneration centred on the creation of low-cost housing, new industries and limited environmental improvement. Even this was no easy task, for most private developers held entirely negative views about East London, and failed to recognize the full potential of the 5,100 acres available. As one businessman remarked:

> You don't spend money on the East side of London, you go to Kensington or Mayfair or Knightsbridge ... You don't spend money in Tower Hamlets. You don't spend money in Newham ... Poplar, Stepney and Bow. The names, you've got to admit it they all sound wrong ... they're all shady Dickens areas or immigrant areas, which is true they are, from the Jews to the West Indians to the Asiatics they're all there and still [there's] that connotation.[60]

With the offer of generous financial packages, some developers reluctantly agreed to a pilot scheme in Beckton. So startlingly successful was this (every house was sold before it was completed) that the developers immediately clamoured for more sites; almost overnight the largest single private house-building programme ever seen in Britain was launched, and Docklands redevelopment took off. Some low-cost housing was offered to local council tenants, a few of whom exploited the lack of controls and rapidly increasing property values to make a quick killing. Stories circulated of tenants buying houses only to sell them on immediately at inflated prices, or 'lending' their rent books to prospective buyers from outside for £50. For the majority of local residents, however, the houses were well beyond their means, and so were snapped up by young professionals keen to live in attractive surroundings with riverside views close to the City.

The obvious success of this venture encouraged the LDDC to consider commercial development. Reg Ward, Chief Executive of the Corporation, approached developers in the north and abroad who were less likely to share old prejudices about East London, and persuaded them that Docklands was not the desolate East End but a vital area no more than a mile and a half away from the City. It was something of a false promise, since with no communications infrastructure Docklands remained inaccessible; but then in 1982 permission was granted to start work on a Docklands Light Railway which opened up the area by providing a fast, regular service linking Docklands to Bank and the Tower, and interconnecting with underground and overland railway lines, and thus commercial development was instantly secured. Encouraged also by hugely advantageous tax breaks, firms began to settle, primarily in sites around the old West India Docks on the Isle of Dogs.

Some on the LDDC were sympathetic to the idea of establishing a dialogue with local communities on schemes which were going to transform people's lives, but, faced with the prospect of endless meetings and debates on every substantive policy issue, decided that the only way forward was to impose their vision of regeneration. In this they were aided by a fractured opposition. The most prominent of the local groups was the Association of Island Communities (AIC), which had fought effectively in the interests of local residents for years and yet found it impossible to work effectively with the more militant Joint Docklands Action Group and the Docklands Forum, which were dominated by Labour Party activists from outside the area and attracted funding from borough councils. And local opinion was rather more ambivalent than activists wished to acknowledge. Among those most concerned about redevelopment there was a desire to preserve the dockland communities, but with the closure of the docks and manufacturing industry this was an increasingly forlorn hope. Some reconciled themselves to change by looking optimistically at the potential benefits which had already been delivered:

> Well it's progress innit really. It has made a lot of difference I mean I've worked in the City ... and it was a hell of a job to get off the Island because [of the] bridges ... and there was always boats and that going through ... But now you see they've got the Docklands Light Railway and ... the bridges are open and they've rerouted the buses so you can go straight to town ... from the light railway ... it's a lot better now.[61]

Influential figures like Ted Johns, chair of the AIC, probably expressed the feelings of many when he admitted that their best course of action was to get what they could from the developers.[62] By the mid-1980s, however, it was apparent that few local people were going to benefit from regeneration. For a time anger against the LDDC became more focused and drew upon

a wider base, then in 1986 Liberals were returned to power on the Tower
Hamlets Council, negotiations with the Corporation resumed, and the
land rush began. Within less than five years, as speculators and developers
moved in, the price of land and accommodation soared, and Docklands
was transformed. Fashionable riverside residences sprang up, to be overshadowed only by massive modernist office blocks and towers, the greatest
of which, the inappropriately named Canary Wharf, was built after several
false starts by the Canadian financial giant Olympia and York. Its magnificent 850-foot tower has come to symbolize in the minds of most what
Docklands regeneration was – a shimmering monument to unfettered
greed, or to the triumph of planning over adversity.

By the late 1980s it was apparent to local residents that they were
excluded not only from the process of consultation, but also from the
houses and jobs created by development. One Islander described well the
sense of betrayal and alienation created at the time:

> We keep hearing we're gonna build so many homes and so many flats
> and there's gonna be squash courts and swimming pools and all
> wonderful things you know and shops [laughs] … In the housing
> boom the houses got put up all right but what I was promised to go
> with 'em – you know it'll contain walks round the side and restaurants
> and all this sort of thing – all very well [but] it's meaningless to the
> average working class person around here.[63]

Demonstrations were organized. One imaginative protest took place in the
summer of 1986 when, much to the horror of the American guests, a flock
of sheep and 150,000 bees were let loose on the open-air launch of the
Canary Wharf development scheme. But it was too little, too late, and,
unmoved, the developers surged ahead. In the period 1981–2006 the population of Docklands increased from 40,000 to 107,000, mostly affluent
young families. The newcomers had a mixed reception from established
residents, some of whom resented being forced into a corner of their
neighbourhood, while others welcomed the arrival of new blood. Some of
the hostility was created by class tensions, but it was evident that the
powerful senses of localism played their part. When a former council
tenant from Bethnal Green moved into a new house on the Isle of Dogs, he
found an alien environment:

> [I]f you move from Bethnal Green to Poplar, Poplar to Stepney, and
> Stepney to the Isle of Dogs they're all different people they've all got

different ways strangely enough, although there's four or five miles in it … These Islanders are very cliquey [and] did resent these people coming in.[64]

In the early 1990s Bengali families were moved to council accommodation on the Island and unsurprisingly were also met with hostility. The extent to which their presence added a racial dimension to an already complicated response was uncertain, but significantly Britain's first councillor representing the British National Party was elected from an Island ward in September 1993.

On a smaller scale, but with no less an impact on the local community, Spitalfields has also been transformed in the past twenty years. Under the rubric of urban regeneration, large developers have hastily moved into the spaces rendered obsolete by protracted economic decline to create new sites of bourgeois pleasure. Along Bishopsgate, marking the historical boundary with the City, the massive Broadgate development and the sudden appearance of glass-towered banks have brought to the area a predominantly young office-based working population whose needs are catered for by the inevitable coffee shops, sandwich bars and smart restaurants. Close by, the Old Spitalfields market, which in 1991 had been made redundant by the opening of the new fruit and vegetable market in Leyton, has been converted by Ballymore Properties into a haven for trendy and expensive food, designer clothes and furniture stalls much frequented by day trippers.

In the meantime, the ancient Brick Lane market is no more. True, stalls are still erected there every Sunday morning, but the market has been sanitized and transformed; no longer the place for cheap merchandise with no questions asked, or of people selling from blankets laid on the ground any items of little worth which they have acquired in the course of the week; the stallholders are now mostly reputable and closely monitored, their clientele mostly tourists. Two hundred yards to the south, Grand Metropolitan decided in the early 1990s to close the historic Truman's Brewery and redevelop it as a tourist attraction.[65] The Brick Lane Music Hall – 'the home of British Music Hall' (sic) – was opened in 1992, and has now found larger and perhaps more fitting premises next to the London City Airport in Silvertown. Other parts of the brewery's grounds have been converted into fashionable eateries.

This transformation of Spitalfields has been accompanied, and in part boosted, by the gradual gentrification of the area. Professional and artistic elites such as Gilbert and George and Tracey Emin have settled, many occupying the Georgian townhouses originally built by master silk weavers but which had since been allowed to deteriorate. Thirty years ago, they were semi-derelict; many today have been restored to their original splendour. Two in Princelet and Wilkes Streets have recently been sold for £2.15m each. At the time of writing (2011), a three-bedroom townhouse with a ground-floor shop in Fashion Street is being advertised for £2.6m.

These redevelopments may have created jobs and wealthy enclaves, but the vast majority of local residents have fared poorly in the labour market. Statistics, at best incomplete, suggest that between 1981 and 1994 the numbers employed in banking, finance, insurance and business services increased from 1,500 to over 20,000; few of these jobs went to local people. Rather they were offered traditional low-quality jobs in distribution, hotels and catering, the numbers of which rose from 4,000 to 9,500 over the same period. Despite these increases, unemployment levels were higher than in the period before redevelopment, in large part because redevelopment had done little to improve the prospects of the long-term unemployed created by closure of the docks and local manufacturing.[66] Combined with the rationalization of many manufacturing industries, closures have dealt a blow to the East London labour market from which it has yet to recover. This does not mean to say that manufacturing is dead. A 1995 survey estimated that there were approximately 3,000 manufacturing firms, employing 48,000 people, in East London and its immediate neighbourhood. A detailed investigation of twenty-one of them revealed that their survival from the recessions of the 1980s and 1990s had depended upon diversification and a reduction of labour costs, namely, cuts in the labour force and intensification of work.[67]

These changes have done little to mitigate the seemingly endemic poverty of East London. Using a range of socio-economic indices to rank 354 local authorities, Hackney, Tower Hamlets and Newham emerge as respectively the second, third and sixth most deprived areas of the country.[68] Here is the most fundamental of continuities which serves to temper unduly optimistic visions of regeneration.

For a time, regeneration of Docklands seemed to provide hope of a boost to the local labour market, but the promise was never realized. East London now stands at the dawn of a regeneration provided by the 2012 Olympics and visions of a transformed Thames Gateway. We turn finally in a brief epilogue to the question of whether or not this is a false dawn.

Epilogue: The Promise of Regeneration?

OVER THE next twenty years East London will be influenced by two schemes of regeneration. We can put it no stronger or more precisely than that, for although the 2012 Olympics and Thames Gateway plan are unprecedented in their sheer scale and ambition, it is anyone's guess how they will actually impact on the lives of East Enders. The idea for the regeneration of Thames Gateway was initially – and significantly – hinted at by Michael Heseltine at the opening of Canary Wharf in 1991, when he suggested that the barren areas of the East Thames Corridor should be brought into more valuable use.[1] But it was not until the Labour government took power and John Prescott at the Office of the Deputy Prime Minister assumed responsibility in 2002 that the project began to take shape.

In every respect the Thames Gateway project is a massive undertaking, by far the largest urban regeneration scheme ever seen in Britain. The area stretches eastward from Tower Hamlets along the northern and southern foreshores of the Thames until, forty miles downstream, it reaches Southend and Sittingbourne. The gateway has known better days, for along the Thames were located many of the nation's great armaments, engineering, shipbuilding, and telegraph and cable industries before twentieth-century deindustrialization and the loss of lucrative colonial markets forced them to close or move to more favourable locations, leaving behind a wilderness of brownfield sites – a cockney Siberia, as it has been called. Fifteen boroughs are included within the boundaries of the scheme, housing a total of 1.6m people, many of whom live in areas which were never able to recover from the loss of industries upon which their communities depended. The intent is to increase this number to over 2m by providing 160,000 new houses, 225,000 new jobs and appropriate infrastructures to create sustainable communities. To kick-start this, the government committed £9bn in the hope that £43bn of private investment would follow; the shadow of recession has since approached, however, and now hangs over the proceedings, forcing planners to revise their estimates.[2]

Tower Hamlets and Newham are embraced by the scheme, and for good reason. Not only do they contain areas of long-standing deprivation, but, as Heseltine hinted, the experience of Docklands redevelopment offered prospects for the regeneration of the region as a whole, and the Olympics has acted as a welcome fillip. The achievements so far are not encouraging. A number of housing projects have been completed piecemeal on brownfield and waterside sites which have gone some way to meeting the need for more affordable accommodation in the London region; but small, often poor-quality flats predominate which have not created mixed and balanced social communities, nor, in the absence of employment opportunities and appropriate infrastructures, are they likely to promote sustainable regeneration.[3] Too many of the developments are isolated and likely to attract a disproportionate number of families on low incomes. Without a more integrated approach based on a strategic alliance between public and private sectors, Thames Gateway could become yet another planning disaster.

The danger is in part that regeneration has been led by housing rather than industry. Relatively little thought has been given to how the region is to be revived economically. Few believe that in a post-industrial age there is any hope of resurrecting the region's astonishing industrial past; more confidence has been placed in a 'cockney cyberia', namely, a commercial redevelopment based on the knowledge and creative economies which have underpinned the success of Docklands and the resurgent fashion trade around Brick Lane. There is something in this, although it will require considerable investments in finance and imagination which have heretofore been lacking. Care must be taken to ensure the region does not become merely an adjunct of the City and Canary Wharf, or a dormitory suburb for those who work elsewhere.

Amidst jubilant celebrations on 9 July 2005, London was rather unexpectedly announced as the host for the 2012 Olympic Games. The bid had identified Stratford as the site of the Olympic Park, with sporting venues in other parts of Newham, and in the neighbouring boroughs of Greenwich, Tower Hamlets, Hackney and Waltham Forest. Its success owed much to the case put forward that the games would act as a catalyst for the renewal of areas of East London which had long suffered social and educational deprivation, and leave a beneficial legacy of a transformed urban environment and a culture of sporting prowess to inspire future generations.

At face value, these schemes seem to offer much to East London. According to much of the hyperbole, some of the most deprived areas in the country are to attract unprecedented levels of public and private investment which will not only transform their built environment but offer thousands of new jobs to local people. Various observers, however, have advised a more cautious approach in thinking about the progress of this regeneration and its likely benefits. In a typically acerbic piece, Iain Sinclair has told of how the Olympics has begun to transform the environment and lives of East Londoners, although in ways few welcome.[4] Speculative capital has rushed in to buy plots of land cheaply which are ruthlessly cleared before gimmicky apartments spring up:

> The urban landscape of boroughs anywhere within the acoustic footprints of the Olympic Park in the Lower Lea Valley has been devastated, with a feverish beat-the-clock impatience unseen in London since the beginnings of the railway age. Every civic decency, every sentimental attachment, is swept aside for that primary strategic objective, the big bang of the starter's pistol.

Hackney Marshes, Sinclair continued, long the site of football matches among enthusiastic local teams, has been prematurely sequestered for the construction of a parking lot, with the loss of eleven pitches. Without any form of redress, long-established businesses have been closed down, allotment holders forced to move on, and houses demolished or mysteriously burnt down to make way for new road infrastructures or buy-to-let accommodation financed by Russian money.

There was a certain inevitability to the financial difficulties faced by the project. Initial estimates of the cost were too low, and would almost immediately be revised upwards. The original operating budget of £2.4bn had reached £3.3bn by 2006, and by late 2010 stood at no less than £9.35bn. In retrospect, it is clear that calculations in the original budget contained major errors which have been compounded by the failure of the private sector to deliver anticipated levels of financial investment. Government departments have thus been forced to step in with extra funding, and major cutbacks have been introduced in the programme of urban renewal, including the provision of affordable housing, which now looks unlikely.[5] Were it felt that such public expenditure was justified by the potential legacy of the games, then the opposition might be muted, but sadly there is little from the experience of previous Olympic cities to suggest this will be the case.[6] Barcelona (1992), Atlanta (1996), Sydney (2000), Athens (2004) and Beijing (2008) all promised much, and to an extent delivered major infrastructural improvements, and yet at the heavy cost of increasing social inequalities and inflated public debts. In a sober assessment of what is realistically achievable, Gavin Poynter has claimed that the recession, incompatibilities between commercialization and Olympic ideals, and confusion over what the legacy actually means are unlikely to provide decent jobs and housing as a precondition for the enhancement of life chances for local people. This failure will merely exacerbate the social and economic inequalities of the area.[7]

The narratives of these regeneration schemes will take time to unfold. The Olympics will be over by the late summer of 2012; it will be another few years before we know whether they have been a success. The course of Thames Gateway regeneration will run for at least another ten years, far too long for idle speculations of historians. All we can do is remind planners, government officials and local communities that the places now in the process of being obliterated by development have a history which is worth recording, preserving and hence remembering. This is what the most eloquent raconteur, Patrick Wright, had in mind when writing *The River* and the accompanying BBC TV series.[8] Subtitled *The Thames in Our Time*, the book provides a brief account of a journey along the length of the river from its source near Ewen to the opening out into the English Channel at the Isle of Grain. Much of the travelogue therefore describes locations along the estuary that would be familiar to planners of the Thames Gateway. Less familiar, however, are the hidden histories and stories which Wright excavates from local people and the crumbling monuments which have survived from a previous age, and which structure and challenge the myths surrounding the Thames riverscape.

Similar concerns have informed this history of East London. In writing it I have attempted to uncover the historical forces which shaped its creation, growth, demise and potential regeneration. Thus its intimate relationship to the metropolis, the richness and diversity of its various districts, the critical role of imperial endeavour, the impact of the Industrial Revolution, the mythologies of outcast London, the devastation of the Blitz and the subsequent re-formation, and the making of what has become a unique diasporic centre have all been explored, not merely as a means of explaining the history but equally to register that this history is a vital one which cannot be allowed to vanish under fleets of mechanical diggers.

Notes

Introduction: O Thomas Cook

1. Jack London, *The People of the Abyss*, Pluto Press, 2001 [1903], p. 1.
2. Charles Booth (ed.), *Life and Labour of the People*, vol. 1, *East London*, Williams and Norgate, 1889.
3. Charles Booth (ed.), *Life and Labour of the People of London*, Third Series, *Religious Influences*, vol. 1, *London North of the Thames: the Outer Ring*, Macmillan, 1902, p. 11.
4. Walter Besant, *East London*, Chatto and Windus, 1901, p. 3.
5. Ibid., p. 256.
6. Robert Sinclair, *East London. The East and North East Boroughs of London and Greater London*, Hale, 1950, p. 33.
7. Millicent Rose, *The East End of London*, Cresset Press, 1951, p. v.

Chapter 1: The Parish of Stepney to 1700

1. Roger Finlay, *Population and Metropolis: The Demography of London, 1580–1650*, Cambridge, Cambridge University Press, 1981; Roger Finlay and Beatrice Shearer, 'Population growth and suburban expansion', in A.L. Beier and Roger Finlay (eds), *London 1500–1700. The Making of the Metropolis*, Longman, 1986, pp. 37–59.
2. For good general accounts of this period see Norman Brett-James, *The Growth of Stuart London*, Allen & Unwin, 1935; Roy Porter, *London. A Social History*, Hamish Hamilton, 1994; Francis Sheppard, *London: A History*, Oxford, Oxford University Press, 1998.
3. Sheppard, *London*, p. 97. During recent excavations between Bishopsgate and the old Spitalfields Market, the remains of the priory were discovered, and have been preserved for all to see.
4. Bedlam moved from Bishopsgate to Moorfields in 1675. After several moves it is now located in Beckenham, South London, where it enjoys a reputation as a pioneer in the treatment of mental disorder.
5. *Stebunheath, otherwise Stepney Manor*, 1894. Several members of the Colebrooke family were closely involved in the affairs of India. Sir George's son George was a director of the East India Company, and his youngest son, Henry Colebrooke, was a Company servant and a respected authority on Indian languages and husbandry. We shall have much more to say about the intimate connections between East London and the East Indies. For details of the rather complex story of the manor and its lands, see the chapter on Stepney, *Victoria County History of Middlesex*, vol. 11, *Stepney and Bethnal Green*, Institute of Historical Research, 1998, pp. 19–22. Happily, this valuable reference work is also available at British History Online (www.british-history.ac.uk).
6. John Stow, *A Survey of London*: reprinted from the text of 1603 with introduction and notes by C.L. Kingsford, 2 vols, Oxford, Clarendon Press, 1908, vol. I, pp. 98–9. Although not the most readily available of the various editions of Stow, this is generally recognized to be the best.

7. Council of the Citizens of East London, *Our East London*, Schools' Committee of the Council, 1951, p. 3.
8. Richard Grafton, *Grafton's Chronicle, or, History of England. From the Year 1189 to 1558*, 2 vols, Johnson, 1809 [1569], vol. II, p. 466.
9. Even Shakespeare showed little interest in having his plays published (A.L. Rowse, *The Elizabethan Renaissance: The Cultural Achievement*, Macmillan, 1972, p. 4).
10. W.H. and H.C. Overall (eds), 'Plays and players', *Analytical Index to the Series of Records known as the Remembrancia: 1579–1664*, Francis, 1878, p. 350.
11. Cited in John Jeaffreson (ed.), *Middlesex County Records*, vol. 2, Greater London Council, 1972 [1886], p. xlvii.
12. Antima Galli, 'Letters from a Florentine correspondent', cited in Andrew Gurr, *Playgoing in Shakespeare's London*, Cambridge, Cambridge University Press, 1987, p. 71.
13. Overall (eds), 'Plays and players', p. 355.
14. Ibid., p. 352.
15. T.M. Parker, *The English Reformation to 1558*, Oxford, Oxford University Press, 1966, p. 20.
16. *Victoria County History of Middlesex*, vol. 11, 'Stepney churches'.
17. Champlin Burrage, *The Early English Dissenters in the Light of Recent Historical Research, 1550–1641*, Cambridge, Cambridge University Press, 1912; Parker, *The English Reformation to 1558*. The Reformation is conventionally linked primarily with Henry VIII's break with the Pope, but in so doing he drew upon much deeper currents of dissent.
18. [William Bohun], *Privilegia Londini: or, The Laws, Customs and Privileges of the City of London*, Browne, 1702, p. 313. Conventicles were illegal religious gatherings.
19. John Foxe, *Acts and Monuments*, Josiah Pratt (ed.), Religious Tract Society, 1877, vol. VIII, p. 458.
20. Ibid., p. 459.
21. Stow, *Survey of London*, p. xx; see also Pennant, *London*, pp. 240–41.
22. Charles Knight mentions a satirical account of the fair in 1658 entitled *A Faire in Spittlefields* which claimed the fair was originally established by pedlars as a means of selling their dubious wares ('Spitalfields', in Charles Knight (ed.), *London*, 6 vols, Knight, 1841–4, vol. 2, p. 390). I have, however, been unable to track down the pamphlet.
23. [John Strype], *A Survey of the Cities of London and Westminster and the Borough of Southwark … Written at first in the Year 1698* [sic] *by John Stow, Citizen and Native of London, corrected, improved and very much enlarged, in the year 1720 by John Strype a Native also of the Said City*, vol. II, book IV, Innys, Richardson et al., 1754, p. 33.
24. Ibid., p. 34.
25. Proclamation of Elizabeth I, 7 July 1580, quoted in ibid., p. 34.
26. M. Dorothy George, *London Life in the Eighteenth Century*, Harmondsworth, Penguin, 1965 [1925], p. 79.
27. Stow, *Survey of London*, vol. II, p. 72.
28. The proclamations have been usefully brought together in Paul Hughes and James Larkin (eds), *Tudor Royal Proclamations*, 3 vols, New Haven, Yale University Press, 1964–9, and James Larkin and Paul Hughes (eds), *Stuart Royal Proclamations*, 2 vols, Oxford, Clarendon Press, 1973–83.
29. [Strype], *A Survey of the Cities of London and Westminster*, vol. II, book IV, pp. 35–6.
30. George, *London Life*, p. 80.
31. Hughes and Larkin, *Tudor Royal Proclamations*, vol. II, pp. 245–8.
32. Thomas Dekker, *The VVonderfull Yeare. Wherein is shewed the picture of* London, *lying sicke of the Plague*, Creede, 1603, in F.P. Wilson (ed.), *The Plague Pamphlets of Thomas Dekker*, Oxford, Clarendon Press, 1925, p. 31.
33. Ibid., pp. 32, 35.
34. Ibid., p. 51.
35. Larkin and Hughes, *Stuart Royal Proclamations*, vol. I, pp. 47–8.

36. Ibid., pp. 111–12.
37. *Acts of the Privy Council*, 1615/16, p. 460, quoted in Brett-James, *Growth of Stuart London*, p. 92.
38. Quoted in ibid., pp. 98–9.
39. [Strype], *A Survey of the Cities of London and Westminster*, p. 37; George, *London Life*, p. 81. We have in Daniel Defoe another contemporary chronicler of a London plague, this of 1665. Defoe was only a young child in 1665 but his *A Journal of the Plague Year*, Harlow, Longman, 1984 [1665], has all the qualities of an eye-witness account. He claims that the infection started in west London, later spreading to the populous eastern parishes, where it raged in its most violent form.
40. Ibid., p. 82.
41. Finlay and Shearer, 'Population growth and suburban expansion', p. 45. The data are summarized below.

Population of the City and suburbs, and as percentages of the total London population, 1560–1680

Date	City	Suburbs	London total
1560	80,000 (73%)	30,000 (27%)	110,000
1600	100,000 (54%)	85,000 (46%)	185,000
1640	135,000 (38%)	220,000 (62%)	355,000
1680	105,000 (24%)	330,000 (76%)	435,000

Source: Extracted from Finlay and Shearer (1986), Table 3.

42. Beier and Finlay, 'The significance of the metropolis'.
43. Andrew Pettegree, *Foreign Protestant Communities in Sixteenth-Century London*, Oxford, Clarendon Press, 1986, p. 96.
44. 13 & 14 Car. II cap. 2.
45. 12 Anne cap. 20.
46. Sheppard, *London*, pp. 142–7.
47. *Victoria County History of Middlesex*, vol. 11, p. 13.
48. Ibid., p. 63.
49. *Survey of London*, vols 43 and 44, *Poplar, Blackwall and the Isle of Dogs*, Athlone Press, 1994, pp. 548–52, also available at British History Online (www.british-history.ac.uk).
50. K.N. Chaudhuri, *The English East India Company: The Study of an Early Joint Stock Company 1600–1640*, Cass, 1965, p. 99.
51. T.M. [Thomas Mun], *A Discovrse of Trade, from England unto the East-indies; answering the Diuerse Obiections which are vsually made against the same*, 1621, in J.R. McCullough (ed.), *Early English Tracts on Commerce*, Cambridge, Cambridge University Press, 1954 [1856], p. 25.
52. *Survey of London*, vols 43 and 44, 'Blackwall yard development, to c. 1819', pp. 553–65.
53. Ibid., p. 549.
54. [Mun], *A Discovrse of Trade*, p. 30.
55. William Foster, *John Company*, Bodley Head, 1926, p. 142.
56. [Mun], *A Discovrse of Trade*, p. 35.
57. Foster, *John Company*, p. 143.
58. Ibid., p. 158.
59. *Survey of London*, vols 43 and 44, 'Blackwall yard', pp. 558–9.
60. G.W. Hill and W.H. Frere (eds), *Memorials of Stepney Parish, that is to say, the Vestry Minutes from 1579 to 1662*, Guildford, privately published, 1890–91, p. 141.
61. Brett-James, *Growth of Stuart London*, p. 196.
62. Hill and Frere (eds), *Memorials of Stepney Paris*; Thomas Downs, 'Maritime Stepney', in Walter Locks (ed.), *East London Antiquities, East London Advertiser*, 1902, pp. 107–20.
63. [Strype], *Survey of the Cities of London and Westminster*, vol. II, book IV, p. 48.

64. Thomas Pennant, *London*, Faulder, 1790, p. 281.
65. Stow, *A Survey of London*, vol. II, pp. 70–72.
66. I have relied on two sources. *Ancient Songs and Ballads, written on various subjects and printed between the years 1560 and 1700 …, 1774*, comprises a substantial collection of ancient ballads collected by Robert Earl of Oxford. Better known as the *Roxburghe Ballads*, it later appeared during the nineteenth century but in heavily edited editions. For this reason it is advisable to consult the original unexpurgated collection in the British Library. This is well supplemented by the online collection of ballads available from the Bodleian Library, Oxford (www.bodley.ac.uk).
67. Paddy's Goose was the popular name given to the White Swan, a tavern on the Ratcliff Highway frequented by Irish labourers.
68. Richard Head, *The English Rogue Described, in the Life of Meriton Latroon; a Witty Extravagant, Comprehending the Most Eminent Cheats of Both Sexes*, Marsh, 1665. Three other editions follow, the last appearing in 1680.
69. Norman Brett-James, *The Growth of Stuart London*, Allen & Unwin, 1935, p. 211.
70. *Victoria County History of Middlesex*, vol. 11, 'Stepney churches', p. 74.
71. 13 & 14 Car. II cap. 4.
72. 16 Car. II cap. 4.
73. 17 Car. II cap. 2.
74. Cited in G. Lyon Turner (ed.), *Original Records of Early Nonconformity under Persecution and Indulgence*, Fisher Unwin, 1911, vol. 3, p. 70.
75. Ibid., pp. 88–9.
76. Ibid., p. 90.
77. *Victoria Country History of Middlesex*, vol. 11, 'Protestant nonconformity to 1689', p. 82.
78. Ibid., pp. 82–3.
79. Simon Dixon, 'Quaker communities in London, 1667–c. 1714', PhD thesis, University of London, 2006.
80. 1 Will. III cap. 18.
81. 7 & 8 Will. III cap. 9.
82. *A Vindication of the case of Spittle-Fields, against an uncharitable paper privately printed, called a true narrative of the case of Sir George Wheler, &c. Humbly offered to the Honourable House of Commons*, privately published, 12 October 1694.
83. Knight, *London*, vol. 2, pp. 391–2.
84. Knight, *London*, vol. 2, p. 392; J. Trevers, *An Essay to the Restoring of our decayed Trade*, 1675; Daniel Defoe, *Review*, 20 March 1705, quoted in George, *London Life*, p. 178.
85. *Calendar of State Papers Domestic, James I*, 1616, p. 397.
86. Ibid.
87. Valerie Pearl, *London and the Outbreak of the Puritan Revolution*, Oxford, Oxford University Press, 1961.
88. William Lithgow, *The Present Surveigh of London … with the several Fortifications thereof*, 1643, cited in Alfred Plummer, *The London Weavers' Company, 1600–1970*, Routledge & Kegan Paul, 1972, p. 177. The line of defence was strengthened by four forts at strategic locations, one of which stood just south of the Whitechapel Road. At the end of hostilities the defences were demolished, but a mound remained adjacent to the newly constructed London Hospital as a distinctive reminder of past resolve until it in turn was levelled early in the nineteenth century. Mount Terrace remains as a reminder.
89. Cited in ibid., p. 181.
90. Ibid., p. 190.
91. Knight, *London*, vol. 2, p. 392.
92. Based on plans prepared by John while working as a weaver in Italy, and secretly smuggled over to England in 1717, the machinery was never able to replace completely the Italian organzine preferred by many weavers, but it did enhance production, and was the archetype for the cotton mills of the late eighteenth century that kick-started the industrial revolution.
93. [Strype], *A Survey of the Cities of London and Westminster*, vol. II, book IV, p. 48.

94. Ibid., p. 47.

95. Brett-James, *The Growth of Stuart London*, p. 489.

96. Richard Dunn, 'The London weavers' riots of 1675', *Guildhall Studies in London History*, 1:1 (1973), pp. 13–23.

97. K.N. Chaudhuri, *The Trading World of Asia and the English East India Company, 1660–1760*, Cambridge, Cambridge University Press, 1978.

98. Plummer, *The London Weavers' Company*, p. 292.

99. [Daniel Defoe], *Manufacturer: or, The British Trade fully Stated, wherein the Case of the Weavers, and the Wearing of Callicoes, are considered*, 30 October 1719, cited in ibid., p. 299.

100. East London History Group, 'The population of Stepney in the early seventeenth Century', *East London Papers*, 11:2 (1968), p. 76. Such data have to be treated with caution since they would not have included sections of the population excluded from the Anglican church, for example, nonconformists.

101. Ibid., p. 84.

102. Michael Power, 'The east and the west in early-modern London', in E.W. Ives, R.J. Knecht and J.J. Scarisbrick (eds), *Wealth and Power in Tudor England*, Athlone Press, 1978, pp. 167–85.

103. Elizabeth McKellar, *The Birth of Modern London: The Development and Design of the City, 1660–1720*, Manchester, Manchester University Press, 1999, p. 39.

104. Nicolas Barbon, *An Apology for the Builder Or a Discourse Shewing the Cause and Effects of the Increase of Building*, Barbon, 1685, p. 2, cited in ibid., p. 33.

105. Michael Power, 'The development of a London suburban community in the seventeenth century', *London Journal*, 4:1 (1978), pp. 29–46.

106. [Strype], *A Survey of the Cities of London and Westminster*, vol. I, book II, p. 346.

107. Ibid., vol. II, book IV, p. 47. One useful indicator of the growth of Stepney is the timing of the formation of new parishes from within its boundaries. Such a parish could be formed by separation from a mother parish only when it had a suitable church and a sufficiently large community to sustain a viable congregation. The dates of the formation of East London parishes – Shadwell (1670), Wapping (1694), Stratford (c. 1720), Spitalfields (1729), St George's-in-the-East (formerly Wapping-Stepney) (1729), Limehouse (1730) and Bethnal Green (1743) – therefore give a rough guide to how the area as a whole developed.

Chapter 2: Industrialization and the spirit of improvement, 1680–1800

1. Roger Finlay and Beatrice Shearer, 'Population growth and suburban expansion', in A.L. Beier and Roger Finlay (eds), *London 1500–1700: The Making of the Metropolis*, Longman, 1986, pp. 38–9. Immigration to London is only part of a complex picture of demographic change in this period. Birth and death rates, related in turn to the standard of living and state of medical knowledge, have to be considered. Happily, such concerns are beyond my brief, but for a recent review of the literature see L.D. Schwarz, *London in the Age of Industrialisation: Entrepreneurs, Labour Force and Living Conditions, 1700–1850*, Cambridge, Cambridge University Press, 1992, in particular Chapter 5, 'The population of London'.

2. M. Dorothy George, *London Life in the Eighteenth Century*, Harmondsworth, Penguin, 1965 [1925], pp. 409–10. The early data are highly speculative. Based on extrapolation from estimates of the number of families, many of the totals for individual parishes are exaggerations, and boundary changes compromise direct comparison.

3. Extracted from ibid., pp. 409–10.

4. *The Foreigners Guide: or, a Necessary and Instructive Companion both for the Foreigner and the Native, in their tour through the Cities of London and Westminster*, Kent, Hope and Joliffe, 1763, p. 156.

5. William Maitland, *The History of London from its Foundation to the Present Time*, Wilkie, Lowndes, Kearsley and Bladon, 1772, p. 1007.

6. John Marriott, 'Smokestack: the industrial history of the Thames Gateway', in Philip Cohen and Michael Rustin (eds), *London's Turning: The making of the Thames Gateway*, Aldershot, Ashgate, 2008, pp. 17–30.

7. George, *London Life*, p. 162.

8. George Rudé, *Hanoverian London, 1714–1808*, Secker & Warburg, 1971, p. 26.

9. Sir William Petty attributed the westward migration of City elites to the foul atmosphere created by the burning of coal. John Evelyn went as far as to suggest, in *Fumifugium*, Exeter, University of Exeter Press, 1976 [1661], that all works using coal should be removed at least five miles downstream from London.

10. Roy Porter, *London: A Social History*, Hamish Hamilton, 1994, p. 138. The significance of this trade to both London and Newcastle is suggested by the fact that in 1650 approximately 8,000 miners, sailors and coal heavers were employed by it (E.A. Wrigley, 'A simple model of London's importance in changing English society and economy, 1650–1750', *Past and Present*, 37 (1967), pp. 44–70). Oddly, Dorothy George fails to mention the significance of coal, but for a general survey see R. Smith, *Sea Coal for London: History of the Coal Factors in the London Market*, Longman, 1961.

11. Mary Mills, *The Early East London Gas Industry and its Waste Products*, M. Wright, 1999.

12. M.W. Flinn, *Men of Iron: The Crowleys in the Early Iron Industry*, Edinburgh, Edinburgh University Press, 1962.

13. *Survey of London*, vols 43 and 44, *Poplar, Blackwall and the Isle of Dogs*, Athlone Press, 1994, pp. 548–52.

14. Thomas Pennant, *London*, Faulder, 1790, p. 255.

15. The opening was somewhat delayed by the discovery underground of a bank of prostrate trees in a remarkable state of preservation. At the time they were thought to be remains of a prehistoric forest struck down by a calamitous natural disaster, and because of this they created great public interest, but it seems more likely they were placed there in the sixteenth century as a means of strengthening the riverbank. Similar trees had been found twelve feet underground when the Blackwall Yard was excavated approximately a hundred years earlier. Johnson showed them to Samuel Pepys, who was clearly fascinated (*Diary and Correspondence of Samuel Pepys*, New York, Dodd, Mead & Co., 1885, vol. V, p. 150).

16. At a time when a personal estate of £100 represented considerable wealth, land tax assessments of Wapping merchants in 1760 revealed that 56 had a personal estate of that figure, 15 were assessed at £150, 10 at £200, 3 at £250 and 5 at £300 (Derek Morris and Ken Cozens, *Wapping, 1600–1800: A Social History of an Early Modern London Maritime Suburb*, East London History Society, 2009, p. 6).

17. Ibid., pp. 52–5. Credit is due to the authors for uncovering the records of this important firm, and, indeed, for providing a mine of useful information on eighteenth-century Wapping.

18. Ibid., p. 136.

19. Porter, *London*, p. 140.

20. *Proposals for Establishing a Charitable Fund for the City of London*, privately published, 1706, p. 13, quoted in George, *London Life*, p. 180.

21. Schwarz, *London in the Age of Industrialisation*, p. 204.

22. George, *London Life*, pp. 42–3.

23. *Order Book*, Middlesex Sessions, January 1735–36, printed in *Distilled Spirituous Liquors the Bane of the Nation*, Roberts, 1736, and cited in ibid., p. 47. George argues that since the figures were gathered by constables, about half of whom were retailers themselves, this total is a gross underestimate.

24. Given the decline which subsequently beset East London industries, it is perhaps surprising that many of those established in this pre-industrial era survived well into the post-Second World War years. The Whitechapel Bell Foundry was founded in 1420, and to this day has occupied the same site on the Whitechapel Road since 1728. The Mile End distillery dates back to 1769, the sugar confectioner Batger in Limehouse to 1748, a knacker's yard along the Mile End Road to 1786, and the Cock Hill glasshouse at Ratcliff to 1780. Several small paint, metal, chemical and canvas firms started

production around this time (D.L. Munby, *Industry and Planning in Stepney*, Oxford, Oxford University Press, 1951, pp. 18–19).
25. 9 Anne cap. 17.
26. More complete data as follows:

Occupations of adult males (expressed as percentages of the total) in the Spitalfields and Riverside areas of East London, 1770

Area	Clothing	Maritime	Transport & building	Upper and middle class	Provisioners	Other
Spitalfields	64.0	0.8	12.3	3.0	10.0	9.9
Riverside	5.9	45.7	19.5	4.0	9.2	15.7

Spitalfields comprised the parishes of Christ Church, Bethnal Green and Mile End New Town; Riverside, St George's, Wapping, Limehouse, Shadwell, Ratcliff and Poplar. Of those engaged in clothing, 86 per cent were in silk manufacture. Upper and middle classes included professionals and gentlemen. Provisioners included bakers, butchers and brewers.
Source: Based on data in L.D. Schwarz, 'Occupations and incomes in late-eighteenth-century East London', *East London Papers*, vol. 14, no. 2, 1972, pp. 87–100.

27. William Maitland, *The History of London from its Foundation to the Present Time*, revised by John Entick: 'A Continuation … bringing the History to the Present Time and describing the Vast Improvements made in every part of this Great Metropolis', 2 vols, Wilkie et al., pp. 4–5.
28. Ibid., p. 17.
29. Ibid., p. 22.
30. Ibid., p. 37.
31. Ibid., p. 51.
32. Samuel Lewis (ed.), *A Topographical Dictionary of England*, 'Stepney', Lewis, 1848.
33. *Survey of London*, vol. 27, *Spitalfields and Mile End New Town*, Athlone Press, 1957, p. 2.
34. George, *London Life*, p. 76. Returns from parish clerks reveal that the number of houses fell from 2,500 in 1729 to 2,012 in 1800. The data are unreliable and take no account of any changes to the housing stock, but they do tend to deny significant expansion.
35. *Survey of London*, vol. 27, p. 4.
36. Michael Power, 'Urban development of East London, 1550–1700', PhD thesis, University of London, 1971, pp. 176–9.
37. *Victoria County History of Middlesex*, vol. 11, *Stepney and Bethnal Green*, Institute of Historical Research, 1998, p. 92.
38. Ibid., p. 94.
39. David Mander, *More Light, More Power: An Illustrated History of Shoreditch*, Sutton, 1996, p. 12.
40. Joanna Smith and Ray Rogers, *Behind the Veneer: The South Shoreditch Furniture Trade and its Buildings*, English Heritage, 2006, p. 7.
41. George, *London Life*, p. 93.
42. Sir William Petty, *Taxes and Contributions*, Brooke, 1662, repr. Charles Hull (ed.), *The Economic Writings of Sir William Petty*, Thoemmes Press, 1997 [1899], p. 41.
43. Capt. John Graunt, *Natural and Political Observations … made upon the Bills of Mortality*, Royal Society, 1676, repr. ibid., p. 381. Doubts remain over the authorship of this tract, many believing that it was actually written by Petty.
44. Somewhat ironically the great northern road through Islington was promoted by Charles Dingley, a wealthy Russia merchant in the City who owned a sawmill at Wapping (Maitland, *The History of London*, 'A continuation', p. 147).
45. Ibid., p. 3.
46. Peter Earle, *The Making of the English Middle Class: Business, Society and Family Life in London, 1660–1730*, Methuen, 1989, pp. 240–42.

47. Derek Morris, *Mile End Old Town, 1740–1780. A Social History of an Early Modern London Suburb*, East London History Society, 2002, p. 4.

48. Idem, 'Mile End Old Town residents and the East India Company', *East London Record*, 9 (1986), p. 20.

49. Ibid., p. 26.

50. J. Wm. Archenholtz, *A Picture of England*, Dublin, Byrne, 1791, p. 77.

51. George, *London Life*, p. 319, suggested their combined populations increased from under 10,000 in 1700 to 123,000 in 1801.

52. J. Richardson, *Recollections of the Last Half Century*, Mitchell, 1856, pp. 3–4.

53. Henry Fielding, *An Inquiry into the Causes of the Late Encrease of Robbers and Related Writings*, M.R. Zirker (ed.), Oxford, Oxford University Press, 1988 [1751], p. 116.

54. 11 Geo. I cap. 22.

55. Father Poussin, *Pretty Doings in a Protestant Nation*, Roberts, 1734, quoted in Dan Cruickshank, *The Secret History of Georgian London*, Windmill, 2010, p. 25. Cruickshank provides a comprehensive and persuasive account of the extent to which the sex trade intruded into virtually every corner of the social and cultural life of the eighteenth-century metropolis.

56. Ibid., p. 166.

57. George, *London Life*, pp. 91–5, and John Marriott, 'The spatiality of the poor in eighteenth-century London', in Tim Hitchcock and Heather Shore (eds), *The Streets of London: From the Great Fire to the Great Stink*, Rivers Oram, 2003, pp. 129–30.

58. Ibid., p. 129.

59. John Spranger, *A Proposal or Plan for an Act of Parliament for the Better Paving, Cleansing, and Lighting of the Streets, Lanes, Courts and Alleys ... Within the Several Parishes of the City and Liberty of Westminster*, privately published, 1754.

60. 2 Geo. III cap. 21.

61. Miles Ogborn, *Spaces of Modernity: London's Geographies, 1680–1780*, New York, Gildford, 1998, pp. 30–31.

62. John Pugh, *Remarkable Occurrences in the Life of Jonas Hanway*, Payne, 1787, p. 139, cited in ibid., p. 108.

63. 8 Geo. III cap. 15.

64. 12 Geo. III cap. 38.

65. 18 Geo. III cap. 80.

66. 22 Geo. III cap. 43.

67. 28 Geo. III cap. 60.

68. Maitland, *A History of London*, vol. II, p. 147.

Chapter 3: The culture and politics of dissent, 1650–1800

1. John Marriott, 'Sensation of the abyss: the urban poor and modernity', in Mica Nava and Alan O'Shea (eds), *Modern Times: Reflections on a Century of English Modernity*, Routledge, 1996, pp. 88–9. The best historical discussion is Peter Burke, *Popular Culture in Early Modern Europe*, Maurice Temple Smith, 1978.

2. John Brown, 'Essay on ridicule', *Essays on the Characteristics of the Earl of Shaftesbury*, Davis, 1751, quoted in Vic Gatrell, *City of Laughter: Sex and Satire in Eighteenth-century London*, Atlantic, 2006, p. 191. Lest we get carried away with the idea that carnival was a joyous – if unruly – celebration, it is worth remembering that it often involved acts of cruelty, particularly to animals such as dogs, cocks and cats which were routinely slain. The human cost could also be high; three deaths during the celebration was not unusual.

3. 28 Geo. III cap. 60.

4. Thomas Downs, 'The Stepney Fair', in Walter Locks (ed.), *East London Antiquities, East London Advertiser*, 1902, p. 159.

5. Matthew Mead, *Good of Early Deliverance*, Ponder, 1683.

6. Henry Morley, *Memoirs of Bartholomew Fair*, Chapman and Hall, 1859, p. 384.

7. Downs, 'Stepney Fair', p. 159.

8. Quoted in Frederick Wood, 'Goodman's Field Theatre', *Modern Language Review*, 25:4 (1930), pp. 443–56.

9. The name of the theatre derived from its location at the northern edge of Goodman's Fields, a small plot of land once farmed by Goodman where in the sixteenth century John Stow had frequently fetched milk.

10. Thomas Pennant, *London*, Faulder, 1790, p. 250.

11. Peter Thomson, *The Cambridge Introduction to English Theatre, 1660–1900*, Cambridge, Cambridge University Press, 2006, p. 87.

12. Pennant, *London*, p. 250.

13. *Victoria County History of Middlesex*, vol. 11, *Stepney and Bethnal Green*, Institute of Historical Research, 1998, p. 147.

14. PP 1840 (639), *Hand-loom Weavers*, 1840. *Assistant Commissioners' Reports*, vol. II, p. 216.

15. William Waller, 'Early Huguenot friendly societies', *Proceedings of the Huguenot Society of London*, VI:3 (1901), pp. 201–35.

16. A story is told that after publication of his work on fluxions Simpson was sought by a gentleman from the Royal Arsenal to teach mathematics to the cadets. He was eventually tracked down at a garret in Angel Alley off Bishopsgate Street. The gentleman could not believe that the meanly dressed man in a green baize apron was the author until he was taken upstairs and shown the original manuscript. Satisfied, the gentleman offered Simpson the post. When asked when he could start Simpson replied: 'When I have finished the piece of goods in the loom.' (Ibid., p. 217.)

17. J.W.S. Cassels, 'The Spitalfields Mathematical Society', *Bulletin of the London Mathematical Society*, 11 (1979), pp. 241–58; L. Stewart and P. Weindling, 'Philosophical threads: Natural philosophy and public experiment among the weavers of Spitalfields', *British Journal of the History of Science*, 28:1 (1995), pp. 37–62. The London Mathematical Society currently organizes regular symposia on specialist topics for the general mathematical community. They are known as Spitalfields Days.

18. PP 1840, *Hand-loom Weavers*, pp. 216–18; see also W.H. Manchee, 'Memories of Spitalfields', *Proceedings of the Huguenot Society of London*, X:1 (1912), pp. 298–345.

19. George Rudé, *Hanoverian London, 1714–1808*, Secker & Warburg, 1971, pp. 188–90.

20. Trial of Robert Page, Thomas Putrode and William Rod, 13 October 1736, *Proceedings of the Old Bailey*. Details of the trial appear in *Proceedings of the Old Bailey*, which are included in the valuable online resource www.oldbaileyonline.org. Do note, however, that the record is far from complete.

21. Nicholas Rogers, 'Popular disaffection in London during the Forty-Five', *London Journal*, 1:1 (May 1975), pp. 5–27.

22. Peter Linebaugh, *The London Hanged. Crime and Civil Society in the Eighteenth Century*, Allen Lane, 1991, pp. 270–87.

23. *Proceedings of the Old Bailey,* 18 October 1769.

24. Linebaugh, *The London Hanged*, pp. 275–9, has begun to sketch out the details.

25. William Maitland, *The History of London from its Foundation to the Present Time*, vol. II, Wilkie et al., 1772, p. 130.

26. *The Middlesex Journal*, December 1769, cited in Linebaugh, *The London Hanged*, p. 281.

27. Maitland, *The History of London*, p. 103.

28. 13 Geo. III cap. 68.

29. Plummer, *The London Weavers' Company*, pp. 328–31; John Clapham, 'The Spitalfields Acts, 1773–1824', *The Economic Journal*, XXVI (1916), pp. 459–71.

30. John Fielding, *A Brief Description of the Cities of London and Westminster*, Wilkie, 1776, pp. 28–9.

31. For a wonderful account of the revolutionary tradition of sea-borne labourers see Peter Linebaugh and Marcus Rediker, *The Many-Headed Hydra: The Hidden History of the Revolutionary Atlantic*, Verso, 2000.

32. *Victoria County History of Middlesex*, vol. 11, p. 18; Brett-James, *The Growth of Stuart London*, 1926, p. 205.

33. The cases are mentioned in Linebaugh, *The London Hanged*, p. 126, and details of the trials appear in www.oldbaileyonline.org.

34. 31 Geo. II cap. 76.
35. Linebaugh, *The London Hanged*, pp. 311–15; Rudé, *Hanoverian London*, pp. 196–7.
36. Maitland, *The History of London: A Continuation*, p. 76.
37. Ibid., p. 76.
38. Rudé, *Hanoverian London*, pp. 220–27.
39. *Proceedings of the Old Bailey*, 28 June 1780.
40. The best account remains George Rudé, *Wilkes & Liberty: A Social Study of 1763 to 1774*, Oxford, Clarendon Press, 1962, on which I have relied heavily.
41. Cited in ibid., p. 26.
42. *Proceedings of the Old Bailey*, 18 May 1768. The trial is unusually well reported.
43. Ibid., 6 July 1768.
44. 9 Geo. III cap. 29.
45. John Appleby, 'Charles Dingley, projector, and his Limehouse sawmill', *London Topographical Record*, XXVII (1995), pp. 179–93. Dingley received compensation from parliament and was able to complete the rebuilding by the summer. It could not have lasted long, however, for Daniel Lysons, *Environs of London* (1795), mentions that the sawmill still stood, but had not been in use for many years.
46. Rudé, *Wilkes & Liberty*, p. 63.
47. Ibid., p. 69.
48. Desmond Chapman-Huston, *Through a City Archway: the Story of Allen & Hanbury's*, Murray, 1954.
49. *Life of William Allen, with Selections from his Correspondence*, 3 vols, Gilpin, 1846, I, pp. 33–4.
50. The monitorial system of education was decisive in enabling the extension of elementary schooling to the working classes. By employing class monitors – invariably older children – teachers could manage much larger numbers of pupils. It was also known as the Madras System because pioneered by Andrew Bell, who as a missionary had observed how pupils were taught in India. Joseph Lancaster developed and extended the system while squabbling with Bell over the question of whose idea it was originally.
51. Benjamin Haydon's wonderful painting of the Anti-Slavery Society Convention, 1840, shows Allen sitting next to Samuel Gurney. Also at the convention was their fellow Quaker abolitionist Thomas Fowell Buxton.
52. J. Fayle, *The Spitalfields Genius: The Story of William Allen*, Hodder & Stoughton, 1884; *Life of William Allen*, 1846.

Chapter 4: Modernization and its discontents, 1800–1860

1. L.D. Schwarz, *London in the Age of Industrialisation: Entrepreneurs, Labour Force and Living Conditions, 1700–1850*, Cambridge, Cambridge University Press, 1992, p. 9. Colquhoun's figure is almost certainly an overestimate.
2. Philip Banbury, *Shipbuilders of the Thames and Medway*, David and Charles, 1971, p. 20.
3. PP 1796, *Report from the Committee appointed to enquire into the best Mode of providing sufficient Accommodation for the increased Trade and Shipping of The Port of London, &c. &c. &c.*, Appendices D and G.
4. Ibid., Appendix E.
5. Ibid., p. 44.
6. Ibid., p. 148.
7. Ibid., p. 52.
8. *Survey of London*, vol. 43, *Poplar, Blackwall and the Isle of Dogs*, Athlone Press, 1994, Chapter 10, 'The West India docks', p. 248.
9. Edward Ogle, for example, chairman of the Committee of Proprietors, Lessees and Wharfingers of the Legal Quays, proposed a new dock at Wapping, and extension and improvement in the quays by wholesale clearance of riverside houses; Ralph Walker, a former slave trader and plantation owner, designed a wet dock at Wapping enclosed by warehouses and a perimeter wall, with a canal across the Isle of Dogs which could be

converted into a timber dock; the Merchants Committee planned an enclosed dock at Wapping with two entrances, and surrounded by a high wall; and the Corporation of London proposed enclosed, T-shaped docks on the Isle of Dogs and at Rotherhithe. Faced with these and the opinions of authoritative bodies such as Trinity House, the committee, while recognizing the urgency of the matter, declined to make a choice, preferring instead simply to present the evidence.

10. Ibid., p. 249.
11. PP 1799, *First Report from the Select Committee appointed to consider evidence taken on Bills for the Improvement of the Port of London*.
12. 39 Geo. III cap. 69.
13. *Survey of London*, vol. 43, pp. 252–3.
14. *Morning Chronicle*, 28 August 1802.
15. Thomas Shepherd and James Elmes, *Metropolitan Improvements; or, London in the Nineteenth Century: being a series of Views of the New and Most Interesting Objects in the British Metropolis and its Vicinity*, Jones, 1827, pp. 115–16.
16. *Survey of London*, vol. 44, p. 575; George Pattison, 'The East India Dock Company, 1803–1838', *East London Papers*, 7:1 (1964), p. 31.
17. 43 Geo. III cap. 126.
18. *Survey of London*, vol. 44, p. 576.
19. Pattison, 'The East India Dock Company', p. 32.
20. Sarah Palmer, 'Port economics in an historical context: The nineteenth-century Port of London', *International Journal of Maritime History*, XV:1 (2003), p. 34.
21. Ibid., p. 42.
22. Sidney Pollard, 'The decline of shipbuilding on the Thames', *Economic History Review*, III:1 (1950), p. 72.
23. John Marriott, ' "West Ham: London's industrial centre and gateway to the world". I. Industrialisation, 1840–1910', *London Journal*, 13:2 (1988), pp. 130–31. The *Warrior* had armour plates 4.5 inches thick which were capable of resisting all naval armaments at the time. Within ten years, however, advances in naval technology rendered the ship obsolete, and it had an active service for only two more years. Happily the *Warrior* has survived, and now fully restored is berthed at Portsmouth Historic Dockyard.
24. Pollard, 'The decline of shipbuilding', p. 88.
25. *London as it is Today: Where to go, and what to see, during the Great Exhibition*, H.G. Clarke, 1851, p. 174.
26. George Sala, *Gaslight and Daylight, with some London Scenes they Shine Upon*, Chapman and Hall, 1859, pp. 55–6.
27. Gareth Stedman Jones, *Outcast London: A Study of the Relations between Classes in Victorian Society*, Oxford, Clarendon Press, 1971, pp. 111–12. Because of the seasonality of work, however, and despite measures to eliminate the degrading influence of casual labour, companies were reluctant to phase out casualism entirely.
28. I am greatly indebted to Chris Ellmers who has given me sight of a draft of his major new study on the West India Docks, which contains these data.
29. Henry Mayhew, *London Labour and the London Poor*, Cass, 1967 [1861], vol. III, p. 310.
30. There is now a considerable body of literature recognizing the significance of Mayhew's contribution, including Bernard Taithe, *The Essential Henry Mayhew: Representing and Communicating the Poor*, Rivers Oram, 1996, Regina Gagnier, *Subjectivities: A History of Self-Representation in Britain, 1832–1920*, Oxford, Oxford University Press, 1991, Karel Williams, *From Pauperism to Poverty*, Routledge, 1981, Anne Humpherys, *Travels into the Poor Man's Country: The Work of Henry Mayhew*, Maryland, University of Georgia Press, 1977, John Marriott, *The Other Empire: Metropolis, India and Progress in the Colonial Imagination*, Manchester, Manchester University Press, 2003.
31. Mayhew, *London Labour and the London Poor*, vol. III, p. 300.
32. Ibid., p. 301.
33. Ibid., p. 303.
34. Ibid., p. 300.

35. Ibid., p. 308.

36. Ibid., p. 309.

37. 13 Geo. III cap. 68.

38. J.H. Clapham, 'The Spitalfields Acts, 1773–1824', *Economic Journal*, 26:104 (1916), p. 462.

39. PP 1818 (134), *Minutes of Evidence taken before the Committee appointed to consider of the several Petitions relating to Ribbon Weavers*, p. 40.

40. PP 1818 (211), *Second Report of Minutes of Evidence taken before the Committee appointed to consider of the several Petitions relating to Ribbon Weavers*, p. 52.

41. Ibid., p. 59.

42. Ibid., p. 55.

43. Alfred Plummer, *The London Weavers' Company, 1600–1970*, Routledge and Kegan Paul, 1972, p. 335.

44. Ibid., p. 358.

45. PP 1840 (639), *Hand-loom Weavers: Copy of Report by Mr. Hickson, on the Condition of the Hand-loom Weavers*, pp. 14–17.

46. Plummer, *The London Weavers' Company*, pp. 370–71.

47. Charles Knight (ed.), *London*, 1841–44, vol. 2, Chapter XLIX, 'Spitalfields', pp. 386–7; PP 1818 (134), *Minutes of Evidence taken before the Committee appointed to consider of the several Petitions relating to Ribbon Weavers*, p. 42.

48. *Tribune*, XXIX, 23 September 1795, cited in E.P. Thompson, *The Making of the English Working Class*, Harmondsworth, Penguin, 1980 [1963], p. 157.

49. Bernard, 'Excerpt from an account of a charity in Spitalfields for supplying the poor with soup and potatoes', 30 March 1798, and A Magistrate [Patrick Colquhoun], *An Account of a Meat and Soup Charity in the Metropolis*, Fry, 1797.

50. *Report of the Committee of the Spitalfields Soup Society*, 1813.

51. Ibid., p. 18. On the reluctance to apply for poor relief see the evidence of William Hale; PP 1818 (134), *Minutes of Evidence taken before the Committee appointed to consider of the several Petitions relating to Ribbon Weavers*, 1818, p. 42.

52. Thomas Folwell Buxton, *Speech of T.F. Buxton Esq. at the Egyptian Hall, 16 November 1816 on the Subject of the Distress in Spitalfields*, Phillips, 1816; see also *London Review and Literary Journal*, December (1816), pp. 521–6.

53. PP 1835 (492), *Analysis of the evidence taken before the Select Committee on Hand-Loom Weavers' Petitions*, p. 4.

54. PP 1837 (376), *Distress, Spitalfields and Nottingham. Copies of the report of Dr. Kay to the Poor Law Commissioner on the subject of Distress in Spitalfields*, pp. 1–2.

55. Henry Mayhew, 'Letter II', *Morning Chronicle*, 23 October 1849. The letter is usefully reproduced in www.victorianlondon.org, and an extract is included in E.P. Thompson and Eileen Yeo (eds), *The Unknown Mayhew. Selections from the* Morning Chronicle *1849–50*, Harmondsworth, Penguin, 1984, pp. 122–36.

56. PP 1840 (639), *Hand-loom Weavers*, Appendix 7.

57. Schwarz, *London in the Age of Industrialisation*, p. 47.

58. Mayhew, *London Labour and the London Poor*, vol. I, pp. 457–68.

59. Ibid., p. 458.

60. Ibid., pp. 151–2. The interview has been the subject of detailed analysis by Carolyn Steedman, 'The watercress seller', *Past Tenses*, Rivers Oram, 1992.

61. Mayhew, 'The slop-workers and needlewomen', Letter VI, *Morning Chronicle*, 6 November 1849, reprinted almost in its entirety in Thompson and Yeo (eds), *The Unknown Mayhew*, pp. 137–50.

62. Ibid., pp. 200–12.

63. Ibid., 'The tailors', Letter XVI, 11 December 1849, ibid., p. 220.

64. See Schwarz, *London in the Age of Industrialisation*, Chapter 7, for a useful overview.

65. Mayhew, 'The woodworkers: Cabinet makers', Letter LXIII, *Morning Chronicle*, 1 August 1850, in Thompson and Yeo (eds), *The Unknown Mayhew*, p. 432.

66. Stedman Jones, *Outcast London*, p. 22.

67. This is the argument of both Schwarz and Stedman Jones.

68. Charles Booth (ed.), *Life and Labour of the People*, Williams and Norgate, 1889. See also Stedman Jones, *Outcast London*, Table 16, pp. 389–90, for a more recent classification based on categories of the Registrar General.

69. Schwarz, *London in the Age of Industrialisation*, pp. 50–57.

70. Ibid., p. 46.

71. Mayhew, 'The tailors', in Thompson and Yeo (eds), *The Unknown Mayhew*, pp. 226–9.

72. Idem, 'The boot and shoe makers', Letter XXXII, 4 February 1850, ibid., pp. 284–7.

73. Idem, 'The woodworkers: Sawyers', Letter LIX, 4 July 1850, in ibid., pp. 399–403.

74. Idem, 'The woodworkers: Carpenters and joiners', Letter LX, 11 July 1850, and Letter LXI, 18 July 1850, in ibid., pp. 389–429.

75. Idem, 'The woodworkers: Cabinet-makers', Letter LXIII, 1 August 1850, Letter LXIV, 8 August 1850, and Letter LXV, 15 August 1850, in ibid., pp. 416–64.

76. Idem, 'The woodworkers: Ship and boat builders', Letter LXVIII, 5 September 1850, in ibid., pp. 483–500.

Chapter 5: The spectre of cholera, 1830–1875

1. Anthony Wohl, *Endangered Lives: Public Health in Victorian Britain*, Dent, 1983, p. 145.

2. *Morning Chronicle*, 27 February 1832.

3. PP 1847–48 (888), *Metropolitan Sanitary Commission: First Report of the Commissioners appointed to Inquire whether any and what Special Means may be Requisite for Improvement of the Health of the Metropolis, Minutes of Evidence,* pp. 1–4.

4. Ibid., p. 2.

5. These instructions were delivered in circulars issued on 14 November 1831, 13 December 1831 and 14 February 1832 (*Morning Chronicle*, 20 February 1832).

6. See the small selection included in PP 1831–32 (155), *Cholera: Copies of Certain Papers relating to Cholera; together with the Report of the Central Board of Health thereupon.*

7. Robert Higgins, 'The 1832 cholera epidemic in East London', *East London Record*, 2 (1979), p. 4.

8. Ibid., pp. 3, 9.

9. Henry Jephson, *The Sanitary Evolution of London*, Unwin, 1907, p. 13.

10. The Stepney Union originally employed eight medical officers, but in 1842 these were reduced to five despite the fact that each had attended an average of over 8,000 patients annually. Their salaries totalled £420 (Ruth G. Hodgkinson, *The Origins of the National Health Service: The Medical Services of the New Poor Law, 1834–1871*, Wellcome Historical Medical Library, 1967, p. 27).

11. *Morning Chronicle*, 15 February 1832.

12. Ibid., 18 February 1832.

13. Ibid., 26 May 1832.

14. *The Standard*, 30 March 1832, cited in Higgins, 'The 1832 cholera epidemic', p. 12.

15. *Morning Chronicle*, 18 February 1832.

16. Ibid., 15 March 1832.

17. PP 1847–48 (888), *Metropolitan Sanitary Commission: First Report, Minutes of Evidence,* pp. 26–7. Since incorrect diagnoses were frequently made on the cause of death, and there was a systematic failure to record accurately, the figures were very unreliable.

18. PP 1834 (584), *Report from the Select Committee on Metropolitan Sewers.*

19. The seventy-five Commissioners for Blackwall in 1833, for example, comprised overwhelmingly significant ratepayers, a large minority of whom lived outside the area. A similar picture obtained for the 182 Commissioners for Tower Hamlets (ibid., Appendix, pp. 57–8, 61–2).

20. Ibid., p. 165.

21. Ibid., Appendix, pp. 66–7.

22. Ibid., p. 160.

23. Ibid., pp. 160–62.

24. Ibid., p. 146.

25. Arnott had served as a surgeon in the East India Company, Kay had written the pioneering study of cotton weavers, *The Moral and Physical Condition of the Working Class Employed in the Cotton Manufacture of Manchester*, Ridgway, 1832, and Southwood Smith was a surgeon at the London Fever Hospital and had written *Treatise on Fever*, Longman Rees, 1830, generally regarded as the standard work. All, coincidentally, had studied at Edinburgh, and were committed to the application of science to social improvement.

26. 11 & 12 Vic. cap. 63.

27. PP 1837–38 (147), T. Frankland Lewis, John G.S. Lefevre and George Nicholls, 'Report as to payment of certain expenses out of rates', in *Fourth Annual Report of the Poor Law Commissioners for England and Wales*, p. 63. Lewis, Lefevre and Nicolls were the Commissioners, Chadwick the secretary.

28. Ibid., pp. 75–9.

29. PP 1837–38 (147), Thomas Southwood Smith, 'Report on some of the physical causes of sickness and mortality to which the poor are particularly exposed; and which are capable of removal by sanatory regulations, exemplified in the present condition of the Bethnal Green and Whitechapel Districts', *Fourth Annual Report of the Poor Law Commissioners*, p. 84.

30. PP 1839 (239), Thomas Southwood Smith, 'Report on the prevalence of fever in twenty metropolitan unions or parishes, during the year ended 20th March 1838', *Fifth Annual Report of the Poor Law Commissioners*, pp. 100–106.

31. PP 1840 (384), *Report from the Select Committee on the Health of Towns*.

32. Ibid., pp. 15–20.

33. Ibid., pp. 20–25.

34. Ibid., p. 37.

35. Ibid., p. 69.

36. Ibid., pp. 77, 81.

37. 9 & 10 Vic. cap. 96.

38. 9 & 10 Vic. cap. 74.

39. 10 & 11 Vic. cap. 34.

40. Wohl, *Endangered Lives*, pp. 148–9.

41. The Health of Towns Association was established in 1844 under the inspiration of Southwood Smith. It brought together doctors and leading politicians, and aimed to disseminate the latest scientific information as a means of tackling the physical and moral problems found in urban environments.

42. Hector Gavin, *Sanitary Ramblings, being Sketches and Illustrations of Bethnal Green*, Cass, 1971 [1848], p. 3.

43. Ibid., p. 4.

44. Ibid., pp. 7–8.

45. Ibid., p. 11.

46. Ibid., pp. 34–5.

47. Ibid., p. 56.

48. Ibid., p. 114.

49. 11 & 12 Vic. cap. 123.

50. 12 & 13 Vic. cap. 111.

51. 11 & 12 Vic. cap. 63.

52. PP 1833 (448), *Report of the Select Committee appointed to consider the best means of securing open spaces in the vicinity of populous towns, as public walks and places of exercise*, p. 5.

53. Ibid., pp. 15–18.

54. Albert Fein, 'Victoria Park: its origin and history', *East London Papers*, 5:2 (1962), pp. 73–90; Charles Poulsen, *Victoria Park: A study in the History of East London*, Journeyman Press and Stepney Books, 1976, pp. 16–20.

55. Ibid., pp. 26–32.

56. To put the park in some historical perspective it is worth recalling that it was, with the exception of Regent's Park, the largest public park in the country, and would remain so

until the completion of Battersea Park in 1856 (Hazel Conway, *People's Parks: The Design and Development of Victorian Parks in Britain*, Cambridge, Cambridge University Press, 1991, Appendix 2).

57. Gareth Stedman Jones has described well the changes in *Outcast London: A Study in the Relationship between Classes in Victorian Society*, Oxford, Clarendon Press, 1971, although referring to the process as a transformation tends to overstate their cumulative impact; ultimately, a small but significant minority of the population was affected. See also Francis Sheppard, *London: A History*, Oxford, Oxford University Press, 1998, pp. 270–73.

58. John Marriott, ' "West Ham: London's industrial centre and gateway to the world". I: Industrialisation, 1840–1910', *London Journal*, 13:2 (1988), pp. 121–42.

59. *Tenth Annual Report of the Medical Officer of Health*, Bethnal Green, p. 4, cited in ibid., p. 163.

60. 17 Geo. 3 cap. 13.

61. See, for example, PP 1813–14 (355), *Papers relating to Parochial and District Assessments for Paving, Lighting and Cleansing of Streets, Lanes, &c., within the Bills of Mortality*; PP 1825 (240), *Sums collected and disbursed for Lighting, Watching and Paving, 1818–1824*; PP 1830–31 (387), *An Account of all sums raised by the Commissioner of Sewers for the Tower Hamlets ..., between the years 1821 and 1830*.

62. In 1818, for example, a considerable but unspecified sum of money was borrowed by the Commissioners of Wapping Pavement to repair and alter pavements in Shadwell, *Sums collected and disbursed for Lighting, Watching and Paving*, p. 82.

63. PP 1837–38 (661), *Second Report from the Select Committee on Metropolitan Improvements*.

64. Ibid., p. iv.

65. Geoffrey Tyack, *Sir James Pennethorne and the Making of Victorian London*, Cambridge, Cambridge University Press, 1992.

66. It was originally to be called Spital Street, but this duplicated the name of an existing street. For a good chronology of the events, see *Survey of London,* vol. 27: *Spitalfields and Mile End New Town*, Athlone Press, 1957, Chapter XIX, 'Commercial Street'.

67. 'Metropolitan improvements', *Westminster Review*, XXXVI (1841), p. 428. The reviewer also expressed relief that responsibility for a royal park in East London had been taken over by the government or, in the 'struggle of parties, it would have dwindled down to a tea-garden' (p. 429). Similar criticisms of how petty local and personal interests undermine metropolitan improvements appeared in the *Athenaeum*, 5 February 1842, p. 131, and 18 November 1843, p. 1026.

68. PP 1847–48 (888), (895), *Metropolitan Sanitary Commission. First Report of the Commissioners appointed to Inquire whether any and what Special Means may be Requisite for Improvement of the Health of the Metropolis*, p. iii.

69. Ibid., p. 21.

70. PP 1850 (1273), (1274), (1275), *Report of the General Board of Health on the Cholera Epidemic of 1848 and 1849*.

71. Ibid., Appendix B, R.D. Grainger, 'Sanitary report on the epidemic cholera as it prevailed in London, 1848–49', p. 30. Just prior to the series of letters in the *Morning Chronicle* which mapped the condition of the working poor, Henry Mayhew submitted a piece describing with customary indignation his visit to the notorious Jacob's Island in Bermondsey where the incidence of cholera was particularly high (*Morning Chronicle*, 24 September 1849, reproduced in John Marriott and Masaie Matsumura (eds), *The Metropolitan Poor: Semi-factual Accounts, 1795–1910*, 6 vols, Pickering & Chatto, 1999, vol. 2, pp. 3–5).

72. Ibid., p. 141.

73. Ibid., p. 112.

74. Ibid., Appendix B, pp. 39, 46.

75. Ibid., p. 92.

76. PP 1854–55 (1893), *General Board of Health. Letter of the President ..., accompanying a report from Dr. Sutherland on Epidemic Cholera in the Metropolis in 1854*, p. 73.

77. Ibid., pp. 36, 60.
78. PP 1854–55 (1980), *General Board of Health. Medical Council: Report of the Committee for Scientific Inquiries in relation to the Cholera Epidemic of 1854*, p. 48.
79. Margaret Pelling, *Cholera, Fever and English Medicine, 1825–1865*, Oxford, Oxford University Press, 1978; Sandra Hempel, *The Medical Detective. John Snow and the Mystery of Cholera*, Granta, 2006.
80. PP 1854–55 (1980), *General Board of Health. Medical Council: Report of the Committee for Scientific Inquiries in relation to the Cholera Epidemic of 1854*, p. 52.
81. PP 1866 (3645), *Public Health: Eighth Report of the Medical Officer of the Privy Council*.
82. PP 1867–68 (4072), *Report on the Cholera Epidemic of 1866 in England: Supplement to the Twenty-ninth Annual Report of the Registrar General*, p. 169.
83. Ibid., p. 84.
84. Ibid., pp. 68–72.
85. Ibid., pp. xi–xii.
86. *Reynolds's News*, 12 August 1866.
87. T.C. Garland, 'London life', in *Leaves from my Log of Twenty-five Years' Christian Work among Sailors and others in the Port of London*, Woolmer, 1882, pp. 163–5.
88. Jephson, *The Sanitary Evolution of London*, p. 189.
89. PP 1854–55 (1980), *Report on the Cholera Epidemic of 1854*, p. 171.
90. Ibid., pp. 186–7.

Chapter 6: The myth of outcast London, 1800–1900

1. I have explored this matter at greater length in John Marriott, 'The imaginative geography of Whitechapel murders', in Alex Werner (ed.), *Jack the Ripper and the East End*, Chatto and Windus, 2008, pp. 31–63. The term 'Outcast London' was most famously employed by Andrew Mearns, an evangelical missionary, in his tract *The Bitter Cry of Outcast London*, London City Mission, 1883, which created a sensation when first published.
2. Charles Booth (ed.), *Life and Labour of the People*, Williams and Norgate, 1889, vol. 1, p. 66. Booth's reference to the new wave of Jewish immigration attendant upon the arrival in the 1880s of tens of thousands fleeing from eastern Europe touched on a matter of renewed concern which was to intensify fears of racial degeneration, and feature prominently in the panic created by the murders. This is explored in detail later (Chapter 8).
3. The *Star*, 1 September 1888. The murder of Nichols was seen here to be the third in a series. Only later was Nichols seen as the first of the five 'canonical' murders committed by the Ripper. Extensive press coverage of the murders is available online from the www.casebook.org website, an invaluable aid to anyone interested in researching the topic.
4. *Evening Standard*, 1 September 1888.
5. *City Press*, 5 September 1888.
6. *Penny Illustrated Paper*, 8 September 1888.
7. *The Times*, 10 October 1888.
8. See, for example, *Daily News*, 11 September 1888.
9. The *Star*, 1 October 1888. A Thug was understood as an Indian thief who garrotted his victims as an act of devotion to the goddess Kali, while Sicarius was a Jew who had employed terror tactics in fighting Roman repression.
10. Peter D'Sena, 'Perquisites and casual labour on the London wharfside in the eighteenth century', *London Journal*, 14:2 (1989), pp. 131–47.
11. John Marriott, 'Policing the poor: Social inquiry and the discovery of the residuum', *Rising East*, 3:1 (1999), pp. 23–47.
12. [Patrick Colquhoun], *A Treatise on the Police of the Metropolis, explaining the Various Crimes ... which are Felt as Pressure upon the Community, and Suggesting Remedies for*

their Prevention. By a Magistrate, Fry, 1795. In subsequent editions Colquhoun was identified as the author.

13. Ibid., 1797, p. v.
14. Ibid., p. vi.
15. Ibid., pp. xi–xii.
16. The incident is recounted in the autobiography of John Harriott, the first resident magistrate (*Struggles through Life*, Longman, 1813, p. 116).
17. Patrick Colquhoun, *A Treatise on the Commerce and Police of the River Thames*, Mawman, 1800, p. 41.
18. John Marriott, *The Other Empire: Metropolis, India and Progress in the Colonial Imagination*, Manchester, Manchester University Press, 2003, Chapter 4.
19. Thomas Beames, *The Rookeries of London*, Bosworth, 1850.
20. Ibid., p. 17.
21. John Garwood, *The Million Peopled City; or, One Half of the People of London made known to the Other Half*, Wertheim and Macintosh, 1853.
22. Ibid., pp. 256, 260.
23. The lectures were published as F. Meyrick, *The Outcast and the Poor of London*, Rivingtons, 1858, p. 13.
24. Ibid., p. 241.
25. Joseph Mullens, 'London Irreligion and Heathenism at Home', *London and Calcutta, compared in their Heathenism, their Privileges and their Prospects*, Nisbet, 1869, p. 15.
26. Ibid., p. 53.
27. Watts Phillips, *The Wild Tribes of London*, Ward, 1855, p. 65.
28. Ibid., p. 55.
29. Ibid., p. 56.
30. Ibid., p. 32.
31. Ibid., p. 12.
32. John Hollingshead, *Ragged in London in 1861*, Smith, Elder and Co., 1861, p. 41.
33. H.O. Davies, 'The Way Out': A Letter Addressed (by permission) to the Earl of Derby in which the Evils of the Overcrowded Town Hovel and the Advantages of the Suburban Cottage are Constrained, Longman Green, 1861, p. 6.
34. Stedman Jones, *Outcast London*, pp. 15–16.
35. Thomas Archer, *The Pauper, the Thief and the Convict; sketches of some of their Homes, Haunts and Habits*, Groombridge, 1865, p. 133.
36. James Greenwood, 'A visit to Tiger Bay', in *The Wilds of London*, Chatto and Windus, 1874, p. 1.
37. Ibid., p. 9.
38. James Greenwood, 'A night in the workhouse', in *The Amateur Casual*, Diprose and Bateman, 1877, p. 6.
39. *Wonderful London; its Lights and Shadows of Humour and Sadness*, Tinsley, 1878, p. 215.
40. [Andrew Mearns], *The Bitter Cry of Outcast London: An Inquiry into the Condition of the Abject Poor*, London City Mission, 1883, p. 2.
41. Ibid., p. 7.
42. George Sims, *How the Poor Live, and Horrible London*, Chatto and Windus, 1889, p. 44.
43. Charles Booth (ed.), *Life and Labour of the People of London*, 17 vols, Macmillan, 1902. This and the following discussion relies upon my *The Other Empire*, Chapter 6.
44. See David Englander and Rosemary O'Day (eds), *Retrieved Riches: Social Investigation on Britain, 1880–1914*, Scolar, 1995, and Judith Walkowitz, *City of Dreadful Delight: Narratives of Sexual Danger in Late-Victorian London*, Virago, 1994, for useful critical assessments.
45. Walkowitz, *City of Dreadful Delight*, p. 31.
46. Charles Booth, 'The docks', in idem (ed.), *Life and Labour of the People*, vol. 1, p. 193.
47. Arnold White, *The Problems of a Great City*, Remington, 1886, p. 227.

48. White had worked with Andrew Mearns in the London Congregational Union, and would later campaign energetically against Jewish immigration, helping in particular to frame the 1905 Aliens Act.
49. William Booth, *In Darkest England and the Way Out*, Salvation Army, 1890.
50. Ibid., p. 9.
51. Ibid., p. 10.
52. Charles Masterman (ed.), *The Heart of the Empire: Discussion of Problems of Modern City Life in England*, Fisher Unwin, 1901.
53. Ibid., p. 7.
54. Charles Masterman, *From the Abyss; of its Inhabitants by One of Them*, Johnson, 1902, p. 5.
55. Ibid., p. 17.
56. Jack London, *The People of the Abyss*, Pluto Press, 2001 [1903], p. 20.
57. The *Graphic*, 12 August 1871.
58. 'Leaves from the life of a "poor Londoner" ', *Good Words*, 1885, p. 532.
59. E. Nixon, 'A Whitechapel street', *English Illustrated Magazine*, February 1890, p. 355.
60. Rev. R.H. Haddon, *An East End Chronicle*, Hatchard, 1880, pp. 1–2. Cited in Katy Pettit, 'The food culture of East London, 1880–1914', PhD thesis, University of East London, 2009.
61. Clara Grant, *Farthing Bundles*, privately printed by the author, 1929, pp. 39–40. This incident occurred *circa* 1908. Cited in Katy Pettit, 'The food culture of East London'.
62. George Sims, 'Human London: II. Behind the Scenes in Stepney', *London Magazine*, November (1907), p. 287.
63. *The Times*, 19 September 1888.
64. [Henrietta Barnett], *Canon Barnett: His Life, Work and Friends. By his Wife*, 2 vols, John Murray, 1918, p. 304.
65. *Daily Mail*, 16 July 1901.
66. 'Worst street in London', a pamphlet published in summer 1901. The original is in Tower Hamlets Library, but a full transcription is available on the www.casebook.org. uk website.

Chapter 7: From dissent to respectability, 1820–1914

1. Francis Place, British Library Additional MSS, 27828, f. 120, cited in M.D. George, *London Life in the Eighteenth Century*, Harmondsworth, Penguin, 1965 [1925], pp. 345–6.
2. British Library Additional MSS, 27834, ff. 86–7, cited in David Goodway, *London Chartism, 1838–1848*, Cambridge, Cambridge University Press, 1982, p. 4.
3. James Grant, *Lights and Shadows of London Life*, Saunders and Otley, 1841, pp. 166–73.
4. The argument has been put most influentially by Gareth Stedman Jones, *Outcast London. A Study of the Relations between Classes in Victorian Society*, Oxford, Clarendon Press, 1971.
5. Ibid., p. 343.
6. For a critical appreciation of the life and times of Egan, see John Marriott, 'Introduction', in idem (ed.), *Unknown London: Early Modernist Visions of the Metropolis, 1815–45*, 6 vols, Pickering and Chatto, 2000, pp. xv–xlix.
7. Pierce Egan, *Life in London, or, The Day and Night Scenes of Jerry Hawthorn, Esq. And his Elegant Friend Corinthian Tom, accompanied by Bob Logic, the Oxonian, in their Rambles and Sprees through the Metropolis*, Sherwood, Neely & Jones, 1821.
8. Ibid., p. 24.
9. The name was one of many verbal tricks. 'All-Max' was an old name for gin, and a counterpoint to Almack's, a respectable club in the West End. It has been traced to the Ratcliff Highway.

10. Ibid., p. 286.
11. Ibid., p. 290.
12. Peter Linebaugh and Marcus Rediker, *The Many-Headed Hydra: The Hidden History of the Revolutionary Atlantic*, Verso, 2000.
13. For a discussion of Egan's legacy, see John Marriott, 'Introduction', in John Marriott and Masaie Matsumura (eds), *The Metropolitan Poor: Semifactual Accounts, 1795–1910*, 6 vols, Pickering & Chatto, 1999.
14. Henry Mayhew, *London Labour and the London Poor*, 4 vols, Cass, 1967 [1861], vol. 1, pp. 11–22.
15. James Grant, *Sketches in London*, Orr, 1838, p. 226.
16. Ibid., p. 161.
17. Ibid., p. 189.
18. Ibid., p. 319.
19. James Grant, *Lights and Shadows of London Life*, p. 165.
20. Graham Wallas, *Life of Francis Place, 1771–1854*, Longman Green, 1898, p. 195, cited in Thompson, *Making of the English Working Class*, p. 63.
21. Ibid., p. 669.
22. Prothero, *Artisans and Politics*, pp. 90, 115.
23. Ibid., p. 211.
24. Goodway, *London Chartism*, p. 188.
25. See *Poor Man's Guardian*, 30 July 1831 and 25 December 1831, for reports of meetings attended by weavers. The latter was addressed by William Lovett, who described the deleterious impact of machinery on the livelihood of the weavers. The meeting resolved that 'most of the present evils of society, are to be attributed to corrupt legislation, coupled with uncontrolled machinery, and individual competition'. Early in 1832 the NUWC appointed a number of persons to receive subscriptions. Of the 82 appointed in London, no fewer than 27 lived in Bethnal Green and Spitalfields. Although it is unlikely all were weavers, many would have been, and the figures thus provide a crude indicator of their presence in the union (*Poor Man's Guardian*, 11 February 1832).
26. Prothero, *Artisans and Politics*, pp. 274, 279.
27. *Poor Man's Guardian*, 3 March 1832.
28. Prothero, *Artisans and Politics*, p. 217.
29. Ibid., p. 302.
30. Ibid., pp. 312–13; Goodway, *London Chartism*, p. 23.
31. *The London Despatch*, 26 March 1837.
32. Prospectus of the East London Democratic Association, January 1837, reproduced in Dorothy Thompson (ed.), *The Early Chartists*, Macmillan, 1971, pp. 55–6.
33. Prothero, *Artisans and Politics*, p. 274.
34. Ibid., p. 324.
35. *The Charter*, 17 November 1838.
36. Ibid., 10 November 1838.
37. Prothero, *Artisans and Politics*, p. 324.
38. Goodway, *London Chartism*, pp. 13–17.
39. Ibid., p. 188.
40. British Library, Additional MSS, 34,245B, fos 3–20, quoted in D.J. Rowe, 'Chartism and the Spitalfields silk weavers', *Economic History Review*, 20:3 (1967), p. 488.
41. Ibid., p. 487.
42. Goodway, *London Chartism*, p. 189.
43. Ibid., p. 48.
44. Ibid., pp. 164–9.
45. Ibid., p. 70.
46. Goodway has estimated that of the 57 branches in London in 1848, no fewer than 25 were in East London (ibid., p. 13).
47. *The Times*, 13 June 1848, cited in ibid., p. 87.

48. Stedman Jones, *Outcast London*, pp. 44–5.

49. John Lovell, *Stevedores and Dockers: A Study of Trade Unionism in the Port of London, 1870–1914*, Macmillan, 1969, p. 66.

50. John Marriott, 'London over the border: A study of West Ham during rapid growth, 1840–1910', PhD Thesis, University of Cambridge, 1985.

51. Gareth Stedman Jones, 'Working-class culture and working-class politics in London, 1870–1900: Notes on the remaking of a working class', reproduced in idem, *Languages of Class*, Cambridge, Cambridge University Press, 1983, pp. 179–238.

52. Lovell, *Stevedores and Dockers*, p. 67.

53. Sidney and Beatrice Webb, *History of Trade Unionism*, Longman, 1950 [1920], p. 402.

54. For more recent accounts, see A. Stafford, *A Match to Fire the Thames*, Hodder and Stoughton, 1961, and R. Beer, *The Matchgirls' Strike of 1888*, Manchester, National Museum of Labour History, 1979.

55. Paul Thompson, *Socialists, Liberals and Labour: The Struggle for London, 1885–1914*, Routledge, 1967, p. 46.

56. Llewellyn Smith and Nash, *The Story of the Dockers' Strike*, p. 29.

57. Quoted in ibid., p. 109.

58. Stedman Jones, *Outcast London*, p. 347.

59. Ibid., p. 315.

60. Llewellyn Smith and Nash, *The Story of the Dockers' Strike*; Sidney and Beatrice Webb, *History of Trade Unionism*.

61. Trades Union Congress, *Centenary History*, TUC, 1968, p. 43.

62. Beatrice Webb, *Diary*, 19 November 1889, cited in Thompson, *Socialists, Liberals and Labour*, p. 51.

63. Peter Bailey, 'Custom, capital and culture in the Victorian music hall', in Robert Storch (ed.), *Popular Culture and Custom in Nineteenth-Century England*, Croom Helm, 1982, pp. 180–208; Dagmar Kift, *The Victorian Music Hall: Culture, Class and Conflict*, Cambridge, Cambridge University Press, 1996.

64. 6 & 7 Vic. cap. 68.

65. 10 Geo. II cap. 28.

66. Kift, *Victorian Music Hall*, pp. 140–42.

67. Bailey, 'Custom, capital and culture', p. 186.

68. See programme of the New National Standard Theatre, 1870, available on the website of the East London Theatre Archive (www.elta-project.org).

69. Paragon Theatre of Varieties programme, 1887, on ibid.

70. McDonald's Music Hall programme, 1866, on ibid.

71. Garrick Theatre programme, 1830, on ibid.

72. Garrick Theatre programme, 1880, on ibid.

73. Garrick Music Hall programme, 1893, on ibid.

74. Stedman Jones, 'Working-class culture and working-class politics', p. 224.

75. See, for example, Bailey, 'Custom, capital and culture', Kift, *Victorian Music Hall*, J.S. Bratton (ed.), *Music Hall: Performance and Style*, Milton Keynes, Open University Press, 1986, and Peter Bailey (ed.), *Music Hall: The Business of Pleasure*, Milton Keynes, Open University Press, 1986.

76. Peter Bailey, 'Champagne Charlie: Performance and ideology in the music hall swell song', in Bailey (ed.), *Music Hall*, p. 64.

77. Jim Davis and Victor Emeljanow, *Reflecting the Audience. London Theatregoing, 1840–1880*, Hatfield, University of Hertfordshire Press, 2001, p. x.

78. Ibid., p. 48.

79. *All the Year Round*, 25 February 1860, cited in ibid., p. 78.

80. Ibid., p. 91.

81. Dagmar Höher, 'The composition of music hall audiences, 1850–1900', in Bailey (ed.), *Music Hall*, p. 76.

82. J.M. Weylland, *Round the Tower, or, The Story of the London City Mission*, Partridge, 1875, p. 69.
83. Ibid., p. 71.
84. James Greenwood, *The Wilds of London*, Chatto and Windus, 1874, pp. 12–20.
85. For the following I have relied on Gareth Stedman Jones, 'The "cockney" and the nation, 1780–1988', in David Feldman and Gareth Stedman Jones (eds), *Metropolis. London: Histories and Representations since 1800*, Routledge, 1989.
86. *Temperance Penny Magazine*, January 1836, p. 6.
87. Weylland, *Round the Tower*, pp. 73–4.
88. Greenwood, *The Wilds of London*, p. 8.
89. *Alliance News*, 21 October 1871, quoted in Brian Harrison, 'Pubs', in H.J. Dyos and Michael Wolf (eds), *The Victorian City: Images and Realities. Vol. I. Past and Present/ Numbers of People*, Routledge and Kegan Paul, 1973, p. 181.
90. Harrison, 'Pubs', pp. 161–90.
91. William Fishman, *East End 1888*, Duckworth, 1988, p. 305.
92. Katy Pettit, 'The food culture of East London, 1880–1914', PhD thesis, University of East London, 2009.
93. [Barnett], *Canon Barnett*. The Barnetts were also prolific authors whose books included *Making of the Home*, Cassell & Co., 1884, *Practicable Socialism*, Longmans, Green & Co., 1888, *The Service of God*, Longmans, Green & Co., 1897, *Religion and Progress*, Adam & Charles Black, 1907, and *Towards Social Reform*, Fisher Unwin, 1909.
94. [Barnett], *Canon Barnett*, vol. 1, pp. 73–4.
95. Ibid., p. 21.
96. Ibid., pp. 75–6.
97. Ibid., p. 101.
98. Fishman, *East End 1888*, p. 230.
99. The emergence of this ideal of service is usefully explored in Georgina Brewis, 'The making of an imperial ideal of service: Britain and India before 1914', PhD Thesis, University of East London, 2009.
100. Seth Koven, *Slumming: Sexual and Social Politics in Victorian London*, Princeton, Princeton University Press, 2004, p. 237.
101. [Barnett], *Canon Barnett*, vol. 2, p. 6.
102. Koven, *Slumming*, p. 248. Among other settlements in East London were Mansfield House, Canning Town, Magdalen College Mission, Shoreditch, Eton Manor, Hackney, Fairbairn House, West Ham, Mayfield House, Bethnal Green and St Margaret's House, Bethnal Green; the last two were exclusively for women.
103. In 1895 Oxford House could claim 800 working men as members, and ran a sick fund, two bands (string and brass), a Shakespeare Club, a dramatic society, a children's club, and clubs for a wide variety of sports. Mayfield House, founded by Cheltenham Ladies' College in 1889, could also claim 800 members. Its activities included home arts and industries, district visiting, mothers' meetings, choral classes, penny dinners, ambulance and nursing work, invalid children's aid, and board school work (John M. Knapp (ed.), *The Universities and the Social Problem: An Account of the University Settlements in East London*, Rivington, Percival & Co., 1895).
104. Jonathan Rose's account in *The Intellectual Life of the British Working Classes*, New Haven, Yale University Press, 2001, is replete with examples of the joy and sense of fulfilment ordinary people derived from reading.
105. Michelle Johansen, 'The public librarian in modern London (1890–1914): The case of Charles Goss at the Bishopsgate Institute', PhD Thesis, University of East London, 2008.
106. Ibid., section 2.1.
107. Rose, *The Intellectual Life of the British Working Classes*.
108. Alan Palmer, *The East End: Four Centuries of London Life*, Murray, 1989, p. 87.

109. G.P. Moss and M.V. Saville, *From Palace to College: An Illustrated History of Queen Mary College*, Queen Mary College, 1985, p. 21.

Chapter 8: Migrants and sweaters, 1860–1914

1. PP 1887 (331), John Burnett, *Report to the Board of Trade, on the Sweating System of the East End of London by the Labour Correspondent of the Board*, p. 3. The term sweater was used inconsistently. Originally, it referred pejoratively to journeymen tailors who chose to work at home, but gradually the sweater came to be thought of as a generic subcontractor employing people who were ruthlessly exploited and forced to work in appalling conditions, although confusingly many unemployed people still referred to themselves as sweaters.

2. David Kynaston, *The City of London*, vol. 1, *A World of its Own, 1815–1890*, Chatto and Windus, 1994, pp. 237–43; Geoffrey Elliott, *The Mystery of Overend & Gurney: A Financial Scandal in Victorian London*, Methuen, 2006.

3. Elliott, *Overend & Gurney*, pp. 185–7.

4. London correspondent of the *New York Times*, 3 September 1866, cited in Sidney Pollard, 'The decline of shipbuilding on the Thames', *Economic History Review*, III:1 (1950), pp. 77–8.

5. Gareth Stedman Jones, *Outcast London: A Study of the Relations between Classes in Victorian Society*, Oxford, Clarendon Press, 1971, p. 103.

6. Jesse Argyle, 'Silk manufacture', in Charles Booth (ed.), *Life and Labour of the People*, vol. 1: *East London*, Williams and Norgate, 1889, pp. 389–405.

7. Stedman Jones, *Outcast London*, p. 123.

8. Beatrice Potter, 'The docks', in Booth (ed.), *Life and Labour of the People*, p. 186.

9. Ibid., pp. 190, 196.

10. Ibid., p. 204.

11. Duncan Blythell, *The Sweated Trades: Outwork in Nineteenth-Century Britain*, Batsford, 1978; James Schmiechen, *Sweated Industries and Sweated Labor: The London Clothing Trades, 1860–1914*, Croom Helm, 1984.

12. Andrew Godley, 'Immigrant entrepreneurs and the emergence of London's East End as an industrial district', *London Journal*, 21:1 (1996), pp. 38–45.

13. Charles Booth, 'Sweating', in Booth (ed.), *Life and Labour of the People*, pp. 481–500; PP 1888 (361), (448); 1890 (169), *Select Committee of the House of Lords on the Sweating System*.

14. Booth, 'Sweating', pp. 483–6.

15. PP 1888 (361), *Select Committee of the House of Lords on the Sweating System*, evidence of Arnold White, p. 35.

16. Ben Tillett, evidence, PP 1888 (448), *Select Committee of the House of Lords on the Sweating System*, pp. 111–47.

17. Barbara Harrison, 'Women's work and health in the East End, 1880–1914', *Rising East*, 2:3 (1999), pp. 20–46.

18. Burnett, *Report to the Board of Trade*, p. 9.

19. PP 1888 (361), *Select Committee of the House of Lords on the Sweating System*, evidence of Samuel Wildman, pp. 65–8.

20. This is not to suggest there was a steady decline in the earning of sweated labour in the course of the century. In 1849 Henry Mayhew interviewed a slop-house worker making body waistcoats. In an average week she earned 3s for a working day of 9am to 11pm. She had worked there for twenty-six years, during which time average prices had fallen from 1s 9d to 1s 1d, largely because of a slackening of work (E.P. Thompson and Eileen Yeo (eds), *The Unknown Mayhew*, Harmondsworth, Penguin, 1973, p. 148). This suggests that market conditions, rather than a tendency systematically to reduce wages, explain levels of earnings in sweated industries. The 1880s witnessed recession.

21. The sewing machine was first introduced by Singer in 1856. It saved enormous amounts of time in seaming and stitching. A sewer could average 35 stitches per

minute, a machine 1,000–2,000. This meant that a shirt with 20,000 stitches could be finished five times faster. Other machines were later developed for specialist tasks such as buttonholing. A shoe-sewing machine was introduced by McKay in 1861. Contemporary observers noted that the machines greatly increased the earnings of workers, and the employment of many more (Blythell, *The Sweated Trades*, p. 69, Schmiechen, *Sweated Industries and Sweated Labor*, p. 26).

22. Ibid., p. 7; PP 1888 (361), *Select Committee of the House of Lords on the Sweating System*, evidence of Charles Solomon, pp. 68–79.
23. PP 1903 [Cmnd 1742], *Royal Commission on Alien Immigration, vol. II, Minutes of Evidence,* evidence of Herbert Evans, p. 393.
24. Joseph Leftwich, 'The Tailor', reproduced in Chris Searle (ed.), *Bricklight. Poems from the Labour Movement in East London*, Pluto Press, 1980. The poem was written in Yiddish.
25. Burnett, *Report to the Board of Trade*, p. 12.
26. PP 1888 (361), *Select Committee of the House of Lords on the Sweating System*, evidence of Charles Solomon, pp. 68–79.
27. Beatrice Potter, 'The tailoring trade', in Booth (ed.), *Life and Labour of the People*, pp. 230–31.
28. The calculations on which I have relied have been done by Schmiechen, *Sweated Industries and Sweated Labor*, pp. 37–43.
29. The Census underestimates the numbers of female workers since many of them, by working in hidden workshops, simply evaded census enumerators.
30. Stedman Jones, *Outcast London*, Tables 5 and 6.
31. Burnett, *Report of the Board of Trade on the Sweating System*, p. 4.
32. Potter, 'The tailoring trade', p. 232.
33. Arnold White, *The Problems of a Great City*, Remington, 1886.
34. PP 1888 (361), *Select Committee of the House of Lords on the Sweating System*, evidence of Arnold White, pp. 35–55.
35. Ibid., pp. 119–20.
36. See, for example, the evidence of Lewis Lyons, a tailor's machinist and regular contributor of articles to the press on the sweating system, in which he blames masters for exploiting the ready supply of pauper migrant labour, be it Irish, English or Jewish, but favours restrictions on immigration chiefly because it is in the interests of the migrants themselves (ibid., pp. 163–4).
37. PP 1890 (169), *Select Committee of the House of Lords on the Sweating System*, pp. cxxxiv–cxlii.
38. White, *The Problems of a Great City*.
39. Bernard Gainer, *The Alien Invasion: The Origins of the Aliens Act of 1905*, Heinemann, 1972, pp. 119–20.
40. Cited in ibid., p. 95.
41. M.A. Shepherd, 'How Petticoat Lane became a Jewish market', in Aubrey Newman (ed.), *The Jewish East End, 1840–1939*, Jewish Historical Society, 1981, pp. 125–31.
42. For a detailed description of the market at the time, see Henry Mayhew, *London Labour and the London Poor*, vol. II, Cass & Co., 1967 [1861], pp. 36–9.
43. Harold Pollins, 'East End Jewish working men's clubs affiliated to the Working Men's Club and Institute Union, 1870–1914', in Newman (ed.), *The Jewish East End*, pp. 173–92.
44. These figures bear little relation to the numbers who actually arrived, for organizations such as the Jewish Board of Guardians and the Russian Committee worked vigorously and successfully to repatriate immigrant Jews or provide them with passage to the USA. Data from the Hebrew Ladies' Protection Society suggest that between December 1888 and March 1889 they met 173 Jewish arrivals, 87 of whom were subsequently passed to the USA. The net result, according to a survey conducted in 1889, was that emigration exceeded immigration (H. Llewellyn Smith, 'Influx of population', in Booth (ed.), *Life*

and Labour of the People, p. 555). Overall, approximately twice as many arrived as settled.

45. David Feldman, *Englishmen and Jews: Social Relations and Political Culture, 1840–1914*, New Haven, Yale University Press, 1994, pp. 148–9, 157.
46. PP 1888 (361), *Select Committee of the House of Lords on the Sweating System*, p. 62.
47. Ibid., pp. 45, 55, 61 and 83.
48. A. Weiner, 'Jewish industrial life in Russia', *Economic Journal*, XV (1905), p. 582.
49. William Fishman, *East End 1888*, Duckworth, 1988.
50. C. Russell and H. Lewis, *The Jew in London: A Study of Racial Character and Present-day Conditions*, Fisher Unwin, 1900.
51. Llewellyn Smith, 'Influx of population', p. 543.
52. Sholom Aleichem, *Adventures of Mottel, the Cantor's Son*, Abelard-Schuman, 1958, p. 199, cited in Feldman, *Englishmen and Jews*, p. 167. Such accounts have to be treated with caution, coloured as they are by a certain nostalgic romanticism. Others recall quite different reactions, for example, Lew Grade, the impresario, who found Brick Lane dark and bleak when he migrated from Russia in 1912 (Lew Grade, *Still Dancing*, Collins, 1997).
53. Avram Stencl, 'Whitechapel in Britain', reproduced in Searle (ed.), *Bricklight*. The poem was written in Yiddish.
54. Lloyd P. Gartner, *The Jewish Immigrant in England, 1870–1914*, Allen & Unwin, 1960, p. 85.
55. 'Report of the Lancet Special Sanitary Commission on the Polish colony of Jew tailors', *The Lancet*, 3 May 1884.
56. The impact of the report was immediate; the *Jewish Chronicle* thought it exaggerated but called on the Jewish Board of Guardians to deal with unscrupulous sweaters, and ensure that the sanitary authorities applied the full weight of their powers.
57. The phrase is used in Russell and Lewis, *The Jew in London*, p. 9.
58. Beatrice Potter, 'The Jewish community', in Booth (ed.), *Life and Labour of the People*, pp. 565–6.
59. Figures on the numbers relieved by the Jewish Board are revealing. In 1883, 2,882 received relief, 56 per cent of whom were natives or had been in London for more than seven years. In 1886 the corresponding figures were 4,139 and 46 per cent, suggesting that greeners were worst affected by the downturn (PP 1888 (361), *Select Committee of the House of Lords on the Sweating System*, evidence of Morris Stephany, Secretary to the Board, p. 8).
60. Raymond Kalman, 'The Jewish East End – where was it?', in Newman (ed.), *The Jewish East End*, p. 11, and Aubrey Newman, 'Synagogues of the East End', in ibid., p. 219. The Federation was distinct from the United Synagogue movement which was founded in 1870 and comprised the larger synagogues, becoming the main instrument of orthodox opinion.
61. Potter, 'The Jewish community', pp. 567–69.
62. A. Rosebury, 'Jewish friendly societies; a critical survey', *Jewish Chronicle*, 8 September 1905. The article is reproduced in David Englander (ed.), *A Documentary History of Jewish Immigrants in Britain, 1840–1920*, Leicester, Leicester University Press, 1994.
63. Gartner, *The Jewish Immigrant*, pp. 221, 224.
64. Feldman, *Englishmen and Jews*, pp. 338.
65. Gartner, *The Jewish Immigrant*, pp. 251–61. In what follows I am heavily indebted to his discussion.
66. The political landscape of Jewish labour is rather better documented than its literary culture. Among useful studies are Feldman, *Englishmen and Jews*, Chapters 9 and 10, William Fishman, *East End Jewish Radicals, 1875–1914*, Duckworth, 1975, Gartner, *The Jewish Immigrant*, Chapter 4, Schmiechen, *Sweated Industries and Sweated Labor*, Chapter 4.
67. Cited in Fishman, *East End Jewish Radicals*, p. 104.
68. Lieberman's distrust of Jewish orthodoxy was well known. His sometime colleague Valerian Smirnov reported that while in London Lieberman had opposed the publication

of socialist literature in Hebrew on the grounds that it was 'unintelligible to the majority of people' within the community, being 'only accessible to … a small number of cultivated hypocrites' (quoted in ibid., p. 127). This sits uneasily with the fact that *HaEmet* had been published in Hebrew, and reflects awkward questions on whether Jewish socialists should work within the community, or towards a proletarian internationalism.

69. Perhaps one of the reasons why we know so much about Lieberman and the Union was that he had a sense of historical significance and wished to record as fully as possible the activities of this early period. See Fishman, *East End Jewish Radicals*, Chapter 4, and Gartner, *The Jewish Immigrant*, pp. 103–7, for good accounts on which I have drawn.
70. *Polishe Yidl*, 19 September 1884, cited in Fishman, *East End Jewish Radicals*, p. 144.
71. *Arbeiter Freind*, 15 July 1885, cited in ibid., p. 109.
72. Fishman, *East End Jewish Radicals*, pp. 151–8.
73. Schmiechen, *Sweated Industries and Sweated Labor*, pp. 81–3.
74. Curiously and disappointingly, no work has been undertaken on this important question.
75. *East London Advertiser*, 23 March 1889, cited in Fishman, *East End Jewish Radicals*, p. 166.
76. *Jewish Chronicle*, 22 March 1889.
77. Gartner, *The Jewish Immigrant*, p. 123. The committee was led by Lewis Lyons, an independent and knowledgeable machinist who had given evidence to the Lords inquiry, with William Wess, a printer and anarchist, as secretary, and rank-and-file workers.
78. *Jewish Chronicle*, 6 September 1889.
79. The detailed course of the strike is well described in Fishman, *East End Jewish Radicals*, Chapter 6.
80. *Arbeiter Freind*, 16 December 1892, cited in Gartner, *The Jewish Immigrant*, p. 131.
81. Fishman, *East End Jewish Radicals*, p. 267, and *passim* for the career of Rocker in London.
82. Cited in ibid., p. 268. Fishman was able to interview several such members of the club.
83. Hymie Fagan, 'An autobiography', Brunel University Library, cited in Jonathan Rose, *The Intellectual Life of the British Working Classes*, New Haven, Yale University Press, 2001, pp. 83–4.

Chapter 9: The ascent of Labour, 1880–1920

1. Gareth Stedman Jones, *Outcast London: A Study of the Relations between Classes in Victorian Society*, Oxford, Clarendon Press, 1971, p. 169.
2. For a general survey, see H.A. Shannon, 'Migration and the growth of London, 1841–91: A statistical note', *Economic History Review*, 5:2 (1935), pp. 79–86.
3. More detailed information as follows:

Population of parishes and boroughs within Tower Hamlets and Shoreditch, 1861–1931

Parish/borough	1861	1881	1911	1931
Shoreditch	129,364	126,591	111,390	97,042
Mile End Old Town	78,061	47,491	–	–
Whitechapel	78,970	71,311	–	–
Stepney	56,572	58,122	279,804	225,238
St George's-in-the-East	48,891	49,382	–	–
Bethnal Green	105,101	–	128,123	108,194
Poplar	79,196	73,661	162,442	155,089
Limehouse	–	56,318	–	–
Bow and Bromley	–	82,819	–	–
Total	**576,155**	**565,695**	**681,759**	**585,563**

Source: Censuses of Population.

4. Hubert Llewellyn Smith, 'Influx of population', in Charles Booth (ed.), *Life and Labour of the People, Vol. 1: East London*, Williams and Norgate, 1889, pp. 521-63.

5. Stedman Jones, *Outcast London*, p. 176.

6. Llewellyn Smith, 'Influx of population', p. 501.

7. Cited in Charles Masterman (ed.), *The Heart of Empire*, 1901, p. 29, and Stedman Jones, *Outcast London*, p. 177.

8. Jerry White's study of Rothschild Buildings provides a rich and vivid evocation of its background and resident community (*Rothschild Buildings: Life in an East End Tenement Block, 1887-1920*, Routledge, 1980).

9. Charlotte was Rothschild's mother. On her death bed in 1884 she was rumoured to have instructed her son to devote his energies to the provision of housing for Jewish workers.

10. Llewellyn Smith, 'Influx of population', p. 507.

11. W.R. Powell, 'West Ham', *Victoria County History of Essex*, Institute of Historical Research, VI (1973), provides a comprehensive survey.

12. See John Marriott, ' "West Ham: London's industrial centre and gateway to the world", I Industrialisation, 1840-1910', *London Journal*, 13:2 (1988), pp. 121-42.

13. John Marriott, 'London over the border': A study of West Ham during rapid growth, 1870-1910', University of Cambridge, PhD thesis, 1985.

14. A. Hugill, *Sugar and All That: A History of Tate and Lyle*, Gentry Books, 1978, p. 38.

15. Henry Morley, 'Londoners over the border', *Household Words*, 12 September 1857.

16. John Marriott, 'Smokestack: The industrial history of Thames Gateway', in Philip Cohen and Michael Rustin (eds), *London's Turning: The Making of the Thames Gateway*, Aldershot, Ashgate, 2008, pp. 17-30. Other firms in the neighbourhood such as Siemens at Woolwich (with 7,000), the Arsenal (70,000) and later Ford at Dagenham (15,000) emphasize that this industrialization rivalled any in the country.

17. For the details see John Davis and Duncan Tanner, 'The borough franchise after 1867', *Historical Research*, 69 (1996), pp. 306-27.

18. The details are given in Marc Brodie, *The Politics of the Poor: The East End of London, 1885-1914*, Oxford, Clarendon Press, 2004, Chapter 2.

19. Davis and Tanner, 'The borough franchise after 1867'.

20. Calculations are based on date in the 1891 Census and electoral statistics given in PP 1887 (124), *Parliamentary Constituencies*, and PP 1895 (288), *Parliamentary Constituencies (Electors)*.

21. Tower Hamlets had Bow and Bromley, Limehouse, Mile End, Poplar, St George's, Stepney and Whitechapel; Hackney had Bethnal Green North East and South West, Hackney Central, North and South, Haggerston, and Hoxton.

22. Brodie, *The Politics of the Poor*, pp. 51-3.

23. **Winning parties from the constituencies of East London and West Ham in the general elections of 1885-1910 (L Liberal, C Conservative, La Labour)**

Constituency	1885	1886	1892	1895	1900	1906	1910J	1910D
Bethnal Green NE	L	L	L	C	C	L	L	L
Bethnal Green SW	L	L	L	L	C	L	L	L
Bow & Bromley	L	C	L	C	C	L	C	La
Limehouse	C	C	L	C	C	L	L	L
Mile End	C	C	C	C	C	L	C	C
Poplar	L	L	L	L	L	L	L	L
St George's	C	C	L	C	C	L	L	L
Stepney	L	C	C	C	C	C	C	L
West Ham N					C	L	L	L
West Ham S			La	C	C	La	La	La
Whitechapel	L	L	L	L	L	L	L	L

Source: Based on tables in Brodie, *The Politics of the Poor*, Appendix 2. 1910 had elections in January and December.

24. Brodie has explored the correlations between a number of socio-economic and cultural indicators and a 'progressive' vote, for the most part demonstrating there were none (Brodie, *The Politics of the Poor*, Chapter 3).

25. *Stratford Express*, 2 April 1892.

26. The story is told fully in my 'London over the border' PhD thesis.

27. *Stratford Express*, 22 January 1887.

28. Ibid., 19 April 1890.

29. Paul Thompson, *Socialists, Liberals and Labour: The Struggle for London, 1885–1914*, Routledge and Kegan Paul, 1967, p. 131.

30. *Stratford Express*, 27 October 1894.

31. Ibid., 3 November 1894.

32. Ibid., 6 November 1897.

33. Ibid., 5 November 1898.

34. Ibid., 12 November 1898.

35. Election manifesto of the Municipal Alliance, 1900.

36. Julia Bush, *Behind the Lines: East London Labour, 1914–1919*, Merlin Press, 1984; John Marriott, 'The political modernism of East London', in Tim Butler and Michael Rustin (eds), *Rising in the East: The Regeneration of East London*, Lawrence and Wishart, 1996.

37. See, for example, Ross McKibbin, *The Evolution of the Labour Party, 1910–24*, Oxford, Oxford University Press, 1974; Bush, *Behind the Lines*; James Gillespie, 'Poplarism and proletarianism: Unemployment and Labour politics in London, 1918–34', in David Feldman and Gareth Stedman Jones (eds), *Metropolis: London: Histories and Representations since 1800*, Routledge, 1989; John Marriott, *The Culture of Labourism: The East End between the Wars*, Edinburgh, Edinburgh University Press, 1991; Duncan Tanner, *Political Change and the Labour Party, 1900–1918*, Cambridge, Cambridge University Press, 1990.

38. *Lax of Poplar: The Story of a Wonderful Quarter of a Century, told by Himself*, Epworth Press, 1927, p. 197.

39. Ibid., p. 197.

40. Ibid., pp. 197–9.

41. *Stratford Express*, 3 February 1917, cited in Graham Hill and Howard Bloch (eds), *The Silvertown Explosion: London 1917*, Stroud, Tempus, 2003, pp. 106–7, which is a useful collection of primary materials.

42. *Report of the Committee Appointed by the Right Honourable the Secretary of State for the Home Department to Inquire into the Cause of the Explosion which occurred on Friday 19 January 1917, at the Chemical Works of Messrs. Brunner, Mond and Company, Crescent Wharf, Silvertown in the County of Essex*. The report, without the evidence submitted by witnesses, is reproduced in ibid., pp. 171–210.

43. E. Sylvia Pankhurst, *The Home Front: A Mirror to Life in England during the First World War*, Cresset Library, 1987 [1932], p. 19.

44. Bush, *Behind the Lines*, pp. 110–11.

45. David Cesarani, 'An embattled minority: The Jews in Britain during the First World War', in Tony Kushner and Kenneth Lunn (eds), *The Politics of Marginality: Race, the Radical Right and Minorities in Twentieth-Century Britain*, Frank Cass, 1900, p. 73.

46. Raphael Samuel, *East End Underworld: Chapters in the Life of Arthur Harding*, Routledge & Kegan Paul, 1981, p. 237.

47. Gillespie, 'Poplarism and proletarianism'.

48. C.R. Attlee, 'Labour and the municipal elections', *New Leader*, 13 October 1922; George Lansbury, 'Foreword' to C.W. Key, *Red Poplar: Six Years of Socialist Rule*, Labour Publishing, 1925, quoted in Gillespie, 'Poplarism and proletarianism', pp. 169–70.

49. Marriott, *The Culture of Labourism*, p. 39.

50. *Cooperative News*, 6 January 1917.

51. Ibid., 19 June 1915.
52. Marriott, *The Culture of Labourism*, pp. 46–53.
53. Bush, *Behind the Lines*, p. 103.
54. Ibid., p. 139.
55. Ibid., pp. 44–9, and Marriott, *The Culture of Labourism*, pp. 29–35. Both these studies tend to focus on the experience of West Ham.
56. Bush, *Behind the Lines*, p. 153. Significantly, Thorne's candidature could not be taken for granted. An alliance of ILP and BSP members on the selection committee refused to nominate him on the grounds of his consistent pro-war stance. Thorne was an Hon. Colonel of the 1st Essex Volunteers, and often appeared in uniform at public meetings. It was only when he turned to his union for support that his candidature was confirmed. (See Marriott, *The Culture of Labourism*, pp. 31–2.)
57. *Stratford Express*, 25 October 1919.
58. *Railway Review*, 3 September 1919.
59. Ibid., 23 May 1919.

Chapter 10: Recession, mass culture and the entrepreneurial spirit, 1920–1939

1. Hubert Llewellyn Smith (ed.), 'Introduction', in *New Survey of London Life and Labour*, II, *London Industries I*, pp. 1–44, P.S. King, 1931. This massive survey, led by one of Charles Booth's co-workers, was designed to assess the profound changes that had taken place in the intervening years. Recognizing the growth that had taken place in London, it wisely decided to extend the inquiry beyond the LCC boundary to embrace nine surrounding boroughs, including West Ham, Leyton, Tottenham and Willesden.
2. PP 1903 [Cmnd 1742], *Royal Commission on Alien Immigration*, 1903, Minutes of Evidence, p. 391.
3. Peter Hall, *The Industries of London Since 1861*, Hutchinson, 1962, Chapter 4; D.L. Munby, *Industry and Planning in Stepney*, Oxford, Oxford University Press, 1951, p. 40. Stepney Borough was the entire district of East London bounded by Bethnal Green to the north and Poplar to the east.
4. Ibid., pp. 61–2.
5. Llewellyn Smith, *New Survey of London Life and Labour*, II, p. 244.
6. A survey carried out by the Factory Department of the Home Office in 1930 estimated that 2,277 factories and workshops were engaged in the furniture trade; of these approximately two thirds were workshops, the majority of which we can assume were in East London (ibid., p. 216).
7. Ibid., p. 290. Such aggregate figures tend to disguise even greater fluctuations in the demand for more specialist dock labour.
8. PP 1920 [Cmnd 936], *Transport Workers – Court of Inquiry*, p. x.
9. Llewellyn Smith, *New Survey of London Life and Labour*, II, p. 400.
10. Munby, *Industry and Planning in Stepney*, p. 275.
11. Llewellyn Smith, *New Survey of London Life and Labour*, II, pp. 430–31.
12. John Marriott, '"West Ham: London's industrial centre and gateway to the world", II, Stabilization and decline, 1910–1939', *London Journal*, 4:1 (1989), pp. 43–58.
13. Hall, *The Industries of London*, Chapter 8.
14. Llewellyn Smith, *New Survey of London Life and Labour*, III, p. 22. Given this, it is curious that the survey undertook no systematic review of unemployment levels.
15. Ibid., I, pp. 36–8, and Appendix Table 1.
16. Marriott, '"West Ham: London's industrial centre and gateway to the world"', II, pp. 52–3.
17. Llewellyn Smith, *New Survey of London Life and Labour*, III, p. 81. Bermondsey was the other borough.
18. Ibid., p. 353.
19. Ibid., p. 409.

20. Ken Young and Patricia Garside, *Metropolitan London: Politics and Urban Change, 1837–1981*, Arnold, 1982, pp. 153–5.
21. Henrietta Barnett, *Matters that Matter*, Murray, 1930, p. 95, cited in A. Olechnowicz, *Working-Class Housing in England between the Wars: The Becontree Estate*, Oxford, Clarendon Press, 1997, p. 3.
22. Phil Cohen, 'A history of disillusionment: The Becontree Estate', *Rising East*, 3:1 (1999), pp. 107–21. The article comes from an extended interview with Denise Riley, who was researching the estate.
23. Olechnowicz, *Working-Class Housing in England*, p. 6.
24. Cohen, 'A history of disillusionment', p. 113.
25. Grace Foakes, *My Life with Reuben*, Shepheard-Walwyn, 1975, p. 37.
26. The record of the struggles of Poplar councillors is described in Noreen Branson, *Poplarism, 1919–1925: George Lansbury and the Councillors' Revolt*, Lawrence and Wishart, 1979.
27. Ibid., p. 79.
28. The full details are in ibid., p. 108. Interestingly, Whitechapel and Hackney were among those which experienced increases.
29. Jerry White, *London in the Twentieth Century*, Vintage, 2008, p. 370.
30. The story of the struggle of West Ham guardians is told in John Marriott, *The Culture of Labourism: The East End Between the Wars*, Edinburgh, Edinburgh University Press, 1991, Chapter 4.
31. The Metropolitan Common Poor Fund had been introduced in 1867 as a step in equalizing the poor rates between rich and poor boroughs, but the inadequate sums of money made available meant it was little more than a palliative.
32. See, for example, his classic account, Wal Hannington, *Unemployed Struggles, 1919–1936*, Lawrence and Wishart, 1977 [1936].
33. See the first issue of *Out of Work*, the newspaper of the LDCU, 19 March 1921.
34. *Stratford Express*, 11 February 1922, cited in ibid., p. 142.
35. Ibid.
36. Weekly outdoor relief fell from £28,000 to just under £4,000, and the numbers on relief from 66,500 to 14,500 (Marriott, *The Culture of Labourism*, p. 159). West Ham was one of three boards superseded at the time, the others being Chester-le-Street in Durham and Merthyr Tydfil, both in areas which had been devastated by catastrophic levels of unemployment.
37. *Stratford Express*, 31 July 1926, cited in ibid., p. 162.
38. For a brief but solid overview, see Eric Hobsbawm, *Age of Extremes: The Short Twentieth Century, 1914–1991*, Michael Joseph, 1994, pp. 192–8. Ross McKibbin, *Classes and Cultures: England 1918–1951*, Oxford, Oxford University Press, 1998, and Mica Nava and Alan O'Shea (eds), *Modern Times: Reflections on a Century of English Modernity*, Routledge, 1996, offer more detailed – and contrasting – accounts.
39. Llewellyn Smith, *New Survey of London Life and Labour*, IX, 1935, p. 5.
40. Robert Graves and Alan Hodge, *The Long Weekend: A Social History of Great Britain, 1918–1939*, Hutchinson, 1985 [1940], p. 133.
41. *Victoria County History of Middlesex*, vol. 11, *Stepney and Bethnal Green*, Institute of Historical Research, 1998, p. 149.
42. *Kinematograph Year Book*, 1921, cited in Marriott, 'Sensation of the abyss', in Nava and O'Shea (eds), *Modern Times*, p. 95.
43. 'The possibilities of cinema', *Mansfield House Magazine*, 27, 1921, cited in ibid., p. 96.
44. Stanley Reed, 'Notes on a working life', unpublished manuscript, n.d., cited in ibid., p. 96.
45. This is a strong impression conveyed by two studies of families migrating out of East London: Michael Young and Peter Willmott, *Family and Kinship in East London*, Harmondsworth, Pelican, 1962, and A. Olechnowicz, *Working-Class Housing in England between the Wars*. We shall return to these later.
46. Llewellyn Smith (ed.), *New Survey of London Life and Labour*, IX, p. 257.
47. Ibid., p. 28.

48. Peter Radford, 'The time a land forgot', *The Observer*, 2 May 2004.
49. In 1787, a runner by the name of Powell bet 1,000 guineas that he could run the mile in under four minutes. We do not have evidence whether he won, but in a time trial just prior to the race he ran 4 minutes 3 seconds. 1,000 guineas is worth well over £1m today, using earnings as an index.
50. Pierce Egan, *Boxiana; or, Sketches of Ancient and Modern Pugilism*, Smeeton, 1812. Written two hundred years ago by an enthusiastic devotee, this remains a vivid evocation of eighteenth-century boxing and its heroes.
51. Stan Shipley, *Bombardier Billy Wells: The Life and Times of a Hero*, Tyne and Wear, Bewick Press, 1993.
52. Cited in Richard Holt, *Sport and the British: A Modern History*, Oxford, Clarendon Press, 1989, p. 67.
53. McKibbin, *Classes and Cultures*, p. 363; R. Seebohm Rowntree and G.R. Lavers, *English Life and Leisure: A Social Study*, Longmans, Green & Co., 1951, p. 124.
54. Charles Dimont, 'Going to the dogs', *New Statesman*, 30 November 1946.
55. Llewellyn Smith (ed.), *New Survey of London Life and Labour*, IX, p. 56.
56. Such was their popularity that Chitty and Wilkinson later had streets named after them.
57. Colm Kerrigan, *Teachers and Football: The Origins, Development and Influence of Schoolboy Football Associations in London, 1885–1918*, Routledge, 2004.
58. Jerry White, *London in the Twentieth Century*, Vintage, p. 318.
59. Llewellyn Smith (ed.), *New Survey of London Life and Labour*, I, p. 34.
60. Between 1893 and 1928 indictable offences, including violence to the person, burglary, larceny, robbery and forgery, expressed as a percentage of the population, had fallen by approximately half, while 'non-indictable offences akin to indictable offences', such as assault, malicious damage, stealing and unlawful possession, had dropped by two thirds. Only with the less serious – and much more numerous – offences, including drunkenness, begging, betting and gaming, and offences against the education acts and police regulations, was there an increase, albeit a small one (ibid., pp. 400–402). We are now rather more sensitive to the contingent nature of such data, determined as they are by the diligence of the authorities in pursuing and recording such offences. There can be little doubt that much of the crime was unreported by the poor, and under-recorded by the police (White, *London in the Twentieth Century*, p. 265).
61. Llewellyn Smith (ed.), *New Survey of London Life and Labour*, I, p. 36.
62. Take, for example, statistics on crime between 1920 and 1928 which suggest that, while metropolitan levels fell, those experienced by the neighbouring parishes of Essex, Hertfordshire, Surrey and Kent all soared by at least 300 per cent. The explanation offered for these rather unexpected findings was that London burglars had switched their activities to the surrounding countryside, where there was less of a police presence, access and escape by car were easier, and more houses could be robbed in a shorter time (ibid., pp. 392–3).
63. White, *London in the Twentieth Century*, p. 245.
64. Dick Hobbs, *Doing the Business: Entrepreneurship, the Working Class, and Detectives in the East End of London*, Oxford, Oxford University Press, 1989, p. 117.
65. Ibid., p. 8.
66. Raphael Samuel, *East End Underworld: Chapters in the Life of Arthur Harding*, Routledge and Kegan Paul, 1981. Arthur Harding was a pseudonym, as were many of the names of characters who featured in Samuel's book.
67. The area featured prominently in contemporary accounts of the condition of East London, but more importantly gained a mythical reputation as the 'Jago' after Arthur Morrison's hugely popular *Child of the Jago*, published in 1896 just as the area was under demolition. Sara Wise has recently explored and vividly revealed the lives of its inhabitants (*The Blackest Streets: The Life and Death of a Victorian Slum*, The Bodley Head, 2008).
68. Samuel, *East End Underworld*, p. 9.
69. Ibid., p. 71.
70. Ibid., p. 106.

71. Ibid., p. 108. On one occasion Murphy pointedly asked Harding how many women Jack the Ripper had killed.

72. Ibid., p. 108. 'Chiv' is slang for a knife.

73. For the best discussion of social banditry, see E.J. Hobsbawm, *Primitive Rebels: Studies in Archaic Forms of Social Movement in the 19th and 20th Centuries*, Manchester, Manchester University Press, 1959.

74. A good, if fictional, example of urban social banditry was Macheath's gang in John Gay's play *The Beggar's Opera*, first staged in 1728.

75. Frederick Wensley, *Detective Days*, Cassell & Co., 1931, p. 136.

76. James Morton, *Gangland: London's Underworld*, Little, Brown & Co., 1992, p. 2. See also Morton's *East End Gangland*, Little, Brown & Co., 2000, and *Gangland: The Early Years*, Time Warner, 2003, although they recycle much of his earlier material.

77. Morton, *East End Gangland*, Chapter 3.

78. Quoted in ibid., p. 78.

79. Morton, *East End Gangland*, p. 149. A recent study of the Chinese in Britain has argued persuasively that Chang's trial was framed by a range of concerns over the extent to which this relatively small community was popularly linked to opium and prostitution (Sascha Auerbach, *Race, Law and 'The Chinese Puzzle' in Imperial Britain*, New York, Palgrave, 2009).

80. Morton, *East End Gangland*, p. 157.

81. Ibid., p. 171.

82. John Pearson, *The Profession of Violence: The Rise and Fall of the Kray Twins*, Grafton, 1990.

Chapter 11: Fascism and war, 1920–1945

1. Phil Piratin, *Our Flag Stays Red*, Lawrence and Wishart, 1978 [1948], p. 18.

2. Thomas Linehan, *East London for Mosley: The British Union of Fascists in East London and South-West Essex, 1933–40*, Frank Cass, 1996, p. 198.

3. For this I have relied on Thomas Linehan, *British Fascism, 1918–1939: Parties, Ideology and Culture*, Manchester, Manchester University Press, 2000.

4. Bernard Gainer, *The Alien Invasion: The Origins of the Aliens Act of 1905*, Heinemann, 1972, p. 61. White had previously founded the Society for the Suppression of the Immigration of Destitute Aliens, but it soon faded into obscurity.

5. Ibid., p. 69.

6. *Stratford Express*, 8 August 1914, cited in Howard Bloch and Graham Hill (eds), *Germans in London*, All Points East, 2000, p. 53. For general surveys see Stella Yarrow, 'The impact of hostility on Germans in Britain, 1914–1918', in Tony Kushner and Kenneth Lunn (eds), *The Politics of Marginality: Race, the Radical Right and Minorities in Twentieth-Century Britain*, Frank Cass, 1990, and Panikos Panayi, *The Enemy in our Midst: Germans in Britain during the First World War*, Berg, 1991.

7. *East Ham Echo*, 14 May 1915. One of the shopkeepers attacked had just lost a son, killed while fighting for the British army in France.

8. Julia Bush, *Behind the Lines: East London Labour, 1914–1919*, Merlin Press, 1984, p. 166.

9. Cited in ibid., p. 171.

10. Linehan, *British Fascism*, pp. 49–50.

11. Piratin, *Our Flag Stays Red*, p. 18.

12. G.D.H. and M.I. Cole, *The Condition of Britain*, Victor Gollancz, 1937, pp. 420–21.

13. Ibid., pp. 235–6.

14. Wal Hannington, *The Problem of the Distressed Areas*, Victor Gollancz, 1937, p. 239.

15. R.J. Benewick, *The Fascist Movement in Britain*, Allen Lane, 1972.

16. For coverage of the debate, see Colin Holmes, 'Anti-semitism and the BUF', in Kenneth Lunn and Richard C. Thurlow (eds), *British Fascism: Essays on the Radical Right in Interwar Britain*, Croom Helm, 1980, pp. 114–34.

17. Linehan, *East London for Mosley*, p. 48.

18. Ibid., p. 276. This and the extracts which follow come from taped interviews with former BUF members.
19. Ibid., p. 277.
20. Ibid., p. 55.
21. David Mayall, 'Rescued from the shadows of exile: Nellie Driver, autobiography and the British Union of Fascists', in Kushner and Lunn (eds), *The Politics of Marginality*, pp. 19–39.
22. Linehan, *East London for Mosley*, p. 298.
23. The contrasting attitudes are illustrated well in the memoirs of Phil Piratin, who, as we have seen, was in favour of continued work with the trade unions and local organizations, while Joe Jacobs, another prominent local communist, advocated physical resistance to fascist provocation (see Piratin, *Our Flag Stays Red*, and Joe Jacobs, *Out of the Ghetto: My Youth in the East End, Communism and Fascism, 1913–39*, Simon, 1978).
24. For a brief assessment of the episode, see Nicholas Deakin, 'The vitality of a tradition', in Colin Holmes (ed.), *Immigrants and Minorities in British Society*, Allen & Unwin, 1978, pp. 158–85.
25. Linehan, *British Fascism*, p. 107.
26. Stuart Hylton, *Their Darkest Hour: The Hidden History of the Home Front, 1939–1945*, Stroud, Sutton, 2001, p. 31. This estimate exceeded the total dropped on Britain in the whole of the war, but clearly attempted to take account of advances in the technology of mass murder.
27. J.F.C. Fuller, *The Reformation of War*, Hutchinson, 1923, p. 50. Interestingly, Bertrand Russell, who in 1936 was at the forefront of the peace movement, used an identical passage in *Which Way to Peace?*, Michael Joseph, 1936, p. 37.
28. Tom Harrisson, *Living Through the Blitz*, Harmondsworth, Penguin, 1978, p. 26.
29. Quoted in Joanna Mack and Steve Humphries, *The Making of Modern London, 1939–1945: London at War*, Sidgwick and Jackson, 1985, p. 40.
30. Quoted in Peter Stansky, *The First Day of the Blitz, September 7th, 1940*, New Haven, Yale University Press, 2007, p. 36.
31. Bryan Forbes, *Notes for a Life*, Collins, 1974, p. 53, cited in ibid., p. 36.
32. Quoted in Mack and Humphries, *The Making of Modern London*, p. 41.
33. *New Yorker*, 14 September 1940, cited in Angus Calder, *The Myth of the Blitz*, Cape, 1991, pp. 33–4.
34. Gareth Stedman Jones, 'The "cockney" and the nation, 1780–1988', in David Feldman and Stedman Jones (eds), *Metropolis: London: Histories and Representations since 1800*, Routledge, 1989, pp. 272–324, presents a detailed survey of the changing fortunes of the cockney in the public imagination.
35. These accounts are taken from testimony gathered by Mass Observation during the Blitz, and included in Harrisson, *Living Through the Blitz*, p. 96.
36. Ibid., pp. 61–3.
37. Ibid., p. 103.
38. Mass Observation, 'Survey of the activities of official and voluntary bodies in the East End, during the intensive bombing, September 7–27, 1940'.
39. Ritchie Calder, 'The war in East London', *New Statesman*, 21 September 1940, cited in ibid., p. 11.
40. The disaster sent shock waves around the community, the reverberations of which are still felt, and to an extent around government circles, particularly when Ritchie Calder used it to expose gross 'official blundering' (Stansky, *The First Day of the Blitz*, p. 112). The official blundering of West Ham Council is skilfully revealed in Doreen Idle, *War Over West Ham*, Faber and Faber, 1943.
41. 'East End at war', *Picture Post*, 28 September 1940, cited in ibid., p. 24.
42. Mack and Humphries, *The Making of Modern London*, p. 79.
43. Quoted in ibid., p. 19.
44. Mass Observation, 'Survey of the activities of official and voluntary bodies', pp. 47–8.

45. Phil Piratin, one of the leaders, describes the episode in *Our Flag Stays Red*, pp. 73–5.
46. Quoted in Stansky, *The First Day of the Blitz*, p. 142.
47. Ibid., p. 143.
48. Mack and Humphries, *The Making of Modern London*, pp. 140–41.
49. Calder, *The Myth of the Blitz*, pp. 39–40. Of these 30,000, West Ham, which experienced 194 raids, had 1,207 fatalities, 0.4 per cent of the 1939 population. To put these figures in some sort of perspective, over 40,000 Germans were killed in the British incendiary attack on Dresden, 13 February 1945, and British Bomber Command lost 55,500 airmen in the course of the war.
50. Ken Young and Patricia Garside, *Metropolitan London: Politics and Urban Change, 1837–1981*, Arnold, 1982, p. 225.
51. W.A. Powell, 'West Ham', *Victoria County History of Essex*, Institute of Historical Research, VI (1973), p. 256.
52. Vera Leff and G.H. Blunden, *The Story of Tower Hamlets*, Research Writers, 1967.

Chapter 12: Postwar decline and the rise of the cosmopolis, 1945–

1. Michael Young and Peter Willmott, *Family and Kinship in East London*, Harmondsworth, Penguin,1962, pp. 89, 91.
2. *The Times*, 18 January 1945.
3. Ibid., 26 July 1945.
4. Ibid., 2 February 1946.
5. Happily, *Neighbourhood 15* is available on the Newham Heritage and Archives Library website, www.newhamstory.com. In plans for reconstruction, the borough was divided into sixteen neighbourhoods, each with a projected population of 10,000. Neighbourhood 15 was the area of Tidal Basin adjacent to Canning Town which was the worst affected by bombing.
6. Bill Riseboro, 'Architecture in East London', in Tim Butler and Michael Rustin (eds), *Rising in the East: Regeneration of East London*, Lawrence and Wishart, 1996, pp. 215–31.
7. Ken Young and Patricia Garside, *Metropolitan London: Politics and Urban Change*, Arnold, 1982, contains a useful overview.
8. Young and Willmott, *Family and Kinship in East London*, pp. 123–4. The figures have been rounded. Note that aggregate levels give no information on the loss of population through other causes, or the extent of inward migration.
9. Ibid., p. 36.
10. Ibid., p. 111.
11. Ibid., p. 127.
12. Ibid., p. 145.
13. Ibid., p. 160.
14. **Population of the Boroughs of Tower Hamlets and Newham, 1951–81**

	1951	1961	1971	1981
Tower Hamlets	230,790	205,682	164,349	139,996
Newham	294,017	265,388	233,699	209,128

Source: Relevant Censuses of Population. For convenience I have used 'Newham' although it was not actually created by a merger between West Ham and East Ham until 1965.

15. For a useful survey of recent work, see Paul Watt, 'Move to a better place? Geographies of aspiration and anxiety in the Thames Gateway', in Philip Cohen and Michael Rustin (eds), *London's Turning: The Making of the Thames Gateway*, Aldershot, Ashgate, 2008, pp. 149–67.
16. See, for example, Peter Fryer, *Staying Power: Black People in Britain since 1504*, Pluto Press, 1981; Rosina Visram, *Asians in Britain: 400 Years of History*, Pluto Press, 2002.

17. White, *London in the Twentieth Century*, Chapter 4, 'The remaking of the Londoner: 1948–99'.
18. Ibid., pp. 130–31.
19. John Seed, 'Limehouse blues: Looking for "Chinatown" in the London docks, 1900–40', *History Workshop Journal*, 62 (2006), pp. 58–85.
20. Michael Banton, *The Coloured Quarter: Negro Immigrants in an English City*, Cape, 1955, p. 18.
21. The whole question of ethnicity at the time is bypassed by Young and Willmott, *Family and Kinship in East London*, and by Millicent Rose's otherwise fine *The East End of London*, Cresset Press, 1951. Even the latest work, dealing specifically with the problem of race, could claim 'immigration was not a significant dimension of East End life in the 1950s' (Geoff Dench, Kate Gavron and Michael Young, *The New East End: Kinship, Race and Conflict*, Profile Books, 2006, p. 18).
22. The work was vividly recalled by Salter himself in J. Salter, *The Asiatic in England; Sketches of Sixteen Years' Work among Orientals*, Seeley, Jackson and Halliday, 1873.
23. Dulip Singh was the son of the last Sikh emperor, Ranjit Singh, on whose death he was enticed to migrate to England with a generous allowance, where he mingled with the aristocracy and became a firm favourite of Victoria.
24. Visram, *Asians in Britain*, pp. 292–4.
25. Banton, *The Coloured Quarter*, p. 77.
26. Phyllis Young, *Report on an Investigation into the Conditions of the Coloured Population in a Stepney Area*, privately published, 1944. The report was commissioned by a committee of 'concerned residents' chaired by the Rev. St J. Groser, Rector of St George-in-the-East.
27. Ibid., p. 17.
28. Cited in Banton, *The Coloured Quarter*, p. 81.
29. *John Bull*, 6 December 1947, cited in ibid., p. 83.
30. Bertha Sokoloff, *Edith and Stepney: The Life of Edith Ramsay*, Stepney Books, 1987, pp. 140–41.
31. Derek Bamuta, 'Report on an investigation into conditions of the coloured people in Stepney', 1949, prepared for the warden of Bernhard Baron Settlement. It was later published anonymously in *Social Work*, January 1950, pp. 387–95. Cited in ibid., p. 84. The classic account of the daily life of a black immigrant in the 1950s is Sam Selvon, *The Lonely Londoners*, Harmondsworth, Penguin, 2006 [1956], while the writings of black Londoners are explored in Sukhdev Sandhu, *London Calling: How Black and Asian Writers Imagined a City*, Harper Collins, 2003.
32. White, *London in the Twentieth Century*, pp. 137–41.
33. Yousuf Choudhury (ed.), *The Roots and Tales of the Bangladeshi Settlers*, 1993, p. 70. Unlike other accounts, Choudhury provides valuable insights into the history of Bengali settlement based on personal experience.
34. Cited in Caroline Adams, *Across Seven Seas and Thirteen Rivers: Life Stories of Pioneer Sylhetti Settlers in Britain*, THAP Books, 1987, p. 41.
35. Ali's brief autobiography is one of many remarkable stories collected in Yousuf Choudhury (ed.), *Sons of the Empire: Oral History from the Bangladeshi Seamen who served on British Ships during the 1939–45 War*, Birmingham, Sylheti Social History Group, 1995.
36. As part of the deal leading to Indian independence in 1947, the subcontinent was partitioned into India and Pakistan. The latter was divided into West Pakistan, located in the Punjab on the north-western edge of the subcontinent, and East Pakistan, the former area of East Bengal at the north-eastern edge. After an independence struggle in 1971, East Pakistan became the People's Republic of Bangladesh.
37. For worthy accounts see Adams, *Across Seven Seas and Thirteen Rivers*, Katy Gardner, *Global Migrants, Local Lives: Travel and Transformation in Rural Bangladesh*, Oxford, Clarendon Press, 1995, and Dench, Gavron and Young, *The New East End*.
38. The data are from the 2001 Census of Population and are also usefully to be found online (www.neighbourhood.statistics.gov.uk). A degree of caution is necessary in

using them. Numbers of foreign-born did not include Bangladeshis born in the UK, so tended to underestimate the Bangladeshi population as a whole. And the Muslim population would have included small numbers from other countries, in particular Somalia.

39. Ansar Ahmed Ullah and John Eversley, *Bengalis in London's East End*, Swadhinata Trust, 2010, provides a brief and nicely illustrated overview.
40. Dench, Gavron and Young, *The New East End: Kinship, Race and Conflict*, 2006. Michael Young died in 2002 and so did not live to see its publication.
41. Ibid., p. 173.
42. Ibid., p. 180.
43. Ibid., p. 87.
44. Ibid., p. 87.
45. John Widdowson and Howard Block, *People Who Moved to Newham*, London Borough of Newham, n.d. This is a pack for teachers containing copies of interesting primary sources.
46. Newham Monitoring Project, *The Forging of a Black Community*, NMP, 1991, p. 16.
47. Ibid., pp. 17–18.
48. Local authority data published by the Office for National Statistics (www.neighbour-hood.statistics.gov.uk). The latest data are estimates.
49. Alice Bloch, 'Refugees in Newham', in Butler and Rustin (eds), *Rising in the East*, pp. 146–69.
50. Vikki Rix, 'Social and demographic change in East London', in Butler and Rustin (eds), *Rising in the East*, pp. 20–60. Note, however, that these aggregate data disguise major variations in racial composition across the boroughs which reflect their historical development. In Newham, for example, the population of the East Ham North Ward comprises white (15 per cent), black (11 per cent) and Asian (69 per cent), compared to that of Canning Town South with white (61 per cent), black (25 per cent) and Asian (7 per cent) (London Borough of Newham, *Joint Strategic Needs Assessment*, LBN, 2009).
51. PP 1940 [Cmnd 6153], *Royal Commission on the Distribution of Industrial Population* [Barlow Commission]; Patrick Abercrombie, *The Greater London Plan 1944*, HMSO, 1945.
52. For the background, see Graham Lomas, 'Labour and life in London', in David Donnison and David Eversley (eds), *London: Urban Patterns, Problems, and Policies*, Heinemann, 1973, pp. 51–85.
53. Canning Town Community, *Canning Town's Declining Community Income: The Cost of Industrial Closures, 1966–76*, Canning Town Community Publications, 1979.
54. Arthur Bryant, *Liquid History: To Commemorate Fifty Years of the Port of London Authority, 1909–1959*, privately published, 1960.
55. Ibid., p. 69.
56. Ibid., p. 66.
57. White, *London in the Twentieth Century*, pp. 204–5.
58. In the following I have relied heavily on Janet Foster's account in *Docklands: Cultures in Conflict, Worlds in Collision*, Routledge, 1999, but see also Bob Colenutt and Jean Lowe, 'Does London need the Docklands Urban Development Corporation? A London debate continued', *London Journal*, 7:2 (1981), pp. 235–8, and M. Hebbert, 'One "planning disaster" after another: London Docklands 1970–1992', *London Journal*, 17:2 (1992), pp. 115–34.
59. R. Travers Morgan and Partners, *Docklands Redevelopment Proposals for East London*, vol. 1, Travers Morgan, 1973, p. i.
60. Cited in Foster, *Docklands*, p. 69.
61. Ibid., p. 103.
62. Ibid., p. 101.
63. Ibid., p. 144.
64. Ibid., p. 179.

65. John Eade and Chris Mele, 'The "Eastern promise" of New York and London', *Rising East*, 1:3 (1998), pp. 52–73.
66. Rix, 'Social and demographic change', pp. 56–8.
67. Gavin Poynter, 'Manufacturing in East London', in Butler and Rustin (eds), *Rising in the East*, pp. 288–315.
68. Government Office for London, *Indices of Deprivation*, 2007.

Epilogue: The promise of regeneration?

1. William Mann, 'One hundred and twenty years of regeneration, from East London to the Thames Gateway', in Cohen and Rustin (eds), *London's Turning*, pp. 31–51. This collection is the most useful overview of the project.
2. Edward Platt, 'The Cockney Siberia', *New Statesman*, 5 March 2010, provides a good survey of the state of play on the eve of the victory of the Conservative Party in the general election, the impact of which on Thames Gateway regeneration will take some time to unfold.
3. Penny Bernstock, 'Homing in on housing', in Cohen and Rustin (eds), *London's Turning*, pp. 169–87.
4. Iain Sinclair, 'The Olympics Scam', *London Review of Books*, 19 June 2008.
5. Gavin Poynter, 'The Olympics: East London's renewal and legacy', in Helen Lenskyj and Stephen Wragg (eds), *A Handbook of Olympic Studies*, Routledge, forthcoming (2011). I am in Dr Poynter's debt for allowing me to see this thoughtful chapter before publication.
6. Gavin Poynter, 'The 2012 Olympic Games and the reshaping of London', in Rob Imrie, Loretta Lees and Mike Raco (eds), *Regenerating London: Governance, Sustainability and Community in a Global City*, Routledge, 2009, and Iain McRury and Gavin Poynter, *London's Olympic Legacy: A 'Thinkpiece' Report prepared for the OECD and Department for Communities and Local Government*, London East Research Institute, University of East London, 2009.
7. Poynter, 'The Olympics'.
8. Patrick Wright, *The River: The Thames in Our Time*, BBC Worldwide, 1999.

Bibliography

(Published in London unless otherwise stated)

Books, Reports and Articles

Abercrombie, Patrick, *The Greater London Plan 1944*, HMSO, 1945
Adams, Caroline, *Across Seven Seas and Thirteen Rivers: Life Stories of Pioneer Sylhetti Settlers in Britain*, THAP Books, 1987
Aleichem, Sholom, *Adventures of Mottel, the Cantor's Son*, Abelard-Schuman, 1958
Ancient Songs and Ballads, written on various subjects and printed between the years 1560 and 1700 … [The Roxburghe Ballads], 1774
Appleby, John, 'Charles Dingley, projector, and his Limehouse sawmill', *London Topographical Record*, XXVII (1995), pp. 179–93
Archenholtz, J. Wm, *A Picture of England*, Dublin, Byrne, 1791
Archer, Thomas, *The Pauper, the Thief and the Convict; Sketches of some of their Homes, Haunts and Habits*, Groombridge, 1865
Argyle, Jesse, 'Silk manufacture', in Charles Booth (ed.), *Life and Labour of the People*, pp. 389–405
Attlee, C.R., 'Labour and the municipal elections', *New Leader*, 13 October 1922
Auerbach, Sascha, *Race, Law and 'The Chinese Puzzle' in Imperial Britain*, New York, Palgrave, 2009
[Bailey, Nathan], *The Antiquities of London and Westminster … by N.B.*, Tracy, 1722
Bailey, Peter, 'Custom, capital and culture in the Victorian music hall', in Robert Storch (ed.), *Popular Culture and Custom in Nineteenth-Century England*, Croom Helm, 1982, pp. 180–208
——, 'Champagne Charlie: Performance and ideology in the music hall swell song', in Bailey (ed.), *Music Hall*
Bailey, Peter (ed.), *Music Hall: The Business of Pleasure*, Milton Keynes, Open University Press, 1986
[Bamuta, Derek], 'Report on an investigation into conditions of the coloured people in Stepney', *Social Work*, January 1950, pp. 387–95
Banbury, Philip, *Shipbuilders of the Thames and Medway*, David and Charles, 1971
Banton, Michael, *The Coloured Quarter: Negro Immigrants in an English City*, Cape, 1955
Barbon, Nicolas, *An Apology for the Builder Or a Discourse Shewing the Cause and Effects of the Increase of Building*, Barbon, 1685
[Barnett, Henrietta], *Canon Barnett: His Life, Work and Friends. By his Wife*, 2 vols, John Murray, 1918
Barnett, Henrietta, *Matters that Matter*, Murray, 1930
Barnett, S. and H., *Making of the Home*, Cassell & Co., 1884
——, *Practicable Socialism*, Longmans, Green & Co., 1888
——, *The Service of God*, Longmans, Green & Co., 1897

——, *Religion and Progress*, Adam & Charles Black, 1907

——, *Towards Social Reform*, Fisher Unwin, 1909

Beames, Thomas, *The Rookeries of London*, Bosworth, 1850

Beer, R., *The Matchgirls' Strike of 1888*, Manchester, National Museum of Labour History, 1979

Beier, A.L. and Roger Finlay, 'The significance of the metropolis', in idem (eds), *London, 1500–1700*, pp. 3–25

Benewick, R.J., *The Fascist Movement in Britain*, Allen Lane, 1972

Benn, Caroline, *Keir Hardie*, Richard Cohen Books, 1997

Bernard, Thomas, 'Excerpt from an account of a charity in Spitalfields for supplying the poor with soup and potatoes', 30 March 1798, in *The Reports of the Society for Bettering the Condition and Increasing the Comforts of the Poor*, vol. 1, Bulmer, 1805

Bernstock, Penny, 'Homing in on housing', in Cohen and Rustin (eds), *London's Turning*, pp. 169–87

Besant, Walter, *East London*, Chatto and Windus, 1901

Bloch, Alice, 'Refugees in Newham', in Butler and Rustin (eds), *Rising in the East*, pp. 146–69

Bloch, Howard, and Graham Hill (eds), *Germans in London*, All Points East, 2000

Blythell, Duncan, *The Sweated Trades: Outwork in Nineteenth-Century Britain*, Batsford, 1978

[Bohun, William], *Privilegia Londini: or, The Laws, Customs and Privileges of the City of London*, Browne, 1702

Booth, Charles, 'Sweating', in idem (ed.), *Life and Labour of the People*

Booth, Charles (ed.), *Life and Labour of the People*, vol. 1, *East London*, Williams and Norgate, 1889

——, *Life and Labour of the People of London*, 17 vols, Macmillan, 1902

Booth, William, *In Darkest England and the Way Out*, Salvation Army, 1890

Branson, Noreen, *Poplarism, 1919–1925: George Lansbury and the Councillors' Revolt*, Lawrence and Wishart, 1979

Bratton, J.S. (ed.), *Music Hall. Performance and Style*, Milton Keynes, Open University Press, 1986

Brett-James, Norman, *The Growth of Stuart London*, Allen & Unwin, 1935

Brodie, Marc, *The Politics of the Poor: The East End of London, 1885–1914*, Oxford, Clarendon Press, 2004

Brown, John, 'Essay on ridicule', *Essays on the Characteristics of the Earl of Shaftesbury*, Davis, 1751

Bryant, Arthur, *Liquid History: To Commemorate Fifty Years of the Port of London Authority, 1909–1959*, privately published, 1960

Burke, Peter, *Popular Culture in Early Modern Europe*, Maurice Temple Smith, 1978

Burrage, Champlin, *The Early English Dissenters in the Light of Recent Historical Research, 1550–1641*, Cambridge, Cambridge University Press, 1912

Bush, Julia, *Behind the Lines: East London Labour, 1914–1919*, Merlin Press, 1984

Butler, Tim, and Michael Rustin (eds), *Rising in the East: The Regeneration of East London*, Lawrence and Wishart, 1996

Calder, Angus, *The Myth of the Blitz*, Cape, 1991

Calder, Ritchie, 'The war in East London', *New Statesman*, 21 September 1940

Calendar of State Papers Domestic, James I, 1616

Canning Town Community, *Canning Town's Declining Community Income: the Cost of Industrial Closures, 1966–76*, Canning Town Community Publications, 1979

Cassels, J.W.S., 'The Spitalfields Mathematical Society', *Bulletin of the London Mathematical Society*, 11 (1979), pp. 241–58

Cesarani, David, 'An embattled minority: The Jews in Britain during the First World War', in Kushner and Lunn (eds), *The Politics of Marginality*, pp. 61–81

Chapman-Huston, Desmond, *Through a City Archway: The Story of Allen & Hanbury's*, Murray, 1954

Chaudhuri, K.N., *The English East India Company: The Study of an Early Joint Stock Company 1600–1640*, Cass, 1965

——, *The Trading World of Asia and the English East India Company, 1660–1760*, Cambridge, Cambridge University Press, 1978

Choudhury, Yousuf (ed.), *The Roots and Tales of the Bangladeshi Settlers*, Birmingham, privately published, 1993

——, *Sons of the Empire: Oral History from the Bangladeshi Seamen who served on British Ships during the 1939–45 War*, Birmingham, Sylheti Social History Group, 1995

Clapham, John, 'The Spitalfields Act, 1773–1824', *Economic Journal*, XXVI (1916)

Clegg, H.A., A. Fox and A.F. Thompson, *A History of British Trade Unions. I. 1889–1910*, Oxford, Oxford University Press, 1964

Cohen, Phil, 'A history of disillusionment: The Becontree Estate', *Rising East*, 3:1 (1999), pp. 107–21

Cohen, Philip, and Michael Rustin (eds), *London's Turning: The Making of the Thames Gateway*, Aldershot, Ashgate, 2008

Cole, G.D.H. and M.I., *The Condition of Britain*, Victor Gollancz, 1937

Colenutt, Bob, and Jean Lowe, 'Does London need the Docklands Urban Development Corporation? A London debate continued', *London Journal*, 7:2 (1981), pp. 235–8

[Colquhoun, Patrick], *A Treatise on the Police of the Metropolis, explaining the Various Crimes … which are Felt as Pressure upon the Community, and Suggesting Remedies for their Prevention. By a Magistrate*, Fry, 1795

Colquhoun, Patrick, *A Treatise on the Commerce and Police of the River Thames*, Mawman, 1800

Conway, Hazel, *People's Parks: The Design and Development of Victorian Parks in Britain*, Cambridge, Cambridge University Press, 1991

Council of the Citizens of East London, *Our East London*, Schools Committee of the Council, 1951

Cruickshank, Dan, *The Secret History of Georgian London*, Windmill, 2010

Davies, H.O., *'The Way Out': A Letter Addressed (by permission) to the Earl of Derby in which the Evils of the Overcrowded Town Hovel and the Advantages of the Suburban Cottage are Constrained*, Longman Green, 1861

Davis, Jim, and Victor Emeljanow, *Reflecting the Audience: London Theatregoing, 1840–1880*, Hatfield, University of Hertfordshire Press, 2001

Davis, John, 'Slums and the vote, 1867–1890', *Historical Research*, 65 (1991), pp. 375–88

Davis, John, and Duncan Tanner, 'The borough franchise after 1867', *Historical Research*, 69 (1996), pp. 306–27

Deakin, Nicholas, 'The vitality of a tradition', in Colin Holmes (ed.), *Immigrants and Minorities in British Society*, Allen & Unwin, 1978, pp. 158–85

Defoe, Daniel, *A Journal of the Plague Year*, Harlow, Longman, 1984 [1665]

Dekker, Thomas, *The VVonderfull Yeare. Wherein is shewed the picture of* London, *lying sicke of the Plague*, Creede, 1603, in Wilson (ed.), *The Plague Pamphlets of Thomas Dekker*

Dench, Geoff, Kate Gavron and Michael Young, *The New East End: Kinship, Race and Conflict*, Profile Books, 2006

Diary and Correspondence of Samuel Pepys, New York, Dodd, Mead & Co., 1885

Dimont, Charles, 'Going to the dogs', *New Statesman*, 30 November 1946

Distilled Spirituous Liquors the Bane of the Nation, Roberts, 1736

Downs, Thomas, 'The Stepney Fair', and 'Maritime Stepney' in Locks (ed.), *East London Antiquities*

D'Sena, Peter, 'Perquisites and casual labour on the London wharfside in the eighteenth century', *London Journal*, 14:2 (1989), pp. 131–47

Dunn, Richard, 'The London weavers' riots of 1675', *Guildhall Studies in London History*, 1:1 (1973), pp. 13–23

Eade, John, and Chris Mele, 'The "eastern promise" of New York and London', *Rising East*, 1:3 (1998), pp. 52–73

Earle, Peter, *The Making of the English Middle Class: Business, Society and Family Life in London, 1660–1730*, Methuen, 1989

East London History Group, 'The population of Stepney in the early seventeenth century', *East London Papers*, 11:2 (1968)

Egan, Pierce, *Boxiana; or, Sketches of Ancient and Modern Pugilism*, Smeeton, 1812

——, *Life in London, or, The Day and Night Scenes of Jerry Hawthorn, Esq. And his Elegant Friend Corinthian Tom, accompanied by Bob Logic, the Oxonian, in their Rambles and Sprees through the Metropolis*, Sherwood, Neely & Jones, 1821

Elliott, Geoffrey, *The Mystery of Overend & Gurney: A Financial Scandal in Victorian London*, Methuen, 2006

Engels, Friedrich, *The Condition of the Working Class in England in 1844*, Cosimo Classics, 2007 [1845]

Englander, David (ed.), *A Documentary History of Jewish Immigrants in Britain, 1840–1920*, Leicester, Leicester University Press, 1994

Englander, David, and Rosemary O'Day (eds), *Retrieved Riches: Social Investigation on Britain, 1880–1914*, Scolar, 1995

Evelyn, John, *Fumifugium*, Exeter, University of Exeter Press, 1976 [1661]

Fagan, Hymie, 'An autobiography', Brunel University Library, cited in Rose, *The Intellectual Life of the British Working Classes*

Fair in Spittlefields, 1658

Fayle, J., *The Spitalfields Genius: The Story of William Allen*, Hodder & Stoughton, 1884

Fein, Albert, 'Victoria Park: Its origin and history', *East London Papers*, 5:2 (1962), pp. 73–90

Feldman, David, *Englishmen and Jews: Social Relations and Political Culture, 1840–1914*, New Haven, Yale University Press, 1994

Feldman, David, and Gareth Stedman Jones (eds), *Metropolis: London: Histories and Representations since 1800*, Routledge, 1989

Fielding, Henry, *An Inquiry into the Causes of the Late Encrease of Robbers and Related Writings*, ed. M.R. Zirker, Oxford, Oxford University Press, 1988 [1751]

Fielding, John, *A Brief Description of the Cities of London and Westminster*, Wilkie, 1776

Finlay, Roger, *Population and Metropolis: The Demography of London, 1580–1650*, Cambridge, Cambridge University Press, 1981

Finlay, Roger, and Beatrice Shearer, 'Population growth and suburban expansion', in A.L. Beier and Roger Finlay (eds), *London 1500–1700: The Making of the Metropolis*, Longman, 1986, pp. 37–59

Fishman, William, *East End Jewish Radicals, 1875–1914*, Duckworth, 1975

——, *East End 1888*, Duckworth, 1988

Flinn, M.W., *Men of Iron: The Crowleys in the Early Iron Industry*, Edinburgh, Edinburgh University Press, 1962

Foakes, Grace, *My Life with Reuben*, Shepheard-Walwyn, 1975

Forbes, Bryan, *Notes for a Life*, Collins, 1974

The Foreigner's Guide: or, a Necessary and Instructive Companion both for the Foreigner and the Native, in their tour through the Cities of London and Westminster, Kent, Hope and Joliffe, 1763

Foster, Janet, *Docklands: Cultures in Conflict, Worlds in Collision*, Routledge, 1999

Foster, William, *East London*, The Historical Association, 1935

——, *John Company*, Bodley Head, 1926

Foxe, John, *Acts and Monuments* (ed.), Josiah Pratt, Religious Tract Society, 1877.

Fryer, Peter, *Staying Power: Black People in Britain since 1504*, Pluto Press, 1981

Fuller, J.F.C., *The Reformation of War*, Hutchinson, 1923

Gagnier, Regina, *Subjectivities: A History of Self-Representation in Britain, 1832–1920*, Oxford, Oxford University Press, 1991

Gainer, Bernard, *The Alien Invasion: The Origins of the Aliens Act of 1905*, Heinemann, 1972

Galli, Antima, 'Letters from a Florentine correspondent', cited in Gurr, *Playgoing in Shakespeare's London*, p. 106

Gardner, Katy, *Global Migrants, Local Lives: Travel and Transformation in Rural Bangladesh*, Oxford, Clarendon Press, 1995

Garland, T.C., *Leaves from my Log of Twenty-five Years' Christian Work among Sailors and others in the Port of London*, Woolmer, 1882

Gartner, Lloyd P., *The Jewish Immigrant in England, 1870–1914*, Allen & Unwin, 1960

Garwood, John, *The Million Peopled City; or, One Half of the People of London made known to the Other Half*, Wertheim and Macintosh, 1853

Gatrell, Vic, *City of Laughter: Sex and Satire in Eighteenth-century London*, Atlantic, 2006

Gavin, Hector, *Sanitary Ramblings, being Sketches and Illustrations of Bethnal Green*, Cass, 1971 [1848]

George, M. Dorothy, *London Life in the Eighteenth Century*, Harmondsworth, Penguin, 1965 [1925]

Gillespie, James, 'Poplarism and proletarianism: Unemployment and labour politics in London, 1918–34', in Feldman and Stedman Jones (eds), *Metropolis: London*, pp. 163–88

Godley, Andrew, 'Immigrant entrepreneurs and the emergence of London's East End as an industrial district', *London Journal*, 21:1 (1996), pp. 38–45

Goodway, David, *London Chartism, 1838–1848*, Cambridge, Cambridge University Press, 1982

Government Office for London, *Indices of Deprivation*, 2007

Grade, Lew, *Still Dancing*, Collins, 1997

Grafton, Richard, *Grafton's Chronicles, or, History of England. From the Year 1189 to 1558*, 2 vols, Johnson, 1809 [1569]

Grant, Clara, *Farthing Bundles*, privately published, 1929

Grant, James, *Sketches in London*, Orr, 1838

——, *Lights and Shadows of London Life*, Saunders and Otley, 1841

Graunt, John, *Natural and Political Observations … made upon the Bills of Mortality*, Royal Society, 1676, repr. Charles Hull (ed.), *The Economic Writings of Sir William Petty*, Thoemmes Press, 1997 [1899]

Graves, Robert, and Alan Hodge, *The Long Weekend: A Social History of Great Britain, 1918–1939*, Hutchinson, 1985 [1940]

Greenwood, James, *The Wilds of London*, Chatto and Windus, 1874

——, *The Amateur Casual*, Diprose and Bateman, 1877

Gurr, Andrew, *Playgoing in Shakespeare's London*, Cambridge, Cambridge University Press, 1987

Haddon, Rev. R.H., *An East End Chronicle*, Hatchard, 1880

Hall, Peter, *The Industries of London Since 1861*, Hutchinson, 1962

Hannington, Wal, *Unemployed Struggles, 1919–1936*, Lawrence and Wishart, 1977 [1936]

——, *The Problem of the Distressed Areas*, Victor Gollancz, 1937

Harriott, John, *Struggles through Life*, Longman, 1813

Harrison, Barbara, 'Women's work and health in the East End, 1880–1914', *Rising East*, 2:3 (1999), pp. 20–46

Harrison, Brian, 'Pubs', in H.J. Dyos and Michael Wolf (eds), *The Victorian City: Images and Realities*, vol. I, *Past and Present/Numbers of People*, Routledge and Kegan Paul, 1973, pp. 161–90

Harrisson, Tom, *Living Through the Blitz*, Harmondsworth, Penguin, 1978

Head, Richard, *The English Rogue Described, in the Life of Meriton Latroon; a Witty Extravagant, Comprehending the Most Eminent Cheats of Both Sexes*, Marsh, 1665

Hebbert, M., 'One "planning disaster" after another: London Docklands 1970–1992', *London Journal*, 17:2, pp. 115–34

Hempel, Sandra, *The Medical Detective: John Snow and the Mystery of Cholera*, Granta, 2006

Higgins, Robert, 'The 1832 cholera epidemic in East London', *East London Record*, 2, 1979

Hill, G.W., and W.H. Frere (eds), *Memorials of Stepney Parish, that is to say, the Vestry Minutes from 1579 to 1662*, Guildford, privately published, 1890–91

Hill, Graham, and Howard Bloch (eds), *The Silvertown Explosion: London 1917*, Stroud, Tempus, 2003

Hitchcock, Tim, and Heather Shore (eds), *The Streets of London: From the Great Fire to the Great Stink*, Rivers Oram, 2003

Hobbs, Dick, *Doing the Business: Entrepreneurship, the Working Class, and Detectives in the East End of London*, Oxford, Oxford University Press, 1989

Hobsbawm, E.J., 'The British standard of living', in idem, *Labouring Men: Studies in the History of Labour*, Weidenfeld and Nicolson, 1968, pp. 64–104

——, *Primitive Rebels: Studies in Archaic Forms of Social Movement in the 19th and 20th Centuries*, Manchester, Manchester University Press, 1959

——, *Age of Extremes: The Short Twentieth Century, 1914–1991*, Michael Joseph, 1994

Hodgkinson, Ruth G., *The Origins of the National Health Service: The Medical Services of the New Poor Law, 1834–1871*, Wellcome Historical Medical Library, 1967

Höher, Dagmar, 'The composition of music hall audiences, 1850–1900', in Bailey (ed.), *Music Hall*, p. 76

Hollingshead, John, *Ragged in London in 1861*, Smith, Elder and Co., 1861

Holmes, Colin, 'Anti-semitism and the BUF', in Lunn and Thurlow (eds), *British Fascism*, pp. 114–34

Holt, Richard, *Sport and the British: A Modern History*, Oxford, Clarendon Press, 1989

Hughes, Paul, and James Larkin (eds), *Tudor Royal Proclamations*, 3 vols, New Haven, Yale University Press, 1964–9

Hugill, A., *Sugar and All That: A History of Tate and Lyle*, Gentry Books, 1978

Humpherys, Anne, *Travels into the Poor Man's Country: The Work of Henry Mayhew*, Maryland, University of Georgia Press, 1977

Hylton, Stuart, *Their Darkest Hour: The Hidden History of the Home Front, 1939–1945*, Stroud, Sutton, 2001

Idle, Doreen, *War Over West Ham*, Faber and Faber, 1943

Jacobs, Joe, *Out of the Ghetto: My Youth in the East End, Communism and Fascism, 1913–39*, Simon, 1978

Jeaffreson, John (ed.), *Middlesex County Records*, 2 vols, Greater London Council, 1972 [1886]

Jephson, Henry, *The Sanitary Evolution of London*, Unwin, 1907

Kalman, Raymond, 'The Jewish East End – where was it?', in Newman (ed.), *The Jewish East End*, pp. 3–16

Kay, James, *The Moral and Physical Condition of the Working Class Employed in the Cotton Manufacture of Manchester*, Ridgway, 1832

Kerrigan, Colm, *Teachers and Football: The Origins, Development and Influence of Schoolboy Football Associations in London, 1885–1918*, Routledge, 2004

Kift, Dagmar, *The Victorian Music Hall: Culture, Class and Conflict*, Cambridge, Cambridge University Press, 1996

Knapp, John M. (ed.), *The Universities and the Social Problem: An Account of the University Settlements in East London*, Rivington, Percival & Co., 1895

Knight, Charles (ed.), *London*, 6 vols, Knight, 1841–2

Koven, Seth, *Slumming: Sexual and Social Politics in Victorian London*, Princeton, Princeton University Press, 2004

Kushner, Tony, and Kenneth Lunn (eds), *The Politics of Marginality: Race, the Radical Right and Minorities in Twentieth-Century Britain*, Frank Cass, 1990

Kynaston, David, *The City of London*. Vol. 1: *A World of its Own, 1815–1890*, Chatto and Windus, 1994

Lansbury, George, 'Foreword' to C.W. Key, *Red Poplar: Six Years of Socialist Rule*, Labour Publishing, 1925

Larkin, James, and Paul Hughes (eds), *Stuart Royal Proclamations*, 2 vols, Oxford, Clarendon Press, 1973–83

Lax of Poplar: The Story of a Wonderful Quarter of a Century, told by Himself, Epworth Press, 1927

'Leaves from the life of a "poor Londoner"', *Good Words*, 1885

Leff, Vera, and G.H. Blunden, *The Story of Tower Hamlets*, Research Writers, 1967

Lewis, Samuel (ed.), *A Topographical Dictionary of England*, Lewis, 1848

Life of William Allen, with Selections from his Correspondence, 3 vols, Gilpin, 1846

Linebaugh, Peter, *The London Hanged: Crime and Civil Society in the Eighteenth Century*, Allen Lane, 2001

Linebaugh, Peter, and Marcus Rediker, *The Many-Headed Hydra: The Hidden History of the Revolutionary Atlantic*, Verso, 2000

Linehan, Thomas, *East London for Mosley: The British Union of Fascists in East London and South West Essex, 1933–40*, Frank Cass, 1996

——, *British Fascism, 1918–1939: Parties, Ideology and Culture*, Manchester, Manchester University Press, 2000

Lithgow, William, *The Present Surveigh of London … with the several Fortifications thereof*, printed by J.O., 1643

Llewellyn Smith, H., *New Survey of London Life and Labour*, 9 vols, P.S. King & Son, 1930–35

Llewellyn Smith, H., 'Influx of population', in Charles Booth (ed.), *Life and Labour of the People*, pp. 521–63

Llewellyn Smith, H., and V. Nash, *The Story of the Dockers' Strike, told by Two East Londoners*, Fisher Unwin, 1889

Locks, Walter (ed.), *East London Antiquities*, East London Advertiser, 1902

Lomas, Graham, 'Labour and life in London', in David Donnison and David Eversley (eds), *London: Urban Patterns, Problems, and Policies*, Heinemann, 1973, pp. 51–85

London as it is Today: Where to go, and what to see, during the Great Exhibition, H.G. Clarke, 1851

London Borough of Newham, *Joint Strategic Needs Assessment*, LBN, 2009

London, Jack, *The People of the Abyss*, Pluto Press, 2001 [1903]

Lovell, John, *Stevedores and Dockers: A Study of Trade Unionism in the Port of London, 1870–1914*, Macmillan, 1969

Lunn, Kenneth and Richard C. Thurlow (eds), *British Fascism: Essays on the Radical Right in Interwar Britain*, Croom Helm, 1980

Lysons, Daniel, *Environs of London, being an Historical Account of the Towns, Villages, and Hamlets within Twelve Miles of that Capital*, 1795

McCullough, J.R. (ed.), *Early English Tracts on Commerce*, Cambridge, Cambridge University Press, 1954 [1856]

McKellar, Elizabeth, *The Birth of Modern London: The Development and Design of the City, 1660–1720*, Manchester, Manchester University Press, 1999

McKibbin, Ross, *The Evolution of the Labour Party, 1910–24*, Oxford, Oxford University Press, 1974

——, *Classes and Cultures: England 1918–1951*, Oxford, Oxford University Press, 1998

McRury, Iain, and Gavin Poynter, *London's Olympic Legacy: A 'Thinkpiece' Report prepared for the OECD and Department for Communities and Local Government*, London East Research Institute, University of East London, 2009

Mack, Joanna, and Steve Humphries, *The Making of Modern London, 1939–1945: London at War*, Sidgwick and Jackson, 1985

A Magistrate [Patrick Colquhoun], *An Account of a Meat and Soup Charity in the Metropolis*, Fry, 1797

Maitland, William, *The History of London from its Foundation to the Present Time*, revised by John Entick: 'A continuation … bringing the history to the present time and describing the vast improvements made in every part of this great metropolis', 2 vols, Wilkie, Lowndes, Kearsley and Bladon, 1772

Manchee, W.H., 'Memories of Spitalfields', *Proceedings of the Huguenot Society of London*, X:1 (1912), pp. 298–345

——, 'Wheler's Chapel, St. Mary's, Spital Square', *Proceedings of the Huguenot Society of London*, X:1 (1912), pp. 55–61

Mander, David, *More Light, More Power: An Illustrated History of Shoreditch*, Sutton, 1996

Mann, William, 'One hundred and twenty years of regeneration, from East London to the Thames Gateway', in Cohen and Rustin (eds), *London's Turning*, pp. 31–51

Marriott, John, '"West Ham: London's industrial centre and gateway to the World". I. Industrialisation, 1840–1910', *London Journal*, 13:2 (1988), pp. 121–42

——, '"West Ham: London's industrial centre and gateway to the world", II: Stabilization and decline, 1910–1939', *London Journal*, 14:1 (1989), pp. 43–58

——, *The Culture of Labourism: The East End between the Wars*, Edinburgh, Edinburgh University Press, 1991

——, 'Sensation of the abyss: The urban poor and modernity', in Nava and O'Shea (eds), *Modern Times*, pp. 77–100

——, 'The political modernism of East London', in Butler and Rustin (eds), *Rising in the East*, pp. 108–22

——, 'The spatiality of the poor in eighteenth-century London', in Hitchcock and Shore (eds), *The Streets of London*, pp. 119–34

——, 'Policing the poor: Social inquiry and the discovery of the residuum', *Rising East*, 3:1 (1999), pp. 23–47

——, *The Other Empire: Metropolis, India and Progress in the Colonial Imagination*, Manchester, Manchester University Press, 2003

——, 'Smokestack: The industrial history of Thames Gateway', in Cohen and Rustin (eds), *London's Turning*, pp. 17–30

——, 'The imaginative geography of Whitechapel murders', in Werner (ed.), *Jack the Ripper and the East End*, pp. 31–63

Marriott, John (ed.), *Unknown London: Early Modernist Visions of the Metropolis, 1815–45*, 6 vols, Pickering & Chatto, 2000

Marriott, John, and Masaie Matsumura (eds), *The Metropolitan Poor: Semi-factual Accounts, 1795–1910*, 6 vols, Pickering & Chatto, 1999

Mass Observation, 'Survey of the activities of official and voluntary bodies in the East End, during the intensive bombing, September 7–27, 1940'

Masterman, Charles, *From the Abyss; of its Inhabitants by One of Them*, Johnson, 1902

Masterman, Charles (ed.), *The Heart of the Empire: Discussion of Problems of Modern City Life in England*, Fisher Unwin, 1901

Mayall, David, 'Rescued from the shadows of exile: Nellie Driver, autobiography and the British Union of Fascists', in Kushner and Lunn (eds), *The Politics of Marginality*, pp. 19–39

Mayhew, Henry, *London Labour and the London Poor*, 4 vols, Cass, 1967 [1861]

Mead, Matthew, *Good of Early Deliverance*, Ponder, 1683

[Mearns, Andrew], *The Bitter Cry of Outcast London: An Inquiry into the Condition of the Abject Poor*, London City Mission, 1883

'Metropolitan improvements', *Westminster Review*, XXXVI (1841)

Meyrick, F., *The Outcast and the Poor of London*, Rivingtons, 1858

Mills, Mary, *The Early East London Gas Industry and its Waste Products*, M. Wright, 1999

Morley, Henry, 'Londoners over the border', *Household Words*, 12 September 1857

——, *Memoirs of Bartholomew Fair*, Chapman and Hall, 1859

Morris, Corbyn, *Observations on the Past Growth and Present State of the City of London*, privately published, 1751

Morris, Derek, *Mile End Old Town, 1740–1780: A Social History of an Early Modern London Suburb*, East London History Society, 2002

Morris, Derek, and Ken Cozens, *Wapping, 1600–1800: A Social History of an Early Modern London Maritime Suburb*, East London History Society, 2009

Morrison, Arthur, *Child of the Jago*, Everyman, 1996 [1896]

Morton, James, *Gangland: London's Underworld*, Little, Brown & Co., 1992

——, *East End Gangland*, Little, Brown & Co., 2000

——, *Gangland: The Early Years*, Time Warner, 2003

Moss, G.P., and M.V. Saville, *From Palace to College: An Illustrated History of Queen Mary College*, Queen Mary College, 1985

Mullens, Joseph, 'London Irreligion and Heathenism at Home', London and Calcutta, compared in their Heathenism, their Privileges and their Prospects, Nisbet, 1869

Munby, D.L., Industry and Planning in Stepney, Oxford, Oxford University Press, 1951

Nava, M., and O'Shea, A. (eds), Modern Times: Reflections on a Century of English Modernity, Routledge, 1996

Newham Monitoring Project, The Forging of a Black Community, NMP, 1991

Newman, Aubrey, 'The synagogues of the East End', in idem (ed.), The Jewish East End, pp. 217–21

Newman, Aubrey (ed.), The Jewish East End, 1840–1939, Jewish Historical Society of England, 1981

Nixon, E., 'A Whitechapel street', English Illustrated Magazine, February 1890

Ogborn, Miles, Spaces of Modernity: London's Geographies, 1680–1780, New York, Gildford, 1998

Olechnowicz, A., Working-Class Housing in England between the Wars: The Becontree Estate, Oxford, Clarendon Press, 1997

Overall, W.H. and H.C. (eds), 'Plays and Players', Analytical Index to the Series of Records known as the Remembrancia: 1579–1664, Francis, 1878

Palmer, Alan, The East End: Four Centuries of London Life, Murray, 1989

Palmer, Sarah, 'Port economics in an historical context: The nineteenth-century port of London', International Journal of Maritime History, XV:1 (2003)

Panayi, Panikos, The Enemy in our Midst: Germans in Britain during the First World War, Berg, 1991

Pankhurst, E. Sylvia, The Home Front: A Mirror to Life in England during the First World War, Cresset Library, 1987 [1932]

Parker, T.M., The English Reformation to 1558, Oxford, Oxford University Press, 1966

Pattison, George, 'The East India Dock Company, 1803–1838', East London Papers, 7:1 (1964)

Pearl, Valerie, London and the Outbreak of the Puritan Revolution, Oxford, Oxford University Press, 1961

Pearson, John, The Profession of Violence: The Rise and Fall of the Kray Twins, Grafton, 1990

Pelling, Margaret, Cholera, Fever and English Medicine, 1825–1865, Oxford, Oxford University Press, 1978

Pennant, Thomas, London, Faulder, 1790

Pettegree, Andrew, Foreign Protestant Communities in Sixteenth-Century London, Oxford, Clarendon Press, 1986

Petty, Sir William, Taxes and Contributions, Brooke, 1662, repr. Charles Hull (ed.), The Economic Writings of Sir William Petty, Thoemmes Press, 1997 [1899]

Phillips, Watts, The Wild Tribes of London, Ward, 1855

Piratin, Phil, Our Flag Stays Red, Lawrence and Wishart, 1978 [1948]

Platt, Edward, 'The Cockney Siberia', New Statesman, 5 March 2010

Plummer, Alfred, The London Weavers' Company, 1600–1970, Routledge & Kegan Paul, 1972

Pollard, Sidney, 'The decline of shipbuilding on the Thames', Economic History Review, III:1 (1950)

Pollins, Harry, 'East End working men's clubs affiliated to the Working Men's Clubs and Institute Union, 1870–1914', in Newman (ed.), The Jewish East End, pp. 173–92

Porter, G.R., Treatise on the Silk Manufacture, Rees, Orme, Brown and Green, 1831

Porter, Roy, London: A Social History, Hamish Hamilton, 1994

Porter, Stephen (ed.), Survey of London, vols 43 and 44, Poplar, Blackwall and the Isle of Dogs, Athlone Press, 1994

'The possibilities of cinema', Mansfield House Magazine, 27, 1921

Potter, Beatrice, 'The docks', in Booth (ed.), Life and Labour of the People

—, 'The Jewish community', in Booth (ed.), Life and Labour of the People

—, 'The tailoring trade', in Booth (ed.), Life and Labour of the People

Poulsen, Charles, Victoria Park: A study in the History of East London, Journeyman Press and Stepney Books, 1976

Poussin, Father, *Pretty Doings in a Protestant Nation*, Roberts, 1734

Powell, W.R., 'West Ham', *Victoria County History of Essex*, Institute of Historical Research, VI (1973)

Power, Michael, 'The East and the West in Early-Modern London', in E.W. Ives, R.J. Knecht and J.J. Scarisbrick (eds), *Wealth and Power in Tudor England*, Athlone Press, 1978, pp. 167–85

——, 'The development of a London suburban community in the seventeenth century', *London Journal*, 4:1 (1978), pp. 29–46

Poynter, Gavin, 'Manufacturing in East London', in Butler and Rustin (eds), *Rising in the East*, pp. 288–315

——, 'The 2012 Olympic Games and the reshaping of London', in Rob Imrie, Loretta Lees and Mike Raco (eds), *Regenerating London: Governance, Sustainability and Community in a Global City*, Routledge, 2009

——, 'The Olympics: East London's renewal and legacy', in Helen Lenskyj and Stephen Wragg (eds), *A Handbook of Olympic Studies*, Routledge, forthcoming (2011)

Proceedings of the Old Bailey

Proposals for Establishing a Charitable Fund for the City of London, privately published, 1706

Prothero, Iorwerth, *Artisans and Politics in early Nineteenth-Century London: John Gast and his Times*, Folkestone, Dawson, 1979

Pugh, John, *Remarkable Occurrences in the Life of Jonas Hanway*, Payne, 1787

Radford, Peter, 'The time a land forgot', *The Observer*, 2 May 2004

Reed, Stanley, 'Notes on a working life', unpublished manuscript, n.d.

Report of the Committee Appointed by the Right Honourable the Secretary of State for the Home Department to Inquire into the Cause of the Explosion which occurred on Friday 19 January 1917, at the Chemical Works of Messrs. Brunner, Mond and Company, Crescent Wharf, Silvertown in the County of Essex

Report of the Committee of the Spitalfields Soup Society, 1811–12, 1813

'Report of the Lancet Special Sanitary Commission on the Polish colony of Jew tailors', *The Lancet*, 3 May 1884

Richardson, J., *Recollections of the Last Half Century*, Mitchell, 1856

Rix, Vikki, 'Social and demographic change in East London', in Butler and Rustin (eds), *Rising in the East*, pp. 20–60

Rogers, Nicolas, 'Popular disaffection in London during the Forty-Five', *London Journal*, 1:1 (May 1975), pp. 5–27

Rose, Jonathan, *The Intellectual Life of the British Working Classes*, New Haven, Yale University Press, 2001

Rose, Millicent, *The East End of London*, Cresset Press, 1951

Rosebury, A., 'Jewish friendly societies: a critical survey', *Jewish Chronicle*, 8 September 1905

Rowe, D.J., 'Chartism and the Spitalfields silk weavers', *Economic History Review*, 20:3 (1967), pp. 482–93

Rowse, A.L., *The Elizabethan Renaissance: The Cultural Achievement*, Macmillan, 1972

Rudé, George, *Wilkes & Liberty: A Social Study of 1763 to 1774*, Oxford, Clarendon Press, 1962

——, *Hanoverian London, 1714–1808*, Secker & Warburg, 1971

Russell, Bertrand, *Which Way to Peace?*, Michael Joseph, 1936

Russell, C., and H. Lewis, *The Jew in London: A Study of Racial Character and Present-day Conditions*, Fisher Unwin, 1900

Sala, George, *Gaslight and Daylight, with some London Scenes they Shine Upon*, Chapman and Hall, 1859

Salter, Joseph, *The Asiatic in England; Sketches of Sixteen Years' Work among Orientals*, Seeley, Jackson and Halliday, 1873

Samuel, Raphael, *East End Underworld: Chapters in the Life of Arthur Harding*, Routledge & Kegan Paul, 1981

Sandhu, Sukhdev, *London Calling: How Black and Asian Writers Imagined a City*, Harper Collins, 2003

Schmiechen, James, *Sweated Industries and Sweated Labor: The London Clothing Trades, 1860–1914*, Croom Helm, 1984

Schwarz, L.D., 'Occupations and incomes in late eighteenth-century East London', *East London Papers*, 14:2 (1972), pp. 87–100

——, *London in the Age of Industrialisation: Entrepreneurs, Labour Force and Living Conditions, 1700–1850*, Cambridge, Cambridge University Press, 1992

Searle, Chris (ed.), *Bricklight: Poems from the Labour Movement in East London*, Pluto Press, 1980

Seebohm Rowntree, R., and G.R. Lavers, *English Life and Leisure: A Social Study*, Longmans, Green & Co., 1951

Seed, John, 'Limehouse blues: Looking for "Chinatown" in the London docks, 1900–40', *History Workshop Journal*, 62 (2006), pp. 58–85

Selvon, Sam, *The Lonely Londoners*, Harmondsworth, Penguin, 2006 [1956]

Shannon, H.A., 'Migration and the growth of London, 1841–91: A statistical note', *Economic History Review*, 5:2 (1935), pp. 79–86

Shepherd, M.A., 'How Petticoat Lane became a Jewish market', in Newman (ed.), *The Jewish East End*, pp. 125–31

Shepherd, Thomas and James Elmes, *Metropolitan Improvements; or, London in the Nineteenth Century: Being a series of Views of the New and Most Interesting Objects in the British Metropoli and its Vicinity*, Jones, 1827

Sheppard, Francis, *London: A History*, Oxford, Oxford University Press, 1998

Shipley, Stan, *Bombardier Billy Wells: The Life and Times of a Hero*, Tyne and Wear, Bewick Press, 1993

Sims, George, *How the Poor Live, and Horrible London*, Chatto and Windus, 1889

——, 'Human London, II: Behind the scenes in Stepney', *London Magazine*, November (1907)

Sinclair, Iain, 'The Olympics scam', *London Review of Books*, 19 June 2008

Sinclair, Robert, *East London: The East and North-east Boroughs of London and Greater London*, Hale, 1950

Smith, Joanna, and Ray Rogers, *Behind the Veneer: The South Shoreditch Furniture Trade and its Buildings*, English Heritage, 2006

Smith, R., *Sea Coal for London: History of the Coal Factors in the London Market*, Longman, 1961

Sokoloff, Bertha, *Edith and Stepney: The Life of Edith Ramsay*, Stepney Books, 1987

Southwood Smith, Thomas, *Treatise on Fever*, Longman Rees, 1830

Speech of T.F. Buxton Esq. at the Egyptian Hall, 16 November 1816 on the Subject of the Distress in Spitalfields, Phillips, 1816

Spranger, John, *A Proposal or Plan for an Act of Parliament for the Better Paving, Cleansing, and Lighting of the Streets, Lanes, Courts and Alleys … Within the Several Parishes of the City and Liberty of Westminster*, privately published, 1754

Stafford, A., *A Match to Fire the Thames*, Hodder and Stoughton, 1961

Stansky, Peter, *The First Day of the Blitz, September 7th, 1940*, New Haven, Yale University Press, 2007

Stebunheath, otherwise Stepney Manor, Bradbury, Agnew, 1894

Stedman Jones, Gareth, *Outcast London: A Study of the Relations between Classes in Victorian Society*, Oxford, Clarendon Press, 1971

——, 'Working-class culture and working-class politics in London, 1870–1900: Notes on the remaking of a working class', reproduced in idem, *Languages of Class*, Cambridge, Cambridge University Press, 1983, pp. 179–238

——, 'The "cockney" and the nation, 1780–1988', in Feldman and Stedman Jones (eds), *Metropolis: London*, pp. 272–324

Steedman, Carolyn, 'The watercress seller', *Past Tenses*, Rivers Oram, 1992

Stewart, L., and P. Weindling, 'Philosophical threads: Natural philosophy and public experiment among the weavers of Spitalfields', *British Journal of the History of Science*, 28:1 (1995), pp. 37–62

Stow, John, *A Survey of London*, edited by C.L. Kingsford and reprinted from the text of 1603, Oxford, Clarendon Press, 1908

[Strype, John], *A Survey of the Cities of London and Westminster and the Borough of Southwark … Written at first in the Year 1698* [sic] *by John Stow, Citizen and Native of London, corrected, improved and very much enlarged, in the year 1720 by John Strype, a Native also of the Said City*, Innys, Richardson et al., 1754

Survey of London, vol. 27, *Spitalfields and Mile End New Town*, Athlone Press, 1957; vols 43 and 44, *Poplar, Blackwall and the Isle of Dogs*, Athlone Press, 1994

T.M. [Thomas Mun], *A Discovrse of Trade, from England unto the East-indies; answering the Diuerse Obiections which are vsually made against the same*, Pyper, 1621

Taithe, Bernard, *The Essential Henry Mayhew: Representing and Communicating the Poor*, Rivers Oram, 1996

Tanner, Duncan, *Political Change and the Labour Party, 1900–1918*, Cambridge, Cambridge University Press, 1990

Thompson, Dorothy (ed.), *The Early Chartists*, Macmillan, 1971

Thompson, E.P., *The Making of the English Working Class*, Harmondsworth, Penguin, 1980 [1963]

Thompson, E.P., and Eileen Yeo (eds), *The Unknown Mayhew: Selections from the* Morning Chronicle *1849–50*, Harmondsworth, Penguin, 1984

Thompson, Paul, *Socialists, Liberals and Labour: The Struggle for London, 1885–1914*, Routledge, 1967

Thomson, Peter, *The Cambridge Introduction to English Theatre, 1660–1900*, Cambridge, Cambridge University Press, 2006

Trades Union Congress, *Centenary History*, TUC, 1968

Travers Morgan, R., & Partners, *Docklands Redevelopment Proposals for East London*, vol. 1, Travers Morgan, 1973

Trevers, J., *An Essay to the Restoring of our decayed Trade*, privately published, 1675

Turner, G. Lyon (ed.), *Original Records of Early Nonconformity under Persecution and Indulgence*, Fisher Unwin, 1911

Tyack, Geoffrey, *Sir James Pennethorne and the Making of Victorian London*, Cambridge, Cambridge University Press, 1992

Ullah, Ansar Ahmed, and John Eversley, *Bengalis in London's East End*, Swadhinata Trust, 2010

Victoria County History of Middlesex, vol. 11, *Stepney and Bethnal Green*, Institute of Historical Research, 1998

A Vindication of the case of Spittle-Fields, against an uncharitable paper privately printed, called a true narrative of the case of Sir George Wheler, & c. Humbly offered to the Honourable House of Commons, privately published, 12 October 1694

Visram, Rosina, *Asians in Britain: 400 Years of History*, Pluto Press, 2002

Walkowitz, Judith, *City of Dreadful Delight: Narratives of Sexual Danger in Late-Victorian London*, Virago, 1994

Waller, William, 'Early Huguenot friendly societies', *Proceedings of the Huguenot Society of London*, VI:3 (1901), pp. 201–35

Wallis, Graham, *Life of Francis Place, 1771–1854*, Longman Green, 1898

Warner, F., *The Silk Industry in the United Kingdom*, Dane's, 1921

Watt, Paul, 'Move to a better place? Geographies of aspiration and anxiety in the Thames Gateway', in Cohen and Rustin (eds), *London's Turning*, pp. 149–67

Webb, Sidney and Beatrice, *History of Trade Unionism*, Longman, 1950 [1920]

Weiner, A., 'Jewish industrial life in Russia', *The Economic Journal*, XV (1905)

Wensley, Frederick, *Detective Days*, Cassell & Co., 1931

Werner, Alex (ed.), *Jack the Ripper and the East End*, Chatto and Windus, 2008

Weylland, J.M., *Round the Tower, or, The Story of the London City Mission*, Partridge, 1875

White, Arnold, *The Problems of a Great City*, Remington, 1886

White, Jerry, *Rothschild Buildings: Life in an East End Tenement Block, 1887–1920*, Routledge, 1980

——, *London in the Twentieth Century*, Vintage, 2008

Widdowson, John, and Howard Block, *People Who Moved to Newham*, London Borough of Newham, n.d.

Williams, Karel, *From Pauperism to Poverty*, Routledge, 1981

Wilson, F.P. (ed.), *The Plague Pamphlets of Thomas Dekker*, Oxford, Clarendon Press, 1925

Wise, Sarah, *The Blackest Streets: The Life and Death of a Victorian Slum*, The Bodley Head, 2008

Wohl, Anthony, *Endangered Lives: Public Health in Victorian Britain*, Dent, 1983

Wonderful London; its Lights and Shadows of Humour and Sadness, Tinsley, 1878

Wood, Frederick T., 'Goodman's Fields Theatre', *Modern Language Review*, 25 (1930), pp. 443–56

Wright, Patrick, *The River: The Thames in Our Time*, BBC Worldwide, 1999

Wrigley, E.A., 'A simple model of London's importance in changing English society and economy, 1650–1750', *Past and Present*, 37 (1967), pp. 44–70

Yarrow, Stella, 'The impact of hostility on Germans in Britain, 1914–1918', in Kushner and Lunn (eds), *The Politics of Marginality*, pp. 97–112

Young, Ken, and Patricia Garside, *Metropolitan London: Politics and Urban Change, 1837–1981*, Arnold, 1982

Young, Michael, and Peter Willmott, *Family and Kinship in East London*, Harmondsworth, Pelican, 1962

Young, Phyllis, *Report on an Investigation into the Conditions of the Coloured Population in an Area of Stepney*, privately published, 1944

Parliamentary Papers

PP 1796. *Report of the Committee appointed to enquire into the best Mode of providing sufficient Accommodation for the increased Trade and Shipping of the Port of London, &c. &c. &c.*

PP 1799. *First Report from the Select Committee appointed to consider evidence taken on Bills for the Improvement of the Port of London*

PP 1813–14 (355). *Papers relating to Parochial and District Assessments for Paving, Lighting and Cleansing of Streets, Lanes, &c., within the Bills of Mortality*

PP 1818 (134). *Minutes of Evidence taken before the Committee appointed to consider of the several Petitions relating to Ribbon Weavers*

PP 1818 (211). *Second Report of Minutes of Evidence taken before the Committee appointed to consider of the several Petitions relating to Ribbon Weavers*

PP 1825 (240). *Sums collected and disbursed for Lighting, Watching and Paving, 1818–1824*

PP 1830–31 (387). *An Account of all sums raised by the Commissioner of Sewers for the Tower Hamlets …, between the years 1821 and 1830*

PP 1831–32 (155). *Cholera. Copies of Certain Papers relating to Cholera; together with the Report of the Central Board of Health thereupon*

PP 1833 (448). *Report of the Select Committee appointed to consider the best means of securing Open Spaces in the Vicinity of populous Towns, as Public Walks and Places of Exercise*

PP 1834 (584). *Report from the Select Committee on Metropolitan Sewers*

PP 1835 (492). *Analysis of the evidence taken before the Select Committee on Hand-Loom Weavers' Petitions*

PP 1837 (376). *Distress, Spitalfields and Nottingham. Copies of the report of Dr. Kay to the Poor Law Commissioner on the subject of Distress in Spitalfields*

PP 1837–38 (147). *Fourth Annual Report of the Poor Law Commissioners for England and Wales.* Frankland Lewis, T., John G.S. Lefevre and George Nicholls, 'Report as to payment of certain expenses out of rates'

PP 1837–38 (147). *Fourth Annual Report of the Poor Law Commissioners for England and Wales.* Southwood Smith, Thomas, 'Report on some of the Physical Causes of Sickness and Mortality to which the Poor are particularly exposed; and which are capable of removal by Sanatory Regulations, exemplified in the present condition of the Bethnal Green and Whitechapel Districts'

PP 1837–38 (661). *Second Report from Select Committee on Metropolitan Improvements*

PP 1839 (239). *Fifth Annual Report of the Poor Law Commissioners for England and Wales.* Southwood Smith, Thomas, 'Report on the Prevalence of Fever in Twenty Metropolitan Unions or Parishes, during the year ended 20th March 1838'

PP 1840 (384). *Report from the Select Committee on the Health of Towns*

PP 1840 (639). *Hand-loom Weavers. Copy of Report by Mr. Hickson, on the Condition of the Hand-loom Weavers*

PP 1842 (006). *Report of an Inquiry into the Sanitary Condition of the Labouring Population of Great Britain* [Chadwick Report]

PP 1847–48 (888), (895). *Metropolitan Sanitary Commission. First Report of the Commissioners appointed to Inquire whether any and what Special Means may be Requisite for Improvement of the Health of the Metropolis*

PP 1847–48 (967). *Eighth Annual Report of the Registrar General*

PP 1850 (1273), (1274), (1275). *Report of the General Board of Health on the Cholera Epidemic of 1848 and 1849*

PP 1854–55 (1893). *General Board of Health. Letter of the President ..., accompanying a report from Dr. Sutherland on Epidemic Cholera in the Metropolis in 1854*

PP 1854–55 (1980). *General Board of Health. Medical Council. Report of the Committee for Scientific Inquiries in relation to the Cholera Epidemic of 1854*

PP 1866 (3645). *Public Health. Eighth Report of the Medical Officer of the Privy Council*

PP 1867–68 (4072). *Report on the Cholera Epidemic of 1866 in England. Supplement to the Twenty-ninth Annual Report of the Registrar General*

PP 1868–69 (4218). *First Report of the Royal Sanitary Commission, with the minutes of evidence*

PP 1887 (124). *Parliamentary Constituencies*

PP 1887 (331). John Burnett, *Report to the Board of Trade, on the Sweating System of the East End of London by the Labour Correspondent of the Board*

PP 1888 (361), (448); 1890 (169). *Select Committee of the House of Lords on the Sweating System*

PP 1895 (288). *Parliamentary Constituencies (Electors)*

PP 1903 [Cmnd 1742]. *Royal Commission on Alien Immigration*

PP 1920 [Cmnd 936]. *Transport Workers – Court of Inquiry*

PP 1940 [Cmnd 6153]. *Royal Commission on the Distribution of Industrial Population* [Barlow Commission]

Theses

Brewis, Georgina, 'The making of an imperial ideal of service: Britain and India before 1914', PhD Thesis, University of East London, 2009

Dixon, Simon, 'Quaker communities in London, 1667–c. 1714', PhD thesis, University of London, 2006

Johansen, Michelle, 'The public librarian in modern London (1890–1914): The case of Charles Goss at the Bishopsgate Institute', PhD Thesis, University of East London, 2008

Marriott, John, 'London over the border: A study of West Ham during rapid growth, 1840–1910', PhD Thesis, University of Cambridge, 1985

Pettit, Katy, 'The food culture of East London, 1880–1914', PhD thesis, University of East London, 2009

Power, Michael, 'Urban development of East London, 1550–1700', PhD thesis, University of London, 1971

Websites

www.bodley.ac.uk
Site of the Bodleian Library, Oxford, which contains some useful online resources available to the public including a collection of broadside ballads.

www.british-history.ac.uk
British History Online contains abundant material on metropolitan history, including
    relevant volumes of the *Victoria County History* and *Survey of London*.

www.casebook.org
Many original sources of material on the Whitechapel murders including, most usefully,
    press coverage.

www.eastlondonhistory.org.uk
A miscellaneous collection of snippets on aspects of the history of East London – quirky but
    there is much of interest.

www.eastlondonhistorysociety.org.uk
Site of the East London History Society, edited by Harry Mernicks, and incorporating
    Tower Hamlet History Online. Contains a useful collection of images including maps,
    and historical articles.

www.elta-project.org
Much facsimile material including programmes and posters compiled by the East London
    Theatre Archive Project

www.hidden-histories.org.uk
Site compiled from the work of Eastside Community Heritage with some useful material,
    but framed by a poor historical imagination.

www.hrionline.ac.uk
London Lives, 1670–1800 is produced by the same team responsible for the Old Bailey
    online sources (see below), and brings together items such as wills, pauper settlement
    cases, Middlesex Session records and hospital records kept in various metropolitan
    archives.

www.londonovertheborder.com
Site devoted to the history of Canning Town, compiled by Newham Heritage and Archives
    Library and containing interesting material, including a video of *Neighbourhood 15*.

www.neighbourhood.statistics.gov.uk
Valuable source of detailed socio-economic information compiled by the government on
    neighbourhoods throughout the country.

www.newhamstory.com
An entertaining site containing images and snippets of information on the history of
    Newham, nicely put together by Newham Heritage and Archives Library.

www.oldbaileyonline.org
Reports of the trials of that took place at the Old Bailey between 1674 and 1913, accompa-
    nied by valuable material on their historical background.

www.victorianlondon.org
Highly entertaining and informative site with a large collection of extracts from primary
    sources, compiled by the resourceful Lee Jackson.

Index